CHAOS THEORY IN PSYCHOLOGY AND THE LIFE SCIENCES

CHAOS THEORY IN PSYCHOLOGY AND THE LIFE SCIENCES

Edited by

ROBIN ROBERTSON
Society for Chaos Theory in Psychology
ALLAN COMBS
University of North Carolina at Asheville

LEA LAWRENCE ERLBAUM ASSOCIATES, PUBLISHERS
1995　Mahwah, New Jersey　　　　　　　　　Hove, UK

Lawrence Erlbaum Associates, Inc., Publishers
10 Industrial Avenue
Mahwah, New Jersey 07430

Library of Congress Cataloging-in-Publication Data

Chaos theory in psychology and the life sciences / edited by Robin
    Robertson, Allan Combs.
        p.   cm.
    Includes bibliographical references and index.
    ISBN 0-8058-1736-0 (alk. paper). — ISBN 0-8058-1737-9 (pbk. :
alk. paper)
    1. Chaotic behavior in systems.   2. Psychology.   3. Life sciences.
4. Philosophy.   I. Robertson, Robin, 1944–   .   II. Combs, Allan,
1942–   .
Q172.5.C45C432   1995
003′.85—dc20   95-17298
                                                             CIP

Books published by Lawrence Erlbaum Associates are printed on acid-free paper,
and their bindings are chosen for strength and durability.

Printed in the United States of America
10 9 8 7 6 5 4 3 2 1

Contents

v

Foreword

Walter J. Freeman
University of California, Berkeley

The question is now commonly asked, "Is the brain chaotic?" This is a fuzzy question with a fuzzy answer: "Undoubtedly." The turbulent flow of conscious experience is nothing if not chaotic, and though unpredictable it certainly isn't random. The more penetrating question is: "How might we use the science of chaos as a tool to help us understand the mechanisms of the mind?" This is an open question, for which some compelling answers are given by the chapters in this book.

Another level of question is, "Aren't psychologists a bit naive to suppose they can investigate mind with a tool that even the mathematical physicists who invented it don't fully comprehend?" Physicists are already using their minds as tools to solve their problems, and, like the rest of us, need all the help they can get, particularly now that some of them have naively introduced the psychological notion of "the observer" into quantum mechanics (Albert, 1994). Modern science has become a seamless enterprise. On the one hand most of us accept the view that behavior is formed by electrochemical processes in brains, and we try to explain brain function by using the known laws of physics and chemistry. On the other hand most of us are equally impressed by the unpredictability of individual performance within the lawful regularities of behavior. Now physics has offered us a fresh start.

The conception of what we call deterministic chaos first emerged in the mathematical analysis of the stability of the solar system. Henri Poincare submitted his solution to the problem for a prize offered by King Oscar II of Norway (Peterson, 1993). After winning the prize for solving the stability problem, a colleague discovered an error in Poincare's calculations. Rather than rescind the prize and endure the shame, the committee gave Poincare 6 months to redo his derivation. On reconsideration he found no closed solution. He had encountered intractable complexity in trying to comprehend a homoclinic tangle, which he called a "trellis" (Poincaré, 1898). Chaos was born, but it was swept from sight like a teratological monster. It has re-appeared nearly a century later, partly because Stephen Smale has clothed it in mathematical respectability, and partly because computer graphics has given it aesthetic appeal.

Poincare, and later Lorenz, found that a simple system of ordinary differential equations in three dimensions is sufficient to generate endlessly complex trajectories in its phase space. In its simplest form a three body system has three point masses and a fixed sum of energy. As any two points "fall" toward each other and become infinitesimally close, the potential energy imparted to the third point may cause it to fly off to infinity. This mathematical fiction contains the essence of the sensitivity to initial conditions and the unpredictability of output of a system having at least three degrees of freedom. From this and similar demonstrations follows the hope that complicated behavior may have much simpler sources than we have heretofore supposed. Given a broad power spectrum with multiple peaks, we need no longer seek an independent oscillator to explain each peak. Given an aperiodic and therefore unpredictable time series, we are no longer constrained to model it with a Markov process or a random number generator. This is truly a liberating alternative.

Even more appealing, the word *chaos* traditionally denotes a formless void that is pregnant with forthcoming order. Now we see that disorder in an individual or a society can precede the emergence of new structure instead of leading inevitably to mere anarchy in accordance with the law of entropy, the 19th century "heat death" of the universe. Stochastic systems have proverbially low probability of coming up with any structure of interest. Recall the apocryphal tale of monkeys typing the works of Shakespeare by chance. Deterministic systems operating in the basins of point and limit cycle attractors have no more life expectancy than the pendulum of a clock. It is the aperiodic solutions of deterministic equations that provide the emergent structures, which give us hope that we can come to understand the biological and psychological mechanisms of self-organization in embryos, brains, adolescent boys and girls, social groups, economies, and nations. The best news is that neophytes don't need a 4-year course in higher mathematics to get started. One's flair for high school geometry and a few weeks' study of a tutorial monograph will suffice, if one does the homework and the problem sets.

So fertile is this notion of chaos that variants breed like rabbits, giving rise to a bewildering array of adjectives: deterministic, terminal (Zak, 1991), itinerant (Tsuda, 1991), computational, soft, hard, controlled, graded, etc., and the levels and domains of application seem boundless. An embedding field is becoming apparent as well in the form of complexity theory, in which the degree of chaos is viewed as an adjustable property. An example comes from the olfactory system of the mammalian brain, in which an endogenous "noise" is continuously generated by the bulb at a modest correlation dimension in the absence of input. Upon inhalation of a familiar odor, the system goes to a more ordered, less chaotic state as a step toward pattern classification. When an unfamiliar odor is inhaled, the system becomes less ordered and more chaotic, as a basis for eliciting an orienting reflex and for generating unstructured activity that is essential to drive Hebbian synapses. Thus the degree of chaos is adapted to the circumstances of the behavior (Freeman, 1992). This is called "life at the edge of chaos" (Lewin, 1993).

How is it done in the brain? We don't know. There is so much that we don't know. Two things are immediately clear. First, psychologists have an opportunity and an obligation to explore this new offering from physics. Second, we do not agree on what it means or how it should be used.

This confusion offers no cause for concern. Scientific experiments come in two flavors: exploratory, and confirmatory. School children are taught the rigors of replication, statistical validation, and double blind controls. These techniques have their uses when we know what hypothesis we are trying to falsify, but they are premature if we don't yet know the right questions, let alone the right answers. At present we are in the joyous phase of children let out of school, who are free to wander in a garden of delights just to see what is there. The hard work of proof will come soon enough, but it should not be required before our imaginations have taken wing. Tolerance for the play of ideas is all the more important, because there is something very deep going on in this decade, and none of us immersed in this period can have the historical perspective needed to grasp the enormity of it. Some of us may live to write its history some decades hence. Meanwhile, it is essential to get on with the spadework of discovery and evaluation. Let us make the most of this remarkable opportunity.

REFERENCES

Albert, D.Z. (1994). Bohm's alternative to quantum mechanics. *Scientific American, 270,* 58–67.

Freeman, W.J. (1992). Tutorial in neurobiology: From single neurons to brain chaos. *International Journal of Bifurcation and Chaos, 2,* 451–482.

Lewin, R. (1993). *Complexity: Life at the edge of chaos.* New York: Macmillan.

Peterson, I. (1993). *Newton's clock: Chaos in the solar system.* New York: Freeman.

Poincare, H. (1898). *Celestial mechanics* (Vol. III, p. 1059, sec. 397).

Tsuda, I. (1991). Chaotic itinerancy as a dynamical basis of hermeneutics in brain and mind. *World Futures, 32,* 167–184.

Zak, M. (1991). Terminal chaos for information processing in neurodynamics. *Biological Cybernetics, 64,* 343–351.

CHAOS THEORY IN PSYCHOLOGY AND THE LIFE SCIENCES

INTRODUCTION TO CHAOS THEORY

1 Chaos Theory and the Relationship Between Psychology and Science

Robin Robertson

Issues usually become critical for philosophy long before they impinge on other fields of thought. Philosophy is the mother of the sciences; initially, each was merely an area of interest for philosophy, then each in turn grew independent enough to call itself a separate field. More recently, each of the sciences has fragmented into myriads of tinier subfields. Because the sciences disavow their philosophic underpinnings, each in turn repeats historical philosophic battles. In particular, when the youngest of philosophy's children, psychology, came into existence in the 19th century, it prided itself on following the methods of its older siblings, the "hard" sciences. It was especially anxious to disavow any "philosophy" in its methods. This chapter traces psychology's roots in the sciences from the Renaissance to the 20th century and shows the unnatural limits this has placed on psychology. Finally, it briefly describes how chaos theory, which provides a broader scope for all fields of science, offers unique possibilities for unifying psychology.

THE RENAISSANCE DAWNS AND CREATIVITY REAWAKENS

When a new world view captures the imagination, a rich outpouring of creativity occurs in all areas of life. The Renaissance was such a time. For the first time in the Western World, we began to realize that we were not only God's creation, but creators ourselves. With this realization we were free in a way we hadn't been free since the golden age of Greek philosophy. Although the growth of Christianity had been the greatest unifying force in the history of the Western World, it effectively brought an end to speculative thought about nature. Throughout the Middle Ages, scholastic philosophy instead perfected the analytic methods of Plato and Socrates. Scholastic philosophy proceeded from religious dogma rather than from observed fact, thus the beginnings of science were set back many centuries. During the Middle Ages, God's word was considered a better guide than human experience or reason.

In contrast, the Renaissance ideal was expressed in statements by Leonardo da Vinci (1452–1519) such as "Experience never errs; it is only your judgments that err by promising themselves such as are not caused by your experiments," or "all our knowledge has its origin in our perceptions" (Richter, 1970, p. 288). Leonardo da Vinci was able to combine this belief in the power of experience with a belief in God by a changing view of God. Leonardo da Vinci addressed his God as "O admirable impartiality of Thine, Thou first Mover; Thou hast not permitted that any force should fail of the order or quality of its necessary results" (Richter, 1970, p. 285).

God had created a world of necessity, and it was our responsibility to use reason to discover the rules that governed that world. Leonardo da Vinci said that "the senses are of the earth; Reason stands apart in contemplation" (Richter, 1970, p. 287). Once that step had been taken, it was inevitable that we would eventually turn reason upon itself and try to describe the nature of the mind.

COPERNICUS AND THE OBSERVATIONAL METHOD

At roughly the same point in time, Nicholas Copernicus (1473–1543) stood apart in contemplation of the universe. Before Copernicus, the earth was assumed to be the central object in the universe, eternally fixed and unmoving. Ptolemy (2nd century A.D.) had speculated that a series of clear, perfectly formed, nesting spheres surrounded the earth, and on those spheres were the sun, the planets, and the stars. Because astronomical observations are critical for agriculture, medieval man knew a great deal about the actual positions and movements of the heavenly bodies. Increasingly, calculations based on Ptolemy's perfect spheres didn't fit those observations; more and more complex rationalizations had to be made in order to preserve earth's central position. Copernicus had the brilliant realization that perhaps the movement was, in part, the perception of the viewer. Perhaps the earth was moving around the sun.

The scientific method is now so taken for granted that it is hard to realize that it is not self-evident. It was indisputable to Aristotle that heavier objects fall faster than lighter objects. For the next 1,900 years (!), Aristotle's statement was regarded as so self-evident that it was never tested. It was only in the 17th century that Galileo tested the theory and found that it was false. It had just never occurred to anyone before that such self-evident facts might be wrong and needed to be tested. Without that realization, observation had to be subsumed within theory and dogma. Copernicus' theory was the first intimation that perhaps the nature of reality depended on the position of the observer, a view that Einstein was to make so central in his Theory of Relativity. In a Copernican world, our observations and conclusions became central because, in a world of flux and movement, everything depended on the observer (De Santillana, 1956).

This new method of thought led to the accumulation of more detailed information about the outer world than had been added in the previous eighteen hundred years, since the end of the golden age of Greek philosophy. The need to deal with this new data in a systematic way led to the creation of an explicit scientific method in the 17th century.

GOD SAID: LET NEWTON BE, AND ALL WAS LIGHT!

When Isaac Newton was born in 1642, science as we know it was still a small thing, exciting to those who could see its possibilities, but little known otherwise. When Newton died in 1727, science was the dominant force in human thought, and he was the primary cause for that change in status. In poet Alexander Pope's famous words, "Nature and Nature's laws lay hid in night; God said, Let Newton be! and all was light" (Gamow 1961, p. 51).

The 17th century was a time, in some ways, like our own, an "interesting time," a time of change and unpredictability, when many contradictory ideas fought for supremacy. With the end of the absolute dominance that religion and the "ancients" (the Middle Ages' most characteristic term for the great Greek thinkers) had previously had over Western thought, a vacuum was left, waiting to be filled by something new. Newton, with his *Optiks* and *Principia*, seemed to his contemporaries to have explained all of nature. Before Newton, there were speculations; after Newton, there were laws! Newton's laws of nature explained motion, force, and light in straightforward ways that lent themselves to practical application. His laws concerned material particles, their motion, and their interaction. His was a world of absolutes: absolute space and time and perfect, indivisible particles moving in that absolute space and time. In Newton's words from the *Principia*, "Absolute space, in its own nature, without relation to anything external, remains always similar and immovable. Absolute, true, and mathematical time, in itself, and from its own nature, flows equably without relation to anything external" (Gamow, 1961, p. 174).

It should be obvious that such a world is a construct of thought. Absolute space and time are concepts that Newton used in order to develop general theories of nature. Those general theories could then be applied to particular cases. The power of Newton's concept of absolute space and time is less in its possible truth than in its broad utility.

Perhaps of equal importance with Newton's laws was the development of practical mathematical tools with which those laws could be applied to nature.

First came Rene Descartes' discovery of analytic geometry early in the 17th century. Euclid's geometry had stood alone as the first and, for nearly 2,000 years, the only known complete, self-consistent scientific system. Descartes had the brilliant realization that geometric locations could be represented by numeric coordinates, much as we can today identify any location in a city by a pair of crossing streets. Using this coordinate method, geometric problems could be transformed into numeric problems. A great jump in abstraction had taken place.

Building on Descartes' method, Newton and German mathematician and philosopher, Gottfried Wilhelm Leibniz (1646–1716; often called "the last universal man"), independently developed calculus. Although analytic geometry could present a numeric snapshot of physical reality, it couldn't deal with irregularity or change. As far back as the Babylonians, mathematicians had approximated the area of an irregular shape by covering it with a large number of shapes whose area they did know. Newton and Leibniz saw that, if the number of such covering shapes was extended infinitely, an exact area could be found. Calculus was a method of extending this approximation method to infinity. Similarly, calculus could calculate rates of change of virtually any quantity that could be described in analytic geometric terms. Calculus provided physical science, especially physics and astronomy, with a tool of incredible versatility. Bishop George Berkeley, whose philosophy of idealism is discussed later, claimed " . . . the method of fluxions [i.e., Newton's term for calculus] is the general key by help whereof the modern mathematicians unlock the secrets of Geometry, and consequently of Nature" (Bell, 1979, p. 90).

After Newton, science began to supplant philosophy and religion as the dominant force in human thought. As psychology began to emerge in embryonic form over the next three centuries, it was to science that it turned for its model, not to philosophy. Although this had great advantages for the eventual emergence of psychology as a separate science in the 19th century, it also left psychology with some critical areas of ignorance, as is seen later.

THE FIRST EMPIRICIST AND THE ASSAULT ON EMPIRICISM

Influenced by his friend Newton, philosopher John Locke (1632–1704) first voiced the empiricist's creed, a philosophy that, in many ways, is still implicit in the view of reality shared by too many scientists. Locke described the human mind as an initially empty vessel that gradually accumulates separate and distinct particles called ideas, which derive either directly or indirectly from sensory experience. Locke was trying to apply Newton's view of the material world as closely as possible to the mind. Although full of difficulties, Locke perfectly expressed the spirit of the new age of science; his views are representative of the mainstream of scientific thought prior to the 20th century (Berlin, 1956, pp. 30–112).

Problems surfaced when two brilliant philosophers—Bishop George Berkeley (1685–1753) and David Hume (1711–1776)—took Locke's ideas to their logical conclusions. Berkeley agreed with Locke's assertion that all our ideas are derived from sensory experience, but he went one step further and said that it was, therefore, nonsense to speak of a physical world separate from our perceptions. As far as each of us is aware, there is no world unless we think of it. Because Berkeley was deeply religious, however, he avoided total solipsism by arguing that the world must necessarily exist, because it always exists in God's mind. This religious answer satisfied few who found his basic argument that we can never prove the existence of an outer world inordinately difficult to resolve (Berlin, 1956, pp. 115–161).

Although Berkeley denied the existence of the material world, David Hume denied causality. He pointed out that, although we might assert that one event caused another, all we really know is that the two events are roughly contiguous in time and space. It is only from habit that we assert that one event caused the other—there is no logical and necessary connection between the two events. "The sole criterion of necessary truth, according to Hume is the law of non-contradiction. If a proposition cannot be denied without contradiction, it is necessarily true" (Aiken, 1956, p. 32).

The "sole criterion of necessary truth" is what, a century earlier, Leibniz had called *analytic judgment;* that is, where the conclusion is contained in the subject. But the conclusion that one event caused another is only a *synthetic judgment;* that is, an observation about the outer world. Leibniz was the first to specifically identify these as separate types of judgment (alternately termed *a priori* and *a posteriori*). An a posteriori, synthetic judgment can never have the necessity of an a priori, analytic judgment. But all that can be known of the world is a posteriori, derived from experience. Hume's argument seemed unassailable. If there could be no logical necessity in any judgment about the outer world, anything could happen at any time. Hume's argument had to be answered by philosophers, or philosophy was at a dead end. And, of course, it is the assumption of such necessary causality that forms the core of all of Newton's Laws, of all science prior to the 20th century (Berlin, 1956, pp. 162–260).

Immanuel Kant (1724–1804) inaugurated modern philosophy with his answer in his *Critique of Pure Reason* in 1781. Kant agreed that analytic truth and synthetic truth are indeed separate and distinct. It is within the human mind that both are experienced, thus Kant argued that there also existed a third category of judgments that were neither analytic nor synthetic. There is an actual world out there that we observe, but we can see it only through the lens of our own mental perceptions. In effect, Kant was arguing that human psychology should be the most important of all the sciences, since our innate psychological makeup inherently colors all observations of nature and all logical conclusions we make about those observations. We might never be able to experience *das ding an sich* (i.e., the thing in itself), but our minds are themselves structured much as the world is structured and contain necessarily true categories with which we perceive the world. This was an argument that would have been unthinkable before the Renaissance and even before the birth of the science. Kant's argument changed the direction of philosophy to a degree comparable only to that of Plato over two millennia earlier. Unfortunately, it had little or no impact on science.

Scientists felt that Newton's Laws, by their very existence, proved an effective counterargument to Berkeley and Hume. Although Berkeley and Hume denied that man could ever speak with necessity about the psychical world, Newton seemed to have done just that. Meanwhile, it was sufficient for scientists to propose provisional theories about the world within the framework of Newton's Laws. As evidence came along that the theories didn't answer, well then, modify the theories. If this presented logical difficulties, they would eventually be resolved. It was a wonderfully pragmatic way to deal with reality. And because it was so inordinately successful, who was to argue.

THE BIRTH OF ASSOCIATIONISM

In Scotland, a contemporary of Hume's, Thomas Reid (1710–1796), founded a school of philosophy that advocated "common sense" and "instinct" and threw out the whole argument. If Berkeley and Hume denied the existence of physical reality, then their arguments weren't worth considering. A quote attributed to Dr. Thomas Brown, one of Reid's followers, however, shows the difficulty in accepting either Reid's or Hume's view wholeheartedly. "Yes, Reid bawled out we must believe in an outward world; but added in a whisper, we can give no reason for our belief. Hume cries out we can give no reason for such a notion; and whispers, I own we cannot get rid of it" (Heidbreder, 1933, p. 52).

Reid's common-sense position led to an emphasis on empirical research, which would eventually culminate in experimental psychology. Associationism proper can be traced less to a reaction against Hume, however, than to an acceptance of Locke's empiricism. David Hartley founded a school of thought based on Locke's concept of the mind as a *tabula rasa* (i.e., blank slate). "[David Hartley] took Locke's little-used title for a chapter, 'the association of ideas,' made it the name of a fundamental law, reiterated it, wrote a psychology around it, and thus created a formal doctrine with a definite name" (Boring, 1950, pp. 193–194).

> The general law of association is that if sensations have often been experienced together, the corresponding ideas will tend to occur together . . . association may be either successive or simultaneous. The former determines the course of thought

in time; the latter accounts for the formation of complex ideas. These few principles form the basis of associationism. (Heidbreder, 1933, p. 54)

CHEMISTRY AND JOHN STUART MILL'S CREATIVE SYNTHESIS

It is one thing, however, to believe that complex ideas all derive ultimately from simple, sensory perceptions; it is quite another to show how this actually operates in even the simplest situation. Dr. Thomas Brown tried to discover under just what specific circumstances association operates. "The laws of recency, frequency, and intensity—that much-used trio—are among them" (Heidbreder, 1933, p. 55). This "much-used trio" formed the core, not only of associationism, but also of its successors, functionalism and behaviorism, which have dominated much of 20th century psychology in America.

Just as physics had emerged from natural philosophy as a separate science in the 17th century, chemistry developed as a separate field of study in the 2nd half of the 18th century and the early days of the 19th century. Antoine Lavoisier (1743–1794) conducted methodical experiments in combustion, which led, among other things, to the first version of the law of conservation of matter. Daniel Rutherford (1749–1819) and Henry Cavendish (1731–1810) discovered nitrogen; Karl Wilhelm Scheele (1742–1786) and Joseph Priestly (1733–1804), oxygen. It was an exciting era when discoveries came tumbling out one after another, and chemistry begin to take shape as a separate, fully quantitative science. By the time philosopher John Stuart Mill (1806–1873) developed his view of the mind in the 19th century, chemistry was firmly in place as not only a theoretical, but a practical science. Mill was convinced that there was more to the mind than associationism's mechanical combination and turned to chemistry for an explanatory principle, much as Locke had turned to physics a century and a half earlier. Mill argued that the mind has an active role in acquiring and assimilating sensory data, not merely through association, but also through a "creative synthesis" that was reminiscent of the formation of a chemical compound. In Mill's words:

> When many impressions or ideas are operating in the mind together, there sometimes takes place a process of a similar kind to chemical combination . . . those ideas sometimes melt and coalesce into one another, and appear not several ideas but one . . . the Complex Idea, formed by the blending together of several simpler ones, should . . . be said to *result from*, or be *generated by*, the simple ideas not to *consist of* them. (Boring, 1950, p. 230)

So a second science, chemistry, had enriched the view of the mind; a third, biology, was next to follow.

DARWIN AND THE TRIUMPH OF EVOLUTION

When Charles Darwin (1809–1882) published *The Origin of the Species* in 1859, the concept of evolution by natural selection changed the course of science forever. But Darwin's discovery didn't emerge from nowhere; debate had already been going on for decades over Lamarck's theory that acquired characteristics could be inherited. Although Darwin's work was meticulously detailed, it needed the support of a large body of patient work, which had already laid the basis for evolution; for example, naturalist Henry Bates' earlier careful studies of insect mimicry. Inspired by Darwin's idea, German biologist and philosopher Ernst Haekel (1834–1919) argued that "ontogeny recapitulates phylogeny"; that is, that an individual's development goes through the same stages as the evolutionary development of the species (Reese, 1980, p. 206). Although Haekel's wonderful catchphrase is somewhat overstated, it is nevertheless true that each of us carries much of the record of our evolutionary history within the structure of our bodies. For example, our alimentary tract functions much like the tubular creatures that swam in the primeval oceans over half a billion years ago; like our alimentary tract, they were little more than a tube through which nutrients could pass and be absorbed for use as food. The most elementary part of our brain— our spinal cord, hindbrain, and midbrain (which neuroscientist Paul MacLean called the "neural chassis"), wouldn't have been out of place in fish swimming the oceans 400 million years ago.

Certainly Haekel's view wasn't far from what was believed by many of the early psychologists. In the late 19th century, when psychology started to branch off from medicine and philosophy and form a separate science, it was to biology that thinkers turned for their understanding of the mind. To them, it was so obvious that it was almost beyond examination, that mind and behavior had biological roots.

PSYCHOLOGY EMERGES AS A NEW SCIENCE

Psychology surfaced as a separate science with twin spheres of interest: experimental and clinical. Both looked to the hard sciences, especially biology, for direction. There is probably no single figure who stands more clearly at the cut-off point between psychology as a branch of philosophy and psychology as a science, than William James (1842–1910). His magnum opus, *Principles of Psychology* (1890), reflects this perfectly. While rejecting views he considered wholly philosophical, such as associationist and vitalist theories, James drew on philosophy to a greater extent than in any other psychological text published either before or after. Yet *Principles* was also the first major text to make use of the vast amount of experimental scientific work that was then underway, as well as the first psychological text to be directly impacted by biology.

Two biological principles, evolution and the reflex arc, both attracted James, principles that would later lead other psychologists to opposing psychological positions. Add one philosophical principle, free will, and you have not only most of what occupied James for the 1,300 plus pages of *Principles,* but also the core of the three major directions psychology would take in the 20th century. "It has been said that there are three schools of psychology, 'the conscious, the unconscious and the anti-conscious,' referring to the introspective, the psychoanalytical, and the behavioristic schools. It is easy to find all three in James" (Perry, 1954, p. 196). The concept of will led to an emphasis on consciousness; evolution toward an emphasis on psychoanalysis or depth psychology; and the reflex arc is, of course, at the heart of behaviorism. Although today we might substitute the cognitive or rational schools for the introspective, these three primary directions still define most of psychology. And James somehow combined them into a single interrelated whole. *Principles of Psychology* was enormously influential, not only among psychologists, but also among the educated public. Reaction for and against James' many idiosyncratic positions helped define the new field of psychology. In a letter to a friend, James expressed his own view that his ideas would be short-lived:

> It seems to me that psychology is like physics before Galileo's time—not a single *elementary* law yet caught a glimpse of. A great chance for some future psychologue to make a greater name than Newton's, but who then will read the books of this generation? Not many, I trow. meanwhile they must be written. (Perry, 1954, p. 197)

Perhaps no elementary law had emerged because psychology looked to the other sciences for elementary laws. At the point when psychology appeared, science reigned supreme, seemingly on the verge of answering all the ultimate philosophical questions about the nature of reality. Trouble was on the horizon, however. The entire edifice of science was largely based on the stability of the Newtonian concept of reality. Chemistry and biology could be secure in their separate levels of investigation because they knew that ultimately all science could be reduced to Newtonian mechanics. Unfortunately, at roughly the same time that psychology so willingly accepted the scientific rules laid down by its older siblings, physics began to find that reality was more complex than was previously thought. The joint discoveries of relativity and quantum mechanics would lead to the dissolution of the Newtonian concept of reality. With that dissolution went a great deal of the unity that traditionally underlay science. Science began to split into increasingly smaller and more specialized areas, each speaking its own language and each largely ignorant of anything outside its domain. Psychology, both experimental and clinical, again followed the lead of its older siblings, and itself split into a wide variety of different paradigms. Will the biblical story of the Tower of Babel be repeated in science and psychology?

CHAOS THEORY AS HEALER

Psychology has grown to maturity with much the same scientific underpinnings it had when it came into existence late in the 19th century. Meanwhile, science has been changed dramatically—physics, by relativity and quantum mechanics; biology, by the discovery of the structure of the genetic code. While chemistry has been less affected, Ilya Prigogine's discovery of dissipative structures may, in the long run, transform it equally. Because psychology has been unaffected by any of these changes, why should chaos theory be any different? (In this chapter, I take the tack of most contemporary writers and use the term *chaos theory* as a shorthand description for nonlinear dynamics in general, as well as a wide variety of related ideas, that spread in a penumbra around the concept of chaos theory.)

Perhaps it is because chaos theory is the broadest of all of the great scientific discoveries of the 20th century! Chaos theory has already entered each of the older sciences through the back door, so to speak. As each has advanced to the point where it has needed to deal with complexity in its many forms, each has discovered some aspect of chaos theory. After an early intoxication in which chaos theory seemed fascinating but peripheral, the older sciences are starting to discover that most of their particular science's assumptions are reasonable limit case conditions in a more general world view offered by chaos theory. Because this enables them to accept chaos theory without rejecting their current views, chaos theory is being accepted with more alacrity than is traditional with new paradigms. The number of papers on chaos theory is increasing in exponential fashion in each of the major sciences. It is time for the same process to occur in psychology.

It is not the purpose of this chapter to present chaos theory in any detail or to present explicit psychological applications of chaos theory. That task is taken up by other chapters in this volume. However, I present here three very basic principles of chaos theory that have relevance for clinical psychology. Psychology prides itself on being a science every bit as much as its elder siblings. Science is traditionally concerned with discovering the deterministic rules that underlie natural phenomena, which can then be used to predict and control nature. How then to deal with unpredictable change? If everything in nature is based on causal chains, then with enough information, nature should be fully predictable. But, of course, it isn't in any but the simplest of situations. And certainly human psychology hasn't yielded to such reductionistic aims. Perhaps the reason is that nature is more complex than such goals allow. Chaos theory's contributions include the following discoveries:

Change isn't necessarily linear; that is, small causes can have larger effects.

Determinism and predictability are not synonymous—deterministc equations can lead to unpredictable results—chaos—when there is feedback within a system.

In systems that are "'far-from-equilibrium" (i.e., chaotic), change does not have to be related to external causes. Such systems can self-organize at a higher level of organization.

Famed hypnotherapist, Milton Erickson, loved to tell a story about an event he had been privileged to observe as boy, which he felt exemplified how major psychological change really takes place. It illustrates all three of these principles of chaos theory. In brief, when Erickson was a boy, there was a young man named Joe who had progressed from petty crimes as a boy, which led him to juvenile detention homes, to felonies as a young man, which led him to prison. Even in prison Joe stood out as being beyond the pale; he refused to obey any of the rules that prisons imposed and spent most of his jail time in solitary confinement. Upon Joe's recent release from prison, he had returned to town and immediately robbed several local stores, although the police had not yet identified him as the thief. One day soon afterward, a lovely young woman about Joe's age walked down the street. Joe walked up to her, eyed her, and asked if he could take her to an upcoming dance. She looked Joe up and down, then said calmly, "You can if you are a gentleman." Well, when the day for the dance arrived, Joe got dressed up in his best clothes, took her to the dance, and behaved like a gentleman. The next week, he took the stolen goods back to the storekeepers, who were so surprised that they didn't press charges. Joe then asked the girl's father, a prosperous farmer, for a job. The farmer must have seen something new in Joe because he gave him a job. Joe worked hard and the town's view of him began to change. Eventually he married the young woman, took over the farm when her father died, and made it even more prosperous than it had been before. In fact, he became one of the community's leaders and an example for the young (Zeig, 1980, pp. 211–216).

A great many major branches taken in a person's life are like Joe's story. They don't yield to easy causal explanation. Instead, the whole fabric of a person's life interacts with his or her total environment, and something new emerges that wasn't predictable from previous behavior. In Joe's case, a small cause (an attractive young woman and her admonition) certainly led to a large effect. Although his life had proceeded within a rather predictable criminal attractor, it suddenly changed in a less predictable direction. Finally, this bifurcation clearly had to be a result of self-organization from within.

Until now, a psychological paradigm could only be scientific by severely limiting its view of human beings and their potential. In contrast, paradigms, such as existential psychology, humanistic psychology, transpersonal psychology, analytic psychology, and so on, were often viewed as outside the pale of scientific respectability. There was no common ground for the two sides to meet within the traditional framework of science. Now chaos theory offers the more "scientific" psychological paradigms a chance to deal with aspects of human psychology they have previously ignored. The less "scientific" paradigms now have support for their recognition of the full variety of human psychology and behavior. Hopefully, they will also want to understand the science that underlies that expanded view of human nature.

C. G. Jung felt that traditional science's search for ultimates such as quarks, GUTs, and so forth, was essentially a religious search, doomed to failure because it attempted to reduce something greater to something smaller. Instead, a new symbol was needed, a living symbol, which could include everything from the material to the spiritual, from physics to depth psychology.

> . . . Since, for a given epoch, it [the living symbol] is the best possible expression for what is still unknown, it must be the product of the most complex and differentiated minds of that age. But in order to have such an effect at all, it must embrace what is common to a large group of men. This can never be what is most differentiated, the highest attainable, for only a very few attain to that or understand it. The common factor must be something that is still so primitive that its ubiquity cannot be doubted. (Jung, 1971, par. 820)

I would like to suggest that perhaps chaos offers science, in general, and psychology, in particular, a new living symbol that is for our time "the best possible expression for what is still unknown." What can be more primitive, more ubiquitous than chaos, from which everything emerged? Chaos theory has begun to emerge as any true symbol emerges, from all directions at once, from the "most complex and differentiated minds" of our age. What else could unite meteorologists, economists looking at market trends, doctors studying heart rhythms, and now, hopefully, psychologists, and others in the life sciences. As you will discover as you read this book, it is astonishing just how large a theoretical "umbrella" chaos theory provides. Thinkers who otherwise have little in common can at least agree on the centrality of chaos theory. Within this book alone, we have research psychologists, psychotherapists of varied schools, evolutionary theoreticians, mathematicians, social scientists, and much more. I hope you enjoy the rich mixture of ideas.

REFERENCES

Aiken, H. D. (Ed.). (1956). *The age of ideology: The 19th century philosophers*. New York: Mentor Books, Houghton Mifflin.

Bell, E. T. (1979). *Men of mathematics*. New York: Simon & Schuster.

Berlin, I. (Ed.). (1956). *The age of enlightenment: The 18th century philosophers*. New York: Mentor Books, Houghton Mifflin.

Boring, E. G. (1950). *A history of experimental psychology* (2nd ed.). New York: Appleton-Century-Crofts.

De Santillana, G. (Ed.). (1956). *The age of adventure: The Renaissance philosophers.* New York: Mentor Books, Houghton Mifflin.

Gamow, G. (1961). *Biography of physics.* New York: Harper & Row.

Heidbreder, E. (1933). *Seven psychologies.* New York: Appleton-Century-Crofts.

James, W. (1950). *The principles of psychology.* New York: Dover. (Original work published 1890)

Jung, C. G. (1971). *Collected works, vol. 6: Psychological types.* Princeton, NJ: Bollingen Series, Princeton University Press.

Perry, R. B. (1954). *The thought and character of William James: Briefer version.* New York: Braziller.

Reese, W. L. (1980). *Dictionary of philosophy and religion.* Atlantic Highlands; NJ: Humanities Press.

Richter, J. P. (1970). *The notebooks of Leonardo da Vinci* (2 vols.). New York: Dover.

Zeig, J. K. (Ed.). (1980). *Teaching seminar with Milton H. Erickson, M.D.* New York: Brunner/Mazel.

2 Chaos, Evolution, And Deep Ecology

Sally Goerner

The goal of this chapter is to bring home a single point—chaos is part of a much bigger and more important revolution in understanding than has been popularized currently. It is, in fact, part of a fundamental change in vision, a change from a controlled machine vision of the world to an evolving ecological vision of the world. Chaos is but the tip of the physical science branch of this change.

This is a tutorial, so I stick to basics. This is as it should be because any truly revolutionary change of vision must be fundamentally simple. And so the revolution. . .we stand at a turning point in human civilization, the magnitude of which we are only barely aware but whose importance cannot be doubted. The changes in thinking will affect every segment of the culture. And the key factor is an understanding of how order emerges and change is driven. The bigger picture, of which chaos is a part, is the physical understanding of how order evolves naturally, why change is inevitable, and what factors underlie transformations. Specifically, science is in the process of developing the physical understanding of the order-producing side of the universe.

The applications and implications of this advance in physical understanding are vast. Pragmatically, it means a whole new array of principles for how change occurs and how complexity grows. Scientifically, it means the connecting of the various disciplines that have come to seem quite disjointed but are, in fact, connected. And finally, in the human domain it means the coming together of science and spirituality because, above all, what the new understanding suggests is that everything is interconnected and everything evolves together. Suddenly "science" suggests that humankind is embedded in, and is part of, a vast interconnected process that created, and is still creating, all the intricate order we see about us and the order we have yet to envision. All our frames of reference are irrevocably altered.

Is this hyperbole? There is, in fact, a relatively simple explanation of the radical change I am predicting. The explanation is scientific, but it is also commonsensical. The goal of this presentation is to outline that common sensical story in a form that you can carry away.

Let me begin with the end. As you came in today, you almost certainly were outdoors at least momentarily. You saw grass, trees, sky, wind, people, buildings, etc. Where did all that come from? The two most common answers to this question are God and an initial accident called life that miraculously runs toward ordering in an otherwise passive, directionless, physical universe. If one believes in a physically real world, neither of these explanations, one nonphysical and the other a physical anomaly, is acceptable. The emerging answer is that everything we see is part of an ongoing physical order-building process that has produced everything from molecules, to life, to galaxies, to civilization. Evolution is more than biological evolution. Rather evolution is the result of a general pressure toward increasing levels of tightly integrated ordered energy flows—"ordered complexity." Evolution is a general process that proceeds inexorably and opportunistically to higher and higher levels of ordered complexity. It is still going on today. It will go on tomorrow.

That is the end of the story. The path to this end goes through chaos, self-organization theory, the thermodynamics of evolution, and biological evolution. The goal is to make these titles and their roles accessible. This means brevity and a lot of references to other work with more detail. I end with two examples, one economic and one metaphysical, of how the new understanding changes our perspective. For the economics, I describe how the rules for growth of complexity apply to the current crisis in business. For the metaphysics, I show how the new view fits with traditional spiritual insights.

Most people here are familiar with chaos and many with self-organization theory. I also use work in the thermodynamics of evolution that is much less well-known. I introduce what I believe is a very pivotal piece of theory, Swenson's (1989a, 1989b) Principle of Maximum Entropy Production (MEP). MEP provides an explanation of why order emerges and complexity grows. Interestingly enough, MEP crystallizes the physical understanding of order production by adding a rate factor to the second law of thermodynamics—the very law that has long been viewed as an antiorder principle. The net result is a fully physical understanding of ordering that can be traced from the mechanical to the biological.

THE NONLINEAR REVOLUTION AND THE EVOLVING ECOLOGICAL UNIVERSE

This story begins with chaos, that is, modern nonlinear dynamics. As this book is centered around chaos, there are numerous chapters that introduce the concepts of attractors, bifurcations, fractals, the butterfly effect (technical chaos), etc. I do not review these concepts here. I start more basically—with the concept of *nonlinearity*. The concept of nonlinearity is key because order building is primarily a product of nonlinear dynamics. The term *nonlinear* sounds complicated. I start with the basics because to fully understand the revolution at hand, one must fully understand just how simple, common, and basic nonlinearity is.

The first thing to know about nonlinearity is that, despite its distressing name, it is utterly simple. Technically, a nonlinear system is any system in which input is not proportional to output, that is, an increase in *x*, does not mean a proportional increase or decrease in *y*. A simple example of a nonlinear system is the headache system. If you have a headache and you take one aspirin, it will reduce your headache by a certain amount. If you take 2 aspirins, they will reduce it somewhat more, and 8 aspirins somewhat more. But it is quite obvious that 64 aspirins will not reduce your headache 64 times as much as one will. A headache is, therefore, a nonlinear system. Nonlinearity is as simple as that. It is everything whose graph is not a straight line—and this is essentially everything.[1]

The second thing to know about nonlinearity is that, from a linear perspective, it is quite a paradoxical beast. Humankind's first-position thinking is linear. In linear thinking, if something works well, then more of it is better; if something has a bad effect, less is better. And while this is an extremely reasonable place to start, one quickly learns that the world is much more subtle than this. The rise of nonlinear models means the rise of a more subtle and, consequently, a more realistic vision of the world. For example, nonlinear modeling has helped engineers see why adding a new road sometimes increases traffic congestion. This and similarly contrary phenomenon have long been observed, but without nonlinear models they seem to defy logic, law, and reason. Time and again, nonlinear models show that apparently aberrant, illogical behavior is, in fact, a completely lawful part of the system. Nonlinear models make such behavior more concrete, and, consequently, more reasonable. They make nonlinear behavior logical.

The last thing to know about nonlinearity is that it is virtually impossible to pin it down as a whole to any one type of effect. I mention this because with the advent of chaos there has been a disturbing tendency to make sweeping statements about nonlinear effects. Nonlinearity is, in fact, quite contrary. Thus,

---

[1]Linear models are actually an idealization. There are no completely linear systems, just linear models. Linear models, however, are very useful, especially over very short ranges and for certain types of systems. A great deal of scientific knowledge is based on linear models because that is the best early tools could do. The nonlinear revolution highlights the fact that a large number of hidden scientific assumptions have consequently also come out of linear models. Modern nonlinear dynamics is most important, not because of fractals or the butterfly effect per se, but because it opens up the nonlinear realm. And in the process, it shows how much of our world view was biased by linear assumptions.

nonlinearity can produce either positive (amplifying) or negative (dampening) feedback. It can produce stability or instability. It may produce coherence (e.g., convergence, coupling, or entrainment) but it may also produce divergence and explosion. The key to understanding nonlinearity is that, quite unlike linear systems, opposing tendencies may be built into a single system. This means a nonlinear world is extremely versatile.

Nonlinearity is simple, nonmagical, lawful, and yet extremely versatile. The concept of nonlinearity is important because once one realizes that everything is fundamentally nonlinear and that nonlinearity has the potential for behavior quite out of line with linear expectations, then one understands how classical science might have missed some of the things we are exploring. And all of this is true before one gets to chaos, per se. Until modern computational power made it accessible, science saw but a tip of the nonlinear world. This meant that the bulk of the world's subtlety was unapproachable. Chaos, self-organization theory, and the thermodynamics of evolution make up a "nonlinear revolution" because nonlinearity lies behind the insights that each of these divisions brings to the fore. The theme for this revolution is that when you broaden science with insights of the nonlinear world, you get a very different picture of how the world works.

This is nonlinearity. But there is another concept that is also critical to the nonlinear revolution: interdependence. Popular chaos literature often confounds interdependence and nonlinearity, but actually they are not related. Nonlinearity has to do with proportionality. Interdependence has to do with whether or not two things mutually affect each other (or, in mathematical terms, whether or not the two are functions of one another). A conversation is an interdependent (also called interactive) communication between two people—both people are affected, and the exchange becomes a reciprocating mutual effect system. In theory, a soliloquy is an independent (unidirectional) communication—one can speak of the message having an effect only on the receiver. Independent systems like linear systems are actually just useful idealizations. In the real world there are no truly linear systems and there are no truly independent systems—not even soliloquies. The notion of truly independent systems has also tended to create erroneous assumptions about how the world (vs. our models) works.

Interdependence is important because it too is critical part of chaos and order building. The nonlinear revolution's most radical insights come out of nonlinear interdependent systems. For example, the phenomenon of chaos (sensitive dependence) itself occurs only in nonlinear interdependent systems. Nonlinearity alone is not enough. In point of fact, classical physics was able to deal with most nonlinear independent systems. The nonlinear revolution, then, is about exploring the nature of nonlinear interdependency, which, in the final analysis, is what all real world systems are.

How does this relate to a new vision of things? Classical approaches such as calculus and linear approximations first broke down when people tried to make their models more realistic, which meant including nonlinear interdependent aspects that had been there all along. The classic example of this is the three-body problem. Newton established the classical vision of precise prediction by applying equations of motion to the solar system. He did this using a simple two-body model; he looked at the effects of a massive body, the sun, on individual smaller bodies, the planets, taken one at a time. Chaos was first discovered when people tried to increase the precision of the model by adding the affects of just one more body (say, a moon or another planet). This model of the solar system is a three-body problem. The problem was that this minutely more sophisticated model could not be solved by approximation methods and had unexpected behaviors that did not appear in the two-body model. The three-body problem exhibits chaos. Newtonian predictability is an illusion of the simpler model.

So, note that the classical vision of the world is a result of the models used. It is a false impression resulting from successfully approximating certain relatively simple systems with simple models. And it is obvious that the three-body problem is a more correct (that is, more realistic) model of the solar system than is the two-body model. Thus, while the new vision of things may have limitations of its own, it is clearly a more accurate rendition than the classical vision. The classical Newtonian clockwork vision was built on an excruciatingly limited-case set of systems and (retrospectively) primitive early models.[2]

So, how does science's vision change? Classical science emphasized linear, independent, closed, and equilibrium models, and these created a particular image of the world. The Newtonian machine world is regular, predictable, controllable, completely knowable (in principle), passive, directionless, and incapable of spontaneously producing order. The classical injunction against order has forced scientists to invoke accident, anomaly, or various mysterious makers of order—for example, selfish genes, the human brain, and life—as the origin of the particular directed orderly phenomenon that they examine. An order-hostile universe makes it hard to explain where coordination comes from. It also tends to make human beings see themselves as separate from the world. Whether God

---

[2]It is interesting to note that the Newtonian view is not a line-shaped view per se but a calculus-shaped view. Calculus, the quintessential tool of the first scientific revolution, works its miracles by breaking down and approximating complex curves with straight lines or simple curves. This approach works both on linear and many nonlinear systems. Classical physics was not limited by nonlinearity per se but by the inability of calculus (and related approximation methods) to solve certain types of problems—nonlinear interdependent ones. What Poincare showed with the famous three-body problem was that even a very simple nonlinear interdependent system (three interacting bodies) could not be broken down and approximated by simpler curves. Why? Because approximation by simpler curves, the very basis of classical tools, often does not work in even very simple interdependent cases. For example, the three-body problem could not be solved because it is a "fractal," and a fractal is a mathematical object that is equally complex at all levels. No matter how small a piece you take, it is no simpler. Mandelbrot (1983) suggested that most naturally occurring geometries are fractal.

created us or we were an accident, we were not part of the mundane physical world. The Newtonian view resulted form calculus being able to precisely predict certain limited-case systems and then extrapolating the characteristics of limited-case systems to the world at large.[3]

Collectively, western civilization is shaking off Newtonian clockwork-machine images and beliefs and replacing them with evolutionary and ecological images and beliefs. This shift to ecological thinking is happening in the culture in general. Images of ecology and change (evolution) are everywhere. The non-linear revolution represents the physical science branch of this transformation. It creates a profound form of ecologism by making the evolving ecology metaphor fully physical. The next sections make the meaning of these statements very concrete, but I summarize the differences.

The nonlinear revolution creates a very non-Newtonian image of the world. The first message of chaos is that physical and lawful does not mean predictable, controllable, or completely knowable. This alone shakes the classical firmament. Thus, an evolving ecological universe is lawful and physical but not completely predictable, controllable, or knowable. It is a bit more illusive, more endlessly mysterious than a Newtonian world. Chaos' second message is that there is order hidden in complexity. Nonlinear interdependent dynamics have penchants for creating such things as patterns, coherence, stable dynamic structures, networks, coupling, synchronization, and synergy. This is why when nonlinear interdependence is restored to the world, the miracle of order production is made part of the world, not some kind of accident. Self-organization and the thermodynamics of evolution expand the vision of order that chaos implies. They suggest that order production is driven by the rules of energy flow. An energy-driven evolving ecological universe moves toward higher and higher levels of complexity. It is active, creative, goes in a direction, and is capable of producing both order and disorder. It is not regular, but it is lawful and patterned. Change is not gradual, but punctuated, it moves through periods of stable sameness and qualitative change. And above all, such a universe is a vastly more integrated, holistically interconnected unity than was previously realized.

In summary, the nonlinear revolution is about shifting our sense of how things work from models based on excruciatingly limited and idealized systems (linear, independent, closed, equilibrium) to lessons learned from the most common types of system, nonlinear interdependent ones. To reduce the jargon overhead and to underscore the idea that the real world is nonlinear interdependent, substi-

---

[3]Newton-bashing has been a favorite theme of new age writers and chaos writers also often play this game. By way of correction then, it is important to note that Newton does not go away. The findings of classical physics remain, they are just seen in a very different context. The systems that succumbed to the classical paradigm were a more limited case than was previously appreciated. The characteristics of these systems do not extrapolate well to the broader case. We must remove assumptions based on them from our collective unconscious. Nevertheless, Newtonian findings remain quite intact.

tute the word "most" for nonlinear interdependent. Every place you see "most systems" you can substitute "nonlinear interdependent systems" to be technically accurate.

THE MESSAGES OF CHAOS

How does chaos connect to order building and an ecological sense of how things work? Chaos provides the foundations of an ecological physics with a few rather simple lessons, as follows:

1. *Order is hidden in chaos.* There is order in complexity. Strange attractors show that intricately ordered flows can be hidden in what looks like completely erratic behavior. They also suggest that "most" dynamics have a heretofore unrecognized penchant for producing intricately ordered patterns. Mutually affecting variables tend to coeffect themselves into stable, ordered patterns.

2. *The order in chaos is holistic order and results from mutual effects.* The order in chaos is a result of interdependent variables coeffecting each other—push-me-pull-you-fashion—into a coherent pattern. The result is a hidden holistic pattern. It does not come from any one variable, it doesn't go in a straight line, and it does not imply a fixed sequence. It is order of the whole. People didn't even see the order in chaos until they looked at how all the system's variables change together over the whole range of the system's dynamics. Chaos is a holistic order that nevertheless arises from mechanical activity.

3. *The order in chaos provides a mechanical explanation for "mysterious" hidden global ordering (an "invisible hand").* Adam Smith spoke of an invisible hand at work behind the operation of economies. Hegel described the world evolving through dialectics and order hidden beneath surface vicissitudes. Mutual-effect systems that create order of the whole provide a mechanical basis for this type of observation. The activity of the elements of a mutual-effect system creates global order; this mutually created global order creates a pressure on each individual element toward conformity to the global pattern. A treadmill gives a simple example of this global mutual-effect momentum phenomenon. Walking on the treadmill causes it to move but its motion creates a pressure to keep walking and to walk even faster. In a complex mutual-effect system, this you-caused-it/it-causes-you phenomenon tends to be subtle, omnipresent, and quite potent. A corollary to this fact is that mutual-effect systems are created from both the bottom up and the top down.

4. *Nonlinear interdependent dynamics have a penchant for creating wholes out of parts.* Strange attractors give an abstract sense that nonlinear dynamics can create wholes out of parts. The phenomenon of coupling/entrainment provides a more concrete example of this fact. The classic example of entrainment is the

phenomenon of self-synchronizing cuckoo clocks. If you hang a number of cuckoo clocks on a wall with their pendulums out of sync, after a while, their pendulums will become synchronized. As each pendulum swings, it sends small perturbations through the wall that affect its fellows; it is, in turn, affected by similar perturbations from the other clocks. The many independent cuckoo-clock systems "couple" into a larger coordinated clock system; they act as one. Entrainment is the technical term for this tendency to couple into larger wholes. The point here is that the spontaneous creation of assemblies (or "unities") through self-coordination is quite natural even in completely mechanical systems.

5. *Nonlinear systems may exhibit qualitative transformations of behavior (bifurcations).* The idea is simple: a single system may exhibit many different forms of behavior—all the result of the same basic dynamic. One equation, many faces. A corollary to this idea is that a system may have multiple attractors, multiple competing forms of behavior, each perhaps a hairsbreadth away, each representing a stable mutual-effect organization. The classic examples here are horses' gaits: walking, trotting, galloping, and running. Each gait represents a completely different organization of leg motion. The transition between gaits occurs in a sudden reorganization. Generally, the horse goes faster and faster within one gait and then suddenly shifts to a new type of organization that allows an increase in speed—walk to trot, trot to gallop. This last exhibits another phenomenon—that bifurcations frequently occur in a series as a particular parameter is increased. In the case of a horse, gait bifurcation occurs in a series as speed increases. May's (1974) classical bifurcation diagram showed how different population patterns emerged as the fertility rate inceased.

THE MESSAGES OF SELF-ORGANIZATION THEORY

Chaos provides a completely mechanical understanding of ecological dynamics. Self-organization theory adds the dimension of energy flow (usually couched in terms of distance from equilibrium).

Thermodynamics is the science of energy flow. Like classical mechanics, classical thermodynamics grew up around its first-accessible cases, in this case, closed, near-equilibrium systems. Like linear independent systems, closed near-equilibrium systems are an extremely limited idealized case. Here too assumptions derived from this early work were inappropriately extrapolated and have become insidiously woven into everyday thought. Goldstein (1990), for example, outlined how equilibrium thinking affects the work of Sigmund Freud and Kurt Lewin.

Ilya Prigogine (1980, 1984) is the person most singly attributed with self-organization theory. A Nobel-prize winning chemist, Prigogine detailed far-from-equilibrium systems that had certain amazing characteristics—they self-organized. Seen mechanically in chaos, Prigogine detailed the operation of self-organization in chemical and heat transfer systems. He also made the first connections to self-organization in living systems. His systems were not life, but they behaved much like life. Finally, he took the concept to popular audiences. Through his influence, work such as that of Von Bertalanffy (1968) in General Systems Theory was tied to a more formal thermodynamic and simple system base.[4]

Since, in this rendition, chaos already shows self-coordination and the spontaneous creation of wholes out of parts, the messages of self-organization theory are:

1. *Self-organizing, self-maintaining dynamic organizations occur spontaneously far from equilibrium (they do not occur at, or near, equilibrium).* Energy flow plays a fundamental role in the creation of such order in the real world. With large disequilibriums, the far-from-equilibrium situation is key.

2. *Self-organization found in nonliving systems provides both a metaphor and a conceptual model for living systems and supra-living systems (e.g., cities).* Even in simple physical self-organizing systems, such as whirlpools and tornadoes, one finds the basic elements of a "self," a figure distinct from the ground. One finds boundaries, ordered activity that maintains the system's form (identify), and energy exchanges with the environment that maintain its distance from equilibrium. Prigogine described how self-generated, self-maintaining, self-organizing dynamics produce and maintain these phenomenon spontaneously.

3. *New forms of organization emerge through the process of order through fluctuation.* Self-organization is usually a result of "a small fluctuation being amplified into a new form." A simple fluid experiment called the Benard cell gives a concrete example of what this means. The Benard cell is a box containing fluid to which heat is added. At low temperatures, the heat is spread by random molecular collisions. Though it is filled with seething oscillating motion, the fluid appears homogeneous; there is no coordinated motion. Little collections of relatively hot or cold molecules have been coming together and moving apart all along, but at higher temperatures an interesting thing happens—some small collection of hot molecules moves some distance upward as a whole because its relative heat content makes it lighter and therefore more buoyant than those it surrounds. This kind of event begins to happen all over. Eventually, a collection rises all the way to the top, pulls other molecules up in its wake, loses its heat to cooler regions at the top, and sinks back down. Suddenly, the entire region erupts in a coherent coordinated circular motion.

---

[4]In many ways, self-organization theory is primarily a refinement of Von Bertalanffy's (1968) open systems and General System's theory. The basic features are the same: open energy-flow dynamics (vs. closed systems) that result in energy exchanges that allow an identifiable system to maintain its integrity, and resulting common patterns of behavior that hold across levels and types of system.

Prigogine showed that this same type of order-through-fluctuation process occurs in all sorts of systems from heat, to chemical, to living. It is easily seen metaphorically in human situations, such as the recent upheavals in Russia—in the right context, a small collection with a different configuration taps an energy buildup, becomes a conduit, and produces a flow of a very different form. A new configuration emerges from the previous.

THE THERMODYNAMICS OF EVOLUTION AND GENERAL EVOLUTIONARY THEORY

So we have mechanical order production and we have far-from-equilibrium islands of self-organization. To get to a general theory of evolution, we need a reason that self-organizing tendencies come into being, persist and move to higher and higher levels of organization. And we have to have some sense of how the process works as a whole, not just in particular locales.

The emerging answer is that the growth of complexity (evolution) is an energy-flow rate phenomenon. There are several facts that support this answer. First, self-organizations always increase the rate of energy transfer. As Table 2.1 shows, the more intricate the organization, the faster the energy flow.

Second, self-organizing systems are also known to go through a series of organizations and reorganizations as part of accelerating energy flow. Driven energy flow phenomena go in a direction and lead to a series of increasingly complex and intricately ordered patterns. One need only think of boiling water. You have a lot of heat; first you get little bubbles, then strings of bubbles up the side, ripples, undulations, and finally a full, rolling boil. Each stage sets the stage for the next and each transfers energy a little faster.

This same acceleration of energy flow has been observed over the evolution life on earth, the succession of ecosystems (grass plains to oak forests) and the evolution of the universe (atoms to galaxies). For example, Fig. 2.1 shows accelerating energy-flow curve for the succession of dominate life-forms on earth.

Thus, there is a great deal of evidence that evolution of increasingly intricately

TABLE 2.1
Increasing Energy Flow Rates With Increasingly Intricate
Organizations (after Chaisson, 1987, p.254)

Structure	F (ergs s^{-1} gm^{-1})
Milky Way	1
Sun	2
Earth's climasphere	80
Earth's biosphere (plants)	500
Human body	17,000
Human brain	150,000

Accelerating Energy Flow Processing in the Evolution of Life
(Swenson, 1989a).

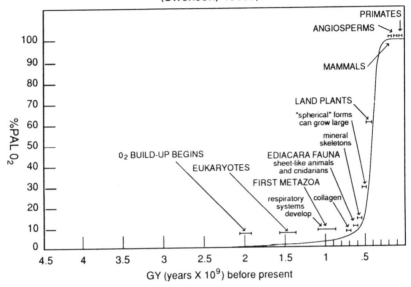

FIG. 2.1. The succession of dominant life-forms on earth has also been a succession of higher-rate metabolizers which effectively amounts to higher rate energy processors. This figure shows that the rate of energy processing for the succession of dominate life-forms on earth has been accelerating. The figure also shows co-evolution of life and the level of atmospheric oxygen. %PAL stands for percent of present atmospheric oxygen levels. Oxygen allows higher rates of metabolism. As higher rate species evolved, they also contributed to higher levels of oxygen which allowed even higher rate species to evolve. (Reprinted with permission from Dr. J. Donald DeRaadt, International Society for Systems Science.)

ordered forms is an energy-flow-rate phenomenon (see Chaisson, 1987; Lotka, 1922; Morowitz, 1968; Odum, 1988; and Pettersson, 1978) over both cosmological and biological time. To use the jargon, increasing levels of "ordered complexity" is intricately tied to increasing rates of energy flow. Ordering and energy-flow efficiency go hand in glove.

The idea that evolution follows a serial pattern of organization and reorganization is in fact quite old. Herbert Spencer (1862) noted that "the instability of the homogeneous . . . the transformation of the incoherent into the coherent hold uniformly from the earliest traceable cosmical changes down to the latest results of civilization." Margulis (1970, 1981, 1982) both strengthened and updated this basic notion with her theory of "serial endosymbiosis." In a nutshell, she showed that the basic path of biological evolution is through the coupling of independent forms into more efficient and more creatively adapted cooperatives. Thus, she noted that the main internal structures of cells such as mitochondria did not originate inside the cell, but reflect a long-standing coupling. Similarly, land plants emerged through symbiotic coupling between lichens and photosynthetic algae. Maturana and Varela (1987) similarly described biology via coupling—single cells to multicellular animals, to families, to herds, to civilizations.

Various other authors have developed the notions of coevolution and the invisibly ordered context. The Gaia hypothesis (Lovelock, 1979) has provided ample evidence that the biosphere functions as an intricately ordered, self-maintaining whole. Material cycles go up through the atmosphere, down through the oceans, in through plant and animal life, both simple and complex—all this is coordinated and interconnected, in a massive self-reinforcing, self-generating way. The point of Gaia is that the biosphere acts like a self-regulating whole (see also Holland, 1978).

And behind the scenes, chaos' vision of nonlinear interdependent dynamics provides a mechanical underpinning. Thus, Eigen and Schuster's (1979) notion of hypercycles describes how self-sustaining cycles develop, increase in coherence, and spread their interconnections. Chemical hypercycles can be seen in living (the Krebs cycle) and nonliving (the carbon cycle) systems and at scales from the microscopic to interplanetary. Like Prigoginian self-organization, such cycles have many behaviors that mirror life. For example, Csanyi (1989) described how cycles begin to reproduce themselves creating widespread replicative networks. The spontaneous emergence of replicating cycles, self-maintained boundaries, self-maintained internal coordination, and internal–external exchanges in nonliving systems makes life seem like a much more natural thing. Even origin of life work is beginning to be recast as a coupling of independent forms into a cooperative with qualitatively new survival enhancing properties (see Dyson, 1985).

To sum up, the image of an intricately interwoven ecological universe—self-ordering and built of nonlinear dynamics—is already well supported. MEP fits into this rather pregnant context like a kind of keystone. It links a number of ideas and dissolves several blocks in one fell swoop. And this gives the whole concept of general evolution greater solidity and continuity.

MEP ties the concept of order building to entropy production and thus to the second law of thermodynamics. Linking order to the second law removes one of the blocks to belief in an order-producing universe. The second law says that entropy increases (is produced) whenever energy flows. MEP adds a rate factor to the second law, it says that not only does entropy increase, it increases at the fastest rate possible, given the constraints. Oddly enough, this simple change makes order and disorder both part of the second law. The faster energy flows, the faster entropy is produced. Ordered flows transfers energy faster than disordered flows; hence, they produce entropy faster. The pressure to go as fast as possible means the second law prefers order because it produces entropy faster; it will produce order whenever possible.

The catch, however, is the word "possible." It takes energy to produce order. Whenever there is a concentration of energy, there is a force, a pressure to flow.

Resistance, however, in its many forms (barriers, weight, momentum, density, inertia), constrains flow. There is always a tug-of-war going on between inertial resistance and the pressure to flow. When the pressure to flow is small, inertia wins out and the system runs downhill (energy flows slower and slower). When the pressure is large, it overcomes resistance and the system runs uphill (energy flows faster and faster).

Whether the system goes downhill, uphill, or creates new order depends on the pressure to flow. At first, if pressure is greater than resistance, energy flows faster and faster within its current form. For example, in the Benard cell, in the beginning, adding more heat means that random collisions occur faster and faster. There is a limit, however, to how fast any particular type of flow can transfer energy. If the pressure to flow is still greater than resistance when that limit is reached, a crisis occurs—the system will drive a new, more efficient form of flow into being. Slightly more efficient fluctuations channel more energy and thus pull more energy into themselves. If a fluctuation taps into a large energy buildup, energy pours in. As in the Benard cell, the field amplifies the fluctuation into a new form of flow. We say a bifurcation occurs. In short, when the conditions are ripe, the field opportunistically amplifies some randomly occurring, minutely more efficient fluctuation into a new form of flow.

Massive disequilibriums create a cycle of evolution. Each new form comes into being, accelerates, reaches its limits, and is succeeded by a yet more efficient form of flow. Such systems or, more accurately, such fields[5] will exhibit "punctuated equilibrium"—periods of sameness followed by sudden change. Such fields will exhibit an accelerating pace of change, accelerating energy-flow efficiency, and increasing complexity. The earth being between the sun and the cold sink of space is in such a massively far-from-equilibrium field. The universe itself, expanding from the big bang, is also a massively far-from-equilibrium field. The biological record exhibits a punctuated equilibrium pattern (see Gould, 1980; Zeeman, 1986).[6]

There another important thing to note—energy-driven evolution is a phenomenon of the whole field. It is the field's (i.e., the whole's) energy configuration that drives general evolution. Thus, complexity grows and flow accelerates in the field as a whole, not necessarily in any given locale. It is the whole that evolves through the seething ecology of its elements. The field is very inhomogeneous. There is great diversity and room for many ecological niches. Particular locales may evolve in relative isolation for a while, but, in the final analysis, all smaller fields are part of the larger fields. There are no closed systems; it is only a matter of time. As locales become more and more tightly integrated, they spread and press outward. In the background, subtle organization (the Gaian type) acts as a

---

[5]*Field* is the technical name for all the matter and energy in a particular region. Fields contain systems.

[6]Such a recursive cycle of order production would help account for the commonness of fractal geometry in nature. Fractals are quintessentially an outcome of recursive processes.

hidden connection. Everything affects everything—eventually. The field's pressure to flow brings us and all other things into being in coevolving ecological interconnectedness.[7]

This is the basic picture of evolution and the order-producing universe—nonlinear dynamics explains the mechanics, self-organization explains particular locales, the thermodynamics of evolution explains why it goes in a series and is interconnected, biology bears it out. How do we use it? The next section is written as a metaphor for business/organizational development. It looks at the pragmatics and some additional rules for the growth complexity.

THE PRAGMATICS OF CHANGE

In a Newtonian view, an organization is a machine. You need to structure it, control its parts (the workers), and you try to predict the future by extrapolating from the present. An evolving ecological view is very different. Order grows. To get new order you need three things: constraints, fluctuations, and energy. No fluctuations, no seeds for the next round of growth. No constraints, no boundary to channel growth—you never get more than random collisions. No energy, no drive, no nothing. In an ecological perspective, organizations are embedded in a field that drives their evolution. Human beings are walking self-organizations in need of energy to keep themselves going. Thus, they are directed (i.e., channeled) by nature. To channel their energies toward a larger organization you primarily need to make their needs and its common. Money does this partially, but it does not capture self-esteem, joy, and curiosity. The current round of management literature is filled with techniques such as "visioning" aimed a developing a coupling between worker and organizational needs. From the ecological perspective, one must also watch out for constraints that block flow or that suppress fluctuations. The following image applies. If one removes all impurities (super-purifies) from a fluid, damps all vibrations, and adds heat, an interesting thing happens. Instead of going through a gradual evolution, the system reaches a critical threshold and explodes. Coordinated, self-sustaining flow grows out of fine-grained mutual relations. If you block self-organization, the pressures will still force a change, it just won't involve the evolution of self-maintaining self-generating flow—it won't involve organization.

The difference between a mechanistic and an ecological vision is striking. In an ecological view, people are intrinsically motivated, self-organization will occur spontaneously if the environment is conducive, emphasis on control is bad for structurally sound growth, the future is not an extrapolation of the present.

---

[7]This is an important point because self-organization theory has a tendency to portray those little islands of organization as pulling themselves up by their bootstraps against the field. This creates an erroneous sense of separation and operation against the flow. Worse, it denies ecological interconnectedness and co-evolution. Self-organization is driven into being by the field.

Ecologism also describes rules for the growth of complexity—reasons that there are plateaus, divisions, and reorganizations. The most fundamental rule is the surface–volume rule. Long known in biology, this rule can now be tied to energy-flow principles. Basically, the rule says that as a self-organization increases in volume, it must also increase in surface area. The ratio of volume to surface area can never be greater than two-thirds power (which is the ratio of the surface of a sphere to the volume of a sphere). The reason for this is that, as the volume grows, the forces that hold the thing together get stretched more and more thinly. The surface–volume ratio is the limit at which the forces of self-organization break. At this limit the organization stops growing, falls apart, or reorganizes.

So, how does self-organization get past the surface–volume limit? The most common answer to the dilemma has been to grow to a certain size and then couple with other similar-sized organizations (similar sized means on the same scale, i.e. molecules couple with other molecules not with atoms). This strategy increases the volume by creating an umbrella around numerous smaller surfaces. The result of this strategy is general oscillation between divergence (small cells developing and spreading) and convergence (coupling between forms or enveloping of smaller forms) in the field at large. It also produces both vertical growth (higher levels) and increasing scope (greater ordered volume). The surface–volume rule is the reason our bodies are composed of cells organized into organs, organized into systems. It's what forces a new levels or types of organization into being—often with characteristics not found in the smaller pieces individually.

The surface–volume rule also brings out the ecological view's different understanding of cooperation and competition. In an ecological world, competition is a survival phenomenon. All self-organizations must compete for enough energy (resources) to hold their boundaries intact and maintain their internal coordination. Yet, here, cooperation is also a survival phenomenon but of a different type. All major increases in efficiency are results of cooperative effects. Molecules are atom collectives, plants are lichen and photosynthetic algal collectives, our bodies are cell collectives, societies are human collectives. Each of these is made up of elements that were separate and independent before they became integrated and interdependent. Each collective vastly increased efficiency over the individual. Because evolution is a matter of increasing efficiency, increasing levels and intricacy of cooperation enhance survival. Thus, competition keeps an organization intact, but cooperation is the route to long-term continuation.

Pantzar (1991) provided an example of ecological evolution in his description of the evolution of U.S. corporations and industry from 1840 to 1910. At the beginning of the 19th century the United States was an insular economy dominated by small unspecialized enterprises. The general merchant, all-purpose businessmen—exporter, importer, wholesaler, retailer, banker and, insurer—dominated the economy. He knew most of the people involved personally. At the end of the same century, the economy was dominated by large industrial corporations and networks of small, specialized enterprises. The modern corporation, with multiple levels of professional management, had come into being. The evolution of the railroad industry shows how this end developed. The general pattern was (a) experimentation phases settling into predictable patterns creating "stable staircases of former industries," (b) coevolution of productive and distributive operations, and (c) ongoing feedback between evolving systems. The message: The evolution of this complexity was a phenomenon of the field as a whole.

Started in 1830, the railroad (transportation) boom paralleled the "'takeoff'" of the U.S. economy in general. Railroads grew 11.38% per year from 1838 to 1910. Each new stage in development solved some problems and created new ones. In railroads, the problem emphasis moved from (a) coordinating "physical objects" (building tracks, designing engines); to (b) coordinating human beings (bureaucratic control, telegraphic communications, formalized operating procedures, timetables); to (c) coordinating interactions between different railroad companies, large customers, and suppliers. As each phase solved and, hence, stabalized its problems, it created a foundation for a new level of problems. For example, by the 1860s, completion of routes and standardizing of operating procedures allowed massive increases in volume and speed of transportation for individual firms. Unfortunately, because it was not integrated, volume in the network as a whole did not increase. And this situation forced a shift of focus— from owned objects to relations with other companies. Price competition on routes drove railroad companies to cooperative alliances that expanded the flow of traffic to the advantage of all. As long as traffic expanded, informal alliances worked well. But, as traffic volumes reached saturation, competitive pressures returned. Faced with ruinous competition, railroad managers moved into formal, well-orchestrated dalliances. In the 1860s, the railway network was not integrated; by the 1880s, a rail shipment could move from one part of the country to another without a single transshipment.

Cooperation appeared to be getting control of competition when suddenly another shift occurred. Railroad alliances were attacked by farmers and traders for attempting to maintain artificially high rates. Additionally, the cartels were unable to handle the complexity of administering cross-network traffic. Pressure intensified not to follow cartel arrangements that, in turn, encouraged the development of professional management. Middle managers provided the administrative coordination that was done poorly by alliances. They subverted the cooperative system by cutting rates to keep traffic. When they were unable to control the oligopolistic pricing by means of formal associations, they pressed to become as self-sufficient as possible. New levels of top management emerged to decide future directions—when to buy or build inter-territorial systems. In the 1860s, small, personally run transportation firms began to be replaced by large, managerially administered enterprises. These enterprises expanded, internalizing large numbers of activities previously handled by hundreds of small enterprises. Enterprises that began as railroads expanded into coal properties, coastal steamers, chains of hotels, and manufacturers of their own sleeping and parlor cars. Interestingly enough, this system building was not done to increase profits but defensively, for survival. As one of the system builders put it:

> I have long been of the opinion that sooner or later the railroads of the country would group themselves into systems [that were] self-sustaining, or in other words, any system that was not self-sustaining would. . .be absorbed by those systems near at hand and strong enough to live alone. . .Each line must own its feeders. (Chandler, 1977, p.159)

The system-building drive grew through the 1880s, but in 1893 things began to change again. Focused on the moves of their rivals and not on estimates of the demand for transportation, system building and the drive to self-sufficiency led many railroads to bankruptcy. By 1906, two thirds of the nation's mileage was operated by seven groups. The system plateaued. The once growing railroad map remained relatively unchanged until railroads became technologically obsolete after World War II. Strategic planning no longer required close attention, pricing and investment became routinized, and management became increasingly bureaucratized. The competitive environment became stable.

Starting as independent enterprises, moving through informal collectives, to formal collectives, to increasing levels and specialization of hierarchy, the railroads stabilized and then declined. The railroad example shows the oscillating pressures between competition and cooperation, the affect of outside and inside influences, and the increase of volume through coupling and increasing levels. It is a study in the growth of complexity.

The current crisis in U.S. industry is also a study in the growth of complexity. In the current case, we have reached the limits of hierarchy itself. This limit is marked by a push to eliminate middle levels of management, to spin off independent cost centers, to encourage teamwork and cooperation. Adding new vertical levels of management is no longer productive. The bonds of coherence are stretched too thin to handle the pace of change. In evolutionary terms, we are seeking a new form of organization that allows the volume to increase by linking smaller, self-organizing surfaces. Toward this end, management theory is changing. Traditional management theory based on Newtonian/Darwinian images emphasizes control as the goal of management and competition as the way to efficiency. Both of these emphases block self-organizing tendencies, as do pressures toward conformity to job titles, pleasing superiors, and parochial self-interest. Traditional information-up, control-down organizations stifle top-to-bottom coupling, and inverted tree organization charts stifle side-to-side coupling. The American corporation is a crisis searching for a new economic form.

The nonlinear revolution has several contributions towards this search. First is the vision of self-organization itself. Self-organization is the most common and most natural form of organization. It is quite possible that management has never really been in a "control" position. The organization-chart image has probably been a very poor model of reality. It is quite likely that simply becoming aware and supportive of existing self-organizing tendencies at all levels can go a long way in producing new levels of productivity.

The nonlinear revolution's second contribution is its vision of cooperation. Competition loses its title as creator of efficiency. This too has been a poor model of reality. Becoming aware and supportive of cooperative tendencies can also go a long way in increasing productivity. This idea abounds in new management literature. There is now a more concrete basis for it.

Changing from a control–competition emphasis to a self-organization–cooperation emphasis will take a lot of training. But there is another, deeper implication of the nonlinear ecological vision. An ecological entrepreneurial system includes understanding the interconnectedness of all the players as a first principle. Connection is not just between the owners and the workers, not just between the workers and the suppliers and the customers, but between all of these and all the people down stream. A successful organization will go through ongoing transformations, a cycle of growth of complexity. It will go from one plateau organization to the next. As it grows, it will tend to interconnect and start to evolve in scope and integration with other entities in the environment, as with the railroads. What constitutes "the organization" and what it does is likely to change. But, there is more. The organization is nothing and goes nowhere except with the rest. Like the current economic and world political crisis, understanding complexity creates an awareness of both the importance and the inescapability of interdependence. This awareness demands a new way of being. this is the metaphor of our time.

And notably, under complexity the importance of interconnection becomes a pragmatic as well as a noble truth. As an example, let us look at both the Communist failure and the capitalist crisis in ecological terms. The key concepts are: *openness, nonlinearity/self-organization,* and *ecological embeddedness.* Communism believed in interconnection (socialism) but pursued economic growth as if it could be done in a closed box (i.e., the Iron Curtain) and with Newtonian principles (i.e., controlled, planned, predicted). The result of such controlled Newtonian planning was an economic system that was rigid, unstable, and overly dependent on the fixed links of the economic chain. In Communism, Newtonian planning blocked ecological growth. Western capitalism on the other hand has long cherished nonlinear images—notions of novelty, spontaneous growth, and amplifying fluctuations. These are the quintessential images of the entrepreneur. Unfortunately, Western capitalism does not understand interdependence or coevolution. Rather, it wallows in separateness. The entrepreneur is a loner; management is separate from workers, workers from customers, and businesses from each other—self-interest is king. But hyper-self-interest also produces a fragile economic ecology. Low quality, cynicism among workers and consumers, leveraged buy-outs that kill productive companies by saddling them with massive debt, scandals, such as the Savings and Loan scandal—the era of the Donald Trumps has produced economic hollowness. In capitalism, the inability to see self-interest as tied to ecological soundness also undermines economic health. Self-interest is best served by being aware of and going with ecological embeddedness. The noble principles of cooperation and interconnection are pragmatic principles as well.

Having looked at the material side of the world, let us now see how the same view also fits with the traditionally nonmaterial side.

HOW DOES THE WORLD WORK? A COSMOLOGY FOR SCIENCE AND SPIRITUALITY

Classical science painted a picture of a purposeless, decaying universe. If one believed this image was fact, then all order–purpose–direction describing traditions were not scientific and not physical. Once order building has a physical basis, this irreconcilable difference falls away. Of course, the new physical image of how the world works does not support all spiritual beliefs, just a much more consonant cosmology.

A Directed Creative Universe   Until its incommensuration ends, the universe is directed toward creation of increasingly ordered forms. We and all "things" that we see are the net result of this creative drive. A sense of direction, of a process larger than ourselves, and of a creative force is restored.

An Opportunistic Universe and a Cooperative One   The delicate balance between forces and flows means that forms will exist in exact proportion to the forces. To the extent that there is force to support it, a form will come into being. In exact opposition to Darwinian thinking, an expanding universe is opportunistic not accidental. Life is no longer an anomaly. Also, in contrast to the Darwinian picture, cooperation is an important part of being and becoming. The coming together of existing entities in a new structure is the basis of all new dimensions of being. Competition and cooperation are partners in the process of being. The world is not simply ruthless and self-interest is dethroned as the sole logic of life.

The One Is Many and the Many Are One   All forms of being are part of one process; they are differentiated aspects of the field that emerge from, contribute to, and then recede back into the ongoing flow. Entity and field are inseparable and coeffecting. The two are like Heidigger's "Being and Being," interplaying aspects of one thing. More strongly, entity, other entities, and field are all inseparable. The intake and output of each and the context locally and globally. . .all these are interplaying aspects of one thing. The process exists and evolves only in the interplay of these many forms. This inseparability of all aspects is essentially an ecological vision but an ecological vision of a deeper level. It is not just that living things are curiously interconnected; our interconnection and our existence, each and all, are part of an unfolding process that carries us, directs us, and to which we contribute. Such a vision denies the religious and scientific anthrocentricism that has stayed with us despite the Copernican revolution. We are not the center, not the power, not the end-all of being. We are members of a community of being—with rights, privileges, duties, and conditions of membership. We are part of a chain of being that will not end with us. We have a role, as all elements of the whole do. If we care to continue, the trick to continued existence is clearly in going with the process, not just ourselves.

Constancy and Change   The process we have outlined shows the basic elements of constancy and change so often noted in our world. Each new space-time crisis gives us a way of being that dominates the field by virtue of its new way of accelerating. During its growth and maturity, before its exhaustion and shortfall, we experience relative constancy. Yet, in fact, existence oscillates between local, relative constancy and inexorable change. Absolute rest and permanence do not exist. Adaptation to a homeostatic status quo is not an appropriate model for survival, especially in critical times. A corollary to constancy and change is that the only real constant is the process. All structure-dependent solutions are doomed to failure. Oddly, if all structural solutions are doomed, one way to serve the pressure to accelerate is to be able to move through forms easily. Forms that change forms (metaforms) are thus most prone to survive because they can accelerate themselves. Both human consciousness and the process we call "science" are such metaforms. They move us distinctly away from fixation on structure because they can change as a result of critically examining themselves. They are forms that change themselves by learning not by changing physically. Such forms are higher, not because they are perfect, but because they find their limitations and can move to a new form with relative ease.

The Codetermined Universe   We are members of a creative unfolding, based in simplicity, but of infinite complexity. Immeasurably small differences will keep evolution forever beyond our control and knowing. Yet, while we cannot be its master, we are not slaves to this process. We cocreate this unfolding. Each living moment arises out of a simultaneous act of effector and effected. Our individual microscale activity in all its uniqueness can count in a way classical science never imagined.

Demystifying and Remystifying the World   The new understanding denies dualism, the separation of human and mind-based dimensions. We are not a mystery apart from the world but part of the mystery of the world. So, although we have significantly demystified ourselves, we have also reenchanted the world and our role in it. Creation is no longer an ancient surrealistic event, but an ongoing mystery unfolding day to day in physical reality. And true to religious description, the mystery is in us, of us, and more than us, all at the same time. Science (our belief in here-and-now facts) and spirituality (our sense of more-to-it-than-this) map to one physically real world.

Conclusion   In classical physics' view, the world has no direction, and order is a highly improbably state. From the classical perspective, Darwinian selection provides a causal explanation of the evolution of species. Before this, life must have started as some initial improbable event. In the classical understanding, the idea of an ordering principle in the universe is pseudoscience nonsense (teleology, vitalism. . .). When we walk about in the world we find order—intricate coherent interrelated structure—everywhere. From ants and grass to cities and civilizations, the facts of the living world conflict with the improbable-order vision in a most obvious way. Now we understand why: Life is not a physical anomaly, classical science had a limited perspective.

Science has been what you can do in a box, what you can do with a straight line, and what you can do if things are independent. The nonlinear revolution from chaos to general evolution produces a very different picture of how the world works. We are embedded in an ongoing evolutionary process that moves inexorably and opportunistically toward increasing levels of ordered complexity. Collectively, western civilization is beginning to take off its Newtonian glasses, and behind them we are finding an evolving ecological world. It is quite a change in vision.

By way of closing I make one last observation. I billed the business section as a metaphoric tour of the growth of complexity in economies. There is the distinct possibility, however, that there is more than metaphor here. Carneiro (1967, 1987), for example, noted that the surface/volume rule holds for the growth of villages and cities—they hit the two-thirds power ratio and either stop growing, fall apart, or reorganize. Real (1990) showed that decision making in lower animals (e.g., bees selecting flowers) follows standard energy-flow curves. The distinct possibility is that we are guided by a more physical, invisible hand than we currently imagine. Although it is hard to digest, the evolving ecological metaphor is real model of the world—and this possibility has profound implications.

Chaos is the tip of the iceberg. The iceberg is the nonlinear revolution and the ecological transformation. The change is an important one.

REFERENCES

Carneiro, R. (1967). On the relationship between size of population and complexity of social structure. *Southwestern Journal of Anthropology, 23,* 234–243.

Carneiro, R. (1987). The evolution of complexity in human societies and its mathematical expression. *International Journal of Comparative Sociology, 28,* 111–128.

Chaisson, E. (1987). *The life era.* New York: Atlantic Monthly Press.

Chandler, A. D. (1977). *The visible hand: The Managerial revolution in American business.* Cambridge, MA: Belknap Press of Harvard University Press.

Csanyi, V. (1989). *Evolutionary systems and society: A general theory of life, mind and culture.* Durham, NC: Duke University Press.

Dyson, F. (1985). *Origins of life.* Cambridge: Cambridge University Press

Eigen, M., & Schuster, P. (1979). *The hypercycle: A principle of natural self-organization*. Berlin: Springer-Verlag.

Goldstein, J. (1990). Freud's theories in light of far-from-equilibrium research. *Social Research, 52*(1), 9–45.

Gould, S. (1980). *Ever since Darwin*. New York: Norton.

Holland, H. (1978). *The chemistry of the atmosphere and oceans*. New York: Wiley.

Lotka, A. J. (1922). Contribution to the energetics of evolution. *Proceedings of the National Academy of Science, 8*, 147.

Lovelock, J. (1979). *Gaia: A new look at life on earth*. Oxford: Oxford University Press.

Mandelbrot, B. (1983). *The fractal geometry of nature*. New York: W. H. Freeman.

Margulis, L. (1970). *Origin of eucaryotic cells*. New Haven, CT: Yale University Press.

Margulis, L. (1981). *Symbiosis in cell evolution*. San Francisco: Freeman.

Margulis, L. (1982). *Early life*. Boston: Science Books International.

Maturana, H., & Varela, F. (1987). *The tree of knowledge*. Boston: Shambhala.

May, R. M. (1974). Biological populations with non-overlapping generations: Stable points, stable cycles, and chaos. *Science, 186*, 645–647.

Morowitz, H. J. (1968). *Energy flow in Biology: Biological organization as a problem in thermal physics*. New York: Academic Press.

Odum, H. T. (1988). Self-organization, transformity, and information. *Science, 242*, 1132.

Pantzar, M. (1991). *Economics and Replicative Evolution*. New York: Gordon & Breach.

Pettersson, M. (1978). Acceleration in evolution, before human times. *Journal of Social and Biological Structures, 1*, 201–206.

Prigogine, I. (1980). *From being to becoming*. New York: W. H. Freeman.

Prigogine, I., & Stengers, E. (1984). *Order out of chaos*. New York: Bantam.

Real, L. A. (1991). Animal choice behavior and the evolution of cognitive architecture, *Science, 252*, 980–985.

Spencer, H. (1862). First Principles. London: Williams & Norgate.

Swenson, R. (1989a). Emergent attractors and the law of maximum entropy production: Foundations to a Theory of General Evolution. *Systems Research, 6*(3), 187–197.

Swenson, R. (1989b). Emergent evolution and the global attractor: The evolutionary epistemology of entropy production. *Proceedings of the 33rd Ann. Meeting of the International Society for the Systems Sciences, 3*, 46–53.

Von Bertalanffy, L. (1968). *General systems theory*. New York: Braziller.

Zeeman, C. (1986). The dynamics of Darwinian Evolution. In S. Diner, D. Fargue, & G. Lochak (Eds.), *Dynamical systems: A renewal of mechanism* (pp. 273–290). Philadelphia: World Scientific Publishing.

3 The Tower of Babel in Nonlinear Dynamics: Toward the Clarification of Terms

Jeffrey Goldstein

And the whole earth was of one language and of one speech. And it came to pass, as they journeyed east, that they found a plain in the land of Shinar; and they dwelt there. And they said one to another, "Come, let us make brick, and burn them thoroughly." And they had brick for stone, and slime they had for mortar. And they said: "Come, let us build us a city, and a tower, with its top in heaven, and let us make a name; lest we be scattered abroad upon the face of the whole earth." And the Lord came down to see the city and the tower, which the children of men builded. And the Lord said: "Behold, they are one people, and they have all one language; and this is what they begin to do; and now nothing will be withholden to them, which they propose to do. Come let us go down, and there confound their language, that they may not understand one another's speech." So the Lord scattered them abroad from thence upon the face of all the earth; and they left off to build the city. Therefore was the name of it called Babel; because the Lord did there confound the language of all the earth; and from then did the Lord scatter them abroad upon the face of all the earth.—Genesis, verse 11

I'll come back to the Tower of Babel in a moment, but for now let's turn to all the enthusiasm surrounding the advent of chaos and related theories. Indeed, it is usually the case that when a new theory is in its early stages of formulation, proponents of it bandy about new terms in a great profusion. This is an important component of creative ferment. A problem, however, can arise when what one person means by a new term is not exactly what another person means by the same term. Then, misunderstanding can exceed understanding, and language can serve to obscure rather than reveal.

For example, in conversations involving *chaos, far-from-equilibrium,* and other related terms, I often have had the experience of not quite understanding what others are talking about, as well as the sense of being misunderstood myself. I (we) believed I (we) were speaking the same language, meant the same things by the words I (we) were using, and that the disagreement was about the content of what I (we) were talking about. Unfortunately, sometimes these conversations have degenerated into "I'm right" and "You're wrong," or "You're right" and "I'm wrong," or "You don't know what you're talking about!" But, the more I thought about these conversations, the more I think the problem primarily stems from my (our) assumption that I (we) were speaking the same language and meant the same things by the words I (we) were using. This assumption, though, in my estimation, was false—we were not speaking the same language, and we failed to recognize that translation from one language to another was what was called for.

With that language misunderstanding in mind, let's return to the story about the Tower of Babel. Here is my commentary (or "midrash" for those talmudicists out there).

When the people had one language they had power, so much power that "nothing will be withholden to them which they propose to do." But God couldn't tolerate this human power, so He confounded their languages with the result that they could no longer understand one another, and, thereby, they lost their power. There is a moral point here, I suppose, about man's arrogance or hubris. But what I want to emphasize, instead, from this story is that when our language becomes confounded, when we talk to each other using different languages but believe we are speaking the same language, we talk past each other, we misunderstand each other, and, thereby, we are threatened with losing our power of concentration and focus. We, so to speak, become scattered, "all over the face of the earth."

Such as quagmire may have faced us in this conference of the Society for the Study of Chaos Theory in Psychology. Perhaps, confusion is ensuing from the situation where we both think we are talking about oranges, but I am presuming the word "orange" refers to orange-colored citrus fruits from Florida, whereas you are telling me I am wrong because oranges are red, hard fruits from Washington. In that case, we are not both talking about oranges, I am talking about oranges and you are talking about what I refer to by the term *apple*. But we didn't know that we were talking about two very, different fruits—oranges and apples. Our assumptions about our terminology had obscured our understanding. So, perhaps it is now in order that we first get clear about terms, not necessarily agreeing but agreeing to disagree, and being clear about what exactly it is we are disagreeing about. Perhaps we can give each other cues about what it is we are referring to when we use the terms we do.

SOURCES OF MISUNDERSTANDING

There are several sources of the problem of how we are not speaking the same language. I have identified three:

Different Schools

We all have different intellectual and theoretical heritages from where we entered into chaos theory, and so on. For example, there is the Prigogine school (from which I come); the mathematical dynamical systems theory school; the chaologists; the complex adaptive systems school; and so on. To borrow Wittgenstein's phrase, each school has a different language game. That is, each school has different research agendas, different questions they are asking, different ways of answering these questions, and different meanings for terms. So to understand what each school means by a term, in a sense, one needs to understand the whole world in which their language game is operating. What you mean by a term in your language game is not necessarily what I mean by the same term in my language game. We first need to recognize that translation between language games is called for, and then we can figure out how to proceed with this translation. I believe that this is not just a problem for those of us in the soft sciences who have appropriated these terms from physics and mathematics, for, as I soon show, there is also a similar problem in how these terms are used in the harder sciences.

Popular Understandings of the New Terms

There are two aspects of this. First, there is the heavily loaded cultural baggage attending the meaning of terms in popular parlance even before the onslaught of the new sciences. For example, the word *chaos* has had all sorts of connotations having to do with turmoil, turbulence, the primordial abyss, the biblical references to Tohu and Bohu, and so on. These associations with chaos don't just disappear because chaos went on to have a specific technical meaning.

Second, there is the meaning these terms have accrued in popular culture as a result of the popularization of the new sciences. Again, the term *chaos* is a case in point—nowadays, people seem to be using the term *chaos* to refer to all sorts of turbulent, unstable, unpredictable behavior in systems. But it is not at all clear whether or not this supposedly chaotic behavior is really able to be depicted on a chaotic attractor.

The affect of both these popular loadings of terms is that it is very difficult, maybe even impossible, to use a term without that term carrying in its trail a whole host of meanings that may not be what's intended in the more scientific usage of the term.

Figurative or Metaphoric Use of Terms

Linguistic confoundedness is amplified when the terms are appropriated and used figuratively or metaphorically. For example, I have said, on occasion, and I have heard a number of people in organizational appropriations of chaos theory say that to facilitate organizational transformation we need to add some chaos into organizations. What exactly is being referred to here by chaos? Most likely, it is not any kind of behavior in a system that could be typified by a chaotic attractor. And even if this addition of chaos did fit such a technical definition, how does one add this kind of chaos to an organization? Isn't chaos per se a matter of a deterministic evolution following some simple nonlinear rules? How exactly is such a thing added to an organization?

The point here is not that the metaphoric use of terms is necessarily erroneous. All scientific terms contain an element of metaphor; consider, for example, "electric current," "spin," or the "charm" of a "quark." As Barbour (1974) suggested, citing the philosopher of science, Max Black, scientific models are *systematically developed metaphors.* What I am suggesting, however, is that we give each other cues when we may be using a term in its more metaphoric meaning than in some kind of scientifically tested way. It seems to me this could clear up a lot of confusion right from the start. But this may require a little bit of thought as to how we are using a term.

These three sources of misunderstandings about terms all show up in the confounding nature of the term *chaos,* so let's turn to chaos.

MAGNITUDES AND REALMS OF CHAOS

Are we referring to the same phenomenon when we use the term *chaos?* How about *weak chaos, mildly chaotic, strong chaos,* or *chaos* itself versus the *edge of chaos?* Ambiguity about chaos actually goes back to the first usages of the term. David Ruelle (1991) noted that in the original coining of the term *chaos* by Li and Yorke (1975), chaos referred to the following mathematical phenomenon: For a large class of maps of a line interval into itself, the existence of a periodic point of period 3 implies the existence of periodic points of every other period (endnote #2, pp. 178, 179). Yet, Ruelle pointed out that: "A time evolution with many periodic orbits often does not show sensitive dependence on initial condition. In fact, the many periodic orbits need not be on an attractor, so that their presence is not relevant to the long-term evolution of the system." But, as Ruelle (1991) wrote, "What we now call chaos is a time evolution with sensitive dependence on initial condition. The motion on a strange attractor is thus chaotic. One also speaks of deterministic noise when the irregular oscillations that are observed appear noisy, but the mechanism that produces them is deterministic"

(p. 67). Thus, Yorke and Li's chaos was not the chaos of sensitive dependence on initial conditions.

Then there is the notion of different magnitudes of chaos. For example, consider the "weak chaos" of Per Bak's theory of self-organized criticality:

> To check the accuracy of predictions in our earthquake model, we conducted two simulations of the critical state. The simulations differ by a small random force on each block, representing a small uncertainty about the initial conditions. When we run the two simulations, the uncertainty grows with time but much more slowly than it does for chaotic systems. The uncertainty increases to a power law rather than an exponential law. The system evolves on the *border of chaos*. This behavior, called *weak chaos*, is a result of self-organized criticality. Weak chaos differs significantly from fully chaotic behavior. Fully chaotic systems are characterized by a time scale beyond which it is impossible to make predictions. Weakly chaotic systems lack such a time scale and so allow long-term predictions. Because we find that all self-organized critical systems are weakly chaotic, we expect weak chaos to be very common in nature. It would be interesting indeed to know whether the inaccuracy of earthquake predictions, economic forecasts and weather forecasts generally increases with time according to a power law rather than an exponential law. (Bak & Chen, 1991; pp. 46–53; italics added)

The difference between increase according to a power law and increase according to an exponential law is no slight matter. So, when we are talking about chaos are we talking about weak chaos or strong chaos?

But weak and strong chaos are not the entire continuum of degrees of chaos. Recently, Ditto and Pecora (1993) wrote about how the mildly chaotic Rossler signal can be used to coax two out-of-phase nonchaotic systems to operate in phase (pp. 82–84). They further described this Rossler signal as "pseudoperiodic." Thus, we now have two more troublesome terms to worry about: "mildly chaotic" and "pseudoperiodic."

Then, there is the term *edge of chaos* from research into complex, adaptive systems (see Lewin, 1992). The edge of chaos refers to a realm of system behavior in "which the components of the system never quite lock into place, yet never dissolve into turbulence, either" (Waldrop, 1992, p. 293). Moreover, notice how, in the quotation from Bak and Chen, they throw in the phrase "border of chaos." This sounds tantalizingly like the edge of chaos but when asked if the evolution toward self-organized criticality is like the edge of chaos, Per Bak said "I think so. . ." (Lewin, 1992, p. 61). Notice the conditionality of Per Bak's answer—"I think so. . ." Well if he's not sure and he's a physicist, a renowned one at that, then where does that leave the rest of us?

Therefore, when we are using the term *chaos* are we referring to weak chaos, mildly chaotic, strong chaos, the edge of chaos, or chaos as a metaphor? We can no longer take it for granted that we are referring to the same thing by chaos. So, we need to discuss terms first, before we can go on to have a lucid and enlightening discussion about what each of us is up to in our research and thinking.

EQUILIBRIUM AND FAR-FROM-EQUILIBRIUM: LANGUAGE GAME?

Another example of the confounding of language can be found in the use of the terms *equilibrium* and *far-from-equilibrium,* which, in my personal experience, can really get people's gander. These terms are particularly liable for causing mischief because they have both a popular presence as well as being key terms in the Prigogine Brussels school, which has been, to some degree, at odds with the American chaos school. In Gleick's (1987) popular account of chaos, he didn't even mention Prigogine; and Briggs and Peat (1989) separated their book into two sections; "Order to Chaos" for chaos theory per se, and "Chaos to Order" for Prigogine and self-organization.

Originally, in ancient Greece "equilibrium" referred to a literal *balance* of weights on a lever such as Archimedes studied (Boyer, 1968). This balance of weights went on to play a role as a determinate condition for scientific research and theorizing. Eventually, with Boltzmann's formulation of the Second Law of Thermodynamics in the 19th century, the concept of equilibrium had made full passage from a simple determinate condition to the final, sought-for state of a system (Broda, 1983).

In psychology, equilibrium also found a linguistic home. In fact, we have a significant heritage of the term in our own social science disciplines, which complicates the picture for us in the modern study of chaos in the social sciences. Equilibrium-based conceptions played a key role in the psychologies of Herbart, Lotke, Freud, Lewin, and Parsons (see Goldstein, chap. 15, this volume). Russett (1966) even recounted how Talcott Parsons exclaimed that the concept of equilibrium was a direct derivation of the concept of a system itself!

We find the use of equilibrium in psychological theory but not much about its opposite condition: non-, dis-, or far-from-equilibrium. Lewin (1951), for instance, tantalizingly mentioned the idea of nonequilibrium in passing, but never developed such a notion in any kind of systematic or clear fashion. Prigogine (Prigogine & Stengers, 1984) popularized the term *far-from-equilibrium* when he referred to the conditions necessary for a system to bifurcate and self-organize. He was using this term against the backdrop of thermodynamics, which was suffused with equilibrium-based concepts. In Prigogine's research, far-from-equilibrium conditions led to systemic behavior different from what was expected by the customary interpretation of the Second Law of Thermodynamics, the emergence of new structures, and ordered configurations instead of a running down of a system into a quiescent equilibrium.

A problem arises, however, in interpreting far-from-equilibrium in a thermodynamic sense. Actually, what Prigogine seemed to have in mind was some other qualification, not simply thermodynamic as the prefix for far-from-equilibrium. For example, in the famous chemical clock behavior of the Belousov-Zhabotinsky experiment, what enables this system to self-organize in the peculiar way that it does is that the system is taken to a far-from-*chemical*-equilibrium condition (Nicolis, 1989). This condition comes about by pumping out from the chemical vessel products of the reaction that are being used to restore detailed balance or chemical equilibrium. This far-from-*chemical*-equilibrium condition serves to bring out or activate the nonlinear factors in the chemical reaction, thereby, enabling bifurcation and self-organization phenomena to take place. Thus, far-from-equilibrium can be used to indicate how some mechanism keeping a system in an equilibrium condition, however equilibrium is defined for that particular system, is being disrupted or interfered with.

Yet, part of the difficulty in using Prigogine's terms is that his own preoccupations with thermodynamic issues seems to bias the expressions in that direction. That is, the terms *equilibrium* and *far-from-equilibrium* have their own cozy home within the context of his specific thermodynamic applications. Problems can occur when such terms are taken on vacation from their home in Prigogine's world and applied to various psychological or sociological phenomena. But it seems very tempting to do so because of the great prevalence of equilibrium-based theories in psychology and sociology, as mentioned above, and the need to transcend the limitations accompanying the concept of equilibrium.

Moreover, another area of confoundedness with the terms "equilibrium" and "far-from-equilibrium" is that they are often used interchangeably for "'stability" and "instability." The latter terms have specific meanings in dynamical theories—stability being defined as a system returning to the same dynamics after a small perturbation, whereas instability referring to a change in the qualitative dynamics of a system after a perturbation (Glass & Mackey, 1988). That is why, for example, a pendulum can be in either stable or unstable equilibrium. But that means that the two sets of terms cannot be purely synonomous.

Still another source of confusion concerning the terms *equilibrium* and *far-from-equilibrium* is their popular connotations. In popular parlance, equilibrium connotes balance, rest, integrity, safety, and so on, whereas disequilibrium (the closest popular term to *far-from-equilibrium*) is associated with being off balance, dizziness, stumbling, vertigo, and so on. this cultural baggage just doesn't go away because of the edict of a scientist and must be reckoned with in order to keep misunderstandings under control.

So, as in the case of chaos, before we can use these terms in meaningful discussions, we first need to discuss what exactly we mean by equilibrium, and non-, dis-, or far-from-equilibrium. And again, the appropriate way to conduct these discussions is not the "I'm right, you're wrong" approach. Instead, let's try to understand the meaning of what is being said in the context of the language game being played.

CONCLUSION

We could keep going on and on with each new term being used in nonlinear systems sciences as to how different people mean different things by it. In fact, here is a partial list of the terms that I believe require our immediate semantic attention:

Complexity
Complex, adaptive system
Attractor
Strange attractor
Information
Energy
Entropy
Noise
Organization
Self-organization
Linear
Nonlinear

In my opinion, we are not going to get too far if we just take it for granted that we are speaking the same language when we are using these terms. So, in order to avoid the fate of a Tower of Babel, I propose we spend some time to agree or agree to disagree about what we mean by the terms we bandy about.

REFERENCES

Bak, P., & Chen, K. (1991, January). Self-organized criticality. *Scientific American,* pp. 46–53.

Barbour, I. (1974). *Myths, models, and paradigms.* New York: Harper & Row.

Boyer, C. (1968). *A history of mathematics.* Princeton, NJ: Princeton University Press.

Briggs, J., & Peat , D. (1989). *Turbulent mirror.* New York: Harper & Row.

Broda, E. (1983). *Ludwig Boltzmann: Man, physicist, philosopher* (L. Gay, Trans.). Woodbridge, CT: Ox Bow Press.

Ditto, W., & Pecora, L. (1993, August). Mastering chaos. *Scientific American,* pp. 78–84.

Glass, L., & Mackey, M. (1988). *From clocks to chaos.* Princeton, NJ: Princeton University Press.

Gleick, J. (1987). *Chaos.* New York: Viking.

Lewin, K. (1951). *Field theory in social science.* New York: Harper & Row.

Lewin, R. (1992). *Complexity.* New York: Macmillan.

Li, T., & Yorke, J. (1975). Period three implies chaos. *American Mathematics Monthly, 82,* 985–92.

Nicolis, G. (1989). Physics of far-from-equilibrium systems and self-organisation. In P. Davies (Ed.), *The new physics* (pp. 316–347). Cambridge: Cambridge University Press.

Prigogine, I., & Stengers, I. (1984). *Order out of chaos: Man's new dialogue with nature.* New York: Bantam.

Ruelle, D. (1991). *Chance and chaos.* Princeton, NJ: Princeton University Press.

Russett, C. (1966). *The concept of equilibrium in American social thought.* New Haven, CT: Yale University Press.

Waldrop, M. (1992). *Complexity.* New York: Macmillan.

II RESEARCH METHODS AND CHAOS THEORY

One of the promises of chaos theory is the application of its mathematical ideas to the analysis of behavior. Traditional descriptive statistics, such as means, standard deviations, and correlations, as well as inferential techniques, such as the analyses of variance and more sophisticated multivariate procedures, all rely on global trends involving many subjects. They are notoriously insensitive to individual differences. Moreover, they deal with structural relationships and, only with difficulty, can be made to analyze processes. The latter is particularly problematic to the psychologist and psychiatrist for, as William James pointed out more than 100 years ago, process is more fundamental to the nature of the mind than is structure. It is also important to all behavioral as well as "natural" sciences.

Of the following four chapters, the first three examine individual differences, using a variety of procedures derived from the mathematics of chaos theory. The first and third approach their topics from a process perspective. The first, by psychologists Allan Combs and Michael Winkler, presents an analysis of the nostril cycle in a demonstration study. Here the nostril cycle—the rough ultradian rhythm of dominant breath from one nostril to the other—is ideal for this because it yields data that, in several ways, is characteristic of what many behavioral scientists are likely to confront in their own work. For example, the data sets of roughly 600 points for each of several participants are small by the standards of chaos theory but large by most behavioral research standards. The data for each subject appears to be chaotic, or at least partially so, but at the same time clearly contains other influences, such as circadian rhythms. Finally, the data was obtained from Likert scales in a fashion typical of many behavioral investigations. In this chapter, the authors construct attractors, compute estimates of Lyapunov exponents and fractal dimensions, and graph power spectra in an experimental examination of individual differences. This is followed by a short chapter by psychologist Tracy Brown, with Allan Combs, that explores the applicability of the fractal dimension as a measure of complexity in an environment that is only partially chaotic.

In the third chapter, psychiatrist Hector Sabelli, along with Carlson-Sabelli, Patel, Levy, and Díez-Martín present a wealth of "traditional" and new procedures for analyzing individual data sets. These range from three-dimensional attractor reconstructions of the changing emotional states of several individuals over significant periods of time, to analyses of human cardiac activity in a range of subjects. Along the way they introduce a variety of analytic procedures that they term *sociodynamics, psychogeometry,* and *electropsychocardiography,* as well as developing a concept of evolving multidimensional patterns called complexes. These are presented in the context of a thoroughgoing processual philosophy of human biology and behavior.

Biomathematican Paul Rapp completes this section with a cautionary discussion of the dangers of over generalization in a field in that procedures themselves are too new for their limitations to be well understood yet. It is standard procedure in traditional courses on statistics, for instance, to emphasize the assumptions that underlie common inferential procedures. The consequences of violating these assumptions are well known, as is the extent to which they are robust in the face of such violations. Chaos scientists, on the other hand, rarely have access to such information. Thus, they are to some extent flying in the dark with regard to the limitations of the procedures upon which they rely. Everyone in the field must to some extent be his or her own mathematician, judging for themselves what is acceptable and what is not. This is a big order in an area where first rate mathematicians do not always agree among themselves, or at least are still in vigorous dialog concerning the correctness and limitations of methods, many of which are already in standard use. Rapp's chapter focuses on single-channel EEG work, but his warnings and suggestions for testing the validity of alternative hypothesis have wide application in this new field.

4

The Nostril Cycle: A Study in the Methodology of Chaos Science

Allan Combs
Michael Winkler

Paul Rapp (1993) suggested that the most important contribution of chaos theory to the life sciences may well turn out not to be its theoretical agenda as much as its methodologies. This conclusion is made upon consideration of the difficulties confronted by researchers faced with the actual problem of demonstrating deterministic chaos in their data. To begin with, it is becoming apparent that traditional methods for demonstrating the presence of deterministic chaos, such as fractal dimension estimates, Lyapunov exponents, and phase portraits, can, under less than ideal conditions, lead to quite unreliable conclusions (Grassberger, 1986; Osborne & Provenzale, 1989; Theiler, 1991). Indeed, some of the early reports of chaotic processes in the life sciences have turned out to be unreliable if not actually spurious (Rapp, 1993). The search for more reliable and meaningful ways to assess complexity is underway (e.g., Grace & Warner, 1992; Havstad & Ehlers, 1989; Judd, 1992; Kurths, Brandenburg, & Feudel, 1993; Parlitz, 1992), but is unlikely to provide the levels of reliability that researchers would desire.

Looked at differently, the complexity of life systems, as opposed to simpler preparations available to the chemist or physicist, rarely yield long runs of stable measurements that now appear necessary for the unequivocal demonstration of a chaotic regimen. This is especially problematic in light of what Rapp refers to as the "data acquisition tragedy." This is that, for each variable added to a dynamical system (in practical terms, any influences that change during a single experiment or recording session), the number of points necessary to resolve that system increases exponentially (Eckmann & Ruelle, 1992; Smith, 1988). Unfortunately, most biological, psychological, and social systems have large numbers of such variables, thus presenting a nearly impossible situation for the researcher.

Given the problems just cited, combined with the rather exotic mathematical

51

demands (to most biologists and behavioral scientists) exacted by chaos theory, one might wonder if the researcher in these fields might give it up entirely. We believe this would be a serious mistake. Based on several years of work with chaos theory in the laboratory, it is our opinion that its principal value is in providing a methodology well-suited to the characterization of many of the complex and fluid processes that are the objects of study in the biological and behavioral sciences. We expand on this point later, doing so from the perspective of our own experience in psychology, and focusing on a particular biological process recently carried out in our laboratory.

ADVANTAGES OF THE CHAOTIC SYSTEMS APPROACH

The chaotic systems approach represents a significant departure from traditional methods used in psychological research. To begin with, it tends to emphasize process rather than structure. Because most phenomena of interest to psychologists would seem at root to be of a process nature—examples include learning, emotion, cognition, perception, psychological development, psychotherapy, and so on (Combs, 1993a, 1993b, 1994)—this approach would seem naturally suited to its topic matter. On the other hand, common practices, such as the computation of means, standard deviations, t-tests, chi-squares, ANOVAs and multivariate procedures, Spearman–Roe correlations, and the like, seem better suited to static situations and are only awkwardly applied to processes. At a minimum, these procedures might beneficially be complemented by those of chaos analysis.

Further, the chaos systems approach shifts analysis towards exquisite nonlinear representations and away from theoretically plain models where relationships are plotted as straight lines that cut through scattered clouds of data. Traditionally, each point in such a cloud is said to represent a mix of treatment effects and error. The chaos systems approach does not recognize "experimental error" but treats the irregularities of real psychological or biological events as complex processes. Despite their intricacy, such processes can sometimes be represented by a surprisingly small number of variables in interaction (e.g., Crutchfield, Doyne, Packard, & Shaw, 1986).

A derivative of this is that differences between individual scores, no longer viewed as error variation, are regarded as essential to the elaborate structure of the process under investigation. A most important result of this is a shift away from traditional nomothetic or group-oriented procedures toward a new emphasis on individual differences. For example, it is not clear at all how one would go about plotting a phase portrait of group data. Presumably, one would need to develop a perspective that allowed the group to be considered as a single system.

A final and vitally important difference with these methods is that they represent events in a *qualitative* fashion, presenting their overall trajectories as topological portraits. Such portraits do not allow detailed prediction but display the overall shapes of highly complex temporal events. For psychological phenomena, such as mood fluctuations, these portraits are often unique for each individual (e.g., Hannah, 1991; Winkler et al. 1991, Winkler, Combs, & Daley, 1994). This being the case, the chaotic systems approach tends to emphasize the uniqueness of individual profiles rather than combining them to form group characterizations.

THE NOSTRIL CYCLE

Nasal Rhythms

The nostril cycle is an ultradian rhythm in which the dominant flow of respiration shifts between the two nostrils. It was selected for investigation both because it is a cyclic event and because its evident irregularity suggests that it may be a chaotic and not simply stochastic process. Beyond this, it is of potential interest to both psychology and neurology, as becomes clear later.

The rhythm is produced as alterations in swelling and shrinking of the nasal mucosa of the nostrils that, in turn, is regulated by the blood flow in these regions (Funk, 1980; Rossi, 1986). Werntz, Bickford, Bloom, and Shannahoff (1981) suggest that it is part of a larger rhythm involving the sympathetic and parasympathetic nervous systems. Others, (Eccles, 1978; Funk, 1980) similarly speculated that it is part of a generalized activity cycle.

There are two unexpected facts concerning this rhythm. The first is that it is highly correlated with the overall EEG amplitude of the contralateral hemisphere (Werntz, Bickford, Bloom, & Shannahoff, 1981, 1982). Indeed, forced breathing through either nostril shifts the distribution of EEG amplitudes within minutes. The second is that traditional yogic scriptures and the closely related ancient Ayur-Vedic medicine associate the nostril cycle with particular states of mind, or dispositions (Ballentine, 1981a; Funk & Clark, 1980; Rossi, 1986). Yogis were, and are still today, trained to regulate their nostril flow by various postures or by application of attention to one or the other of the nostrils. Dominance of the right nostril was associated with an active state and recommended for vigorous and assertive activities, whereas dominance of the left nostril was associated with passive activities such as listening to the teachings of a wise man.

Modern studies have found the nostril rhythm to exhibit wide variation in the length of its cycle, both between and within individuals. These often range from about 1 to 4 hours but can be much longer (Ballentine, 1980a, 1980b; Clark, 1980 et al.; Eccles, 1978; Funk, 1980; Keuning, 1963; Werntz et al. 1981). A common theme throughout these reports is the extreme irregularity of the nostril cycle, even within an individual on a single day (Ballentine, 1980a; Funk & Clark, 1980). Such irregularity suggests the possibility that these rhythms may be the product of deterministic chaos. Even if they are not, and this is central to our theme, the chaotic systems approach is ideally suited for investigating them.

METHOD

Participants

Five trained undergraduate students participated in the study. All were male, with ages ranging from about 20 to 50 years.

Materials and Procedure

The participants observed and recorded their nostril dominance once each 30 min, except when sleeping, for a period of 3 weeks. They found that making observations on the hour and the half hour was not difficult to remember after the first few hours of practice (also see Hannah, 1991). Nostril dominance was estimated by gently pressing one side of the nose and then the other with the index finger, thus closing each nostril successively and allowing the relative amount of air flowing through the opposite nostril to be appraised. The result of each observation was recorded as a vertical slash on a straight line Likert scale 4 cm in length. If both nostrils were judged to be equal in flow the slash was made at the center. If the entire breath was flowing solely through the left nostril the slash was marked to the extreme left, and vise versa for the extreme right, with intermediate judgments marked at intermediate locations. The Likert scales were printed in booklets that contained 1 day's worth on each of 21 pages, the number of days during which observations were carried out. The reliability of this technique had previously been established during pilot studies in our laboratory. Moreover, our findings were consistent with those of other investigators (Clark, 1980; Eccles, 1978; Funk & Clark, 1980; Heetderks, 1927).

DISCUSSION AND FINDINGS

Constructions of attractor portraits were used in combination with frequency spectra to display each individual's characteristic nostril rhythm. Because these portraits appeared chaotic in form, we used a Monte Carlo procedure, to assure ourselves that they were not simply random, and fractal dimension estimates to test for the possible presence of deterministic chaos.

Attractor Constructions

Using Schaffer's Dynamical Software (1988) for the personal computer, attractor portraits were constructed for each participant's record. This involved the inter-

polation of four points between each successive pair
computation of a running 3-point average on the res
produced by this procedure was lagged three units agains\
.3 hr, and the resulting pairs of points were plotted suc
portraits (Fig. 4.1).

Monte Carlo Procedure

To test that the attractor portraits were not purely stochastic, several sets of Likert values were scrambled using a randomization program, and portraits were constructed from these by exactly the same procedures as used on the original sets (Hannah, 1991; Rapp, Albano, Zimmerman, & Jimenez-Montano, in preparation; Fig. 4.1). It was apparent on inspection that the portraits of randomized data lacked the rhythmatic structure and individual patterning seen in the original constructions. This was especially obvious watching the erratic unfolding of these portraits on the computer screen in real time.

Fractal Dimension

Correlation dimension estimations were obtained using Sarraille and DiFalco's (1992) Fd3 program for the PC. These are shown in Table 4.1. They are remarkably consistent for all participants, ranging only from 1.661 to 1.811. The fact that they are not even approximately whole number values allows the possibility that they are the product of deterministic chaotic processes.

To further explore these ideas, correlation dimension estimations were computed for the same data sets after randomly scrambling the order of the Likert values (Table 4.1). Casti (1992) suggested that, in the presence of deterministic chaos, this procedure should yield larger estimates than original data and nearer to the whole number dimensional value of the attractor portraits, in this case, 2. As can be seen, the randomized sequences produced larger dimension estimates nearer to the unitary value of 2. The magnitude of the differences between the original and randomized dimension estimates are small. This later fact, in itself, however, is not discouraging, as only small differences could be expected in the presence of a chaotic process mingled with more constrained elements such as

TABLE 4.1
Correlation Dimension Estimates

Participant	Corr. Dim.	Randomized
1	1.772	1.922
2	1.811	1.842
3	1.784	1.851
4	1.661	1.733
5	1.663	1.864

rcadian and ultradian rhythms exhibited in the power spectra of some of the participants, as is explained below (Peters, 1991). Nevertheless, for reasons explained in the introduction, we consider these findings to be no more than suggestive of the presence of deterministic chaos.

Considering all the information just presented, however, including the attractor portrait constructions as well as the fractal dimension estimates would seem, all limitations aside, to leave little doubt that the nostril cycle is a nonrandom process of significant complexity.

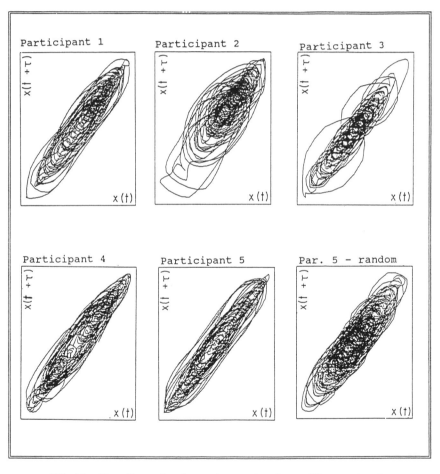

FIG. 4.1. Two-dimensional attractor constructions of the nasal cycle. Responses for participant 5 were randomized and constructed using the same procedure. Maximum and minimum Likert scale values are P_1: 5–35; P_2: 9–37; P_3: 17–24; P_4: 4–36; P_5: 9–40; random: 9–40.

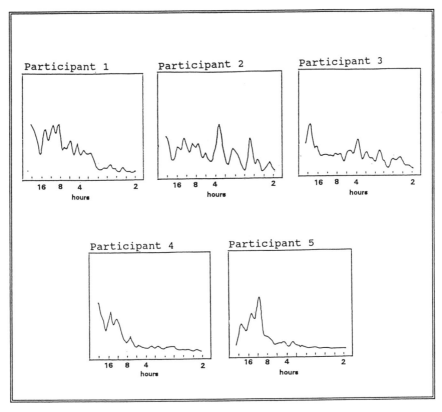

FIG. 4.2.   Power spectra presented as periodicity (1/f) between 2 and 32 hours. Sixteen hours is roughly circadian, as subjects averaged about 8 hours of sleep in a 24-hour day. See text for further discussion.

Frequency Spectra

Our experience has been that, while attractor constructions reveal overall rhythmatic patterns, it is difficult to estimate rates of oscillation without some form of frequency analysis. For these data sets we used Schaffer's Dynamical Software to obtain power spectra for each participant (Fig. 4.2). These were computed as the Fourier transforms of the autocorrelation functions.

Inspection of the power spectra discloses that certain of the participants, numbers 2 and 5, and 3 to a lesser degree, display readily identifiable peak periodicities, whereas 1 and 4 do not. More will be said about these figures in the following section.

Individual Differences

The notable individual differences apparent in the nostril cycle make it ideally suited for a chaotic systems analysis. Inspection of the attractor portraits, for instance, discloses several individual features in the nasal cycle. Participants 4 and 5, for example, display roughly symmetrical portraits, indicating more or less equal amounts of time that each nostril is dominant. Moreover, the low density centers of these two portraits indicate a tendency for the air flow to remain predominantly on one side or the other, oscillating there before crossing over again to the other side. This tendency is very apparent when the portraits are observed unfolding in real time. On the other hand, Participant 1, and especially 2, disclose asymmetrical portraits, indicating a preference for the right nostril. Indeed, Participant 2 spent virtually no time at all with the left nostril dominant. Neither of these portraits displayed the low density central region suggestive of a balanced oscillation ranging on either side of the center.

Another notable feature of the attractor portraits is their amplitude. This is not apparent in Figure 4.2 because here the portraits have been scaled to a yield common maximum display. Participant 5, however, produced a very large attractor portrait, ranging from 9 to 40 Likert scale points out of a possible range from 0 to 40. Participant 4 also produced a relatively large attractor portrait, ranging from 4 to 36 points, similar to Participant 1. This means that these individuals varied widely in their laterality of nostril flow. Participant 3, on the other hand, varied only between 17 and 24 Likert points, spending his entire time within the central 7 points of the potential 40-point range.

Returning to the power spectra, we find that Participant 2 who, as noted earlier, exhibits a chronic bias toward the right nostril, displays two prominent peaks, or periodicities, one at about 4 hours and another at a little less than 3 hours. These agree well with previously reported averages in the general range of 1 to 4 hours (e.g., Clark, 1980; Eccles, 1978; Funk, 1980; Keuning, 1963; Werntz et al. 1981). Participant 5, who displays regular large smooth oscillations into both nostrils, exhibits a strong peak at about 8 hours, with diminishing peaks in the neighborhood of 16 hours. Because this individual, like Participant 2, regularly sleeps about 8 hours each night, the peaks near 16 hours represent a circadian cycle, and the one at 8 hours disclosing a double-cycle or ultradian rhythm within the circadian one. The spectrum of Participant 3 is also suggestive of a tendency toward a double oscillation, one at 4 hours, as seen in Participant 2, and another at less than 20 hours. It is not surprising that this individual's record discloses a shorter than usual sleep cycle, averaging about 5 hours per night.

The records from Participants 1 and 4 exhibit a very erratic sleep cycle. Thus, it is not surprising that their spectra fail to disclose crisp periodicities. Both, however, display modest peaks in the neighborhood of 8 to 16 hours, suggestive of weak circadian rhythmicity.

REFERENCES

Ballentine, R. (1980a). Nasal functioning. *Research Bulletin of the Himalayan International Institute, 2*, 11–12.

Ballentine, R. (1980b). Clinical significance of the nasal cycle. *Research Bulletin of the Himalayan International Institute, 2*, 9–11.

Casti, J. L. (1992). *Reality rules: I; Picturing the world in mathematics—The fundamentals.* New York: Wiley.

Clark, J. (1980). The nasal cycle II: A quantitative analysis of nostril dominance. *Research Bulletin of the Himalayan International Institute, 2*, 3–7.

Combs, A. (1993a, June). *A naturalist's process phenomenology of the human mind.* Papers presented at The First Brandenburg Colloquium on Evolutionary Thought, Potsdam, Germany.

Combs, A. (1993b). The evolution of consciousness: A theory of historical and personal transformation. *World Futures: The Journal of General Evolution, 38*, 43–62.

Combs, A. (1995). Psychology, chaos, and the process nature of consciousness. In F. Abraham & A. Gilgen (Eds.), *Chaos theory in psychology.* Westport, CT: Greenwood.

Crutchfield, J., Doyne, F., Packard, N., & Shaw, R. (1986). Chaos. *Scientific American, 8*, 46–57.

Eccles, R. (1978). The central rhythm of the nasal cycle. *Acta Otolaryngol, 86*, 464–468.

Eckmann, J. P., & Ruelle, D. (1992). Fundamental limitations for estimating dimensions and Lyapunov exponents in dynamical systems. *Physica, 56D*, 185–187.

Funk, E. (1980). Biorhythms and the breath: The nasal cycle. *Research Bulletin of the Himalayan International Institute. 2*, 3–5.

Funk, E., & Clark, J. (1980). The nasal cycle observations over prolonged periods of time. *Research Bulletin of the Himalayan International Institute. 2*, 1–4.

Grace, R. C., & Warner, R. M. (1992, June). *Estimating fractal dimension: A more efficient approach.* Paper presented at the 4th Annual Meeting of The American Psychological Society, San Diego.

Grassberger, P. (1986). Do climatic attractors exist? *Nature, 323*, 609–612.

Hannah, T. (1991). *Mood fluctuations and daily stress: The contribution of a dynamical systems approach.* Paper presented at the Inaugural meeting of The Society for Chaos Theory in Psychology, San Francisco, CA.

Havstad, J. W., & Ehlers, C. L. (1989). Attractor dimension of nonstationary dynamical systems from small data samples. *Physical Review, 39A*, 845–853.

Heetderks, D. (1927). Observations on the reaction of normal nasal mucous membrane. *American Journal of Medical Science, 174*, 231–244.

Judd, K. (1992). An improved estimator of dimension and some comments on providing confidence intervals. *Physica, 56D*, 216–228.

Keuning, J. (1963) Rhythmic conchal volume changes. *International Rhinology, 2*, 57.

Kurths, J., Brandenburg, A., & Feudel, U. (1993). Complexity in inhomogeneous systems. In *The Paradigm of Self-Organization II* (Workshop at Wildbad-Kreuth, September 4–6, 1991). New York: Gordon & Breach.

Osborne, A. R., & Provenzala, A. (1989). Finite correlation dimension for stochastic systems with power-law spectra. *Physica, 35D*, 357–381.

Parlitz, U. (1992). Identification of true and spurious Lyapunov exponents from time series. *International Journal of Bifurcation and Chaos, 2*, 155–156.

Peters, E. (1991). *Chaos and order in capital markets.* New York: Wiley.

Rapp, P. (1993). Chaos in the neurosciences: Cautionary tales from the frontier. *Biologist, 40*(2), 89–94.

Rapp, P., Albano, A. M., Zimmerman, I. D., & Jimenez-Montano, M. A. (in preparation). *Phase-randomized surrogates can produce spurious identifications of non-random structure.*

Rossi, E. (1986). Altered states of consciousness in everyday life: The ultradian rhythms. In M.

Wolman & M. Ullman (Eds.), *Handbook of states of consciousness* (pp. 97–131). New York: Van Nostrand.

Sarraille, J., & DiFalco, P. (1992). *Fd3 fractal factory software.* Department of Philosophy & Cognitive studies; 801 West Vista Ave. Turlock, CA 95381.

Schaffer, W., Truty, G., & Fulmer, S. (1988). *Dynamical systems Software.* P.O. Box 35241, Tucson, AZ, 85740.

Smith, L. A. (1988). Intrinsic limits on dimension calculations. *Physics Letters, 133A,* 238–288.

Theiler, J. (1991). Some comments on the correlation dimension of 1/f noise. *Physics Letters. 155A,* 480–493.

Werntz, D., Bickford, R., Bloom, F., & Shannahoff, D. (1981, February). *Selective cortical activation by altering autonomic function.* Paper presented at Western EEG Society.

Werntz, D., Bickford, R., Bloom, F., & Shannahoff, D. (1982). Alternating cerebral hemisphere activity and lateralization of autonomic nervous function. *Neurobiology, 4,* 225–242.

Winkler, M., Combs, A. L., & Daley, C. (1994) A chaotic systems analysis of rhythm in feeling states. *The Psychological Record, 44,* 359–368.

Winkler, M., Combs, A., Dezern, D., Alstott, T., Burnham, J., Rand, B., & Walker, S. (1991, August). *Cyclicity in moods: A dynamical systems analysis.* Paper presented at the Inaugural meeting of The Society for Chaos Theory in Psychology, San Francisco, CA.

5 Constraint, Complexity, and Chaos: A Methodological Follow-Up on the Nostril Cycle

Tracy L. Brown
Allan Combs

This chapter is written entirely from the perspective of researchers in the behavioral sciences. It is not based on mathematical formalisms, although certainly it is not contrary to them, but arises from considerations faced by the researcher who must interpret real experimental data sets. It arose from an attempt to establish the presence of deterministic chaos in the nostril cycle.

High fractal dimensionality is indicative of random data, a condition of unrestraint in which each point is independent of the others. Random data yields estimates of fractal dimension approaching the value of the embedding dimension, if the data sets are large enough. Low fractal dimensionality, on the other hand, indicates a highly constrained, smooth function, in which each point is more or less continuous with previous ones. For example, a smooth function, such as a sine wave, yields low fractal dimensionality and does so no matter how large the embedding dimension. Classical chaotic functions, such as the Lorenz attractor, fall between these extremes, exhibiting fractal dimension estimates larger than smooth functions, such as the sine wave, but smaller than those produced by random data. Moreover, they "staturate" quickly, meaning that, as the embedding dimension increases, fractal dimension estimates rapidly approach a maximum value and do not continue to grow appreciably.

The previously mentioned material is equivalent to saying that classical chaotic functions lie somewhere between constraint and complexity. First consider constraint. By any reasonable definition, a sine function, which is perfectly predictable and holds no surprises, is highly constrained. Sets of random numbers, on the other hand, are unconstrained and are thus highly complex. A review of the entire literature on complexity in psychology and mathematics would be a lifetime project. One measure of complexity that few would argue with, how-

61

ever, is defined simply as the shortest algorithm, say, a computer program, that can be written to generate the series of numbers in question. This is termed *algorithmic complexity* (e.g., Cambel, 1993). In the case of a sine wave, the shortest algorithm is simply to state the sine function. For a truly random set of numbers, however, each number is unconstrained, that is, unrelated to the others, and the only way to generate the series is to rewrite it. In other words, the shortest algorithm is writing the series itself. Assuming large or unlimited data sets, this algorithm indicates great complexity.

Analyzing the data from the nostril cycle study by Combs and Winkler (chap. 4), the researchers were confronted with the question, typical of the behavioral sciences, of whether it is simply random or in some way constrained. Beyond this, if it is constrained, is it constrained by factors of real interest to the researchers, or only by extraneous factors of little or no interest? In the case of the nostril cycle, the researchers observed evidence of irregular but still modestly smooth individual ultradian rhythms entrained within daily or circadian periods. These in themselves are of interest in terms of the biology of this system and the past literature on it. Beyond this, however, the researchers were interested in whether or not the nostril cycle is regulated in part by complex nonlinear influences, biological or otherwise, that are chaotic. To get at the latter question, fractal dimension estimates were computed, and, in a technique suggested by Rapp, Theiler, and others (Rapp, Albano, Zimmerman, & Jimenez-Montano, 1994; Theiler, Euband, Longtin, Galdrikian, & Farmer, 1992), these were used to generate surrogate date sets to which they were compared.[1]

First, fractal dimension estimates were obtained for embedding dimensions from 1 to 10 for the data sets of each of the five participants. These were correlation dimension estimates using the Grassberger-Procaccia algorithm (Grassberger & Procaccia, 1983) implemented with J. C. Sprott's *Chaos Data Analyzer* program for the personal computer from Physics Academic Software. See the previous chapter for details of the study. A typical set is shown in Table 5.1. There it can be seen that for low embedding dimensions the estimated fractal dimension values are slightly smaller than those of the embedding dimension, but as the latter increases, especially beyond about 5, the fractal values do not continue to grow proportionately. Indeed, the estimated fractal dimension for embedding dimension 10 is slightly smaller than for embedding dimension 9. Though the development of methods for computing individual confidence intervals of fractal dimension estimates is still in progress, this roll-off of the dimension estimates is typical of all participants. Indeed, all the data sets look very similar with respect to fractal dimension.

The failure of the fractal dimension estimates to keep pace with the embed-

---

[1]The authors extend appreciation to Paul Rapp for providing the Fortran programs with which the surrogate data sets were generated. Portions of these were drawn from Press, Teukolsky, Vetterling, and Flannery's *Numerical Recipes* (1992).

TABLE 5.1
Fractal Dimension Estimates of the Nostril Cycle Data[a]

Embedding Dimension	Original Data	Random Shuffle	Controlled Shuffle[b]
1	—	—	1.04
2	1.19	1.29	2.05
3	2.22	3.05	3.07
4	3.11	3.79	3.80
5	4.16	4.18	4.41
6	4.69	4.73	5.20
7	5.09	5.34	5.49
8	5.11	6.06	5.89
9	5.63	6.41	6.33
10	5.59	6.70	6.57

[a] Correlation dimension using the Grassberger-Procaccia algorithm.
[b] Theiler et al. (1992).

ding dimension would seem to be an indication that the data is somehow constrained. Perhaps it is partially the result of deterministic chaos. Unfortunately, however, it could also be due simply to the fact that even random data estimates do not keep up with the embedding dimension if the data sets are not sufficiently large. Both these issues can be addressed by scrambling the original data, producing a random shuffle surrogate, and recomputing fractal dimension estimates. If the new values approach the embedding dimension values, then the original data evidently was not random. If the new values are similar to the original ones, however, it is possible that the data sets are too small.

As can be seen in Table 5.1, the random shuffle values are similar to the original ones but, in every instance, slightly larger. This was typical of data sets from all five participants. In 45 comparisons, there appeared only five instances of inversions and only at embedding dimensions of two and three. (The reasons for the latter are unclear.) The apparent consistency of the random shuffle surrogates to produce slightly higher fractal dimension estimates suggests that the original data was not entirely random but somehow constrained. It does not in itself, however, prove the presence of chaos. The most obvious sources of constraint are the ultradian rhythms themselves, which would of course be entirely lost in the random shuffle.

Thanks to Paul Rapp, the authors were fortunate to have recently acquired another shuffle algorithm, one designed to test hypothesis immaterial to the present study, but that effectively randomizes the data in a controlled shuffle, while preserving its overall temporal form (Theiler et al., 1992). For example, when used on sinusoidal data, it preserves the form of the sine way. The important thing here is that, if the above constraint is due to the ultradian rhythms, substantially preserved in surrogates from the second algorithm, then fractal dimension estimates obtained from these should be essentially the same as those from the original data sets. This, however, was not found to be the case. In fact, as can be seen in Table 5.1, the fractal dimension estimates obtained from the second algorithm were very similar to those obtained from the plain random shuffle, indicating that whatever is showing up in the fractal dimension estimates that constrains this data are not the ultradian rhythms.

Unfortunately, and much to the unhappiness of undergraduate psychology students, null hypotheses never yield confirmations. They only fail to disprove. In this instance, the authors have used the methods available to them at the time of this writing, and with these have in good faith failed to disprove the presence of deterministic chaos in the nostril cycle data. Since chaos in biological systems, and especially in the nervous system, has been widely observed with a variety of procedures (Abraham & Gilgen, 1994; Basar, 1990; Pribram, 1994) it still seems quite possible that chaos may exist here.

REFERENCES

Abraham, F., & Gilgen, A. (Eds.). (1994). *Chaos theory in psychology.* Westport, Ct: Greenwood.

Basar E. (Ed.). (1990). *Chaos in brain function.* Berlin: Springer-Verlag.

Cambel, A. B. (1993). *Applied chaos theory: A paradigm for complexity.* New York: Academic Press.

Grassberger, P., & Procaccia, I. (1983). Characterization of strange attractors. *Physical Review Letters, 50,* 346–349.

Physics Academic Software. American Institute of Physics. 335 East 45th Street; New York, NY, 10017–3483.

Press, W. H., Teukolsky, S. A., Vetterling, W. T., & Flannery, B. P. (1992). *Numerical recipes: The art of scientific computing.* New York: Cambridge University Press.

Pribram, K. H. (Ed.). (1994). *Origins: Brains and self organization.* Hillsdale, NJ: Lawrence Erlbaum Associates.

Rapp, P., Albano, A. M., Zimmerman, I. D., & Jimenez-Montano, M. A. (1994). Phase-random surrogates can produce spurious identifications of non-random structure. *Physics Letters.*

Theiler, J., Euband, A., Longtin, B., Galdrikian, B., & Farmer, J. D. (1992). *Physica. 58D, 77.*

6

Anger, Fear, Depression, and Crime: Physiological and Psychological Studies Using the Process Method

Hector C. Sabelli
Linnea Carlson-Sabelli
M. Patel
A. Levy
Justo Diez-Martin

This chapter presents empirical studies of emotional processes, relevant to affective dysfunctions, cardiac illness and criminal behavior, using a comprehensive process method described herein. The populations studied include normal subjects, psychiatric patients, and inmates at a prison facility. Three novel techniques that apply nonlinear dynamic methods are described: *sociodynamics* (clinical study of social behavior), *psychogeometry* (longitudinal study of emotions), and *electropsychocardiography* (EPCG; mathematical analysis of dynamic electrocardiograms to reveal how emotional patterns determine patterns of cardiac timing). These studies lead us to develop the concept of *complexes* (multidimensional and evolving patterns in interacting processes, in contrast to attractors, that are stable low-dimensional patterns, and apparent only in the absence of interactions) as a model for complex processes. These studies also suggest a multidimensional model of psychobiological energy (libido). In this manner, we hope to develop a *mathematical psychodynamics*.

PROCESS THEORY AND METHOD

Process theory (PT) provides a research methodology, a clinical approach (Sabelli & Carlson-Sabelli, 1989, 1991; Sabelli, Carlson-Sabelli, & Messer 1994) a social program (Sabelli & Synnestvedt, 1991), a mathematical dialectic logic (Sabelli, 1984), and a world view (Sabelli, 1989), by integrating dynamics and psychodynamics within the framework of physiology. Modern physiology provides scientific bases to psychology and to epistemology (Piaget's experimental epistemology) and suggests general physical principles (Pasteur's cosmic asymmetry, see later). In Ancient Greece, physiology was born as a biological model for the laws (logos) of nature (physios), which Heraclitus subsumed under three interlocking principles:

1. *Dynamic Monism*. Matter is alive and creative; it is fire (energy) and logos (information); psyche and body are made of the same stuff. This view was later abandoned in favor of a dualism of inert physical matter and immaterial spirit, and physiology was restricted to the biological realm.

2. *Union of Opposites (harmony and conflict, union and separation, true and false)*. Conflict is the father of all things, and harmony is their mother. This view was later supplanted by the separation of opposites (logical principle of no contradiction), or their mutual neutralization (mechanics), or by unilateral formulations of universal harmony (theology) or of a struggle of opposites (Marxist dialectics and Darwinian evolutionism).

3. *Becoming*. This was the belief in the creation and destruction of structures in opposing processes of evolution and involution (*enantiodromia*). This view was later on displaced by static views (implicit in geometric models of time and in the conceptualization of processes as stable attractors), or by one sided formulations of either progressive evolution or involution towards entropic disorder.

PT adopts and updates the principles of physiology, as can be seen in the following sections.

Oneness of Action

Everything is an action, that is to say, a flow of energy in time, as action is defined in physics. Movement is mechanical action, metabolism is chemical reaction, behavior is organized in action patterns, structures are slowly moving processes. Energy, information, and matter are inseparable aspects of all processes. Each emotion, for instance, consists of a physiological change and an outward behavior (energy), a subjective feeling and an intersubjective communication (information), and a chemical transmitter release in a brain structure (matter); the comprehensive study of emotions includes measurements of physiological changes and neuroamine metabolism. Physical, biological, social and psychological processes, and structures are forms of energy, made of the same stuff, differing only in their organization. The complexity of psychological processes is encoded in sequences of action potentials, which in turn are embodied in the physical movement of ions. Because complex processes organize the simpler levels that, by necessity, encode them, the same forms exist at all levels within an organism. Hence, the EPCG portrays mathematically the physical correlate (electrical currents) of a biological function to characterize psychological processes.

The flow of energy in time is unidirectional. Action is asymmetric, and every structure is asymmetric because it carries the imprint of the action that created it. Having discovered that biomolecules are asymmetric, Pasteur inferred that the most basic components of nature must be asymmetric (Haldane, 1960); the asymmetry of subatomic processes has been found in the nonconservation of parity (Yorke & Li, 1975); asymmetry is also a fundamental feature of biological, social, and psychological processes (Corballis & Beale, 1976; Sabelli, 1989). The oneness of nature is its cosmic asymmetry—action. Asymmetry defines the ordering relation < studied by *lattice* theory, one of the three pillars of mathematics according to Bourbaki (1963). Every process has the structure of a lattice, that is, a sequence of forkings and differentiations, and of reunions and combinations, with a beginning and an end, ordered by the unidirectional flow of time.

Opposition as Information

Processes are driven and organized by the interaction between multiple pairs of inseparable opposites. This *union of opposites,* independently discovered by Heraclitus and Lao-tzu, was adopted by Hegel and Engels in their dialectic logic, and by Niels Bohr to explain quantum complementarity. Group theory, a second pillar of mathematics, according to Bourbaki, studies the relation between opposites (an element and its inverse), and the more complex systems of symmetry they generate. Containing opposites, everything contains information because a difference constitutes a unit of information (Shannon & Weaver, 1964), and two values suffice in traditional and in Boolean mathematical logic. Coexisting in one and the same process, opposites are, by necessity, more similar than different, and partially synergic, as well as partially antagonistic; thus opposites cannot be represented as extreme poles of a linear continuum but should be depicted as orthogonal vectors (decomposable into synergic and opposing components), which may be taken as axes for phase portraits (see later). Opposite actions, each asymmetric, complement each other to create partial symmetries, such as cycles, folds, and structures, rather than neutralizing each other in formless equilibrium. Reformulating theormodynamics, processes move toward symmetry, not only disorder, but also higher dimensional organization; entropy is symmetry, not disorder (Sabelli, 1989, 1994; Sabelli et al., 1994).

Becoming: Cocreation of Tridimensional Matter and Higher Dimensional Organization

The interaction of opposite structures generate new ones: sexes copulate to procreate a new individual; oppositely charged particles bind to create atoms (matter). Similarly, opposite forces interact in a nonlinear manner, thereby cocreating patterns, which can be fairly transient (complexes) or relatively stable (structures). In this manner, organization, complexity, novelty, and diversity emerge. Two forces can produce only change or equilibrium, but the interaction of three or more (partially opposite) forces can create patterns of partial symmetry; thus, complexes and structures have three or more dimensions. In static view of logic, opposites cannot coexist (Kant's absolute principle of no contradiction), and the third is excluded; according to PT, opposites coexist, and interact to create a third entity, which always has one more dimension (nonlinearity), because opposites cannot coexist at the same time, in the same place and in the same respect (Aristotle's local principle of no contradiction). The simplest case is the *catastrophe* (Thom, 1975), in which the nonlinear competition between opposite point attractors creates a distribution of outcomes in a third dimension. Catastrophes and other creative bifurcations not only change form, but also increase (or decrease) dimensions. As opposition is universal, the *trifurcation* of processes, and the existence of tridimensional structures are also universal. More generally, the formation of a $N + i$ dimensional fold results from the interaction of N processes; in this manner, structures of higher dimensionality are generated. In mathematical models, the repetition of bifurcations creates chaotic attractors, and the iteration of simple mathematical calculations creates complex fractal structures; in the same manner, repeated and intense oscillation between opposite processes creates chaos that, in turn, generates novel and complex dissipative structures (Prigogine, 1980). In a similar manner, according to PT, the oppositions inherent in the asymmetry of energy create matter (tridimensional structure) and more complex forms of organization (Molecules, organisms, societies, and psychological individuals)—a divergent and creative process, not a lineal development. Such a portrait of creative evolution contrasts with deterministic and reversible mechanics, and with statistical conceptions that postulate lineal trajectories, and convergence to a point attractor. Processes are trees that branch, becoming more complex as they grow. Physical as well as biological evolution diverge, creating diversity of qualities and complexity of organization. Biological as well as psychological development diverge, creating a variety of healthy and pathological personalities—this is in contrast to the view of pathology as the result of involution or of developmental arrest. Natural patterns are not stable attractors. Opposites interact continuously, so the patterns of organization (complexes) are also constantly changing; structures are fluid, evolving continuously (gradual bifurcation) or discontinuously (sudden bifurcation) into others. These create a complex embedding of patterns and a hierarchy of topologically embedded levels: *mathematical, physical, chemical, biological, social,* and *psychological.* Topology (upon which dynamics is based) is the third pillar of mathematics according to Bourbaki (1963).

The simpler levels have greater energy, extension, and duration (priority); they exist without and within, as well as before, during, and after complex processes. The maximization of entropy has priority, increasing both in simple and complex systems (this is in contrast to Prigogine's explanation of evolution as resulting from a local decrease in entropy in complex systems). The more complex levels are localized, but concentrate free energy from their simpler environment, have greater density of energy and information flow. For instance, the free energy flux density of brain is 150,000 ergs/sec^{-1} gm^{-1} in contrast to 2 ergs/sec^{-1} gm^{-1} in the sun (Chaisson, 1987), and hence organize and control the simpler levels with which they are coextensive (supremacy). Thus, PT postulates the *priority of the simple and the supremacy of the complex* (Sabelli, 1989). In human processes, there is a *biological priority* and a *psychological supremacy* (Sabelli, 1989). Human ideas reflect external reality but include subjective interpretations derived from social and psychological processes; hence the *objective has priority and the subjective has supremacy* (Carlson-Sabelli & Sabelli, 1984). To study a process, one must examine it from the double perspective of its simple foundations and of the more complex processes that control it; the most comprehensive approach includes *mathematics (priority) and psychosocial analysis (supremacy)* (Sabelli & Carlson-Sabelli, 1993).

According to PT, asymmetry, opposition, and topological embedding are three cosmic forms or "logoi"—as Thom calls them in honor of Heraclitus—that repeat at each level of organization, thereby creating a self-similarity characteristic of fractals (Mandelbrot, 1977). Logoi have a numerical form: 1 for oneness and unidirectionality, 2 for opposition and bidirectionality, and groups of 3 and more elements. All processes and structures have the physical dimensions of energy, information and matter, and the corresponding cosmic forms but also create new forms of higher dimensionality: evolution is a process of local dimensiogenesis. Biological, social, and psychological dimensions are as yet poorly identified, yet they are as real as physical dimensions and can be estimated through dynamic portraits (see later).

Based on these hypotheses, the process method investigates all phenomena as processes over time (rather than isolated events, stable structures, or attractors), examining patterns of change in time series data, using a sequence of frameworks of increasing dimensions, as we shall exemplify with current findings of ongoing empirical studies.

BIDIMENSIONAL PORTRAITS OF OPPOSITES

The interaction of coexisting opposites is studied in a bidimensional state space (Sabelli, 1989; Carlson-Sabelli & Sabelli, 1992a, 1992b). Most psychological tests adopt linear scales that implicitly assume that opposing forces balance and neutralize each other. Yet common sense and clinical experience recognizes the coexistence of opposing feelings and preferences, as well as of opposite aspects in each personality (e.g., introversion and extroversion). An increase in positive feelings or personality traits does not necessarily decrease their opposite. Equally powerful opposite motivations do not produce neutral equilibrium but result in

A On the rotated grid below you are asked to take into account both your PULL TO CHOOSE and your PULL NOT TO CHOOSE each person in the group for the activity indicated, and to place a point in the grid which best represents it. Once you have made each point, draw an arrow from the point to a place outside this grid where you will write each person's name. More than one person may be located at the same point.

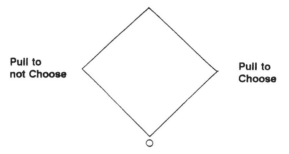

Pull to not Choose

Pull to Choose

B Rank Order

If you had to choose only one person from among this group for the criterion identified, in what order would your choices be? Indicate the order on the continuum below by indicating a point on the line appropriate for each person. Once you have identified the point, draw an arrow from the point to a place above or below the line where you will write their name. Do not place more than one person at the same point. Next, put a C by those persons you choose, N for those you are neutral toward, or R for reject. See the example.

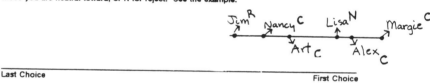

Last Choice   First Choice

C

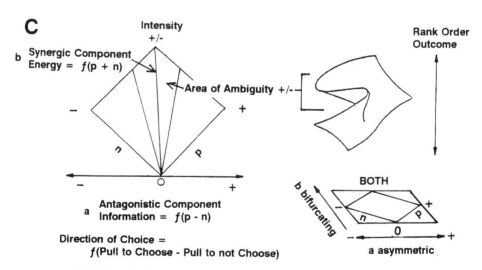

FIG. 6.1. Sociodynamic test using a plane of opposites: (A) Plane of opposites used by subjects to plot their feelings of attraction and repulsion. (B) Linear scale used by subjects to rank the order of their choices. (C) Analysis of the data. Coexisting opposite forces (p, posi-

70

ambivalence and generate complex behaviors that accommodate both. Intrapsychic and interpersonal processes are driven by contradictory feelings of attraction and repulsion and by conflicting behaviors of cooperation and conflict. Assuming a categorical distinction or an inverse linear relation between opposites can be empirically demonstrated to create gross distortions of the data (Sabelli, 1992). To study opposites that can be mutually synergic as well as antagonic, we plot them as orthogonal axes, thereby creating a bidimensional plane. We use such bidimensional scales to study personal history by recording temporal changes in feelings of love and hate toward parents, spouses, and children (Sabelli, 1989) and to study personal networks by recording current and desired feelings of attraction and repulsion, harmony, and conflict toward each significant other (Carlson-Sabelli & Sabelli, 1992a, 1992b); and interpersonal choices for partners within small groups (Sabelli, 1992; Carlson-Sabelli, Sabelli & Hale, 1994a). For instance, the *sociodynamic test* (Fig. 6.1) plots each person's reports of feelings of the attraction and repulsion towards each other group member in a bidimensional construct and his or her choices and rejections on a linear rank on a third axis. The surface created by the relation between them presents a fold that can be modelled by one or another of Thom's elementary catastrophes. The asymmetric parameter of the catastrophe can be calculated as the difference of opposites (attraction and repulsion); it provides information regarding the outcome (choice vs. rejection), except when the opposites are very similar. The sum of these opposites provides the bifurcating parameter, which reflects the total emotional energy involved in the choice and determines the outcome when attraction and repulsion are similar in intensity: neutrality at low values, and ambivalence (choices and rejections changing from one to the other) at high values. Clinically significant events occur in this area of contradiction. These observations suggest to us that the asymmetric and bifurcating parameters in catastrophes represent the union and difference of opposites, a relation that we propose as a general law that applies to all types of bifurcations. We propose that high energy contradictory processes, either intrapsychic or interpersonal, provide the emergent milieu for creativity and destructiveness, and are easily influenced

---

tive attraction, and n, negative repulsion) are represented as orthogonal axes. 0 denotes zero intensity for both opposites. The difference between p and n on the horizontal axis corresponds to the asymmetric factor of a fold catastrophe; when p is greater than n, a choice is expected; conversely, a rejection when n is greater than p. When p and n are similar (symmetry), the sum of opposites (bifurcating factor), becomes the best predictor: low-intensity opposites lead to neutrality—choosing not to choose—and high-intensity opposites unpredictably result in either a choice or a rejection, changes from one to the other occur, and new behaviors emerge. The distribution of outcomes plotted on a third axis has a catastrophe distribution.

by small interventions (butterfly effect). Identifying the areas of unstable contradiction, the sociodynamic test is useful to target issues that are most amenable to therapeutic intervention (Carlson-Sabelli et al., 1994a).

PSYCHOGEOMETRY AND THE CONFLICT THEORY
OF DEPRESSION

Psychogeometry studies mood by portraying the temporal pattern of variation of emotions and behaviors as reported by the subject (Carlson-Sabelli, Sabelli, Hein & Javaid, 1990). With this method, we have studied the relation between anger, fear, and depression. Classic theories portray these behaviors as choices between opposite alternatives. According to Freud, anger can be turned outward, as aggression, or inward, as depression; the union of opposites suggests that inwardly directed and outwardly directed anger coexist and reinforce each other. For Cannon, conflict leads to fight or flight, a dichotomy modelled as a catastrophe (Zeeman, 1977): When a subject experiences both anger and fear simultaneously, these opposites do not cancel each other (as in quantitative theories of opposition), but rather one emotion predominates. The subject either fights or flees. Actually, mammals confronted with conflict may also display submission, which normally terminates the aggressive behavior of the other, avoiding intraspecies killing, and generating social hierarchies. Conflict thus poses a trifurcation: fight, flight or surrender. These behaviors may be mutually exclusive, but alternate, intertwine, and replace each other, according to circumstances. Their subjective components—anger, fear, and sorrow—coexist, consciously or unconsciously, because conflict is their common trigger. The *conflict theory of affect* (Sabelli, 1989; Sabelli & Carson-Sabelli, 1991) postulates that rage, anxiety, and depression are pathological manifestations of these three innate responses to conflict, brought about by external conflicts, and/or triggered by dysfunctions in the metabolism of the neurohormones that mediate these emotional behaviors—in this case, the manifested hostile and depressive behaviors can create interpersonal conflict.

We have tested these hypotheses through the longitudinal study of mood patterns in 16 healthy adult volunteers (28 to 70 y/o, 8 women and 8 men), single and married, with middle class occupations and educations; and 33 adult outpatients (21 to 65 y/0, 24 women and 9 men) of similar class background, treated for depressive and anxiety disorders. Psychodynamic patterns were explored by longitudinal monitoring of levels of joy, depression, anger and rage, fear and anxiety, sexual feelings and behavior, sleep quality, positive and negative feelings toward significant others, and positive and negative events. Each person subjectively evaluated the feelings experienced during the past 24 hours as a single value on a scale from 0 (*none*) to 9 (*very intense*). Records were obtained for periods ranging from 35 up to 700 consecutive days. The entire record of each person, or sequences of 35 consecutive daily self-reports for intergroup comparisons, were analyzed using four methods: correlation analysis; factor analysis (sorted and rotated factors); harmonic analysis (Patel, 1993); and tridimensional phase space portraits, in which reports of anger, anxiety, or depression were the orthogonal axes—the intersection of values for a given day defined a point, and the sequence of points drew the trajectory of mood.

In these phase portraits, we could readily recognize by visual inspection several types of trajectories (Fig. 6.2). The first is an equilibrium pattern (2A and B): tight trajectories occupying a relatively small area of the phase space near the zero point (2A) with occasional spokelike trajectories (2B) that spin off and return rapidly to the origin, suggesting transients. We interpret these trajectories as point attractors. They were extremely rare. The second portrait shows periodic cycles (2C and E): relatively small cyclic trajectories, around the center of the phase space, that we interpret as periodic cycles, as supported by harmonic analysis; we have found this type of trajectories in all groups studied. The third are chaoticlike trajectories (2D and F): large, irregular trajectories that appear random, wandering all over the phase space in an overtly erratic manner. These chaoticlike trajectories were more common in depressed subjects (Table 6.1).

Harmonic analysis confirmed the periodicities observed in phase space trajectories; showed that different emotions and behaviors varied quite independently from each other; and revealed unique configurations for each individual. Women and men showed periodic patterns, sometimes associated with lunar cycles, others of odd number (e.g., 17 days). Most surprising, "external events," a category designed to tease out variations caused by chance events, occurred in a periodic fashion in many individuals, indicating that subjective perceptions were more important than external inputs.

Anger, fear, and depression varied together in phase space trajectories. Statistical analysis showed these emotional opposites were positively correlated (a negative correlation would have been expected from polar opposites) and loaded together in factor analysis, in both male and female, depressed and nondepressed subjects. Anxiety and depression loaded in the same factor and correlated positively (0.50 in controls), consistent with the frequent clinical association of these two symptoms. Anger and anxiety also correlated positively (0.63)—at variance with the fight or flight dichotomy. Depressed subjects experienced more anger than controls but did not associate these two emotions as closely as nondepressed persons: anger and depression were positively correlated to a greater extent in controls (0.70) than in depressed subjects (0.31). These data support Freud's hypothesis, relating depression and anger, but not the conceptualization of depression as a displacement of anger, which implies the replacement of one by the other. These results indicate the need to promote the resolution of conflicts that trigger, or are the consequence of, depression and anxiety. Marital therapy is very often indicated in the treatment of depression, even in those cases initiated by a metabolic dysfunction.

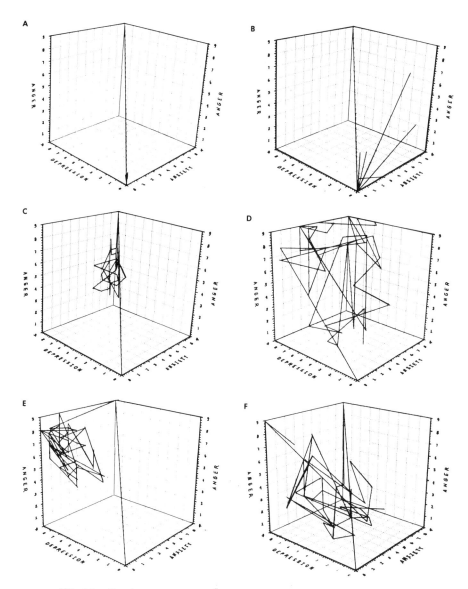

FIG. 6.2.   Psychogeometry: tridimensional phase space portraits self-reported levels of anxiety (right axis), depression (left axis) and anger (vertical axis) for 35 days. The diagonal line is a calibration signal. (A) and (B) are equilibrium patterns observed in jail inmates. (C) is a periodic pattern in a normal individual. (D) is a chaotic pattern in a manic depressive who committed murder two weeks after completing the test. (E) is shifted periodic pattern. (F) is a chaotic pattern in a depressed subject.

TABLE 6.1

Phase Space Portraits of Anger, Anxiety and Depression in Control Subjects,
Depressed Patients, and Prison Inmates

| | | Percent of Subjects for Each Trajectory Type | | |
| | | | | |
Trajectory Type	Controls (n = 16)	Depressed Patients (n = 33)	Nondepressed Inmates (n = 14)	Depressed Inmates (n = 19)
Equilibrium	13	3	67	0
Cyclic	31	15	13	8
Chaotic	56	82	20	92

CHAOS, DEPRESSION AND CRIME

The observed association between anger and depression suggested to us that psychogeometry might be useful to explore the hypothetical relation between conflict, anger, depression, and crime postulated by so many authors. We obtained longitudinal reports of mood from 33 male inmates (20 to 64 y/o) of the Utah state prison (Levy, 1991; Levy, Sabelli & Payne, 1992). The inmate sample was part of a larger study of the relation between depression, violence, and the urinary excretion of phenylacetic acid, the main metabolite of the brain neurohormone phenylethylamine (PEA). PEA may modulate mood, as its administration causes excitement, its plasma levels are increased in sociopathic criminals (Sandler, Ruthven, Goodwin, 1978), the plasma and urinary levels of its metabolite phenylacetic acid are diminished in 60% of depressed subjects (Sabelli et al., 1983), and PEA replacement therapy rapidly relieves depression (Sabelli, Fahrer, Medina, & Frágola, 1994).

Phenylacetic acid excretion was significantly lower (116 ± 11 mg/day) in 59 inmates with severe depression (according to the MMPI, Hamilton and Beck depression scales) than in 49 subjects who were not depressed by any criterion (181 ± 22 mg/day); intermediate values were obtained in subjects with moderate depression. Phenylacetic acid excretion was higher in nondepressed inmates than in noncriminal populations. Forty percent of the inmates had committed violent crimes, ranging from homicide to burglaries with a weapon; in comparison to other inmates, they had significantly higher excretion of phenylacetic acid (Levy, 1991; Levy et al., 1992). These results are compatible with previous observations relating PEA excess to aggression and PEA deficit to depression.

The frequency of the various temporal patterns of mood was dramatically different in inmates than in noncriminal populations. Chaotic patterns were frequent among inmates and often associated with depression, as in other populations (Table 6.1). Nondepressed inmates were unique among all groups studied, in the high frequency of near equilibrium trajectories, with or without transient deviations (67% of cases). In contrast, such dramatic limitation of emotion was never observed in depressed inmates and rarely observed in controls (Table 6.1). Statistical analysis also indicated nondepressed inmates reported significantly less anxiety, depression, or anger than any of the other experimental groups (including healthy controls). The fact that criminals, but not normals, showed equilibrium patterns is at variance with the notion of health as equilibrium and illness as disorder.

The difference between equilibrium, cyclic and chaotic patterns was evident in factor analysis. In inmates with equilibrium patterns, anger, depression, anxiety, negative feelings, and negative events loaded in the first factor; positive emotions loaded in separate factors (e.g., sex was separated from positive feelings and joy). In subjects with periodic or chaotic patterns, joy, positive events, positive feelings, and sex loaded in factor one; factor two loaded for negative feelings, negative events, anger, and depression.

In individual analyses, anger and anxiety loaded together in 33% of subjects; anger and depression in 45%, and anxiety and depression in 55%. Further, all three emotions loaded in the same factor for the entire population of inmates and noninmates, and for all the subgroups of nondepressed subjects, including both women and men. These three emotions, however, did not load in the same factor in the case of depressed subjects (inmates and noninmates). Depressed patients dissociated anger from depression, and depressed inmates dissociated anxiety from depression. The five murderers differ from other prisoners in the existence of a separate factor that loaded for anxiety and depression together with positive feelings toward their significant others.

Joy and depression loaded in separate factors in nondepressed subjects, indicating that they varied separately, while the factor analysis of the depressed subjects showed that they loaded in the same factor, with opposite signs, indicating their dichotomization as opposite ends of a continuum. these data support the view that normality is associated with tolerance for the coexistence of opposites, while black and white thinking is known to predispose to neurosis (Adler) and depression (Beck, Rush, Shaw, & Emery, 1979).

These studies support three main conclusions. First, the association between anger, fear, and depression in most circumstances, and their partial separation in pathological populations. Second, a possible association of chaotic patterns of mood variability with depression. Third, a possible association of emotional blunting with sociopathy. Whereas chaotic patterns and low phenylacetic acid excretion characterized depressed individuals whether patients or prison inmates, aggressive criminals often reported absence of depression, emotional equilibrium, and showed high levels of phenylacetic acid excretion. These differences seem to refute the hypothetical relation between depression and crime. Yet, none of the prison inmates studied had a normal psychiatric history, and many who denied being currently depressed had a history of depression, attention deficit disorder, alcoholism, drug abuse, parental abuse, and combinations thereof.

PHYSIOLOGICAL OBJECTIVITY AND PSYCHOLOGICAL SUBJECTIVITY

Subjective reports, particularly those from prison inmates, are open to conscious and unconscious distortions. An inmate on death row since age 19 for a particularly gruesome murder, reported no negative affects. Although he denied depressive feelings, his urinary excretion of phenylacetic acid was 63 mg/day, in the range observed in patients with major depressive disorder. Our clinical experience indicates that such amine deficits reflect masked depressions that benefit

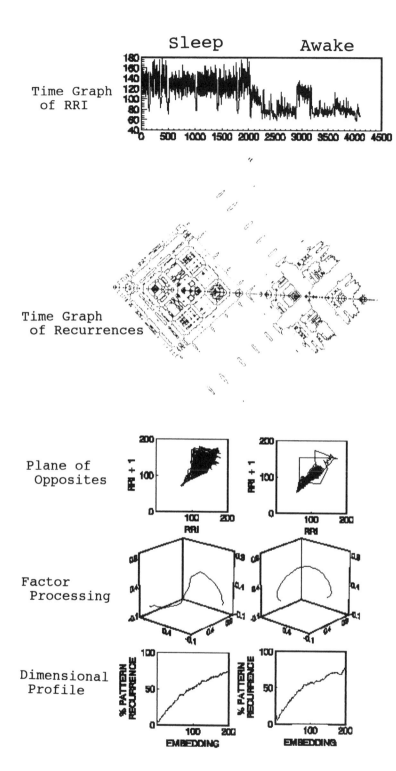

from pharmacological treatment. We thus envision a system of psychiatric diagnosis based on physiological data rather than phenomenological description.

Both the biochemical and the psychological tests described above are of limited clinical usefulness because they are time consuming, and provide very sparse data—insufficient for dynamic analysis. Data are not readily obtainable from children, psychotics, and even from normal persons. A more objective and precise evaluation of the temporal variation of emotions and behaviors may be useful for diagnosis. In principle, the various patterns of emotional behavior may be recognized through monitoring their peripheral physiological components.

ELECTROPSYCHOCARDIOGRAPHY

We thus turned to the study of cardiac timing, as measured by the duration of R-R intervals in 24 hour monitoring of the electrocardiogram (Sabelli et al., 1994; Carlson-Sabelli et al., 1994b; Sabelli et al., in press). Based on PT, we have developed a number of novel mathematical techniques to study the time course and multiple dimensions (Fig. 6.3):

Plane of Opposites

Phase plane portraits can be interpreted in terms of opposing processes of adrenergic acceleration and cholinergic deceleration: the minor axis of the trajectory blob represents the difference between successive beats, determined by the difference of opposites, while the major axis represents the joint variation of successive beats as parts of a pattern (union of opposites). Psychotics often show a reduction in the major axis.

Factor Processing

To reveal the multiplicity of independent factors that modulate cardiac timing, we correlated the original time series with time-delayed replicas from 1 to 30

FIG. 6.3. Electropsychocardiography: The sequence of R-R intervals during awakening in a normal subject. From top to bottom: Unidimensional time graph, showing a marked change in frequency with awakening. Time graph of recurrences (4000 beats, 480 embeddings), demonstrating patterning, its variation from sleep to wakefulness, and its interruption during awakening. Phase plane portrait of R-R I $_i$ versus R-R I $_{i+i}$, during sleep (left) and wakefulness (right). Factor processing during sleep (4 statistically demonstrable factors) and wakefulness (3 factors). Dimensional profile, indicating the percent of patterned recurrences in frameworks from 1 to 200 dimensions; the median embedding dimension was more complex just prior to awakening (89) that immediately afterwards (77).

lags, identified the statistically significant factors that describe these 30 variables, and rotated them to separate orthogonal opposites. This procedure reveals two to five factors in most subjects. Plotting the factor loadings for each factor against the factor loadings of the others, one can draw the trajectories determined by the three most significant factors, thereby identifying various patterns, and interruptions separating them. These patterns are relatively simple, as illustrated by the inverted U shape in the figure, but become extremely disorganized during sleep in a subgroup of depressives, as well as during episodes of angina in patients with coronary artery disease.

Time Graph of Recurrences

Eckmann, Kamphorst, and Ruelle (1987) developed recurrence plots, constructed by the delay technique, as a method to construct graphs of higher dimensions from a time series. For each beat, one constructs a vector that includes the $R–R$ interval itself, and each of the following intervals up to the number $N,$ the number of embeddings, typically 3–10. The time-ordered sequence of vectors is ordered in a square matrix, in which the horizontal axis represents the time index, $x(i)$, and the vertical axis $x(j)$ represents each of the successive vectors forward in time. When two vectors so constructed are approximately equal (within 10%, using the Euclidean norm for the calculation of distances), a dot is plotted to indicate a recurrence. Recurrence plots reveal patterns far from apparent in time graphs of $R–R$ intervals. Based on our process perspective, we connect recurrence plots to generate time graphs of recurrences. These graphs reveal complex patterns consisting of discrete phases (*complexes*), each with a beginning and an end, separated from the others by *interruptions* of pattern during awakening (Fig. 6.3) and other changes in state. We have identified some 20 distinct forms of complexes that repeat in different subjects and that we have labeled with the letters of the alphabet. Comparisons between electrocardiographic recordings and patients' diaries reveal that some of these complexes appear to be specifically associated with particular emotions (regardless of the patient's diagnosis), such as sadness (first identified in a child crying and later seen in depressed subjects) and anxiety (observed in normal, cardiac, anxious, depressed, and schizophrenic subjects). These observations suggest to us the existence of an alphabet of cardiac patterns associated with the action patterns of behavior described by ethology.

Another type of difference exists between psychotic subjects (schizophrenic or manic), whose recurrence graphs are highly organized and simpler, and nonpsychotic subjects, whose graphs contain many fewer recurrences that are more complex. These visual differences are striking even to the naked eye.

Constructing recurrence plots of various durations, using a range of embeddings, we found that these complexes are self-similar, suggesting a fractal structure, as observed in chaotic attractors and more complex forms of organization. This led to the study of complexes in frameworks of multiple dimensions.

Dimensional Profiles

Based on the method of Zbilut and Webber (1992) to quantify recurrences, we measured the following *organization qualities:* (a) the number and percentage of recurrences; (b) the number and percentage of "patterned recurrences" (recurrences contained in lines, with Zbilut and Webber call "determinism"); (c) Shannon's entropy (a measure of information, not disorder) according to the length of line segments; (d) consumption ratio, entropy multiplied by $R-R$ interval), which provides an estimate of the rate of production of entropy as a function of the flow of energy; (e) arrangement ratio, as the ratio between percentages of patterned and total recurrences, which provides an estimate of organization; and (f) productivity, the ratio of arrangement over entropy, estimating how the consumption of energy creates organization. We studied each samples at various embeddings, from 1 to 500.

We found that 20 to 100 embeddings are necessary to account for 50% of the recurrences (i.e., for 50% of the recurrences to be contained in lines); this median embedding dimension is greater in control subjects than in schizophrenics (Table 6.2). As the number of embeddings represents the dimensions of the framework in which the process under study is projected, we concluded that psychophysiological processes include components of tens and even hundreds of dimensions and that illness represents a reduction in dimensionality.

The homeostatic model postulated that cardiac rate tended to a normal average (point attractor), which varied in a cyclic mamner with the sleep wakefulness cycle (periodic attractor); more recently, Goldberger (1991) proposed that normal heart rate represents a chaotic attractor (three or more dimensions). Zbilut and Webber (1992) suggested that cardiac timing consists of transients determined by a number of independent factors (respiration, blood pressure, endocrine, etc.) and only falls into the basin of an attractor under pathological conditions. Our data suggest that cardiac timing is organized in high dimensional, patterned, and transient complexes that are integrated as components of patterned neurophysiological processes, such as behavioral action patterns (emotions), rather than being organized into a single attractor, whether homeostatic, periodic or chaotic, or simply being regulated on a beat-to-beat basis by a number of independent factors. Hence, the possibility and the necessity of studying emotional life to understand cardiac dynamics.

As the embedding dimensions vary so dramatically from subject to subject, we compare all variables measured at the median embedding dimension. These measurements confirm the observed differences between psychotic and non-psychotic subjects (Table 2); these differences were evident regardless of the

TABLE 6.2

Comparison Between Three Normal, Three Bipolar Depressed, and Three Psychotic Subjects During Wakefulness and During Sleep. Average ± S.D. of Variables at the Median Embedding Dimension (Embedding 50, E_{50}). Lag 1, Cutoff 0.1, 7000 Beats Per Patient. Statistical Significance (Mann-Whitney U Test).

Variable	Wakefulness			Sleep				Significance	
	Controls	De-pressed	Psychotic	Controls	De-pressed	Psychotic	Random	Psychotic Versus Non-Psychotic	Awake Versus Asleep
E_{50}	57.7 3.5	51.7 24.7	24.7 10.5	37.3 3.1	36.0 8.5	19.3 6.0		$p < 0.01$	—
Mean RRI (msec)	831 52	1010 305	719 47	1157 235	1194 188	835 122		$p < 0.01$	$p < 0.05$
Mean distance	9.2 0.8	9.9 4.1	4.7 2.3	5.8 0.9	6.2 2.0	3.5 2.3		$p < 0.05$	$p < 0.05$
Number* recurrences	20.3 1.0	21.7 7.7	46.3 31.7	36.8 4.3	34.2 8.5	60.7 25.8		$p < 0.05$	$p < 0.05$
Percent recurrences	0.8 0.0	0.9 0.3	1.9 1.3	1.5 0.2	1.4 0.3	2.5 1.1		$p < 0.05$	$p < 0.05$
Number* lines	35.0 1.5	38.3 13.1	88.5 70.7	71.3 12.9	63.2 15.6	123.0 62.0		$p < 0.05$	$p < 0.01$
Entropy	1.9 0.1	1.8 0.2	1.7 0.3	1.6 0.2	1.7 0.1	1.5 0.3	1.2	—	$p < 0.05$
Arrangement ratio	61.0 2.6	61.7 22.5	34.1 17.0	34.2 3.5	37.8 8.0	23.3 7.8	15.6	$p < 0.05$	$p < 0.01$
Consumption ratio	1588 43	1784 372	1241 272	1796 150	2056 228	1284 236	122.0	$p < 0.001$	—
Productivity	31.2 1.8	36.5 16.1	18.6 8.0	21.8 2.0	22.0 5.1	15.3 5.6	12.7	$p < 0.05$	$p < 0.05$

*× 10^4

activity of the individual at a given time (sleep, resting, active, etc.) and in untreated subjects as well as in psychotics treated with neuroleptics.

MULTIDIMENSIONAL MODEL OF PSYCHOBIOLOGICAL ENERGY

Psychological processes are flows of physical energy in a complex brain. Thus, Freud founded psychodynamics on the concept of psychological energy, which he called libido. Based on the thermodynamics of closed systems, Freud proposed that psychological energy was constant (hence, emotional changes consisted only in displacements) and tended to rest (point attractor) through discharge (catharsis). Actually, biological energy is far from thermodynamic equilibrium and is constantly changing. Physical, sexual, emotional, and mental energy increase together in mania, and decrease together in depression, albeit manic energy and depressive mood can coexist in mixed affective disorders.

Freudian psychodynamics is bidimensional. Freud opposed bonding libido (best exemplified by sexual libido but including all forms of bonding as aim-inhibited sexuality) either to nutrition (early model) or to a destructive death instinct (late model). The results reported here indicate that the emotional world of a person is a multidimensional space, including conflict and harmony, hierarchy and distance; even synergic and interdependent emotions, such as affection, sexuality, and esteem, represent separate dimensions, as they can be in part antagonic (e.g., sexual inhibition by the incest taboo or by childhood affection) and can vary differentially. Opposing emotions, such as love and anger, may reinforce each other, as both increase excitement; a conflictual marriage is often vital. For any two emotions, one must consider both the energy that they provide together (union of opposites) and the information provided by their difference.

Attempting to explain psychobiological regulation, a number of models of increasing dimensionality have being proposed: (a) Homeostasis (static point attractor): health depends on the maintenance of biological and psychological equilibrium by a balance of opposite negative feedback mechanisms, while illness results from disequilibrium and disorder; (b) Periodic attractors (Wirz-Justice & Wehr, 1983): although biological cycles are fundamental to normal function and are obviously enhanced in bipolar illness, they fail to explain creative development, as well pathological conditions in which normal rhythmicity runs away from homeostatic limits; (c) Chaotic attractors: adaptive changes may result from their exquisite sensitivity to initial conditions (Goldberger, 1991); and (d) Patterned complexes: psychobiological processes include some twenty genetically determined action patterns of behavior ("instincts") corresponding to the basic emotions, consisting of an appetitive sequence of actions (modifiable by learning), leading to a consummatory act that terminates the sequence and can be followed by any other action (Barlow, 1977). In our view (Sabelli, 1989), ethological patterns are cyclic (not linear pathways tending to a consummatory attractor), autocatalytic (consummatory acts are reinforcers), and coexist and interact with each other at all times (rather than being mutually exclusive).

PT proposes a multidimensional model of psychobiological processes, which includes unidirectional temporal components (biological development, accumulated experience, etc.), systems of two or more regulatory processes that are both synergic and antagonic (e.g., sympathetic and parasympathetic nerves can produce similar or opposite changes depending on the effector organ and on their level of activity), and complex patterned processes resulting from multiple interactions that often are creative.

Implicit in the monistic hypothesis, each of these multiple components of psychological energy must be embodied on specific chemicals. In fact, the overall levels of physical, sexual, emotional and intellectual energy depend on systemic hormones, particularly those secreted by the thyroid, and perhaps also on specific brain neuromodulators, such as PEA (Fischer, Ludmer, & Sabelli, 1967; Sabelli & Giardina, 1973). Without any experimental evidence, it has been speculated that PEA is the "hormone of love." The results obtained in jail inmates suggest that endogenous PEA may not only be specifically associated with bonding emotions, but may also facilitate aggressivity. Also, testosterone increases sexual libido, mood, and aggressivity. This suggests that psychological energy is indeed one.

The alternation of neurophysiological patterns between opposite states, wakefulness and sleep, is presumably regulated by opposite neuromodulators, such as norepinephrine and serotonin (Brodie & Shore, 1957). That anxiety and depression loaded in the same factor and correlated positively is at variance with the catecholamine theory that attributes depression to norepinephrine deficit (Brodie & Shore, 1957) and anxiety to norepinephrine release (Toman, Everett, & Jeans, 1957), but consistent with the hypothesis that norepinephrine release favors mediates both anxiety and depression. Each neurophysiological pattern, such as sleep, dreaming, and emotions, is modulated by a specific chemical; metabolic disorders and exogenous drugs exert their effects by interfering with their specific actions. Each of these pathways of emotional behavior can be triggered by the release of at least one neurohormone—possibly acetylcholine for anger (Sabelli, 1964, 1990) and norepinephrine for fear (Toman et al., 1957); they are held in abeyance by an inhibitory neuromodulator—possibly GABA inhibits fear (Fuxe et al., 1975), glycine inhibits anger (Sabelli, 1964), and serotonin (Asberg et al., 1976), and PEA (Sabelli & Mosnaim, 1974) inhibit depression.

The dimensional portraits of cardiac complexes, with median embedding dimensions of 40 to 100 in normals and lesser in patients, suggest to us that physiological health is a creative process that generates novelty and complexity, not a low-dimensional attractor that maintains order. Conversely, illness is not disorder but excessive order, a simplification of healthy complexity to simpler chaotic, periodic, and even static attractors—the order and equilibrium that homeostatic models define as health. We thus have three views on the psycho-biological role of chaos: (a) as a pathogenic increase in dimensionality from homeostatic regularity; (b) as the normal process of adaptation that pathology reduces to rigid order (Goldberger, 1991); and (c) as a pathological decrease in the dimensionality of healthy complexity (Sabelli, 1989). The fractal geometry of cardiac complexes confirms the notion that the organization of physiological processes is at least as complex as it is chaoticlike. Chaotic processes may contribute to form novel dissipative structures, both normal (e.g., artistic inspiration) and pathological (e.g., delusions and obsessions in psychoses, Sabelli et al., 1990; multiple personality in dissociative disorders, Raaz, Carlson-Sabelli, & Sabelli, 1992).

A dynamic model of bipolar illness and bipolar personality (Sabelli, Carlson-Sabelli, & Javaid, 1990) postulates that the lowering of energy in depression accounts for the reduction in motor activity, self-love, love, sexual drive, and creativity, as well as for the tendency toward static and cyclic (obsessive) thinking, while the increase in energy in mania accounts for increased spontaneity (flow to goals), reactivity (flow to point attractors), affective and cognitive periodic oscillations (periodic attractors) and swings (catastrophes), creativeness and destructiveness (chaotic attractors). This would explain the core characteristics of bipolarity: elation and irritability, periodicity, seasonality, autonomous course, abrupt shifts, and biphasic time course, in which affective episodes oppose temperament (depressive episodes in hyperthymics [bipolar II] and manic episodes in chronic depressives [bipolar I]. There is no experimental confirmation for such a model; in fact, the empirical data discussed above indicate an increase incidence of chaotic patterns of mood in depressives, and an increase psychocardiological order during the manic phase. Undoubtedly the methodology needs to be refined, but these empirical studies illustrate the possibility of a comprehensive physiology, an objective, and scientific psychodynamics.

MATHEMATICAL PSYCHODYNAMICS

In summary, inspired by Kant's notion that a discipline achieves the status of science only when it utilizes mathematical methods, here we (a) define mathematical psychodynamics as the application of the geometric methods of mathematical dynamics to the description of psychodynamic processes; (b) postulate mathematical priority and psychological supremacy as its determining principle; (c) illustrate its research and clinical potential with the plane and the space of opposites, the time graph of recurrences, and the dimensional profile; (d) develop the concept of complex as a model to study complex processes; and (e) propose a multidimensional model of psychobiological energy.

REFERENCES

Asberg, M., Thoren, P., Traskman, L. (1976). Serotonin depression: a biochemical subgroup within the affective disorders? *Science, 191*, 478–480.

Barlow, G. W. (1977) Model action patterns. In T. A. Sebeok (Ed.), *How animals communicate* (pp. 98–134) Bloomington: Indiana University Press.

Beck, A. T., Rush, A., Shaw, B., & Emery, G. (1979). *Cognitive therapy of depression*. New York: Guilford.

Brodie, B. B., & Shore, P. A. (1957). A concept for a role of serotonin and norepinephrine as chemical mediators in the brain. *Annuals of the New York Academy of Science, 66*, 631–642.

Bourbaki, N. (1963). *Elements de mathematique*. Paris: Hermann.

Carlson-Sabelli, L., & Sabelli, H. C. (1984). Reality, perception and the role reversal. *Journal of Group Psychotherapy Psychodrama and Sociometry, 36*, 162–174.

Carlson-Sabelli, L., & Sabelli, H. C. (1992a). Interpersonal profiles: Analysis of interpersonal relations with the phase space of opposites. In L. Peeno (Ed.), *Proceedings of Thirty-Sixth International Society for the Systems Sciences* (vol. 2, pp. 668–677). Denver, CO: ISSS.

Carlson-Sabelli, L., & Sabelli, H. (1992b). Phase plane of opposites: A method to study change in complex processes, and its application to sociodynamics and psychotherapy. *The Social Dynamicist, 3*, 1–6.

Carlson-Sabelli, L., Sabelli, H. C., & Hale, A. (1994). Sociometry and sociodynamics. In P. Holmes, M. Karp, & M. Watson (Eds.), *Psychodrama since Moreno: Innovations in theory and practice* (pp. 146–185). London & New York: Tavistock/Routledge.

Carlson-Sabelli, L., Sabelli, H. C., Hein, N., & Javaid, J. (1990). Psychogeometry: The dynamics of behavior. In B. H. Banathy & B. A. Banathy (Eds.), *Proceedings of Thirty-fifth International Society for the Systems Sciences* (vol. 2, pp. 769–775). Portland, OR: ISSS.

Carlson-Sabelli, L., Sabelli, H. C., Zbilut, J., Patel, M., Messer, J., Walthall, K., Tom, C., Fink, P., Sugerman, A., & Zdanovics, O. (1994b). How the heart informs about the brain: A process analysis of the electrocardiogram. In R. Trappl (Ed.), *Cybernetics and systems—Proceedings European Meeting on Cybernetics and Systems Research, Vienna,* (vol. 2, pp. 1031–1038). Singapore: World Scientific.

Chaisson, E. (1987). *The life era*. New York: The Atlantic Monthly Press.

Corballis, M. C., & Beale, I., L. (1976). *The psychology of left and right*. Hillsdale, NJ: Lawrence Erlbaum Associates.

Eckmann, J. P., Kamphorst, S. L., & Ruelle, D. (1987). Recurrence plots of dynamical systems. *Neurophysics Letters, 4*, 973–977.

Fischer, E., Ludmer, R. I., & Sabelli, H. C. (1967). The antagonism of phenylethylamine to catecholamines on mouse motor activity. *Acta Fisiologica Latino Americana, 17*, 15–21.

Fuxe, K., Agnati, L. F., Bolme, P., (1975). The possible involvement of GABA mechanisms in the action of benzodiazepines on central catecholamine neurons. In E. Costa & P. Greengard (Eds.), *Mechanism of action of benzodiazepines*. New York: Raven.

Goldberger, A. L. (1991). Is the normal heartbeat chaotic or homeostatic? *News in Physiological Science, 6*, 87–91.

Haldane, J. B. S. (1960). Pasteur and cosmic asymmetry. *Nature, 185*, 87.

Levy, A. B. (1991). *A clinical study of the urinary phenylacetic acid (PAA) test of depression in prison inmates*. Unpublished doctoral dissertation, Department of Clinical Psychology, Brigham Young University, Provo, UT.

Levy, A. B., Sabelli, H. C., & Payne, I. R. (1992). *The biochemistry of crime*. Paper presented at the 145th American Psychiatric Association meeting, Washington, DC.

Mandelbrot, B. B. (1977). *The fractal geometry of nature*. San Francisco, CA: Freeman.

Patel, M. (1993). *Harmonic Analysis* (Fortran Computer Program). Department of Computer Assisted Research. University of Illinois at Chicago.

Prigogine, I. (1980). *From being to becoming. Time and complexity in the physical sciences.* San Francisco, CA: Freeman.

Raaz, N., Carlson-Sabelli, L., & Sabelli, H. C. (1992). Psychodrama in the treatment of multiple personality disorder: A process theory perspective. In E. Kluft (Ed). Expressive and functional therapies in the treatment of *Multiple personality disorder* (pp. 169–188). Springfield, IL: Thomas.

Sabelli, H. C. (1964). A pharmacological strategy for the study of central modulator linkages. In J. Wortis (Ed.), *Recent advances in biological psychiatry* (Vol. 6, pp. 145–182). New York: Plenum.

Sabelli, H. C. (1984). Mathematical dialectics, scientific logic and the psychoanalysis of thinking. In R. S. Cohen & M. W. Wartofsky (Eds.), *Hegel and the Sciences* (pp. 349–359). New York: D. Reidel.

Sabelli, H. C. (1989). *Union of opposites: A comprehensive theory of natural and human processes.* Lawrenceville, VA: Brunswick.

Sabelli, H. C. (1990). Anticholinergic antidepressants decrease marital hostility. *Journal of Clinical Psychiatry, 3,* 127–128.

Sabelli, H. C. (1994). Entropy as symmetry: Theory and empirical support. New systemic thinking and action in a new century. In B. Brady & L. Peeno (Eds.), *Proceedings of the International Systems Society, 38th Annual Meeting* (pp. 1483–1496). Pacific Grove, CA.

Sabelli, H. C., & Carlson-Sabelli, L. (1989). Biological priority and psychological supremacy, a new integrative paradigm derived from process theory. *American Journal of Psychiatry, 146*(12), 1541–1551.

Sabelli, H. C., & Carlson-Sabelli, L. (1991). Process theory as a framework for comprehensive psychodynamic formulations. *Genetic, Social, and General Psychology Monographs, 117,* 5–27.

Sabelli, H. C., & Carlson-Sabelli, L. (1993). Chaos theory in psychology and medicine: Mathematical priority and psychological supremacy as theory, method and mission. *The Social Dynamicist, 4*(3), 1–4.

Sabelli, H. C., Carlson-Sabelli, L., & Javaid, J. I. (1990). The thermodynamics of bipolarity: A bifurcation model of bipolar illness and bipolar character and its psychotherapeutic applications. *Psychiatry: Interpersonal and Biological Processes, 53,* 346–367.

Sabelli, H. C., Carlson-Sabelli, L., & Messer, J. (1994). Process method of comprehensive patient evaluation based on the emerging science of complex dynamic systems. *Theoretic and Applied Chaos Theory in Nursing. 1,* 33–41.

Sabelli, H. C., Carlson-Sabelli, L., Patel, M., Zbilut, J., Messer, J., & Walthall, K. (1995). Psychocardiological portraits: A clinical application of process theory. In F. Abraham & A. Gilgen (Eds.), *Chaos theory in psychology.* Westport, CT: Greenwood.

Sabelli, H. C., Fahrer, R., Medina, R. D., & Frágola, E. O. (1994). Phenylethylamine replacement rapidly relieves depression. *Journal of Neuropsychiatry 6*(2): 203.

Sabelli, H. C., Fawcett, J., Gusovsky, F., Javaid, J. I., Edwards, J., & Jeffriess H. (1983). Urinary phenylacetate: A diagnostic test for depression? *Science 220,* 1187–1188.

Sabelli, H. C., & Giardina, W. J. (1973). Amine modulation of affective behavior. In H. C. Sabelli (Ed.), *Chemical modulation of brain function* (pp. 225–259). New York: Raven.

Sabelli, H. C., & Mosnaim, A. D. (1974). Phenylethylamine hypothesis of affective behavior. *American journal of Psychiatry, 131,* 695–699.

Sabelli, H. C., & Synnestvedt, J. (1991). *Personalization: A new vision for the millennium.* Chicago, IL: Society for the Advancement of Clinical Philosophy.

Sabelli, L. C. (1992). Measuring co-existing opposites: A methodological exploration. (Doctoral dissertation, University of Illinois at Chicago year). *Dissertation Abstracts International,* 9226372

Sandler, M., Ruthven, C. R. J., & Goodwin, B. L. (1978). Phenylethylamine overproduction in aggressive psychopaths. *The Lancet* 1269–1270.

Shannon, C. E., & Weaver, W. (1964). *The mathematical theory of communication.* Urbana, IL: University of Illinois. (Original work published 1949)

Thom, R. (1975). *Structural stability and morphogenesis* (D. H. Fowler, Trans.). Reading, MA: Benjamin/Cummings.

Toman, J. E. P., Everett, G. M., & Jeans, R. F. (1957). Seizure latency method and other procedures for antipsychotic drugs. In H. E. Himwich (Ed.), *Tranquilizing drugs.* Washington, DC: American Association for the Advancement of Science.

Wirz-Justice, A., & Wehr, T. A. (1983). Neuropsychopharmacology and biological rhythms. *Advances in Biological Psychiatry 11,* 20–34.

Yorke, J. A., & Tien-Yen Li (1975). Period three implies chaos. *American Mathematical Monthly, 18,* 985–992.

Zbilut, J. P., & Webber, Jr., C. L. (1992). Embeddings and delays as derived from quantification of recurrence plots. *Physics Letters A, 171,* 199–203.

Zeeman, E. (1977). *Catastrophe theory.* Reading, MA: Addison-Wesley.

7 Is There Evidence for Chaos in the Human Central Nervous System?

Paul E. Rapp

Is there any evidence for chaos in the dynamical behavior of the human central nervous system? In most instances, evidence supporting this hypothesis is based on examinations of EEG records taken in a variety of conditions (Babloyantz & Destexhe, 1986; Duke & Pritchard, 1991; Dvorak & Holden, 1991; Jansen & Brandt, 1993; Rapp, Bashare, Martherie, Albano, & Mees, 1991; Rapp et al., 1985). The purpose of this chapter is to show that many of the results obtained with EEGs can be obtained with filtered noise. Since EEG signals are filtered, these calculations raise important questions about the validity of published demonstrations of chaotic behavior in the EEG.

Preliminary results of a study that combines calculations with EEGs and random-phase surrogates are considered. These surrogates address the null hypothesis that the original signal is indistinguishable from linearly filtered noise. Examined were 220 EEG signals, and 52,800 dimension estimates were obtained from these signals and their surrogates. The null hypothesis was rejected by 35 records (16%) in calculations at a 2.5% confidence level. That is, in these calculations 84% of the EEG records were found to be indistinguishable from linearly filtered noise.

The limitations of these calculations are also discussed. A cautious interpretation is warranted. Nonetheless, it seems clear that the case for chaos in the human central nervous system diminishes with each improvement in analytical technology.

PHASE PORTRAITS

The investigation begins with the measurement of a digitized signal, in this instance an EEG. Let $\{v_1, v_2, ... v_{\text{NDATA}}\}$ denote the time series of voltage measurements. These data are embedded to form $\{X_j\}$, the set of points in N-dimensional space formed by the rule

$$X_j = (v_j, v_{j+L}, \ldots v_{j+(N-1)L})$$

N is the embedding dimension and L is the lag.

In many instances, dynamical analysis consists of the quantitative characterization of the geometrical properties of embedded data. The simplest way of examining the geometry of $\{X_1\}$ is to consider the two dimensional case. The set of (x,y) pairs defined by (v_j, v_{j+L}) connected by line segments is the phase plane trajectory. An example of the trajectory produced by a set of uniformly distributed random numbers is shown in Fig. 7.1. No organized structure is apparent. The random numbers used in Fig. 7.1 were generated by a random number generator (Press et al., 1986) that satisfied tests for randomness. Equivalent results were produced with sets of random numbers produced by measuring ^{60}Co decay. Very different results were obtained with phase portraits of EEG records (Fig. 7.2). The orderly appearance seen in these diagrams has been interpreted as evidence of dynamically significant structure in the EEG.

Although the contrast between Fig. 7.1 and Fig. 7.2 is indisputable, it must be recognized that all structure is not meaningful. In the next set of calculations, the random numbers used to construct Fig. 7.1 were filtered by a simple linear filter similar to the filters routinely used in electroencephalography. The mathematical specification of the filter is given in Rapp and others (1993...). The phase portrait of filtered random numbers is shown in Fig. 7.3. On comparing Fig. 7.2 and 7.3,

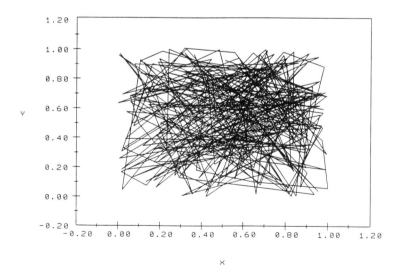

FIG. 7.1.   Phase portrait constructed with 300 points of uniformly distributed random numbers. The ordered pairs $(X, Y) = (X_i, X_{i+6})$ connected by line segments are displayed.

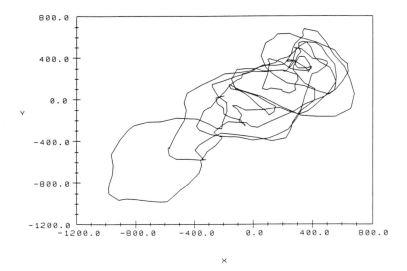

FIG. 7.2. Phase portrait of an EEG signal recorded from a normal adult subject at rest. The ordered pairs $(X, Y) = (X_i, X_{i+6})$ connected by line segments are displayed.

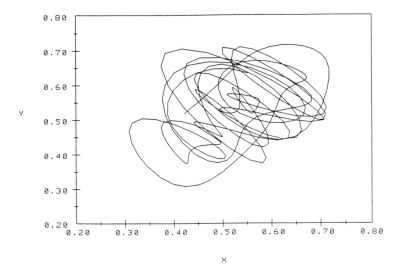

FIG. 7.3. Phase portrait of linearly filtered random numbers. Three hundred points of the form $(X,Y) = (X_i, X_{i+6})$ connected by line segments are displayed.

we must conclude that orderly structure in a phase portrait does not, of itself, demonstrate the existence of meaningful dynamical structure in the data.

PROJECTIONS TO THE PRINCIPAL COORDINATES

The phase plane portraits described in the previous section are limited to two dimensions. Complex dynamical structure could be lost in these low-dimensional projections. In principle, the idea of a phase space trajectory generalizes to higher dimensions. Set$\{X_j\}$ could, for example, be defined with $N = 10$. Visualization of the result then becomes the limiting difficulty. The most commonly employed approach to visualizing higher dimensional structures is to rotate the set of points $\{X_j\}$ to its principal coordinates and construct a two-dimensional projection of the first two principal components. Let E be the embedding matrix. This is the matrix in which point X_j, as previously defined, is the j–th row. The singular value decomposition of E (Golub & Reinsch, 1971) is denoted by $E = VDU^T$. D is the diagonal matrix of the singular values, and matrix U is the corresponding orthogonal transformation. The matrix $E' = EU$ contains the set of N-dimensional points obtained by rotating set $\{X_j\}$ by rotation U to the principal coordinates. After rotation, the maximum variance is in the first component; the next greatest contribution to the variance is in the second component, and so

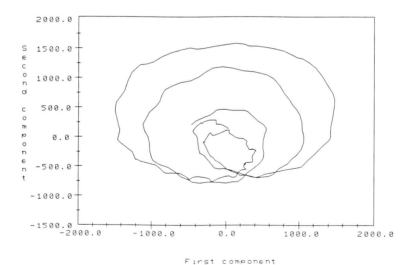

FIG. 7.4.   Phase portrait of the EEG of Fig. 7.2. after projection to the principal coordinates. The data were embedded with $N = 10$ and $L = 6$. The first two components of the rotated embedding are displayed (connected by line segments).

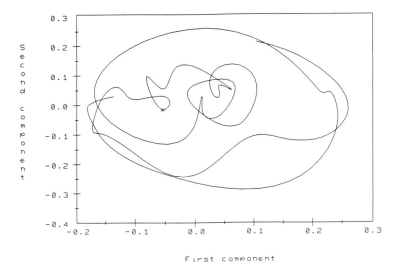

FIG. 7.5. Phase portrait of the filtered noise signal of Fig. 7.3 after projection to the principal coordinates. The data were embedded with $N = 10$ and $L = 6$. The first two components of the rotated embedding are displayed (connected by line segments).

on. The first two columns of rotated matrix E' can be plotted in a two-dimensional phase portrait that gives the maximum representation of the variance of $\{X_j\}$ that can be obtained in two dimensions. This rotation can often result in the appearance of structures in complex data that would have been lost in a tangled two-dimensional phase portrait.

Noise, by definition, has equal variance in all components of the embedding space. If this procedure is applied to the original set of random numbers, a principal component phase portrait results that is similar to that in Fig. 7.1. If the method is applied to the EEG data, a clarified and highly structured trajectory results (Fig. 7.4). Unfortunately, this is also true of a principal component phase portrait of filtered noise (Fig. 7.5). The presence of an orderly structure in a principal component phase portrait does not guarantee the presence of meaningful structure in the data.

VARIANCE SPECTRA

Matrix D of the previous section contains the singular values of matrix E. They are ordered so that $d_j \geq d_{j+1}$. The singular values are related to the variance of each component by the relation

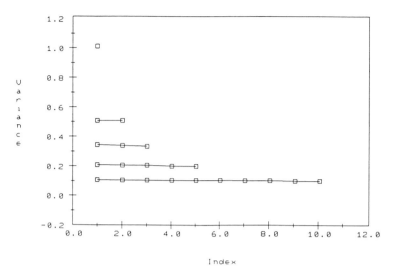

FIG. 7.6. Variance spectra for random numbers. There were 8,192 points embedded with $L = 1$ and $N = 1,2,3,5$, and 10.

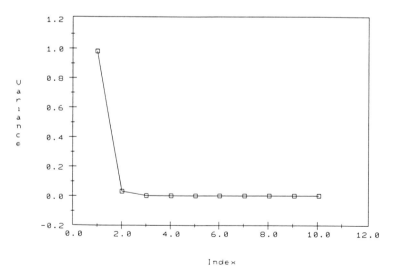

FIG. 7.7. Variance spectrum for a solution of the Mackey–Glass equation (= 23). There were 8,192 points embedded with $L = 1$ and $N = 10$.

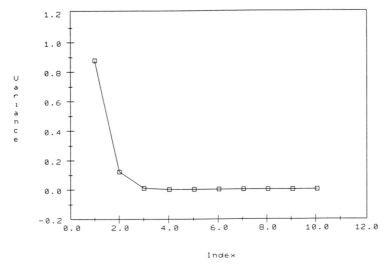

FIG. 7.8.   Variance spectrum of the resting EEG used in Fig. 7.2. Four thousand points were embedded with $N = 10$ and $L = 1$.

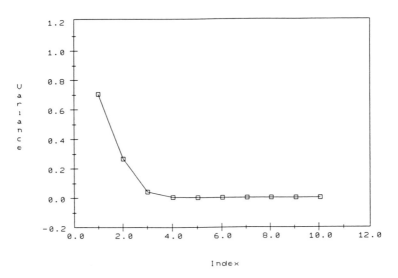

FIG. 7.9.   Variance spectrum of the filtered noise used in Fig. 7.3. There were 8,192 points embedded with $N = 10$ and $L = 1$.

$$Var_j = d_j^2 \Big/ \sum_{k=1}^{N} d_k^2$$

where N is the embedding dimension. The plot of Var_j as a function of index j is the variance spectrum. Noise has equal variance in all directions in the embedding space. For example, if noise is embedded in ten dimensions, $Var_j = .1$ for all values of j (Figure 7.6).

If the time series of a low-dimensional, deterministic system is embedded, there is a nonuniform distribution of variance in the embedding space. Figure 7.7 shows the variance spectrum obtained when a solution of the Mackey–Glass equation (Mackey & Glass, 1977) is embedded in a 10-dimensional space. Nearly all of the variance in the system is in the first principal component. Similar spectra are obtained with EEG signals (Fig. 7.8).

Results like those in Fig. 7.8 have been interpreted as providing significant evidence of meaningful dynamical structure in the EEG. The comparison with the results obtained with filtered random numbers (Fig. 7.9) is therefore disheartening.

CORRELATION DIMENSION

Dimension is a word of many meanings (Hurewicz & Wallman, 1941). It has already been encountered in the definition of embedding dimension. Set $\{X_j\}$ also has a dimension, different from the embedding dimension, that can be measured by performing calculations with the embedded data (Grassberger et al., 1991). If the embedding dimension is large enough, the estimated dimension of set $\{X_j\}$ is independent of the embedding dimension. This estimate will remain the same as the embedding dimension is increased. Noise is an exception to the last statement. The dimension of noise is, by definition, infinite. If a dimension estimation algorithm, for example the Grassberger–Procaccia algorithm (Grassberger & Procaccia, 1983), which estimates the correlation dimension, is applied to embedded noise, the estimated value of dimension should be equal to the embedding dimension. If, in contrast, the dimension estimate remains approximately the same with increasing values of embedding dimension, it is commonly supposed that the underlying signal has low-dimensional, deterministic structure.

The results of Fig. 7.10 shows that this is not the case. The dimension estimates obtained with random numbers, the upper trace, increase with embedding dimension. At higher embedding dimensions the estimated value of the embedding dimension because of the finite data set (8,192 points). The results obtained with filtered noise, shown in the lower trace of Fig. 7.10, display stable values with increasing dimension. Details of the calculations are given in Rapp and others (1993...). We conclude that stable, finite values of dimension result-

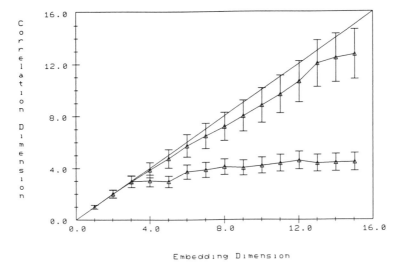

FIG. 7.10.   Correlation dimension as a function of embedding dimension for uniformly distributed random numbers (upper trace) and the same random numbers after filtering (lower trace). There were 8,192 points embedded with $L = 1$.

ing from the application of the Grassberger–Procaccia algorithm do not establish the presence of meaningful low-dimensional behavior in the data.

SURROGATE DATA

The ability of filtered noise and other artifactual signals to produce spurious dynamical results motivated a search for procedures that could be used to test the validity of these calculations. The surrogate data method is an important technique in the effort to bring increased rigor to these investigations. A review of the literature is given in Theiler and others (1992). In its general form, the central idea is elegantly simple. A measure is applied to the original data, for example, estimation of its correlation dimension using the Grassberger–Procaccia algorithm. Surrogate data sets are then constructed from the original data (the procedures used to do this will be described presently), and the same measure is applied to the surrogates. We then ask if the results obtained with the original data and the surrogates are different.

Different classes of surrogates are constructed to address different null hypotheses. Suppose the null hypothesis addressed is: There is no structure in the data. Surrogates can be constructed to address this null hypothesis by performing a random shuffle on the original data. The Grassberger—Procaccia algorithm returns a value of 4.4 when applied to the filtered noise data set (8,192 points, L = 1, N = 2,3,...15). If the algorithm is applied to a random shuffle of this signal, the value of dimension obtained is, approximately, the same as the embedding dimension. Since the results obtained with the original data and the shuffled surrogates are very different, we can reject the null hypothesis. There is structure in filtered noise.

As we previously observed, however, all structure is not meaningful. In this instance the structure was imposed on the random data by the filter. A different class of surrogate is needed to address a different null hypothesis: The original time series is indistinguishable from linearly filtered noise. Random-phase surrogates address this null hypothesis. The procedure form constructing this class of surrogates is given in Theiler and other 1992. When the Grassberger–Procaccia algorithm is applied to random-phase surrogates constructed from the filtered noise example, the results are very nearly the same. We fail to reject the null hypothesis and conclude, as we should, that the signal is, under this measure, indistinguishable from filtered noise (Rapp et al., 1993).

More sophisticated surrogates investigate more exacting null hypotheses. An important additional class is the Gaussian-scaled surrogate (Theiler et al., 1992), which addresses the null hypothesis that the signal is indistinguishable from linearly filtered noise transformed by a static monotone nonlinearity. This is an essential extension. It is possible to construct examples based on random systems that "fool" random-phase surrogates but are correctly identified by Gaussian-scaled surrogates (Rapp et al., 1994, and Rapp, 1994). If calculations with random phase surrogates indicate a nonrandom structure in the original data, calculations with Gaussian scaled surrogates should be considered.

SINGLE CHANNEL EEGS, RANDOM-PHASE SURROGATES AND THE GRASSBERGER-PROCACCIA ALGORITHM

Most evidence for chaos in the human central nervous system is based on the examination of single channel EEGs by the Grassberger–Procaccia algorithm. Preliminary results of a study comparing EEGs against random-phase surrogates, undertaken in collaboration with James Theiler, have called previous results, indicating the presence of low-dimensional structure in the EEG (Rapp et al., 1989) into question. EEG records were obtained from normal adult subjects in three behavioral conditions: resting, performing mental arithmetic in steps of two, and performing mental arithmetic in steps of seven. In the recalculations, 220 EEG signals were examined. Six embeddings were constructed for each signal, and 39 random-phase surrogates were constructed for each signal. A total of 52,800 dimension estimates were thus obtained from the original EEGs and their surrogates.

The null hypothesis was rejected by 35 signals (16%) in a calculation at a 2.5% confidence level; that is, the false-positive rejection rate could be as high as 2.5%. In these calculations, 84% of the EEG records were found to be indistinguishable from linearly filtered noise. Dimension estimates of Gaussian-scaled surrogates have not yet been obtained for the 35 signals classed as nonrandom by the random-phase surrogates. Calculations with Gaussian-scaled surrogates may reduce further the number of signals that are distinguishable from filtered noise. Before rejecting the hypothesis of low-dimensional behavior in the EEG definitively, however, the following limitations of these calculations should be noted.

The absence of convincing evidence of low-dimensional structure could be due to the quality of the data. The signals analyzed in this study are single channel, 12-bit EEGs. Low-dimensional structures may become apparent if 16-bit, multichannel signals are investigated.

The embedding parameters N, the embedding dimension, and L, the lag, used in the recalculations may not have been appropriate. Failure to construct a proper embedding can result in the unnecessary failure to detect dynamical structure (Albano et al., 1988). Even computer-generated data like the Rössler attractor, where low-dimensional structure is inarguably present, can fail to reject the random-phase surrogate null hypothesis if the Grassberger-Procaccia algorithm is applied to inappropriately embedded data. There is no universally successful choice of N and L. Different signals require different embeddings. In these calculations the same six embeddings were used for all signals ($N = 11$, $L = 1,2,3,5,8,10$). There is no consensus as to the best procedure to use for selecting N and L. Several candidate measures, reviewed by Rapp (1994), have been proposed. Additional calculations with different embeddings may reveal structures lost in these calculations.

A nonparametric statistical test was used to evaluate the results of the surrogates and to determine if the null hypothesis was rejected. Surrogate calculations with different data (Rapp, 1994) suggest that different statistical tests may be more appropriate.

All the EEG results summarized here were obtained with the Grassberger–Procaccia algorithm. This algorithm imposes very severe data requirements. The application of different measures to the same data, for example, tests of determinism (Kaplan, 1994; Wayland, et al., 1993) or predictability (Casdagli, 1991; Sugihara & May, 1990), may succeed where the Grassberger–Procaccia algorithm fails.

Is there any evidence for chaos in the human central nervous system? The body of evidence in support of this conclusion continues to decrease as analytic methods improve. If nothing else, however, the dynamical analysis of biological data has taught us the value of caution. Therefore, in response to the question that motivated the investigation we would, at present, be well advised to return a form of verdict available in Scots Law: Not proven.

REFERENCES

Albano, A. M., Muench, J., Schwartz, C. Mees, A. I., & Rapp, P. E. (1988). Singular-value decomposition and the Grassberger–Procaccia algorithm. *Physical Review, 38A,* 3017–3026.

Babloyantz, A., & Destexhe, A. (1986). Low-dimensional chaos in an instance of epilepsy. *Proceedings of the National Academy of Science, U.S.A., 83,* 3513–3517.

Casdagli, M. (1991). Chaos and deterministic versus stochastic nonlinear modelling. *Journal of the Royal Statistical Society, 54B,* 303–328.

Duke, D. W., & Pritchard, W. S. (Eds.). (1991). *Proceedings of the Conference on Measuring Chaos in the Human Brain.* Singapore: World Scientific.

Dvorak, I., & Holden, A. V. (Eds.). (1991). *Mathematical approaches to brain functioning diagnostics.* Manchester: Manchester University Press.

Golub, G. H., & Reinsch, C. (1971). Singular value decomposition and least squares solutions. *Handbook for automatic computation. Vol. II. Linear algebra.* Heidelberg: Springer-Verlag.

Grassberger, P., & Procaccia, I. (1983). Characterization of strange attractors. *Physical Review Letters, 50,* 346–349.

Grassberger, P., Schreiber, T., & Schaffrath, C. (1991). Nonlinear time sequence analysis. *International Journal of Bifurcation and Chaos, 1,* 521–548.

Hurewicz, W., & Wallman, H. (1941). *Dimension theory.* Princeton, NJ: Princeton University Press.

Jansen, B. H., & Brandt, M. E. (Eds.). (1993). *Nonlinear Dynamical Analysis of the EEG.* Singapore: World Scientific Publishers.

Kaplan, D. T. (1994). Exceptional events as evidence of determinism. *Physica D, 73D,* 38–48.

Press, W. H., Flannery, B. P., Teukolsky, S. A., & Vetterling, W. T. (1986). *Numerical Recipes. The Art of Scientific Computing.* Cambridge: Cambridge University Press.

Rapp, P. E. (1994). A guide to dynamical analysis. *Integrative physiological and behavioral sciences, 29,* 308–324.

Rapp, P. E., Albano, A. M., Schmah, T. I., & Farwell, L. A. (1993). Filtered noise can mimic low dimensional chaotic attractors. *Physical Review, 47E,* 2289–2297.

Rapp, P. E. Albano, A. M., Zimmerman, I. D., & Jiménez-Montaño, M. A. (1994). Phase-randomized surrogates can produce spurious identifications of non-random structure. *Physics Letters, 192A,* 27–33.

Rapp, P. E., Bashore, T. R., Martinerié, J. M., Albano, A. M., & Mees, A. I. (1989). Dynamics of brain electrical activity. *Brain Topography, 2,* 99–118.

Rapp, P. E., Zimmerman, I. D., Albano, A. M., deGuzman, G. C., Greenbaun, N. N., & Bashore, T. R. (1985). Experimental studies of chaotic neural dynamics: Cellular activity and electroencephalographic signals. In H. Othmer (Ed.), *Nonlinear oscillations in chemistry and biology* (pp. 175–205). New York: Springer-Verlag.

Sugihara, G., & May, R. M. (1990). Nonlinear forecasting as a way of distinguishing chaos from measurement error in time series. *Nature, 344,* 734–741.

Theiler, J., Eubank, S., Longtin, A., Galdrikian, B., & Farmer, J. D. (1992). Testing for non-linearity in time series: The method of surrogate data. *Physica, 58D,* 77–94.

Wayland, R., Bromley, D., Pickett, D., & Passamante, A. (1993). Recognizing determinism in a time series. *Physical Review Letters, 70,* 580–582.

III | COGNITION AND CHAOS THEORY

It seems inevitable that the cognitive sciences, still burgeoning after almost 50 years, and the rapidly expanding sciences of complexity would meet on a number of fronts but nowhere more energetically than in the investigation of the mind and the brain. Chaos theory, with its computational intensity and inherent complexity, provides a particularly fertile theater for this dialogue, as seen in the following chapters.

William Sulis, who is both a psychiatrist and a mathematician, begins this section with a substantial discussion of computation and what it means in naturally occurring biological systems, as opposed to artificial systems, or computers and virtual computational systems simulated on computers. Sulis seeks to make a beginning toward overcoming the present fragmentation between the many fields that study naturally occurring systems. These include disciplines as seemingly disparate as biology, ecology, economics, sociology, the neurosciences, psychology, and medicine, including psychiatry. He articulates three principal causes of this fragmentation. The first is the need for validation. Many exotic ideas, such as emergence, self-organization, self-organized criticality, and systems on the edge of chaos, are either poorly defined or defined only in very specific situations. Their robustness across a wide range of applications is, for the most part, yet to be established. Next, there is the problem of parochialism in individual disciplines. Each has its own unique history, its own language, models, and theories. The difficulties for interdisciplinary communication of ideas that are brought about by this state of affairs would be enough, in and of themselves, but are further exacerbated by what to most seems to be an esoteric mathematical sophistication required for full participation in the sciences of complexity. Finally, fields, such as clinical psychology and psychiatry, often deal in the problems and situations of unique individuals, while the new approaches have often focussed on the study of generic principles and universal patterns of behavior, as did the previous Newtonian approaches. (It must be admitted, however, that they are more amenable to the examination of individual differences, as indicated by studies reported in the research section of this volume chap. 4–7.) Sulis, by developing the concept of naturally occurring computational systems, attempts to bring order into this house of babble in a way that is both practical and friendly to the wide variety of disciplines involved.

The central two chapters of this section are written by chaos mathematician Ben Goertzel. Over the course of several years, Goertzel has developed a powerful mathematical model of intelligence and the mind. In its final conception, the mind is viewed as a chaotic attractor governed by a cognitive equation that describes its travel through myriad daily trajectories. Such an equation may seem fantastic at first glance, but Goertzel has worked it out with rigor and meticulous attention to detail. The result is not unlike the complex multilobed attractor originally described by Walter Freeman for the olfactory bulb of the rabbit but on a much grander scale. An essential aspect of this construction involves the interaction of beliefs in a competitive process much like that seen in contemporary selectionist models of biological evolution. Cognitive elements interact in an aggressive fashion in which some survive, some do not, and original elements are created. The first of Goertzel's two chapters presents his thinking on the creation and interaction of belief systems, while the second develops the larger concept of the cognitive equation.

In the last chapter in this section, experimental psychologist Fred Abraham demonstrates the possibilities for psychology of a dynamical systems approach to behavior. Chaos theory, especially as it emphasis bifurcations and attractor topologies, can in fact be understood as a subset of the study of dynamical systems. The latter deals with systems for which there exists a rule of change or evolution, so that for each possible state of the system the rule dictates the next state. In plain English, this is the study of how systems change, usually represented geometrically in visual space. Abraham begins his chapter with an overview of key mathematical terms and ideas from dynamical systems theory, such as vectorfields, trajectories, phase portraits, attractors, repellors, various types of bifurcations, and so on. From this beginning, he goes on to articulate a holonomic theory of mind that avoids the traditional dichotomies between mind and brain, and neurology and behavior. He continues to develop this discussion by revisiting Miller, Dollard, and Lewin's classical social conflict theory but here with the conceptual technology of modern dynamical systems theory. The result is rich. Then, in the final pages of the chapter, Abraham explores the possibility of a unified psychology, one with compassion and a humanist perspective and mission.

8 Naturally Occurring Computational Systems

William Sulis

Ideas from nonlinear and complex systems theory have fuelled profound speculation about some of the most deeply personal aspects of existence, such as the origin of life and of biological form and diversity, the origin of order and structure, and the origin and nature of mind and consciousness. Many researchers, however, particularly those in the biological, social, and medical sciences, remain skeptical. There appear to be three principal reasons for this.

The first is methodological. Many of the more striking ideas, such as emergence, self-organization, self-organized criticality, and edge of chaos are ill defined and based upon results that have not been subjected to rigorous scrutiny. For example, Packard and Langton's results about the edge of chaos (Langton, 1990) have only recently been examined and have not been confirmed (Mitchell, Hraber, & Crutchfield, 1993).

The second is parochial. Each discipline possesses its own language and traditions. Each has its own set of criteria by which to assess the worth of questions and the validity of results and methodology. As well, each has aesthetic criteria for determining the form of theories and models. Researchers crossing traditional disciplinary boundaries tend to bring with them the attitudes and criteria of their base disciplines. The result is that the form or focus of their work may be viewed either as unintelligible or irrelevant to those within other disciplines. For example, Murray (1991) pointed out the need for mathematicians to become familiar with the needs and realities of the biologist rather than attempting to force biological phenomena to fit mathematical reality.

The third is pragmatic. Most disciplines seek general principles. Applied disciplines, such as medicine and engineering, have secondary goals, namely, to be able to utilize these principles to bring about directed change, whether to correct illness or dysfunction or to construct a specific structure. The problem is individual diversity. The traditional approach has been to ignore or minimize individual variation and to seek out only average or universal patterns of behavior. The study of individual variation, vital to any applied discipline, has tended to be ignored. This has been true of nonlinear science as well. Additionally, nonlinear ideas are difficult for those who lack mathematical sophistication and are firmly attached to classical Newtonian ideas of determinism and causality. As a consequence, many of the applied disciplines have been slow to embrace these powerful new ideas.

The focus of this chapter is the concept of the naturally occurring computational system. A set of general ideas describing significant constraints upon these systems is discussed in an attempt to delimit the concept. The idea of a naturally occurring computational system provides a unifying concept for many disciplines including biology, ecology, economics, sociology, neuroscience, psychology, and medicine, particularly psychiatry. The goal is to develop criteria that will address some of the problems outlined here, namely to serve as a foundation upon which to develop a set of testable hypotheses, to encourage the development of a theoretical language and methodologies that will be relevant to the life and social sciences and to foster the search, both for general principles, as well as for the mechanisms that result in individual variation.

NATURALLY OCCURRING COMPUTATIONAL SYSTEMS

Presented here are 24 general ideas that serve to delimit the concept of the naturally occurring computational system (NOCS). The use of the term *computational* refers broadly to the apparent ability of the system to respond to the information content inherent in an interaction with its surrounding environment, not merely to the direct physical aspects of the interaction. The term is not used in the narrow mathematical sense of computability, which refers to a much more restricted class of processes than is conceived of here. The term *natural* is used to refer to computational systems, or those possessing putative computational capability, which have arisen in the natural world without direct human intervention. In this group, we consider biological organisms, ecological systems, human and animal societies, and economic systems (although the latter have sometimes been designed, most have arisen through the vicissitudes of life and so qualify as NOCS). Those systems that have arisen through consciously directed design and construction on the part of humans are referred to as artificial computational systems (ACS). In this latter group, we include all mechanical computational devices, as well as all virtual systems simulated on such devices. These general ideas are descriptive and are meant to constrain the concept of a NOCS but not necessarily to define it.

The ideas are organized around five major themes: material constraints (focusing on issues of limitations), environmental constraints (focusing on issues of computational goals and performance), developmental constraints (focusing on issues of origin), hierarchical constraints (focusing on the issue of reducibility), and dynamical constraints (focusing on the issue of dynamical vs. logical computation). These ideas are summarized in Table 8.1.

Computational Competence and Performance

Fundamental to an exploration of these ideas are the dual notions of *computational competence* and *computational performance*. I have discussed these dual notions in several recent papers (Sulis, 1993a, 1993b; Sulis, 1995). computational competence refers to whether or not a system has the ability to perform or support a specific computation. Computational competence addresses the question *what?* Computational performance refers to the exact process through which this specific computation is implemented. Computational performance addresses the question *how?* Computational competence is the primary concept. Computational performance is a secondary concept.

A simple example illustrates this distinction. Two students are asked to multiply *xyz* by 3 to get *rstu*. One student sets up a traditional multiplication array,

$$xyz \cdot 3 = rstu$$

whereas, the second student sets up an addition array,

$$xyz + xyz + xyz = rstu.$$

The students possess the same competence but different performance.

Most research into computation over the past half century has addressed questions of performance. Moreover, most of this work has focused upon computations performed using algorithmic methods. Issues related to computational competence have been largely ignored. One reason for this has been a fundamental misunderstanding of the assertion of the Church–Turing Thesis (Hopcroft & Ullman, 1974). The Church–Turing Thesis asserts that any function that can be effectively computed, no matter how that notion is formulated, is capable of computation by some Turing machine. This has evolved over time into an implicit assertion that all computational processes are carried out in a Turinglike fashion, in other words, algorithmically. This is a strong assertion about computational performance; however the Church–Turing Thesis is, in fact, merely an assertion about computational competence. If one system is competent to carry out a specific computation then there exists a Turing machine that is also competent to carry out that same computation. It does not assert that the performance of the system and of the Turing machine must be identical or even remotely similar.

This fundamental misunderstanding has led to much rancorous debate within the literature. It has impeded the ability of reaserchers to explore novel computational processes and severely limited theoretical development.

TABLE 8.1
Comparison of Naturally Occurring and Artificial Computational Systems

Theme	Criterion	Naturally Occurring Computational System	Artificial Complex Computational System
Material	Material Form	Natural	Engineered or Virtual
	Life Span	Finite	Arbitrary
Environmental	Goals	Environmentally Determined	Arbitrary
	Performance Criteria	Environmentally Determined	Arbitrary (usually optimality)
	Context Effects ('Key-in-lock')	Dominant	Variable ('if loop')
	Quasi-ergodicity	Necessity	Requires Reprogramming
	Response Stability	Present	Absent
	Nonstationary Environment	Common	Uncommon
Developmental	Noise	Creative Force	Destructive Force
	Reproduction	Necessary	Manufactured
	Development	Necessary	None (upgrades?)
	Adaptation	Universal	Limited & Primitive
	Class Behaviour	Idiosyncratic	Stereotyped
	Autonomy	Universal	Virtually Nonexistent
	Self Organization	Universal	Virtually Nonexistent
	Performance Measure	'Good Enough'	Optimality
	Evolution	Universal	Limited & Primitive
	Coevolution	Common	Virtually Nonexistent
	Fitness Criteria	'Life is not fair'	Optimality
Hierarchical	Reducibility	Irreducible	Reducible
	Language	Transient	Chomsky
	Grammar	Stochastic & Dynamical	Chomsky
Dynamical	Response Selection	Competitive Emergence	Programmed

In studying a given NOCS, the most fundamental task is to determine its set of computational competencies. Only then can questions about its set of computational performances be addressed. If it turns out that there exists a Turing machine that is also competent to carry out the same computation as the NOCS, then that Turing machine can serve as a useful benchmark against which to compare and understand the performance of the NOCS. It would be a fatal logical error, however, to assert that the performance of the Turing machine and of the NOCS must a priori be equivalent.

Each NOCS possesses a set of computational competencies reflecting those processes that the NOCS is capable of supporting and a dual set of computational performances that reflect the methods by which these competencies are implemented. The nature of these sets is not addressed here. I refer the reader to Sulis (1995) for further elaboration. Nevertheless, the various constraints are discussed in reference to these two sets.

CONSTRAINTS ON A THEORY OF NOCS

Material Constraints

Theoreticians have largely ignored questions about the relationship between the material form of the agents that constitute a NOCS and the computational processes that NOCS is able to support. Indeed it has been a fundamental tenet of the strong approach to artificial intelligence that knowledge about the physical processes that support a computation are irrelevant to the study of that computation. The assertion is that only the formal aspects of a computational process are of relevance. This neglect arises from the misinterpretation of the Church-Turing Thesis referred to in the previous section.

Nevertheless, every known exemplar of a naturally occurring computational system contains agents that possess a *material form*. Neurons are composed of various chemicals, brains of neurons, and ecologies of various flora and fauna. The material form of these constituent agents of a NOCS exerts a constraint upon its set of computational competencies and its set of computational performances.

The material form of these agents broadly constrains the set of computational competencies. For example, some bats are blind. They have no capacity for visual computation. Nevertheless, they have a remarkable ability for echolocation, a form of auditory computation. Humans, on the other hand, can perform visual computations but only within a limited range of the spectrum and cannot perform echolocation.

The material form of these agents broadly constrains the set of computational performances. For example, human brains are composed of neurons that support computation through their action potentials. These action potentials have a finite velocity setting a lower limit on the duration of computational performance.

More than simply constraining performance, the existence of specific material factors may be required in order for a specific computational competence to be expressed. For example, mating behavior may be a competence of a NOCS but cannot be expressed without the priming induced by exposure to sexual hormones or secondary messengers (Culotta & Koshland, 1992).

These ideas also apply to more abstractly defined systems such as ecosystems, economic systems and human societies. Ecosystems (or societies) arising in distinct geographical environments, such as deserts, rain forests, temperate forests, or plains each develop a differing set of computational competencies and performances. Insect societies demonstrate different computational performances compared to human societies.

In contrast, ACS may or may not be constrained by their material structures. Silicon-chip based computers are limited in quantum mechanical level. Virtual systems, in principle, face no such constraints although, clearly, attempts to model such systems will in practice be limited by the design constraints of the systems in which they are being simulated.

Closely related to the concept of material constraints is that of *life span*. All NOCS possess a finite life span. This is true whether one is studying a biological organism, a social structure, an ecology, or an economic system. Although the actual life span may be difficult to determine for the more abstract NOCS, it can certainly be bounded. This finite life span provides a powerful performance constraint since it demands that any essential computational processes that a NOCS undertakes must be completed within this finite span. Indeed most processes must be carried out within a minute fraction of this span. Many formal models fail to satisfy this most basic performance criterion.

Environmental Constraints

No naturally occurring computational system stands in isolation unto itself. Each operates within the context of some *environment*. The environment possesses geographical and physical structure and usually contains other systems that serve as a source of interaction.

For example, every animal exists within some ecological niche, comprising not only geographical structures but also a mixture of other plants and animals. The interactions take many forms: predation, symbiosis, competition, cooperation, education, mating, establishment of dominance. Each interaction requires specific computational activity on the part of the systems.

The environment affects the computational processes of a NOCS in a myriad of ways. The environment establishes a constraint on the set of computational competencies supported by a NOCS by broadly defining the *goals* of the various computational processes that must be supported by the NOCS. Consider a bat and its prey. Both exist within the same ecological niche. Nevertheless, their relationship within that niche demands different goals of each. The bat must try to catch, in the dark, as many insects as possible. To this end it has acquired a set of computational competencies directed towards echolocation, insect detection, and acrobatic flight. The prey, on the other hand, tries to avoid the bat. Its set of computational competencies are directed towards avoidance.

The environment establishes a constraint on the set of computational performances of the NOCS through several mechanisms. First, in concert with the material form constraint referred to above, a broad set of *performance* criteria is imposed upon each computational performances. For example, bat echolocation must serve to detect flying insects in the dark while the bat is in flight, resulting in specific performance criteria that the echolocation process must meet.

Second, environmental factors may become an integral component of the computational performance. It is well accepted that contextual effects play a significant role in human cognition, particularly in ares of memory and recall (Wilkinson, 1979). Contextual factors may play a central role in the phenomenon known as passive remembering (Spence, 1987) in which arise unbidden memories. Presumably some feature in the environment, not consciously recognized, triggers a specific recollection. This can be regarded as a *key-in-lock phenomenon*. Thus, the environment may be an essential factor in the ability of a NOCS to carry out a specific computational process.

Third, environmental factors constrain the dynamical interrelationships between computational processes. A most significant constraint arises from the fact that all naturally occurring computational systems interact continuously with their environments in real time. They must be able to shift computational processes rapidly in response to changing environmental contingencies. For example, a deer grazing in a field must be able to rapidly alter its behavior in response to the appearance of a predator. This requires that most computational processes can be termed *quasi-ergodicity*. Contrast this with most current models of ACS, which must be reset or sometimes reprogrammed to deal with altered environmental contingencies.

Fourth, the environment frequently exhibits regularities across time. These regularities are seldom exact yet frequently elicit similar responses from the NOCS that interact with them. The NOCS themselves change over time yet maintain regular patterns of response. Consider the responses of an individual over time to the question: "What is your name?" These observations suggest that the computational processes of NOCS must be stable relative to small changes in environmental stimuli and internal states. This *response stability* is another significant constraint on performance. Most current ACS are notoriously unstable. Consider what happens when a single bit is altered in a computer program.

It is important to point out that this notion of stability applies specifically to the response of the system to a specific environmental stimulus. It is not required that the overall dynamical behavior of the system be stable. Indeed, simulation studies utilizing cellular automata (Sulis, 1995) reveal that their responses to external inputs can be stable, yet the underlying autonomous behavior is unstable or chaotic.

Fifth, the environment constrains the sets of computational competencies and performances by virtue of the need to resolve the stability—plasticity dilemma (Grossberg, 1988) in the face of *nonstationarity*. The stability—plasticity dilemma refers to the conflict between the need for a NOCS to maintain stable responses to environmental contingencies while at the same time adapting those responses to changes in the contingencies. An environment is said to be stationary if the probability of occurrence of various events within that environment follows a probability distribution that is fixed over time. It is nonstationary otherwise. Most NOCS must function within nonstationary environments. For example, most ecosystems are subject to fluctuations of varying magnitudes occurring at all scale levels. There are seasonal variations, storms, and natural disasters. They are geographically nonuniform.

A NOCS that is too plastic in a nonstationary environment is at risk for developing a chaotic response pattern. A NOCS that is too stable in a nonstationary environment is at risk for maintaining increasingly inappropriate responses. In the case of organisms in an ecosystem, either case could result in death. For example, consider a driver who habitually approaches stop signs at excessive speed, requiring heavy braking to stop. This works well most of the time. Consider, however, what might happen should the intersection be covered in black ice!

Noise Induced Transitions   There are three major mechanisms by which environmental nonstationarity gives rise to modifications of the sets of computational competencies and performances of a NOCS. They are noise, adaptation, and evolution. The role of *noise* is addressed here. Adaptation and evolution are explored in the next section.

The behavior of any dynamical system can be viewed as taking place on a dynamical landscape in which a location on the landscape refers to a specific set of initial conditions and parameter values and the surface elevation reflects different dynamical trajectories, for example fixed point, periodic, or aperiodic trajectories parameterized by an energy function. The behavior of the system at fixed energy occupies a region of the landscape.

Noise has traditionally been viewed either as irrelevant or as an inconvenience. Its effect upon the dynamical landscape of the system is to introduce a small irregularity onto the surface of the landscape. One can think of it as roughing up the surface. The consequences are minor in general, merely *perturbation*.

Prigogine (1980) and followers radically altered our view of noise when they suggested that noise played a pivotal role in the formation of ordered structures by adjusting the internal parameters of a system in such a way that it could move into another dynamical region in which more regular behavior occurred. This can be visualized as follows. Consider a system having a landscape consisting of two valleys surrounded by high mountains. Left to its own, a system starting out in one valley will remain there regardless of the complexity of the local dynamics. The introduction of noise, however, provides a capacity to drive the system up and over the mountains into the other valley. Once in the new valley, it will remain constrained as before. The overall result, however, is that novel behavior occurs that was previously unavailable to the system. Noise is *order generating*.

Most recently, a third view of noise has arisen (Millonas, 1993). In this view, noise is responsible for the emergence of structure and novel behavior as a result of its ability to induce an entirely novel dynamical structure for a system. This can be visualized as follows. Consider the system described previously. The introduction of noise is akin to a seismic cataclysm in which the mountain range fractures, forming a rift valley between the two original valleys. The system may now move into the other valley as before but for radically different reasons. The entire dynamical landscape has been altered. This is a profound idea. It accords noise a deep and pivotal role in governing the dynamics of complex systems. Noise is *dynamics generating*.

I believe that all three models of noise apply to NOCS under differing conditions. Most often, noise will act according to the first paradigm. Noise plays a role via the second paradigm in adaptation and learning. Noise likely plays a role via the third paradigm in evolution, reproduction, and in competitive emergence.

Once can witness an example of this behavior in simulations of cellular automata under random inputs (Sulis, 1995). Cellular automata are a simple model of a complex computational system. Many cellular automata demonstrate synchronization of their behavior under external inputs. By this I mean that the external input has the capacity to induce a rapid convergence of the responses of the cellular automata arising from distinct initial states, even when the autonomous behavior arising from those initial states in quite distinct. Similar synchronization has been found in other chaotic systems as well (Pecora & Carroll, 1990). This provides a simple example in which the dynamical landscape of a system is radically altered by the introduction of noise.

As a consequence, theoretical formulations of NOCS need to take careful account of the various roles that noise can play in determining behavior. Rather than being dismissed as irrelevant, it is highly likely that noise plays a profound role in the behavior of NOCS. This is likely to have deep repercussions for the kinds of mathematics and methodologies that will be required in order to model, analyze, and ultimately understand the behavior of NOCS.

Developmental Constraints

NOCS do not come into existence spontaneously and complete. Instead, NOCS arise through a process of *reproduction* from preexisting NOCS. In some cases, such as in the majority of plants and animals, this reproduction is sexual. In some species and in the majority of more abstract NOCS such as ecologies, economies, and societies, reproduction is parthenogenic, arising from a single host. In some cases, the host persists; in others the host becomes subsumed into the nascent NOCS.

The nascent NOCS usually arrives into the environment incomplete in regards to its material form and its sets of computational competencies and performances. Over time, the NOCS undergoes a process of *development* whereby both its material form and its sets of computational competencies and performances are modified. As a result, it must be recognized that these sets are themselves dynamical structures. dynamical aspects of NOCS are discussed in a later section. Here are discussed issues that derive directly from the dynamical nature of these sets.

The processes that govern the concept of *adaptation*. Adaptation permits a NOCS to adjust both its set of computational competencies and its set of computational performances in response to changes within the environment. A NOCS will, in general, experience only a finite sample of its environment over time. This perforce results in *idiosyncrasy* in its sets of computational competencies and performances. Adaptation allows these sets to be modified in the light of further experience.

Adaptation is sensitive to the effects of noise. Noise can have a profound effect upon an adaptive process resulting in both failures of adaptation as well as the emergence of novel computational processes. Noise can act as a powerful creative force.

The need for reproduction and adaptation requires that, at the very least, the mechanisms for adaptation be instantiated in a form that is capable of surviving the reproductive process. If the mechanisms for adaptation are not somehow inherent in the system and preserved under reproduction, the nascent NOCS could come into existence without any mechanism in place to acquire sets of computational competencies and performances and ensure an appropriate fit with its environment. This is a very significant constraint on the form of adaptational processes. The same will be true of any fundamental computational processes that the nascent NOCS might require for its immediate survival.

These concerns do not apply in general to ACS. These systems generally come into existence complete and by conscious design. Any necessary structures are incorporated into the system at the time of its implementation. There is no need for reproduction or frequently for adaptation since the ACS is simply reconfigured to meet changing environmental demands.

Most NOCS, having come into existence, acquire their sets of computational competencies and performances *autonomously.* This is true of many animal species, such as sea turtles, that hatch to find themselves on their own, bereft of parents. This is generally true of more abstract NOCS such as ecologies, economies, and societies for which there is no formal teacher. Even for humans, the teacher plays only a small role in shaping the development of these sets. This stands in contrast to ACS that, in general, are externally programmed.

The sets of computational competencies and performances are structured. Computational processes interact and become interrelated. The development of this structure must also, in general, occur autonomously and reflects a basic dynamical process, that of *self-organization*. Again, unlike ACS where structure is imposed externally, NOCS must develop structure as a result of onging interactions, both internally and with its environment. The fundamental processes governing adaptation must be capable of supporting self-organization.

As an example of a self-organizing or emergent computational process, consider human autobiographical memory. Nelson (1987) presented evidence that suggests that the capacity for autobiographical memory in a child requires a specific interaction with parents and peers over a period of time. The capacity for autobiographical memory is neither solely innate nor is it taught. Rather it emerges as a result of a complex interaction between the child and its environment. Most researchers in psychotherapy believe that the same is true of object relations and self-structures.

The result of all these factors is that each NOCS is truly an individual, truly separate from all other exemplars within its class. Each such NOCS will arise from different ancestors, will experience different life histories, will face differing sets of environmental contingencies, and, as a result, will acquire idiosyncratic sets of computational competencies and performances. The study of NOCS demands that attention be paid to individual diversity and the mechanisms by which such diversity arises. The search for robust methods to detect and delineate individual computational competencies and performances becomes an important goal of NOCS research, particularly if such research is to hold nay value for those working with such systems in applied disciplines such as medicine, psychiatry, psychology, and social work.

Adaptation and Optimality   Central to the present theoretical study of adaptation is the concept of optimality. In the case of ACS, optimality has provided the criterion to be used for determining which particular computational processes survive the adaptational process. The notion of optimality has provided a useful heuristic tool for designing adaptational schemes for ACS. This is important for ACS where considerations of precision, reproducibility and minimal use of resources are very important.

When one comes to consider NOCS, however, the concept of optimality appears to be too restrictive. There are certainly examples, such as human photoreceptors, that appear to function optimally given the environmental constraints (Flam, 1993); however, examples abound of suboptimal performance among NOCS. For example, it is difficult to see the optimality in humans dispute resolution processes, in government fiscal policy, in stock market behavior, in teenage sexual habits, in the selection of mates, in driving habits, in the use of electricity and other resources, in the management of waste, in the management of agricultural products, in war. Optimality is another of those beautiful ideas that, like the fabled unicorn, vanish as soon as one looks for them.

Optimality is a very fragile concept. It is not robust under noise. It is difficult to maintain in the face of a nonstationary environment. Many systems possess large number of local optima making a global optimum difficult to achieve. Many situations are governed by multiple parameters. It may be impossible to determine which one to optimize or whether or not an optimal solution is even possible. There may be many frustrations to optimization. For some situations, such as a psychotherapeutic session, the parameters may not even be known. Nevertheless, NOCS still function.

Computational competence provides a way out of the dilemma. As defined (Sulis, 1995), competence requires merely that the system perform within a range of possibilities in response to a range of environments and stimuli. This is similar to James' idea that brains produce ad hoc solutions to problems (Anderson, & Rosenfeld, 1988). Rather than seeking the optimal solution, NOCS seeks out a *good enough response,* given the immediate environmental demands and their internal constraints. NOCS find a solution that works, then get on to the next problem. The determination of the boundaries of the region of adequacy and the selection of adaptational processes that yield adequate computational processes become major foci for study. Theories predicated on optimality might function as useful benchmarks but are unlikely to succeed as significant models of NOCS.

Evolution and Fitness   Noise and adaptation provide two major sources of variation among NOCS. The third is *evolution.* Evolution applies to populations of NOCS as opposed to individual NOCS. Evolution operates at the time of reproduction by selecting out specific adaptational and computational processes for preservation in the nascent NOCS. Most theories of evolution assume that the environment operates in such a manner so as to support the emergence of optimality with respect to the rather ill-defined concept of fitness. Fitness can have many meanings, although it frequently refers to reproductive success. One is fit if one produces lots of offspring. A major problem is that fitness, like optimality, is a relative concept. Fitness must be defined against other NOCS and the environment. If *coevolution* is taking place, in other words, both the NOCS, its environment, and any other NOCS with which it interacts are also evolving, then the relative fitness of these interacting NOCS may also change. A NOCS that is fittest at one juncture may not be fittest at a later juncture.

Like adaptation, evolution too is subject to noise. This aspect tends to be neglected in accounts of evolutionary processes. Noise can have a profound effect upon the evolutionary process. Noise may degrade the reproductive process. Additionally, there is what can best be described as the *life is not fair* paradigm. This is best illustrated with an example. Two wolves are about to compete for dominance and leadership of the pack. To determine this, they both must jump across a fast-moving stream. The survivor will lead. One wolf is clearly larger and more powerful than the other. It is more cunning and intelligent. It has the keener sense of smell. It is faster. It is more sexually potent. The two wolves stand beside each other at the bank. They crouch, fix their attention on the leap before them. Together they hurl themselves into the air, propelling themselves across the bank. Just as the right hind leg of the lead wolf is about to leave the ground, the soil under it shifts, the foot slips, the wolf is thrown off balance, and before it can correct itself, falls into the stream and is carried to its death. The weaker wolf survives. Life is not fair.

Evolution does not result in survival of the fittest, in the sense of optimality. It results in survival of the survivors who, in general, are merely good enough to have survived. Evolution provides a means of hedging bets: Only a select few NOCS can be considered optimal for their environment, whereas many can be considered good enough. The essential unfairness of life constrains evolutionary processes to those that can produce large numbers of adequate NOCS. This provides another significant departure from standard lore.

Hierarchical Organization

Naturally occurring computational systems are composed of lesser systems, agents, that themselves may be composed of subagents and so forth. Additionally, the original NOCS may serve as an agent in a larger metasystem and so forth. The preceding sections should have made it clear that the computational processes of a NOCS cannot be understood in isolation from those of the underlying agents and/or overlying metasystems and environments. These multiple layers of NOCS comprise a hierarchy of structure. Each layer, semiautonomous in itself, nevertheless interacts with all of the layers above and below it in the hierarchy. The result is a very strong *irreducibility*. Focused attention at one level in the hierarchy does not inform fully about the computational processes supported by that or any other level. The hierarchy functions as an integrated whole. Essential to the study of NOCS is an appreciation of the limitations that this hierarchical structure imposes upon our knowledge.

Most disciplines focus attention at one specific level in this hierarchy. Those disciplines, such as physics, that focus on the lowest levels have tended to argue for primacy. They assert that a complete knowledge about their level will answer all questions about every other level. The existence of emergent structures in simple complex systems, such as cellular automata, has falsified this assertion. Novel behaviors may arise that cannot be predicted from a knowledge of low-level structure. Equally, those disciplines, such as cognitive psychology, that function at the higher levels have argued sufficiency. They assert that knowledge about large scale order will answer all of their questions so that knowledge of other levels is irrelevant. However, the requirement of certain computational processes for specific material or environmental factors, such as occurs with mating behavior and sexual hormones, has falsified this assertion.

This same struggle has been replicated in psychiatry between the psychotherapists and the biological psychiatrists with sometimes disastrous consequences. It is absolutely essential that the study of NOCS be viewed as a multidisciplinary endeavor. No level has primacy over any other. The task is to understand the limitations on the knowledge available at any one level and to understand the interactions that exist among levels.

Dynamical Constraints

Naturally occurring computational systems are first and foremost dynamical systems. They are dynamic from the lowest to the highest levels, changing over time according to a hierarchy of constraints and interactions. The entire hierarchy within which a NOCS nests is an extraordinarily complex dynamical system. It comprises a bewildering system of nonlinear interactions. Additionally, unpredictable stochastic events intervene to distort and sometimes profoundly alter its dynamical structure. Such overwhelming complexity would lead one to believe that a study at any level of the hierarchy would reveal utter unpredictable chaos. Yet that is not the case. For, in spite of all of the nonlinearity, regular approximately predictable patterns, coherences, and correlations emerge.

Another major task for the study of NOCS is to understand the origin of order in the midst of stochastic chaos. Many examples of this phenomenon have been found,but no real understanding of the process exists. The quest for such an understanding has only just begun.

Most models of computation are atemporal. They study purely the formal relationship between the individual elements that constitute the computational process. This approach again follows from the aforementioned interpretation of the Church-Turing thesis because, from that perspective, only the formal, algorithmic aspects of the computational process are significant. The failure to appreciate the distinction between computational competence and performance has also resulted in a failure to appreciate the significance of NOCS as complex dynamical systems. This failure bears crucially upon two ideas that are frequently observed in the literature on ACS, namely that of rationality or logicality and that of algorithmicity.

Transient Languages and Dynamical Grammars   The prevailing notion concerning the higher level temporal organization of computational processes is that it follows principles of rationality and logic. This belief informs most of the study of ACS. It underlies most theoretical models of NOCS, especially those rooted in mathematics, physics, and computer science. It seems apparent that the temporal organization of computational processes possesses order and structure. That this structure reflects an underlying logic is more leap of faith than demonstrable fact.

Simple observation raises many doubts about the rationality and logic of NOCS. Drive along any back county highway and observe the road kill. The rationality (certainly optimality) and logic behind those decisions seems elusive. Research into syllogistic reasoning (Johnson-Laird, 1983) has shown that skill in this area is not innate. Even with correction of the underlying assumptions, some subjects still tend to form incorrect judgments. Decisions tend to be based upon local idiosyncratic experience rather than general knowledge. For another example, observe the prescribing practices of physicians.

NOCS, particularly many animal species, including humans, are governed by affective considerations as much or more so than by intellectual considerations. For examples, simple walk into the office of any lawyer or politician. Even science can be influenced by nonrational considerations (consider the debate over the SSC).

Nevertheless, there is form and structure to the temporal organization of computational processes. In Sulis (1993, 1995), it is shown that every dynamical system has a representation as a formal language (Hopcroft & Ullman, 1974). The symbols of the language consist of samples of transient behavior of finite duration. A dynamical trajectory of the system, broken down into finite time segments (transients), can be described by words over these symbols. Two symbols are adjacent only if there is an actual trajectory of the system in which the corresponding transients stand in succession to one another. The relationships that are imposed upon these transients by the dynamical structure of the system determines a dynamical grammar. This grammar consists of those productions that reflect the actual dynamical behavior of the system. Thus, the dynamical activity of a NOCS can be described by a *transient language* governed by a *dynamical grammar*. In general, this grammar will be stochastic.

Logics also form languages with associated grammars (axioms and rules of deduction), but they form a very restricted subset of the set of all formal languages.

The temporal organization of NOCS exhibits linguistic structure imposed by a dynamical grammar. This grammar arises from the myriad interactions governing the NOCS and is idiosyncratic. The study of NOCS requires an elaboration of the determinants that govern the form of the dynamical grammar and the factors that result in modifications to the grammar over time. Issues related to rationality and irrationality become questions about applicability rather than universality.

Competitive Emergence   Rationality and irrationality are questions about the form of a language. Closely related are questions about the mechanisms that generate the language. This involves the debate about algorithmic versus nonalgorithmic production. The existence of a formal language and descriptive grammar suggest that, in principal, the language might be generated in algorithmic fashion. The Church–Turing thesis again rears itself. The transient language might possess a grammar that is quite distinct from the dynamical grammar. This grammar might even be capable of algorithmic implementation. This does not mean that the original grammar was algorithmic. Description and function are not equivalent.

When a NOCS interacts with its environment, computational processes are initiated within its constituent agents. These agents interact not only with features of the environment but with each other as well. The resulting computational process effected by the system is frequently described in terms of these component subprocesses. Specific forms of interaction are sometimes posited as being universal. Several examples illustrate this point.

Consider a presentation of a short segment of a film to a subject for recognition and interpretation. The reception by the retina of photons reflected from the surface of the screen initiates a complex cascade of neuronal activity. Various neurons and cell assemblies activate in response to different features of the image: color, form, motion, context. Each feature detection constitutes a computational subprocess. The final perception of the image by the subject results from an integration of all these separate subprocesses, perhaps through cooperative interactions. This integration is termed *feature binding.*

Now consider motor activity. The subject is asked to carry out a specified task. Multiple possibilities for action present themselves. A variety of neuronal cell assemblies representing various action sequences become activated. As a result of interactions between these cell assemblies, a specific action sequence achieves access to motor neurons resulting in expressed activity. This successful sequence is sometimes viewed as having succeeded in a competitive struggle with the other action sequences, a kind of Darwinian survival of the fittest.

Now consider recollection. On a request to recall an experience from autobiographical memory, a host of cell assemblies are again activated. These assemblies support different features of the memory, different features of the representation process, access to various sensory and semantic descriptors. A complex interaction occurs, neither pure competition nor pure cooperation, out of which results an experience of memory. This experience, however, is never the same twice in succession. It changes over time. Sometimes it contains features from other memories. Sometimes it contains completely novel features. The survival and recollection of memories has been likened to a process of evolutionary selection (Rosenfield, 1988).

None of these examples expresses the full dynamical character of NOCS, yet they have been posited as universal principles. Many of these ideas have been based upon a naive interpretation of the concept of the cell assembly as a fixed implementation of a computational process. This idea garnered support with the discovery of ocular dominance columns in visual cortex. There is evidence, however, that retinotopic and somatotopic representations are dynamic, not static, structures. Neurons are more like actors than workers on an assembly line; they support many different roles at different times. The play is the thing (apologies to Shakespeare). Evolutionary ideas become problematic when there is no fixed role by which to judge fitness.

A better approach recognizes the fundamental dynamical nature of NOCS. Computational processes are viewed as the end result of *competitive emergence.* A computational process is supported by computational subprocesses occurring among the constituent agents of the NOCS, subject to constraints imposed by the global hierarchy in which the NOCS is embedded. These constituent agents and their computational subprocesses interact with one another (and sometimes with the larger environment), and out of that interaction emergences a computational process that is discernable at the level of the NOCS. Sometimes this process of emergence may be reducible into clearly defined metaprocesses such as competition, cooperation, or evolutionary selection. Most of the time, it will be irreducible. In cellular automata, this phenomena gives rise to the notion of emergent computation (Forrest, 1990), in which low-level processes support but do not define the emergent higher level process. A clear illustration of this is the two-dimensional cellular automaton Life, which, at the pattern level, operates as a universal Turing machine, capable of producing any effective computation, yet, at the level of the individual cell, is capable of only the simplest of computations, namely counting the number of active neighbors and either changing state or remaining the same, depending on the number.

The task for a study of NOCS is to develop a qualitative understanding of the various factors that govern competitive emergence and to explore the relationship that exists between the lower level interactions and computational processes and the higher level emergent processes.

CONCLUSION

Let me summarize what I have suggested about the broad structure of naturally occurring computational systems. NOCS must be studied in terms of two dual sets, that of computational competencies and of computational performances.

Material constraints apply to these sets by virtue of the material form of the agents that constitute the NOCS and by its finite life span.

The environment constrains these sets in many ways: by establishing goals and performance criteria, by acting as a key-in-lock, thus, controlling performance, by requiring that the NOCS demonstrate quasi-ergodicity and response stability under nonstationarity.

Noise serves as a fundamental force for change: perturbing, order generating, and ultimately dynamic generating.

Developmental factors constrain, since all NOCS arise by reproduction from preexisting NOCS. The nascent NOCS undergoes developmental changes and must be able to self-organize and adapt autonomously in a manner that permits good enough interactions with its environment. At a metalevel, NOCS undergo evolutionary and coevolutionary changes in the face of the fundamental unfairness of life.

NOCS are organized in a fundamentally irreducible hierarchy of structure. Finally, NOCS are fundamentally complex dynamical systems. They express a transient language governed by a dynamical grammar that gives rise to temporal order. They are fundamentally neither rational nor irrational in their temporal organization of processes. These processes are themselves dynamic and are fundamentally neither algorithmic nor nonalgorithmic in character. They are the result of an interactive emergence of structure arising from an interaction between the hierarchy and its environment.

The discussion in this chapter has, of necessity, been brief and has likely done an injustice to many deep areas of study. Much of the material that I have presented is not new, though I think that the ideas of the unfairness of life, noise as dynamics generating, transient languages, dynamical grammars, and competitive emergence will stimulate curiosity and interest. I hope that by presenting this material in a unified fashion, attention will be focussed upon the issues facing those seeking to study naturally occurring computational systems. The challenge is to build a body of theory and methodology that will provide a unifying language for the life and social sciences. This theory and methodology must be relevant to the above constraints and will serve to illuminate some of the fundamental questions raised concerning naturally occurring computational systems. Such a body of theory and methodology can only serve to enrich, not only the life and social sciences, but also mathematics and the physical sciences by expanding their scope and power.

REFERENCES

Anderson, J. A., & Rosenfeld, E. (1988). *Neurocomputing: Foundations of research.* Cambridge, MA: MIT Press.

Culotta, E. & Koshland, D. E., Jr., (1992). NO news is good news. *Science, 258,* 1862–1863.

Flam, F. (1993). Physicists take a hard look at vision. *Science, 261,* 982–984.

Forrest, S. (1990). Emergent computation: Self-organizing, collective, and cooperative phenomena in natural and artificial computing systems. *Physica D, 42,* 1–11.

Grossberg, S. (1988). Nonlinear neural networks: Principles, mechanisms, architectures. *Neural Networks, 1,* 17–61.

Hopcroft, J. A., & Ullman, J. D. (1974). *Introduction to automata theory, languages and computation.* Reading, MA: Addison-Wesley.

Johnson-Laird, P. N. (1983). *Mental models.* Boston, MA: Harvard University Press.

Langton, C. (1990). *Physica D, 42,* 12–37.

Millonas, M. (1993). A nonequilibrium statistical field theory of swarms and other spatially extended complex systems. *SFI Preprint,* 93–06–039.

Mitchell, M., Hraber, P. T., & Crutchfield, J. P. (1993). Revisiting the edge of chaos: Evolving cellular automata to perform calculations. *SFI Preprint,* 93–03–014.

Murray, J. D. (1991). Mathematics, biology, nonlinearity. *Nonlinear Science Today, 1,* 1–5.

Nelson, K. (1987). The ontogeny of memory for real events. In U. Neisser & E., Winograd (Ed.), *Remembering reconsidered: Ecological and traditional approaches to memory* (pp. 244–276). Cambridge, UK: Cambridge University Press.

Pecora, L. M., & Carroll, T. L. (1990). Synchronization in chaotic systems. *Phys Rev Lett, 64*, 821–824.

Prigogine, I. (1980). *From being to becoming: Time and complexity in the physical sciences.* San Francisco, CA: Freeman.

Rosenfield, I. (1988). *The invention of memory.* New York: Basic Books.

Spence, D. P. (1987). Passive remembering. In U. Neisser & E. Winograd (Ed.), *Remembering reconsidered: Ecological and traditional approaches to memory* (pp. 311-325). Cambridge, UK: Cambridge University Press.

Sulis, W. (1993a). Emergent computation in tempered neural networks 1: Dynamical automata. *Proceedings of the World Congress on Neural Networks.*

Sulis, W. (1993b). Emergent computation in tempered neural networks 2: Computation theory. *Proceedings of the World Congress on Neural Networks.*

Sulis, W. (1995). Driver cellular automata. In D. Stein & L. Nadel, *1993 Lectwiel in Complex Systems.* Reading, MA: Addinson-Wesley.

Wilkinson, J. (1979). Context effects in children's event memory. In M. M. Gruneberg, P. E. Morris, & R. N. Sykes (Eds.), *Practical aspects of memory* (pp. 107-111). New York: Academic Press.

9 Belief Systems as Attractors

Ben Goertzel

Are belief systems attractors? There is something quite intuitive about the idea. Before one settles on a fixed system of beliefs, one's opinions may wander all over the spectrum, following no apparent pattern. But once one arrives at a belief system, one's opinions are unlikely to vary from a narrow range. But of course, if one is to declare that belief systems are attractors, one must specify: attractors of *what* dynamical system? To say "attractors of the brain" is obvious but inadequate: the brain presents us with a system of billions or trillions of coupled nonlinear equations, which current methods are incapable of analyzing even on a qualitative level. If belief systems are to be viewed usefully as attractors, the relevant dynamical iteration must exist on a higher level than that of individual neurons. In the companion chapter (Goertzel, chap. 10, this volume) it is argued that, in order to make headway toward an understanding of psychodynamics, we must shift up from the neural level and consider the dynamics of interacting *mental processes* or *neural maps* (Edelman, 1988). An equation for the evolution of mental processes is proposed, and it is suggested that the mind may be viewed as residing in *strange attractors* of this equation. My goal here is to relate these formal ideas to real-world psychology by considering the sense in which a particular human belief system may be seen as an attractor of this "cognitive equation of motion." A familiarity with the definitions given in (Goertzel, Chap. 10, this volume) is presupposed. In particular, I consider a particular *conspiratorial* belief system. I list seven beliefs central to this system and argue that this group of beliefs delineates a strange attractor for the cognitive equation of motion. Then I explore the relationship between the *irrationality* of this belief system and its *dynamical* properties. It is concluded that irrationality tends to occur when some subset of the mind persists largely due to the fact that *it is itself*

123

an attractor for the cognitive equation rather than due to its interactions with the remainder of the mind. This analysis implies that irrationality is a kind of abstract *dissociation,* a welcome conclusion in the light of recent work relating dissociation with various types of mental illness (van der Kolk & van der Hart, 1991). And, in the final section, I suggest that the relation between systematic belief and dissociation goes even further: I argue, using Neural Darwinist ideas (Edelman, 1987), that personality dissociation may be a selective factor *in favor of* self-supporting belief. Personalities and their associated belief systems are notoriously vague and complicated. It might seem futile to attempt to describe such phenomena with precise equations. But the Church–Turing thesis implies that one can model anything in computational terms if one only chooses the right sort of equation. My claim is that the "cognitive law of motion," properly applied, is adequate for describing the dynamics of mentality.

A CONSPIRATORIAL BELIEF SYSTEM

The particular belief system that I have chosen to illustrate general belief dynamics is the *conspiracy theory* of a real woman, whom I know, suffering from paranoid delusion. As I am a mathematician and not a clinical psychologist, I am not pretending to offer a "diagnosis" of the holder of this belief system. My goal is merely to broaden our conceptual horizons regarding the nature of psychodynamics by giving a specific example to back up the theoretical abstractions of Chap. 10, this volume (Goertzel).

Jane's Conspiratorial Belief System

"Jane" almost never eats because she believes that "all her food" has been poisoned. She has a history of bulimia, and she has lost 25 pounds in the last month and a half; she is now 5′1″ and 85 pounds. She believes that any food she buys in a store or a restaurant or receives at the home of a friend has been poisoned; and when asked who is doing the poisoning, she generally either doesn't answer or says, accusingly, "*You* know!" She has recurrent leg pains, which she ascribes to food poisoning. Furthermore, she believes that the same people who are poisoning her food are following her everywhere she goes, even across distances of thousands of miles. When asked how she can tell that people are following her, she either says "I'm not stupid!" or explains that they give her subtle hints, such as wearing the same color clothing she wears. When she sees someone wearing the same color clothing she is wearing, she often assumes the person is a "follower," and sometimes confronts the person angrily. She has recently had a number of serious problems with the administration of the college that she attends, and she believes that this was caused by the influence of the same people who are poisoning her food and following her. To give a partial list, she believes that this conspiracy involves: (a) a self-help group that she joined several years ago, while attending a college in a different part of the country, for help with her eating problems; (b) professors at this school, from which she was suspended and that she subsequently left; and (c) one of her good friends from high school. Her belief system is impressively resistant to argument. If you suggest that perhaps food makes her feel ill because her long-term and short-term eating problems have altered her digestive system for the worse, she concludes that you must be either stupid or part of the conspiracy. If you remind her that, 5 years ago, doctors warned her that her leg problem would get worse unless she stopped running and otherwise putting extreme pressure on it and suggest that perhaps her leg would be better if she stopped working as a dancer, she concludes that you must be either stupid or part of the conspiracy. If you suggest that her problems at school may have been due partly to the fact that she was convinced that people were conspiring against her and consequently acted toward them in a hostile manner, she concludes that you must be either stupid or part of the conspiracy.

The Cognitive Equation

We have analyzed the structure of Jane's conspiracy theory; now, how does this relate to the "cognitive equation of motion" given in chap. 10, this volume (Goertzel)? This equation of motion says roughly the following:

1. Let all processes that are "connected" to one another act on one another.
2. Take all patterns that were recognized in other processes during Step 1; let these patterns be the new set of processes, and return to Step 1. An *attractor* for this dynamic is then a set of processes X with the property that each element of the set is:

   a) produced by the interaction of some elements of X, or

   b) a pattern in the set of entities produced by the interactions of the elements of X. In order to show that Jane's belief system is an attractor for this dynamic, it suffices to show that each element of the belief system is a pattern among other elements of the system and is potentially producible by other elements of the system. Consider, for instance, the following beliefs:

C_0: There is a group conspiring against me.

C_1: My food is poisoned by the conspiracy.

C_2: My friends and co-workers are part of the conspiracy.

C_3: My leg pain is caused by the conspiracy.

C_4: My food tastes bad.

C_5: My friends and co-workers are being unpleasant to me.

C_6: My leg is in extreme pain.

In the following discussion, it will be implicitly assumed that each of these beliefs is stored *redundantly* in the brain; that each one is contained in a number of different "neural maps" or "mental processes." Thus, when it is said that C_0, C_1, C_2, and C_6 "combine to produce" C_3, this should be interpreted to mean that *a certain percentage of the time,* when these four belief processes come together, the belief process C_3 is the result. Furthermore, it must be remembered that each of the brief statements listed above next to the labels C_i is only a shorthand way of referring to what is in reality a diverse collection of ideas and events. For instance, the statement "'my co-workers are being unpleasant to me" is *short-hand* for a conglomoration of memories of unpleasantness. Different processes encapsulating C_5 may focus on different specific memories.

JANE'S BELIEF SYSTEM AS AN ATTRACTOR

Obviously, the belief C_0 is a pattern among the three beliefs that follow it. To suppose that each of the mental processes corresponding to C_1, C_2, and C_3 is equipped with a generalization routine of the form "When encountering enough other beliefs that contain a certain sufficiently large component in common with me, create a process stating that this component often occurs." If this is the case, then C_0 may also be *created* by the cooperative action of C_1, C_2, and C_3, or some binary subset thereof. One might wonder why the process corresponding to, say, C_1 should contain a generalization routine of this type. The only answer is that such routines are of general utility in intelligent systems and that they add only negligible complexity to a processes such as C_1, which deals with such formidable concepts as "'food" and "conspiracy." In a self-organizing model of the mind, one may not assume that recognitive capacity is contained in a single "generalization center"; it must be achieved in a highly distributed way.

Production of Particular Conspiracies

Next, what about C_1? Taking C_0, C_2, C_3, and C_4 as given, C_1 is a fairly natural inference. Suppose the process corresponding to C_0 contains a probabilistic generalization routine of the form "The greater the number of events that have been determined to be caused by conspiracy, the more likely it is that event X is caused by conspiracy." Then when C_0 combines with C_2 and C_3, it will have located two events determined to be caused by conspiracy. And when this compound encounters C_4, the generalization capacity of C_0 will be likely to lead to the creation of a belief such as C_1. So, C_1 is *produced* by the cooperative action of these four beliefs. In what sense is it a *pattern* in the other beliefs? It is a pattern because it *simplifies* the long list of events that are summarized in the simple statement "My food is being poisoned." This statement encapsulates a large number of different instances of apparent food poisoning, each with its own list of plausible explanation. Given that the concept of a conspiracy is *already there,* the attribution of the poisoning to the conspiracy provides a tremendous simplification; instead of a list of hypotheses regarding who did what, there is only the single explanation "*They* did it." Note that for someone without a bent toward conspiracy theories (without a strong C_0), the cost of supplying the concept "conspiracy" would be sufficiently great so that C_1 would *not* be a pattern in a handful of cases of apparent food poisoning. But for Jane, $I(C_4|C_1,C_0) < I(C_4|/C_0)$. Relative to the background information C_0, C_1 simplifies C_4. Clearly, C_2 and C_3 may be treated in a manner similar to C_1.

Production of Actual Events

Now let us turn to the last three belief processes. What about C_5, the belief that her co-workers are acting unpleasantly toward her? First of all, it is plain that the belief C_2 works to produce the belief C_5. If one believes that one's co-workers are conspiring against one, one is far more likely to interpret their behavior as being unpleasant. Furthermore, *given* C_2, the more unpleasant her co-workers are, the *simpler* the form C_2 can take. If the co-workeres are acting pleasant, then C_2 has the task of explaining how this pleasantry is actually false and is a form of conspiracy. But if the co-workers are acting unpleasant, then C_2 can be vastly simpler. So, in this sense, it may be said that C_5 is a pattern in C_2. By similar reasoning, it may be seen that C_4 and C_6 are both *produced by* other beliefs in the list and by *patterns in or among* other beliefs in the list.

Jane's Conspiracy as a "Structural Conspiracy"

The arguments of the past few paragraphs are somewhat reminiscent of R. D. Laing's *Knots* (1973), which describes various self-perpetuating interpersonal and intrapersonal dynamics. Some of Laing's "knots" have been cast in mathematical form by Francisco Varela (1978). Laing's "knots," however, treat self-referential dynamics in terms of propositional logic, which is of dubious psychological value (Goertzel, 1994). The present treatment draws on a far more carefully refined model of the mind. It follows from the above arguments that Jane's conspiratorial belief system is in fact a *structural conspiracy.* It is approximately a fixed point for the "'cognitive law of motion." A more precise statement, however, must take into account the fact that the specific contents of the belief processes C_i are constantly shifting. So, the belief system is not exactly *fixed:* it is subject to change but only within certain narrow bounds. It is a *strange attractor* for the law of motion. Whether or not it is a *chaotic* attractor is not obvious from first principles; however, this question could easily be resolved by computer simulations. One would need to assume particular *probabilities* for the creation of a given belief from the combination of a certain group of beliefs, taking into account the variety of possible belief processes falling under each general label C_i. Then one could simulate the equation of motion and see what occurred. My strong suspicion is that there is indeed chaos here. The specific beliefs and their strengths most likely fluctuate pseudorandomly, while the overall conspiratorial structure remains the same.

BELIEF AND RATIONALITY

Jane's belief system is clearly irrational, according to the ordinary standards. It is worth briefly asking how this irrationality is tied in with the *dynamical* properties of the belief system, as discussed in the previous section. This investigation will lead to a strikingly general dynamical formulation of the concept of rationality.

Conservatism and Irrelevance

The irrationality of Jane's belief system manifests itself in two properties.; First of all, Jane is simply *too glib* in her generation of theories. Given any unpleasant situation, her belief system has no problem whatsoever reeling off an explanation: the theory is always '"the conspirators did it." New events never require new explanations. No matter how different one event is from another, the explanation never changes. Let us call this property *conservatism*. To put it abstractly, let E_s denote the collection of beliefs that a belief system generates in order to explain an event s. That is, when situation s arises, E_s is the set of *explanatory* processes that the belief system generates. Then one undesirable property of Jane's belief system is that the rate of change of E_s with respect to s is simply too small. The second undesirable property of Jane's belief system is, I suggest, that the theories created to explain an event never have much to do with the specific structure of the event. Formally, the collection of patterns that emerge between E_s and s is invariably very small. Her belief system explains an event in a way that has nothing to do with the details of the actual nature of the event. Let us call this property *irrelevance*.

Of course, Jane would reject these criticisms. She might say "I don't need to change my explanation; I've always got the right one!" A dogmatist of this sort is the exact opposite of the prototypical skeptic, who trusts nothing. The skeptic is continually looking for holes in every argument; whereas Jane doesn't bother to look for holes in any argument. She places absolute trust in one postulate and doesn't even bother to look for holes in arguments purporting to contradict it, for she simply "knows" the holes are there.

This attitude may be most easily understood in the context of the mathematical theory of pattern. The pattern-theoretic approach to intelligence assumes that the environment is chaotic on the level of detailed numerical paramters but roughly *structurally predictable*. In Charles S. Peirce's phrase, it assumes that the world possesses a "tendency to take habits." Under this assumption, it is clear that conservatism, irrelevance, and reluctance to test are, in any given case, fairly *likely* to be flaws. First of all, if change is likely and if old ideas are not necessarily true for the future, then a belief system that does not change is undesirable. Second, if induction is imperfect and if the mind works by induction, then one must always face the fact that one's own conclusions may be incorrect.

The Genesis of Delusion

Why, exactly, is Jane's belief system conservative and irrelevant? To answer this, it is convenient to first ask how Jane's mind ever got *into* the irrational attractor that I have described. The beginning, it seems, was an instance of C_5 and C_2: a professor at school was asking her questions relating to her Overeaters Anonymous group, and she came to the conclusion that people were talking about her behind her back. Whether or not this initial conspiracy was real is not essential; the point is that it was nowhere nearly as unlikely as the conspiracies that she imagined later. Even if no real conspiracy was involved, I would not say that this step was "unjustified." It was only a guess, and there is nothing unjustified about making a wrong guess. After all, the mind works largely by trial and error. What is important is that her initial belief in a conspiracy was not strongly incompatible with the remainder of her sane, commonsensical belief system. After this, all that were needed were a few instances of C_4 or C_6, and a few more instances of C_5. This caused the creation of some C_0 belief processes; then the feedback dynamics implicit in the analysis of the previous section kicked in. The point is that only a small number of C_i is necessary to start a cybernetic process leading to a vast proliferation. Eventually C_0 became so strong that plausible stories about conspiracies were no longer necessary; an all-purpose "them" was sufficient. Most of us weather unpleasant experiences without developing extravagant conspiracy theories. In the initial stages of its growth, Jane's conspiratorial belief system depended crucially on certain other aspects of Jane's personality, specifically, on her absolute refusal to accept any responsibility for her misfortunes. But once this early phase was past, the spread of her belief system may have had little to do with the remainder of her mind. It may have been a process of isolated expansion, like the growth of a cancer.

Rationality and Dynamics

The lesson is that irrational belief systems are self-supporting, self-contained, integral units. Considered as attractors, they are just as genuine and stable as the belief systems that we consider "normal." The difference is that they gain *too much* of their support from internal self-generating dynamics—they do not draw enough on the remainder of the mental process network. This is perhaps the most *objective* test of rationality one can possibly pose (Lakatos, 1978): how much support is internal, and how much is external? Excessive internal support is clearly inclined to cause conservatism and irrelevance. In this way, the *irrationality* of a person's mind may be traced back to the existence of *overly autonomous subattractors* of the cognitive equation. The mind itself is an attractor of the cognitive equation, but small portions of the mind may also be attractors for this same equation. When a portion of the mind survives because it is itself an attractor rather than because of its relations with the rest of the mind, there is a significant danger of irrationality. Another way to put this is that *irrationality is a consequence of dissociation.* This formulation is particularly attractive since dissociation has been used as an explanation for a variety of mental illnesses and strange psychological phenomena—schizophrenia, MPD, posttraumatic stress syndrome, cryptomnesia, hypnosis, hysterical seizure, and so on (van der Kolk & van der Hart, 1991). The general concept of dissociation is that of a "split" in the network of processes that makes up the mind. Here we have seen that this sort of split may arise due to the dynamical autonomy of certain collections of processes.

BELIEF AND DISSOCIATION

In fact, the connection between belief and dissociation may run a little deeper. Recall that the dual network model analyzes mind in terms of two semi-autonomously functioning networks: an *associative memory network,* which self-organizes according to the principle that related entities should be stored "near" each other; and a *perceptual-motor hierarchy,* which operates according to the multilevel logic of a flexible command structure. And it makes the central hypothesis that *these two networks are superposed.* This superposition implies a roughly "fractal" structure for the associative memory network. And, more to the point, it implies that, if a section of memory is somehow split off or "dissociated" from the rest of memory, then a section of the mind's *control network* is also split off, as an automatic consequence. This explains, in one immensely simple step, how the attempt to suppress unpleasant memories can lead to the creation of an autonomously acting and remembering psychological unit. In other words, as will be shown in detail below, it explains the basic phenomenon of *traumatic memory* and posttraumatic stress syndrome. Multiple personality is a little more complex: it has to do with the *self,* an intricate self-referential construction, and a complex belief system; however, we may make a few simple observations. Posttraumatic stress syndrome is often a consequence of a *single painful event* (e.g., watching a close friend die a bloody death). Multiple personality, on the other hand, is generally a consequence of *repeated painful events,* usually *beginning in early childhood.* Very often these events are incestual rape, or severe child abuse. In posttraumatic stress syndrome, the painful event usually occurs *after the person's self is formed.* The person already has a unified self-image, so if his mind wants to shut off offending memories, it has to shut them *away* from the well-formed self. In multiple personality, though, the painful events occur while the person's self is still forming. Therefore, the "split-off" memories are subjected to the self-formation process, just as much as the rest of the dual network. While not a complete explanation, this gives some idea of why multiple personality disorder should exist and why different types of traumas should give rise to different psychological problems.

Dissociation and Personality Dynamics

The writer Somerset Maugham observed: "There are times when I recognize that I am made up of several persons and that the person that at that moment has the upper hand will inevitably give place to another." Maugham did not have multiple personality disorder—each of the "several persons" making up his psyche was aware that its name was Somerset Maugham and was aware of *most,* if not all, of the experiences had by the other "persons." But Maugham was a good enough self-observer to recognize that his mind was to some degree *dissociated,* that it consisted of several largely disconnected "functional personality units." A dissociated personality subnetwork or *subpersonality* is centrally concerned with two things: (a) constructing the reality perceived by the mind; and (b) constructing the self-image "perceived" by the mind.

Separate personality subnetworks are interconnected in the sense that they access, to a great extent, the same memory store. They also have in common certain parts of the self/reality system, particularly the lower and more basic levels. What makes human beings so interesting is that, by altering the common aspects of the self/reality belief system and by altering the associative memory structure, each subpersonality affects the *environment* in which the other subpersonalities live. Thus, relations between subpersonalities of a mind are somewhat more intense than relations between people in the physical world. Perhaps the best physical-world analogy for the subpersonalities of a single mind is a *community of psychokinetics,* each one living a normal life but also continually altering the physical world in response to the alterations made by the others. In such a community, one could never be sure what was "objectively there" and what was merely placed there by somebody else for some particular purpose. This is precisely the situation with which subpersonalities are presented. The way a person deals with any given issue may be determined by *different subpersonalities* at different times. Thus there is a kind of *evolutionary competition* among subpersonalities. The result of this competition, I suggest, is that a subpersonality will flourish to the extent that it can create belief systems that: (a) support its interests; and (b) stand little chance of being destroyed by other subpersonalities. Quite clearly, the best way to achieve (b) is to create structurally conspiratorial belief systems—beliefs systems that, like Jane's, are *attractors* for the cognitive equation. If a belief system depends on outside factors for its survival, these factors may well shift when the controlling subpersonality shifts. But if a belief system can survive on its own, then it has a much better chance of "waiting out" a hostile environment. Subpersonality competition is obviously not necessary for the maintainance of structural conspiracies, which by definition maintain themselves. It may be very useful, however, for the maintenance of belief systems that, while *close* to being structurally conspiratorial, they are not yet truly self-supporting. The iteration of the cognitive equation is *mind wide;* it is not restricted to the individual subnetworks that happen to be converging with attractors on their own. It will tend to mix up subnetworks, even if they are somewhat close to being autonomous. The extra push toward autonomy may often be needed; and personality dissociation may thus be a crucial part of the development of *self-supporting belief systems.*

Possible Dissociative Roots of Jane's Paranoid Belief System

As an illustrative example of this phenomenon, let us return to Jane's paranoid belief system, discussed above. Jane demonstrates many, many different dissociated subpersonalities. Chief among these, however, are: (a) an *obsessive* subpersonality, in which the world is perceived as hostile and in need of constant mocking scrutiny; and (b) a *happy-go-lucky* subpersonality, in which she makes an excellent impression on others, and is good natured almost to the point of being giddy. These are not full personalities; they share most of the same memories. But on the other hand, they are not merely *moods* either; they are alternate systems of perceiving and classifying data. The alternation between these two subpersonalities might be characterized as "manic depression." But the psychiatrists who have observed her have not made this diagnosis. It would seem that, at the very least, there is an unusually complex form of manic depression at work here. In the obsessive subpersonality, Jane is overly attentive to facial expressions, the colors of clothing, the letters on license plates, and so forth; she is constantly categorizing things in unusual ways. She demonstrates perceptual patterns that might be called "compulsive," and her behavior tends toward the unusual and offensive. She will often act out specifically to shock people, cursing, flashing, making faces, and so forth. In the happy-go-lucky subpersonality, on the other hand, Jane is open-minded and accepting toward other people's ideas. She tends not to notice details of her surroundings, and her behavior is generally quite unexceptional, except for perhaps a slight overexuberance. She is a pleasant companion and a good conversationalist. The worst of Jane's depressed moods seem to occur when she is in her obsessive subpersonality, and she is unable to find an *external source* to blame for her problems (most of which are caused, of course, by the paranoid behavior of the obsessive subpersonality). The happy-go-lucky subpersonality is not so concerned about these problems and, thus, is not worried about where to place the blame. But every time the obsessive subpersonality comes back again, it needs to once again begin its quest for an external source to blame. Therefore, obviously, it is in the interest of the obsessive subpersonality to create a blame-placing belief system that will *persist* even when the happy-go-lucky subpersonality is in charge. How can this be done? One way, of course, is to create a *structurally conspiratorial* blame-placing belief system; a system that will maintain itself indefinitely, that will keep itself going even when the reigning subpersonality has no use for it. Perhaps the obsessive subpersonality will experiment with many different strategies for apportioning blame; but those that are less conspiratorial will be less likely to survive the fluctuations of control. Personality dissociation provides a *selective force* in favor of structural conspiracies. In slightly more detail, one may say that the obsessive subpersonality contains the following beliefs:

D_0 = I am unloved.

D_1 = I am good and lovable.

D_2 = They are bad.

This system is not in itself an attractor for the cognitive equation; it is partially self-supporting, but it also relies on other aspects of Jane's mind. The dynamics here are simple enough. D_0 chips away at D_1; but D_1, acting on D_0, helps to produce D_2. And D_2, acting on D_1 and D_0 collectively, helps to produce D_1, thus counteracting the effect of D_0 (if one is not loved by bad people, that increases rather than decreases one's goodness). But the problem is that D_0 is a *self-reproducing* belief: it is a pattern in the behavior that it produces. It would seem that perhaps D_0, and the behavior systems to which it is connected, are *in themselves* an attractor for the cognitive equation, for the behavior system is produced by D_0 and its own internal dynamics; and D_0 is produced by the behavior system. The effect of D_0 on D_1 is so strong that D_1 is powerless to counteract it, even via D_2. so, what could be more natural than to counteract D_0 by making D_2 self-perpetuating, by making it a structural conspiracy. *This* is what is accomplished by the conspiratorial belief system discussed above. This entire belief system, with all its complex dynamics, is merely a way of making D_2 as strong as possible. this, on a deeper level, is the meaning of Jane's refusal to take blame. Taking blame for anything subtracts from D_1, which is already in serious trouble. But the conspiratorial belief system within D_2 works along with D_1 to counteract the powerful effect of the self-reproducing belief D_0, which is, most likely, the root of the whole problem. This is still a very partial, sketchy analysis of Jane's situation. But it does serve to illustrate the perverse complexity of the mind. One sees belief-system attractors grow within subpersonality attractors and spawn new belief-system attractors in the common memory, generating a hierarchy of chaotic pattern dynamics—all to counteract the runaway self-perpetuating growth of a single belief of the utmost simplicity: "I am unloved."

REFERENCES

Edelman, G. M. (1987). *Neural Darwinism.* New York: Basic Books.

Goertzel, B. (1994). *Chaotic logic: Thought and reality from the perspective of complex systems science.* New York: Plenum.

Laing, R. D. (1973). *Knots.* New York: Bantam.

Lakatos, I. (1978). *Philosophical Papers.* Cambridge, England: Cambridge University Press.

van der Kolk, R. & van der Hart, O. (1991). The intrusive past: The flexibility of memory and the engraving of trauma. *American Imago, 48,* (4), 425–454.

Varela, F. (1978). *Principles of biological autonomy.* Cambridge, England: Cambridge University Press.

10 A Cognitive Law of Motion

Ben Goertzel

In a first course on chaos theory (Devaney, 1988), one studies discrete iterations like the tent map, the Baker map, and the logistic iteration. These iterations are completely unpredictable, under anyone's definition. It is obvious that complex systems like the brain are not purely pseudorandom in the same sense that these simple iterations are. In what sense, then, can the brain be called chaotic?

One way to avoid drawing a distinction between the two types of systems is to posit that complex systems like brains present "high-dimensional dynamics with underlying low-dimensional chaos." But this does not really get at the heart of the matter. I argue that complex, self-organizing systems, while unpredictable on the level of detail, are *roughly predictable on the level of structure*. This is what differentiates them from simple iterations that are unpredictable both on the level of detail, and the level of structure.

What this means for chaos psychology is that, even though the dynamics of the brain may be governed by a strange attractor, the *structure* of this strange attractor need not be as coarse as that of the Lorentz attractor, or the attractor of the logistic map. The *structure* of the strange attractor of a complex system contains information regarding the transitions from one patterned state to another.

Unfortunately, there is no apparent way to get at the structure of the strange attractor of a dynamical system like the brain, which presents hundreds of billions of variables even in the crudest formal models. Therefore, I propose, it is necessary to shift up from the level of physical parameters, and consider the mind and brain as *networks of interacting, intercreating processes*. Kampis' (1991) component-system theory integrates this idea with other aspects of general systems theory, and, as will be discussed below, Edelman's (1987) theory of Neural Darwinism places it on a sound neurological basis. Here, however, I will move far beyond Neural Darwinism and component-system theory, and propose a precise "cognitive equation of motion" governing the creative evolution of the network of neural processes.

When one thinks of the mind and brain in terms of "self-generating" process dynamics rather than physical dynamics, one finds that fixed points and strange attractors take on a great deal of psychological meaning (here we focus on the formal aspects; but the companion chapter (Goertzel, chap. 9, this volume) treats a real-life example). Process dynamics give rise to highly structured strange attractors that superimpose on the more finely detailed strange attractors provided by physical dynamics. Chaos is seen to be the substrate of a new and hitherto unsuspected kind of order.

MIND AND PATTERN

Let us begin, rather inauspiciously, with a series of necessary definitions. Gregory Bateson's (1980) "Metapattern," a basic epistemological/ontological axiom, states very simply that *the living world is made of pattern*. This simple idea, in slightly different versions, is central to the philosophy of Charles S. Peirce and the anthropological linguistics of Benjamin Whorf. In this chapter, we will focus almost exclusively on the *psychological* world, but in *The Evolving Mind* (Goertzel, 1993a), the Metapattern is taken more generally and applied to the biological world as well.

Although they thought in terms of pattern, Bateson, Peirce, and Whorf took "pattern" to be a basic undefined term.[1] This is a perfectly good approach. Since we are seeking a model that is mathematical as well as conceptual, we must define "pattern" in terms of the recognized vocabulary of mathematical objects. Here is my definition: *a pattern is a simpler representation of something*. It is not merely a representation; it is a representation as something simpler.

More explicitly: A process w is a *pattern* in an entity x if (1) the result of w is a good approximation of x, and (2) w is simpler than x.

The *intensity* with which w is a pattern in x—a technical quantity that we will have little use for—is the product AB, where A is the ratio of the simplicity of w to the simplicity of x, and B is one plus the error of the approximation of x by w.

This definition begs two question: what's a "result," and what is "simpler"? The easiest way of specifying these concepts is to take a computational point of view. For example, if an "entity" is a binary sequence, and a "process" is a computer program, then the *simplicity* of an entity or a process may be defined as its *length*. This ties in nicely with Gregory Chaitin's (1987) algorithmic informa-

---

[1]Peirce preferred the word *habit* to the word *pattern*, but this is inessential. Hume preferred *regularity*, but his meaning was also the same.

tion theory: The algorithmic information $I(x)$ is the simplicity of the simplest pattern in x. A simple example is the binary sequence

$x=100100100100100100100100100100100100100100100100100100$
    100100100.

The program w = "Repeat '100' 21 times" is a pattern in x, because it results in x, and is shorter. Similarly, we may define w to be a pattern in x *relative to y* if (1) the result of applying w to y is a good approximation of x, and (2) w is simpler than x.

The algorithmic information $I(x|y)$ is the length of the shortest program for computing x given y.

An alternative computational definition of simplicity is Bennett's (1982) "logical depth." In this approach, the simplicity of a binary sequence is still its length, but the simplicity of a program is its *running time*. This has the merit of generalizing nicely to the quantum domain. The British physicist David Deutsch (1985) has constructed (on paper) a "quantum computer" that can simulate any finitely specifiable quantum system to within arbitrary accuracy. Quantum computers cannot compute any functions besides those that ordinary computers can also compute, but they have all the counterintuitive properties of quantum systems—indeterminacy, nonlocality, and so forth. If one considers programs that run on quantum computers rather than on Turing machines, one can still define program simplicity as running time; and, because of the arguments of Deutsch, the definition of pattern still makes sense. This illustrates that the definition of pattern is not tied to any particular model of computation—or, for that matter, to the concept of computation. Tell it what a process is and how simplicity is measured, and it tells you which entities are patterns in what.

Getting back to ordinary computers, one good way to think about the concept of pattern is to look at two-dimensional images rather than binary sequences. Suppose one has a picture on the computer screen, say an image of a black Spleenwort fern. If the screen is 400 by 600 pixels, then to store this picture in a bit-by-bit way requires at least 240,000 bits. But using fractal image generation techniques, one may generate a picture of a black Spleenwort fern from a very short program (which, incidentally, also runs very fast). This program is a pattern in the picture: it is a process that results in the output of the picture, and it is simpler than the picture, where simplicity is measured in terms of length.

Structure and Emergence

Having defined pattern, structure follows immediately. I define the *structure* of an entity as the set of all patterns in that entity. This is a fuzzy set, since different patterns provide different degrees of simplification. Formally, I denote the structure of x as $St(x)$. One may define the *structural complexity* of an entity x as the "size" of the fuzzy set $St(x)$. This is a measure of the "total amount of pattern" in *x:* it captures formally the sense that a person is more complex than a flower, which is more complex than a virus. But the definition of "size" here is a little bit subtle—one has to subtract out for overlapping patterns—and there is no need to go into it here.

Next, one may define the *relative structure St^* of a set $A = \{a, b, c, \ldots\}$ as the set of all *x* which are patterns in some subset of *A* *relative to* some other subset of *A*. This notion will play an integral role in our "cognitive equation of motion."

Finally, having talked about patterns and fuzzy sets of patterns, we must introduce one *operation* relating patterns with fuzzy sets of patterns. This is the operation of emergence. Most simply, a process is *emergent* between *x* and *y* if it is a pattern in the "union" of *x* and *y* but not in either *x* or *y* individually. More generally, a process is emergent between *x* and *y* if the degree to which it is a pattern in the union of *x* and *y* exceeds the sum of the degree to which it is a pattern in *x* and the degree to which it is a pattern in *y*. The set of all patterns emergent between *x* and *y* is denoted $Em(x,y)$, and it is defined by the equation

$$Em(x,y) = St(x \cup y) - St(x) - St(y)$$

PATTERN AND CHAOS

In mathematics, "chaos" is typically defined in terms of certain technical properties of dynamical systems. For instance, Devaney (1988) defines a time-discrete dynamical system to be chaotic if it possesses three properties (1) sensitivity to initial conditions; (2) topological transitivity; and (3) density of periodic points.

Intuitively, however, the concept of chaos—determinism that simulates randomness—seems to have a meaning that goes beyond formal conditions of this sort. The mathematical definitions approximate the idea of chaos but do not capture it.

In physical and mathematical applications of chaos theory, this is only a minor problem. One identifies chaos intuitively and then uses the formal definitions for detailed analysis. But when one seeks to apply chaos theory to psychological or social systems, the situation becomes more acute. Chaos appears intuitively to be present, but it is difficult to see the relevance of conditions, such as topological transitivity and density of periodic points.

I will outline an alternative point of view. For starters, I define a temporal sequence to be *structurally predictable* if knowing patterns in the sequences's past allows one to roughly predict patterns in the sequence's future. And I define a static entity to be structurally predictable if knowing patterns in *one part* of the entity allows one to predict patterns in other parts of the entity. This allows us to finally define an *environment* to be structurally predictable if it is somewhat structurally predictable over time.

One may give this definition a mathematical form, modeled on the standard epsilon-delta definition of continuity (Goertzel, 1993b), but I will omit that here. The only key point is that, if an environment is structurally predictable, then patterns of higher degree have in a certain sense a higher "chance" of being found repeatedly. This shows that the assumption of a structurally predictable environment implies Charles S. Peirce's declaration that the world possesses a "tendency to take habits." The more prominent and rigid habits are, the more likely they are to be continued.

It is interesting to think about the relationship between structural predictability and chaos. For example, one key element of chaotic behavior is *sensitive dependence on initial conditions* (or, in physicists' language, positive Liapunov exponent). Sensitive dependence means, informally, that slightly vague knowledge of the past leads to extremely vague knowledge of the future. In practical terms, if a system displays sensitive dependence, this means that it is hopeless to try to predict the exact value of its future state.

Structural predictability is compatible with sensitive dependence. It is quite possible for a system to possess sensitive dependence on initial conditions, so that one can never accurately predict its future state but still display enough regularity of overall structure that one can roughly predict future patterns. Intuitively, this appears to be the case with complex systems in the real world: brains, ecosystems, atmospheres. Exact prediction of these systems' behaviors is impossible, but rough prediction of the regularities in their behaviors is what we do every day.

But sensitive dependence does not, in itself, make chaos—it is only one element of chaotic behavior. There are many different definitions of chaos, but they all center around the idea that a chaotic dynamical system is one whose behavior *is deterministic but appears random*.

A pattern-theoretic definition of chaos is as follows: An entity x is *structurally chaotic* if there are patterns in x, but if the component parts of x have few patterns besides those that are also patterns in the whole. For instance, consider the numerical sequence consisting of the first million digits of the pi: 3.1415926535. . . There are patterns in this sequence—every mathematical scheme for generating the expansion of pi is such a pattern. But if one takes a subsequence—say digits 100,000 through 110,000—one is unlikely to find any *additional* patterns there. There may be some extra patterns here and there—say, perhaps, some strings of repeated digits—but these won't amount to much.

Structural chaos is a weak kind of chaos. All the commonly studied examples of chaotic dynamical systems have the property that, if one records their behavior over time, one obtains a structurally chaotic series.[2] But on the other hand, the interesting structurally predictable series are *not* structurally chaotic.

---

[2]The easiest way to see this is to use symbolic dynamics.

Attractors, Strange and Otherwise

To probe more deeply into the relation between chaos and prediction, we must consider the notion of an "attractor." Let us begin with the landmark work of Walter Freeman (1991) on the sense of smell. Freeman has written down a differential equations model of the olfactory cortex of a reptile (very similar to that of a human) and studied these equations via computer simulations. The result is that the olfactory cortex is a dynamical system that has a "strange attractor with wings."

Recall that an *attractor* for a dynamical system is a region of the space of possible system states with the property that (a) states "sufficiently close" to those in the attractor lead eventually to states within the attractor, and (b) states within the attractor lead immediately to other states within the attractor.

An attractor that consists of only one state is called a "fixed point." It is a "steady state" for the system—once the system is close to that state, it enters that state; and once the system is in that state, it doesn't leave. On the other hand, an attractor that is, say, a circle or an ellipse is called a "limit cycle." A limit cycle represents oscillatory behavior: The system leaves from one state, passes through a series of other states, then returns to the first state, and so goes around the cycle again and again.

And a "strange attractor," finally, is an attractor that is neither a fixed point nor a limit cycle but rather a more complex region. Behavior of the system within the set of states delineated by the "strange attractor" is neither steady nor oscillatory but continually fluctuating. Sometimes the behavior of a system within a strange attractor is chaotic in the technical sense, but this is not always the case.

Freeman found that the olfactory cortex has a strange attractor—a fixed set of states, or region of state space, within which it varies. But this strange attractor is not a formless blob—it has a large number of "wings," protuberances jutting out from it. Each "wing" corresponds to a certain recognized smell. When the system is presented with something new to smell, it wanders "randomly" around the strange attractor, until it settles down and restricts its fluctuations to one wing of the attractor, representing the smell that it has decided it is perceiving.

This is an excellent intuitive model for the behavior of complex self-organizing systems. Each wing of Freeman's attractor represents a certain *pattern recognized*—smell is chemical, it is just a matter of recognizing certain molecular patterns. In general, the states of a complex self-organizing systems fluctuate within a strange attractor that has many wings, subwings, sub-subwings, and so on, each one corresponding to the presence of a certain pattern or collection of patterns within the system. There is chaotic, pseudorandom movement within the attractor, but the structure of the attractor itself imposes a rough global predictability. From each part of the attractor, the system can rapidly get to only certain other parts of the attractor, thus imposing a complex structural predictability that precludes structural chaos.

In other words, the structure of the dynamics of a complex system consists of the *patterns in its strange attractor*. The strange attractors that one usually sees in chaos texts, such as the Lorentz attractor, have very little structure to them; they are not structurally complex. But that is because these systems are fundamentally quite simple despite their chaos. A truly complex system has a highly patterned strange attractor, reflecting the fact that, in many cases, states giving rise to Pattern *X* are more likely to lead to states giving rise to Pattern *Y* than they are to states giving rise to Pattern *Z*. The states *within* the strange attractor represent patterned states, and the patterns *of* the strange attractor represent patterns of transition.

INTELLIGENCE AND MIND

Next, let us turn from mathematics back toward psychology. In *The Structure of Intelligence* (Goertzel, 1993b) I defined a *mind* as the structure of an intelligent system. Therefore, a mind is a mathematical form—a certain fuzzy set of processes that are patterns in a certain entity.

This definition in itself is obviously incomplete: It merely alters the problem of defining mind into the problem of defining intelligence. But *this* problem, or so I claim, can also be solved by a judicious application of pattern theory.

To see how, let us turn to the branch of engineering called automatic control theory, which is concerned with designing machines that are "intelligent" in very limited ways. In automatic control theory, intelligence is typically defined by some phrase like *the ability to achieve complex goals in an unpredictable environment*.

As a mathematician trained in optimization theory, I prefer to rephrase this as follows: Intelligence is the ability to maximize $f(x_1, x_2, \ldots, x_n)$ given only x_1, $\ldots, x_m$, $m < n$, where f is a "complex" function and $x_1, \ldots, x_n$ is an "unpredictable" sequence.

But this does not solve the problem of question begging: what is "complex"? And what is "unpredictable"? In order to solve this difficulty, I suggest, we must turn to our new, structural chaos theory. We must reformulate our definition of intelligence as follows: *the ability to maximize functions whose graphs are unpredictable in detail, but somewhat structurally predictable, in environments that are unpredictable in detail, but somewhat structurally predictable*. This implies that an intelligent system should be able to achieve complex goals in an environment that is itself a complex self-organizing system.

Mind and Brain

One concrete implication of this approach to the mind is the following: There is almost certainly no hope of methodically building a theory of mind from the neuron level up, based solely on empirical observations of neural behavior, without any "leaps of level." The brain is not predictable on the level of individual neuron behavior. It is somewhat predictable on the level of *pattern dynamics.* The problem of pattern recognition, however, is too hard to be done by exhaustive search; some sort of insight is required to determine what sort of pattern to look for.

One theory as to the type of pattern to look for is Edelman's *Neural Darwinism.* Edelman suggested that the smallest psychologically relevant entity is not the neuron but the *neuronal group,* the cluster of densely interconnected neurons containing say 100–100,000 neurons. If it is indeed the case that neuronal groups tend to act as units, then each neuronal group is a significant pattern in the brain, and hence a part of the mind.

And the next level up, in Edelman's theory, is a *map*—an integrated collection of neuronal groups, which tend to fire together in a certain habitual pattern. These maps are higher-level patterns in the brain, and hence more intense portions of mind. Edelman's central hypothesis is that *neural maps evolve by natural selection:* They mutate by random or chaotic neural fluctuations, and they are reinforced differentially based on their "fitness" (their effectiveness for survival and their harmony with the environment of neural maps that surrounds them). This hypothesis is in the spirit of Hebb's (1948) synaptic reinforcement theory of learning, but, biologically speaking, it is substantially more sophisticated.

In (Goertzel, 1993a, 1993b), it is argued that, although Edelman's basic framework is correct, it provides insufficient structure for the complex dynamics of intelligence. A structure called the *dual network* is outlined, and it is proposed that the network of neural maps must be organized in this way.

The Dual Network

Intelligence, as I have defined it, requires prediction and pattern recognition. And it follows from the pattern-theoretic definitions that prediction and pattern recognition are necessarily based on *analogical reasoning*—reasoning of the form: If the same pattern occurs in two situations, then related patterns may also occur in both situations. This leads up to a crucial observation. If a long-term memory is to be useful for analogical reasoning, it must have the property that, once one has accessed a certain pattern, it is generally easy to access other patterns that are *related* to that pattern. If analogy had to use a memory without this property, it would be uselessly slow. Analogy requires continual search for related patterns.

These considerations yield the idea of a *structurally associative memory*—a memory in which entities are stored "near" to those entities that are related to them by common patterns. In particular, if w is a pattern in x, then a structurally associative memory should usually store w "near" x. This is a very natural idea—it is just the old idea of associative memory, with association defined in terms of pattern. The pattern-theoretic approach resolves a weak point in the association-ist theory of memory because the structurally associative memory is emphatically made of *processes,* not images or tokens.

It has been convincingly demonstrated (Rosenfield, 1989) that one remembers something by applying a complex array of interacting processes, rather than by accessing a "record" that is "stored" as in a file cabinet or a library. Historically, most associationist theories have assumed an imagist view of memory. But the definition of pattern provides a natural, general way to talk about association of processes. The important thing to remember is that "nearby" is defined in terms of memory *access,* not physical memory structure. If w is "near" x in the structurally associative memory, this means that accessing w primes the memory for access of x.

In order to move from the associative memory network to the dual network, I propose a "perceptual hierarchy" of recognitive processes, a sort of pyramidal architecture consisting of a Level 1 containing processes that recognize patterns in sense data, a Level 2 containing processes that recognize patterns emerging from the patterns recognized by Level 1 processes, a Level 3 containing pro-cesses that recognize patterns emerging from the patterns recognized in Level 2 processes, and so on. Of course, this structure need not be strict and orderly—some processes may recognize patterns emerging between patterns on different levels.

And, inversely, I describe a "motor control hierarchy." Suppose the mind wants to carry out a complex plan of action. It needs to somehow *build* this complex action out of tiny, simple actions—out of elementary muscle move-ments and the like. This is a very hard problem, and I propose that the only generally workable way to solve it is hierarchically. The complex action must be decomposed into a collection of simpler actions, which in turn must be decom-posed into a collection of simpler actions, and so on down until a sufficiently elementary level is reached. An act, such as throwing a football or massaging a shoulder, is then a pattern emergent among patterns emergent among . . . pat-terns emergent among muscle movements.

A *dual network,* then, is a collection of processes that is at the same time a perceptual-motor hierarchy and an associative memory. It is organized as a command structure and also as a library in which related subjects are near one another. The only way that this dual structure can be produced is if the associa-tive memory possesses a *fractal* structure, in which clusters of ideas combine to form clusters of clusters, which combine to form clusters of clusters of clusters, etc.

This *dual network structure,* I suggest, is the most intense of the many patterns that make up mind. The structured dynamics of mind, as displayed in the structure of the strange attractor of the brain, reflect the dynamics of the dual network. But what are these dynamics, exactly? In order to approach this ques-tion, one more concept must be introduced into the mix: that of a *self-generating system,* a system of processes that exist to act on one another and create one another.

SELF-GENERATING SYSTEMS

In the Neural Darwinist view, the mind consists largely of a collection of "neural maps," competing with one another and symbiotically reinforcing one another with all the complexity of an ecosystem. The next step, however, is to view neural maps as themselves being *creators* of maps. Nothing in Edelman's framework prevents one from saying that one map acts on another map to produce a third map. Edelman chooses not to focus on this aspect of map dynamics; however, George Kampis (1991) and others have proposed that it is *precisely* this sort of intercreation that is the essence of mind.

The handiest way to model this sort of interaction is to invoke Aczel's *hyperset theory* (Aczel, 1988) and make use of "hyperfunctions." Just as the function $f(x) = x^2$ maps numbers into numbers, and the operator d/dx maps functions into functions, and hyperfunction maps hyperfunctions into other hyperfunctions. For instance, if f, g and h are hyperfunctions, one may write $f(g) = g(f) = h$, or $f(f) = f$. This may seem to be a contradiction, but Aczel has proved that it is not; and in many cases one may model hyperfunctions using ordinary well-founded functions (the cost being added notational complexity).

Given a collection of hyperfunctions $\{f,g,h,. . .\}$, one can form a vast variety of "compounds" of the form $f(g)$, $F(g,h)$, $h(g)$, and so forth. A "self-generating dynamic" is a rule that determines a "range" collection of hyperfunctions from the *compounds* formed by another "domain" collection of hyperfunction. This, I will argue, is the general type of dynamic that emerges from the strange attractors of extremely complex systems, such as brains. The various maps in the brain act on one another, and tomorrow's maps are determined by the maps that were *produced* by the intercreative transformations of today's maps.

The simplest self-generating dynamic consists of the rule: "given a collection of hyperfunctions, replace it with the collection of all compounds which one can form from it." For instance, one might have:

$$f(f) = g$$
$$f(g) = f$$
$$g(g) = g$$
$$g(f) = h$$
$$h(f,g) = g$$

In this case, if one takes $\{f,g\}$time $= 1$

this rule produces the collection $\{f(f), f(g), g(f), g(g)\} = \{g,f,g,h\} = \{f,g,h\}$, or

$\{f,g,h\}$time $= 2$

And iterated once again, the rule produces $\{f(f), f(g), f(h), g(f), g(g), g(h), h(f,g)\}$, or

$\{f,g,h\}$time $= 3$

In this particular case, after two steps, the dynamical rule has reached a fixed point. No matter how many times one iterates, one will keep on obtaining $\{f,g,h\}$.

In the above example, the collection of compounds itself was simply taken as the range collection. But this is not the only way to do things. As an example, one could study the rule: "given a collection of hyperfunctions, replace it with two hyperfunctions *randomly drawn* from the collection of all compounds which one can form from it."

More formally, one may define a general self-generating system by the following equation:

$$\text{System}_{t+1} = T[\ R[\text{System}_t]\ ] \tag{1}$$

Here $R[A]$ is defined as the collection of all compounds formed from the hyperfunctions contained in A, and T is some stochastically computable rule. In the simple example given above, T was assumed to be the identity function. In the future, the term *raw potentiality* may serve as a useful nonmathematical surrogate for the notation "$R[\text{System}]$."

Universal Computation

It is not hard to show that self-generating systems are capable of *universal computation*. This means, in essence, that any finitely describable behavior can be mimicked by some self-generating system. Specifically, in order to obtain universal computation, it is not enough to consider simple examples, such as the one worked out above. One modification is required: One needs to introduce "inverses" or "antifunctions." For instance, in addition to f, g, and h, one might require i, j, and k defined by $i = f^\wedge$, $j = g^\wedge$, $k = h^\wedge$. The dynamical rule then includes two steps: (1) as before, all compounds are formed, and the products collected, and (2) if a hyperfunction and its inverse are both elements of this collection, then the hyperfunction and its inverse are both eliminated.

Step 2 defines a transition function T, which is not the identity.

Systems of this form give one the ability to express the two fundamental operations of *conjunction* (*and*) and *negation* (*not*). The simplest conjunction is:

$f(g,h) = k$
$f(g) = \{\text{null set}\}$
$f(h) = \{\text{null set}\}$

The hyperfunction f creates the hyperfunction k if and only if *both* g and h are present. And, on the other hand, to obtain negation one need only set things up as follows:

$$f(f) = h$$
$$f(g) = h^\wedge$$

Assuming that no other elements of System$_t$ interfere, the presence of f in System$_t$ will cause the presence of h in System$_{t+1}$ if and only if g is not present in System$_t$.

Since all computers can be built of *and* and *not* gates, it follows that this type of system is a universal computer. The easiest way to verify this explicitly is to use the 3-clause conjunctive normal form for Boolean expressions.

Self-Generating Pattern Dynamics

Equation 1, in itself, is much too general to be of any use. If System$_1$ and T are chosen appropriately, equation 1 can describe anything whatsoever. That is, after all, the meaning of universal computation! However, equation 1 is nevertheless the first stop along the path to the equation that we desire. What is needed is merely to *specialize the operator T*.

Instead of taking the compounds formed from System$_t$, I suggest, one must take the *patterns in these compounds*. This completes the picture of the mind as a system that recognizes patterns in itself, which forms its own patterns *from* its own patterns. There might seem to be some kind of contradiction lurking here: after all, how can patterns in hyperfunctions themselves be hyperfunctions? But a moment's reflection reveals that this is precisely the unusual property of hyperfunctions: They subvert the hierarchy of logical types of potentially belonging to their own domain and range. And this unusual property does *not* violate the laws of physical reality, because the hyperfunctions required for practical modeling can be perfectly well modeled in terms of ordinary Boolean functions.

As above, let $St^\wedge (X)$ denote the relative structure of X. Then the simplest self-generating pattern dynamic says that, where System$_t$ is the system at time t,

$$\text{System}_{t+1} = St^\wedge (R[\text{System}_t]) \tag{2}$$

We may call this iteration the *basic deterministic dynamic*. The idea underlying this equation is encapsulated in the following simple yet subtle maxim: In a cognitive system, *time is the process of structure becoming substance*. In other words, the entities that make up the system *now* all act on one another, and thus produce a new collection of entities that includes all the products of the interactions of entities currently existent. Then, the system *one moment later* consists of the *patterns* in this collection.

But this simple iteration is only the beginning. For every type of self-generating system, there is a corresponding type of self-generating pattern dynamic. For example, the basic deterministic dynamic is founded on the type of self-generating system that is so totally "well-mixed" that *everything interacts with everything else at each time step*. But, in general, this is only the simplest kind of self-generating system: A self-generating system may use *any stochastically computable rule* to transform what I have called the Raw Potentiality of time t into the reality of time $t + 1$. Formally, this means:

$$\text{System}_{t+1} = F\ [\ Z_t\ [St^\wedge(\ G[\ R[\text{System}_t]\ ])]\ ] \tag{3}$$

where F and G are any stochastically computable functions, and $Z_t = Z[\text{System}_t]$ is a "filtering operator" that selects certain elements of $St^\wedge$ ($G[\ R[\text{System}_t]$]]), based on the elements of System_t.

Note that the function F cannot make any reference to System_t; it must act on the level of structure alone. This is why the function Z_t is necessary. The particular system state System_t can affect the *selection* of which patterns to retain but not the way these patterns are transformed. If this distinction were destroyed, if F and Z_t were allowed to blur together into a more general $F_t = F[\text{System}_t]$, then the fundamental *structure-dependence* of the iteration would be significantly weakened. One could even define F_t as a constant function on all values of $St^\wedge($ $G[\ R[\text{System}_t]$]), mapping into a future state depending *only* on System_t. Thus, in essence, one would have equation 1 back again.

Equation 3, like the basic deterministic dynamic equation 2, is merely equation 1 with a special form of the transition operator T. T is now assumed to be a some sequence of operations, *one* of which is a possibly filtered application of the relative structure operator $St^\wedge$. This is indeed a bizarre type of dynamic—instead of acting on real numbers or vectors, it acts on *collections of hyperfunctions*. However, it may still be studied using the basic concepts of dynamical systems theory—fixed points, limit cycles, attractors, and so forth.

STRUCTURAL CONSPIRACY

According to the basic deterministic dynamic equation 2, come time $t + 1$, the entities existent at time t are replaced by the patterns in the Raw Potentiality generated by these entities. But this does *not* imply that all the entities from time t completely vanish. That would be absurd—the system would be a totally unpredictable chaos. It is quite possible for some of the current entities to survive into the next moment.

If a certain entity survives, this means that, as well as being an element of the current system System_t, it is also a regularity in the raw potentiality of System_t, that is, an element of $R[\text{System}_t]$. While at first glance this might seem like a difficult sort of thing to contrive, slightly more careful consideration reveals that this is not the case at all.

As a simple example, consider two entities f and g, defined informally[3] by

$f(x)$ = result of executing the command "Repeat x two times"
$g(x)$ = result of executing the command "Repeat x three times"
        Then, when f acts on g, one obtains the "compound"
$f(g)$ = result of executing the command "Repeat x three times"
        the result of executing the command "Repeat x three times"
        And when g acts on f, one obtains the "compound"
$g(f)$ = result of executing the command "Repeat x two times"
        the result of executing the command "Repeat x two times" the result
        of executing the command "Repeat x two times"

Now, obviously the pair (f,g) is a pattern in $f(g)$, since it is easier to store f and g, and then apply f to g than it is to store $f(g)$. And, in the same way, the pair (g,f) is a pattern in $g(f)$. So f and g, in a sense, perpetuate one another. According to the basic deterministic dynamic, if f and g are both present in System$_t$, then they will both be present in System$_{t+1}$.

Note that this indefinite survival is fundamentally a synergetic effect between f and g. Suppose that, at time t, one had a system consisting of only two entities, f and h, where h = "cosmogonicallousockhamsteakomodopefiendoplamicreticulumpenproletariatti"

Then the effect of h acting on f would, by default, be $h(f)$ = {null set}

And the effect of f acting on h would be $f(h)$ = "cosmogonicallousockhamsteakomodopefiendoplasmicreticulumpenproletariatticosmogonicallousockhamsteakomodopefiendoplasmicreticulumpenproletariatti"

Now, (f,h) is certainly a pattern in $f(h)$, so that, according to the basic deterministic dynamic, f will be a member of System$_{t+1}$. But h will not be a member of System$_{t+1}$—it is not a pattern in anything in R[System$_t$]. So there is no guarantee that f will be continued to System$_{t+2}$.

What is special about f and g is that they assist one another in producing entities in which they are patterns. But, clearly, the set $\{f,g\}$ is not *unique* in possessing this property. In general, one may define a *structural conspiracy* as any collection of entities G so that every element of G is a pattern in the Raw

---

[3]One may rephrase this example a little more formally by defining $f(x) = xx$, $g(x) = xxx$. In set-theoretic terms, if one makes the default assumption that all variables are universally quantified, this means that f has the form $\{x,\{x,xx\}\}$, while g has the form $\{x,\{x,xxx\}\}$. So, when f acts on g, we have the ugly-looking construction $\{ \{x,\{x,xxx\}\}, \{\{x,\{x,xxx\}\}, \{x,\{x,xxx\}\} \{x,\{x,xxx\}\}, \}$; and when g acts on f, we have the equally unsightly $\{\{x,\{x,xx\}\}, \{\{x,\{x,xx\}\}, \{x,\{x,xx\}\} \{x,\{x,xx\}\} \{x,\{x,xx\}\}\}$. It is easy to see that, given this formalization, the conclusions given in the text hold.

Potentiality of *G*. It is obvious from the basic deterministic dynamic that *one successful strategy for survival over time is to be part of a structural conspiracy.*

Extending this idea to general *deterministic* equations of the form equation 3, a *structural conspiracy* may be redefined as any collection *P* that is preserved by the dynamic involved, that is, by the mathematical operations *Raw, G, St^*, and *F* applied in sequence.

And finally, extending it to *stochastic* equations of form equation 3, a structural conspiracy may be defined as a collection *P* that has a *nonzero probability* of being preserved by the dynamic. The *value* of this probability might be called the "solidity" of the conspiracy. Stochastic dynamics are interesting in that they have the potential to break down even solid structural conspiracies.

One phrase that I use in my own thinking about self-generating pattern dynamics is "passing through." For an entity, a pattern, to survive the iteration of the fundamental equation, it must remain intact *as a pattern* after the process of universal interdefinition, universal interaction has taken place. The formation of the Raw Potentiality is a sort of holistic melding of all entities with all other entities. But all that survives from this cosmic muddle, at each instant, is the *relative structure*. If an entity survives this process of melding and separation, then it has passed through the whole and come out intact. Its integral relationship with the rest of the system is confirmed.

Conspiracy and Dynamics

What I have called a structural conspiracy is, in essence, a *fixed point*. It is therefore the simplest kind of attractor that a self-generating pattern dynamic can have. One may also conceive of self-generating-pattern-dynamic *limit cycles*—collections *P* so that the presence of *P* in System$_t$ implies the presence of *P* in System$_{t+k}$, for some specific integer $k>1$. Nietzsche's theory of "eternal recurrence" may be interpreted as the postulation of a system limit-cycle—his idea was that the system, with all its variation over time, is inevitably repetitive, so that every moment that one experiences is guaranteed to occur again at some point in the future.

And, pursuing the same line of thought a little farther, one may also consider the concept of a *self-generating-pattern-dynamical strange attractor*. In this context, one may define a "strange attractor" as a group *P* of entities that are "collectively fixed" under a certain dynamic iteration, even though the iteration does not cycle through the elements of *P* in any periodic way. Strange attractors may be *approximated* by limit cycles with very long and complicated periodic paths.

In ordinary dynamical systems theory, strange attractors often possess the property of *unpredictability*. That is, neither in theory nor in practice, is there any way to tell *which* elements of *A* will pop up at which future times. Unpredictable strange attractors are called *chaotic attractors*. But on the other hand, some strange attractors are statistically predictable, as in Freeman's "'strange attractor with wings" model of the sense of smell. Here, chaos coexists with a modicum of overlying order.

It is to be expected that self-generating pattern dynamical systems possess chaotic attractors, as well as more orderly strange attractors. Furthermore, in ordinary dynamics, strange attractors often contain fixed points; and so, in self-generating pattern dynamics, it seems likely that strange structural conspiracies will contain ordinary structural conspiracies (although these ordinary structural conspiracies may well be so *unstable* as to be irrelevant in practice). There is at the present time, however, *no mathematical theory* of direct use in exploring the properties of self-generating pattern dynamical systems or any other kind of nontrivial self-generating system. The tools for exploring these models simply do not exist; we must make them up as we go along.

Fixed points are simple enough that one can locate them by simple calculation or trained intuition. But in classical dynamical systems theory, most strange attractors have been found *numerically,* by computer simulation or data analysis. Only rarely has it been possible to verify the presence of a strange attractor by formal mathematical means, and even in these cases, the existence of the attractor was determined by computational means *first.* So, it is to be expected that the procedure for self-generating dynamics will be the same. By running simulations of various self-generating systems, such as self-generating pattern dynamics, we will *happen upon* significant strange attractors and follow them wherever they may lead.

Structural Conspiracy and the Dual Network

In this section, I take the dual network model of mind briefly described above, and relate it to equation 3 by arguing that *a dual network is a kind of structural conspiracy.* The key to relating self-generating pattern dynamics with the dual network is the filtering operator Z_t. This operator may be defined specifically to ensure that only those elements of $St^\wedge$ (G[System$_t$]]) that are *actually computed by subsystems of System$_t$* are passed through to F and System$_{t+1}$. Under this interpretation, equation 3 says loosely that System$_{t+1}$ consists of the patterns that System$_t$ has recognized in itself (and in the "compounds" formed by the interaction of its subsystems). This brings equation 3 down into the realm of physical reality.

Informally, one may describer the "cognitive equation of motion" obtained by introducing this filtering operation as (a) Let all processes that are "connected" to one another act on one another; and (b) Take all patterns that were recognized in other processes during Step 1, let these patterns be the new set of processes, and return to Step 1.

An *attractor* for this dynamic (a "structural conspiracy") is then a set of processes with the property that each element of the set is (a) produced by the set of processes; and (b) a pattern in the set of entities produced by the set of processes.

It is not hard to see that, with this filtering operation, an associative memory is *almost* a structural conspiracy. For nearly everything in an associative memory is a pattern emergent among other things in that associative memory. As in the case of multilevel control, there may be a few odd men out—"basic facts" being stored that are not patterns in anything. What is required in order to make the whole memory network a structural conspiracy is that these "basic facts" be *generatable as a result of some element in memory acting on some other element.* These elements must exist by virtue of being patterns in *other* things—but, as a side-effect, they must be able to generate "'basic facts" as well.

Next, is the perceptual-motor hierarchy a structural conspiracy? Again, not necessarily. A process on level L may be generally expected to be a pattern in the products obtained by letting processes on Level L-1 act on processes from Level L-2. After all, their purpose is to recognize patterns in these products and to *create* a pattern of success among these products. But what about the bottom levels, which deal with immediate sense-data? If these are present in $System_t$, what is to guarantee they will continue into $System_{t+1}$. And if these do not continue, then under the force of self-generating pattern dynamics, the whole network will come crashing down. . . .

The only solution is that the lower level processes must not *only* be patterns in sense data, they must *also* be patterns in products formed by higher-level processes. One way to achieve this would be for there to exist processes (say on Level 3) that *invert* the actions taken by their subordinates (say on Level 2), thus giving back the contents of Level 1. This inversion, thought, has to be part of a process that is *itself a pattern in Level 2* (relative to some other mental process). None of this is inconceivable, but none of it is obvious either. It is, ultimately, a *testable prediction* regarding the nature of the mind, produced by equation 3.

The bottom line is, it is quite possible to conceive of dual networks that are *not* structural conspiracies. But on the other hand, it is not much more difficult, on a purely abstract level, to envision dual networks that *are.* Equation 3 goes beyond the dual network theory of mind, but in a harmonious way. The prediction to which it leads is sufficiently dramatic to deserve a name: the "'producibility hypothesis." *To within a high degree of approximation, every mental process X which is not a pattern in some other mental process, can be produced by applying some mental process Y to some mental process Z, where Y and Z are patterns in some other mental process.*

This is a remarkable kind of "'closure," a very strong sense in which the mind is a world all its own. It is actually very similar to what Varela (1978) called "'autopoesis"—the only substantive difference is that Varela believes autopoetic systems to be inherently noncomputational in nature. So far, psychology has had very little to say about this sort of self-organizarion and self-production. The companion essay (Goertzel, chap. 9, this volume), however, indicates one direction in which these abstract ideas might be related to every-day psychic life.

CONCLUSION

Let us sum up. The brain, like other extremely complex systems, is unpredictable on the level of detail but roughly predictable on the level of structure. This means that the dynamics of its physical variables display a strange attractor with a complex structure of "wings" or "compartments." Each compartment represents a certain collection of states that give rise to the same, or similar, patterns. Structural predictability means that each compartment has wider doorways to some compartments than to others.

The complex compartment-structure of the strange attractor of the physical dynamics of the brain determines the macroscopic dynamics of the brain. There would seem to be no way of determining this compartment-structure based on numerical dynamical systems theory. Therefore, one must "leap up a level" and look at the dynamics of *mental processes,* perhaps represented by interacting, intercreating *neural maps.* The dynamics of these processes, it is suggested, possess their *own* strange attractors called "'structural conspiracies," represent-ing collections of processes that are closed under the operations of pattern recog-nition and interaction. Process-level dynamics results in a compartmentalized attractor of states of the network of mental processes.

Each state of the network of mental processes represents a large number of possible underlying physical states. Therefore, process-level attractors take the form of *coarser structures,* superimposed on physical-level attractors. If physical-level attractors are drawn in ball-point pen, process-level attractors are drawn in magic marker. On the physical level, a structural conspiracy represents a whole complex of compartments. But only the most densely connected regions of the compartment network of the physical-level attractor can correspond to structural conspiracies.

Admittedly, this perspective on the mind is somewhat speculative, in the sense that it is not closely tied to the current body of empirical data. It is essential in all branches of science to look *ahead* of the data, however, in order to understand what sort of data is really worth collecting. The ideas given here suggest that, if we wish to understand mind and brain, the most important task ahead is to collect information regarding the component structure of the strange attractor of the brain, both on the physical level and the process level and above all, to under-stand the complex relation between the strange attractors on these two different levels.

REFERENCES

Aczel, P. (1988). *Non-well-founded sets.* Palo alto: CSLI Lecture Notes.

Bateson, G. (1980). *Mind and nature: A necessary unity.* New York: Bantam.

Bennett, C. H. (1982). The thermodynamics of computation—A review. *International Journal of Theoretical Physics, 21,* 905–940.

Chaitin, G. (1987). *Algorithmic information theory.* New York: Addison-Wesley.

Deutsch, D. (1985). Quantum theory, the Church-Turing principle and the universal quantum computer. *Proceedings of the Royal Society of London, A400,* 97–117.

Devaney, R. (1988). *Chaotic dynamical systems.* New York: Addison-Wesley.

Edelman, G. M. (1987). *Neural Darwinism.* New York: Basic Books.

Freeman, W. (1991). The physics of perception. *Scientific American,* pp. 34–41.

Goertzel, B. (1993a). *The evolving mind.* New York: Gordon & Breach.

Goertzel, B. (1993b). *The structure of intelligence.* New York: Springer-Verlag.

Hebb, D. O. (1948). *The organization of behavior.* New York: Wiley.

Kampis, G. (1991). *Self-modifying systems in biology and cognitive science.* New York: Pergamon.

Rosenfield, I. (1989). *The invention of memory.* New York: Bantam.

Varela, F. (1978). *Principles of biological autonomy.* New York: Cambridge University Press.

11

Dynamics, Bifurcation, Self-Organization, Chaos, Mind, Conflict, Insensitivity to Initial Conditions, Time, Unification, Diversity, Free Will, and Social Responsibility

Frederick David Abraham

This is my first attempt to construct a dynamical approach to cognition. First, I review some basic notions from dynamical systems theory, important for seeking a unifying language. Then, for illustrative purposes, I follow with some comments on a nonlinear extension of Miller, Dollard, and Lewin's social conflict theory. Finally, I comment on the responsibility and capacity of the dynamical systems approach to contribute to the evolution of a balance between unity and diversity in psychology, to the exercise of free choice, and to the humanist missions of science, psychology, and society.

REVIEW OF BASIC CONCEPTS

Dynamics is properly a branch of mathematics. Sciences borrow the approach as a strategy to observe and model the behavior of complex sets of interrelated phenomena. As a modeling enterprise, the dynamical systems approach measures various aspects of those phenomena (observable variables), and constructs rules for how the behavior of such variables change at each state of the system. Usually this is done by use of differential or difference equations as well as sketches. Hypothetical variables, of course, may also be employed in the models. Thus, a dynamical system is defined by a *vectorfield* of the tendencies of the system to change at each of its states. The system, then, proceeds through a succession of states after a given initial state is specified. The resulting path in the state space is called a *trajectory*. The collection of all such trajectories is called a *phase portrait*.

Phase portraits reveal certain features. For example, all nearby trajectories may depart from a given point or cycle (called point or periodic *repellors*). Likewise, all nearby trajectories may approach a point or a cycle (*fixed point* or *periodic attractors*). *Saddle* points and cycles are regions to which some trajectories approach while others depart. If there is more than one attractor in a phase portrait, *basins* can be seen as regions containing the trajectories going to each, and trajectories not tending to any attractor are *separatrice* because they usually form boundaries separating basins.

Chaotic attractors are neither fixed point nor periodic attractors, and they can vary from nearly periodic to almost totally random behavior. The complex patterns are the result of forces that attract trajectories to a complex surface folded into a region of the space and divergent forces that cause neighboring trajectories to diverge from each other. This divergence from every very close neighboring starting points is called *sensitivity to initial conditions*.

Dynamical systems can change. As the vectorfield changes, so does the result of integrating it over time, the phase portrait. Why does it change? It changes when some parameter, some *constant,* some feature of the system other than the main variables, change. That is, the equations retain their same form, but the value of some constant changes, becomes inconstant. A parameter can be changed over a large range of values while the phase portrait changes but gradually. Alternatively, the value of the control parameter may change by a very small amount and result in a radical transformation in the system's behavior. Such a major transformation is called a *bifurcation.*

There are three main species of bifurcations. A *subtle* bifurcation is where one type of attractor changes to another, as in a Hopf bifurcation (Fig. 11.1), when a fixed point attractor changes to a periodic attractor. A *catastrophic* bifurcation occurs when an attractor either appears or disappears. An *explosive* bifurcation is when the principle feature is the sudden shift in the magnitude of the attractor. In order for bifurcations or chaos to occur in a dynamical system, at least one of the equations must have at least one nonlinear term. Systems at bifurcation points are very unstable; between bifurcation points, they are more stable (including even chaotic attractors).

A *dynamical scheme* is comprised of the changes in the dynamical system as a function of one or more *control parameters.* The visual geometric rendering of the complex system is called a *response diagram* (Fig. 11.1). It is usually shown in partial or ghost form to emphasize the different types of attractors exhibited by the system at representative values of the control parameters, and to highlight the bifurcation sequence. If only the bifurcation points are emphasized, the response diagram may be called a *bifurcation diagram.* Sometimes bifurcation diagrams show the control space divided into regions sharing common attractors, with the boundaries between them being the loci of bifurcation points.

A *complex dynamical system* is comprised of a network of coupled dynamical schemes. Two or more dynamical schemes are considered coupled when one or more control parameters of one scheme are a function of the state of another

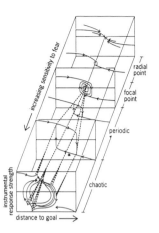

FIG. 11.1. Response diagram of dynamical scheme for conflict. Dimensions of the state spaces (vertical planes) are response velocity and position with respect to a goal. The control parameter is sensitivity to fear. With increasing sensitization to fear, the sequence of subtle bifurcations first exhibits a Hopf (from a fixed point to a periodic attractor) and then excitation of chaos (periodic to chaotic, the chaotic is shown as the collapsed shadow of a trajectory wound around a torus). From Abraham (1993), in *1993 McGraw-Hill Yearbook of Science & Technology.* Courtesy of McGraw-Hill.

scheme. Figures summarizing them are *network diagrams* (Fig. 11.2). It is possible to break a large dynamical system into several components, each with its own control parameters, or to combine several simpler systems into a larger one, as a network with the control parameters of each dependent upon the states of some of the others.

When the control parameter(s) of a system are influenced by the state of the system itself one can speak of *self-control,* or *self-organization.* This self-control can be by means of an immediate route (Fig. 11.2) or by the mediation of a network of complex systems (Fig. 11.2). Note that this concept transcends the usual concept of feedback. The ordinary idea of feedback, such as in the continual interplay of centrifugal brain control of sensory processing, and other features of the continual interplay of environment, brain, and behavior familiar to all students of the brain, are already incorporated into the notion of the interacting variables of the dynamical system. Self-control deals with the reorganizational, bifurcational features of systems, individuals, and societies.

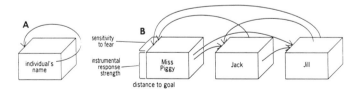

FIG. 11.2. Network diagrams. (A) Self-control (direct), (B) Complex dynamical system comprised of three coupled dynamical schemes (with indirect self-control). The control parameter of each scheme is influenced by the state of each of the other two schemes. The schemes are the same as Fig. 11.1. © Fred Abraham.

MIND: INDIVIDUAL AND COLLECTIVE
AND INSENSITIVITY TO INITIAL CONDITIONS

We start with a generalization of a principle postulate of Vandervert's neurological positivism (Vandervert, 1993), namely that there is a holistic unity involving mind, brain, behavior, and environment; none can be understood as a separate entity. Their mutually interactive and complex processes comprise an organic entity. That is, *mind* is a dynamical system. Internal environment, response produced stimuli, proprioception, centrifugal control (in the nervous system), cognitive attribution, and psychoneuroimmunology, are but a few of the concerns of psychology that show the difficulty of distinctions between mind, brain, behavior and environment. Even the bald term *response* stands for a two-way interaction between organism and environment.

The *mind* of a social organization is also the dynamical system comprised of the interaction of the components of the social system with each other, its and their environments, and the personal *minds* of its participants. The complex patterns of *mind* are conceived to exhibit and be comprised of various attractors along with other features of dynamical systems. Even if it is impossible, as yet, to competently describe them, it is possible to discuss some of their properties from the emerging conjectures of dynamical systems theory. What might be a theorem in mathematical theory usually must remain a conjecture for the science of psychology, although there is experimental support in a few cases (Abraham, Abraham, & Shaw, 1990; Abraham & Gilgen, in press; Barton, 1994; Levine & Fitzgerald, 1992; for general reviews).

From this point of view, there is a number of other benefits and problems that accrue. If a memory is a chaotic attractor, by definition it requires time for expression. How much time does it take the brain to process an attractor? How much time must it integrate to comprehend the attractor? What kind of time spans are required and is it capable of? There has been much discussion of this perplexing issue, and it is raised in part to emphasize the more resolvable context of the dynamical systems point of view but more to relate it to the context of the discriminability problem between attractors representing different processes of *mind,* such as specific memories. It is tempting to say "states of *mind*" instead of "processes of *mind,*" but "state" is a technical term that represents a system at a given instant of time.

My contention, however, is that the attractive properties, the complex pattern in general, the attractor, represents the process of *mind*. Moreover, not a specific trajectory, but any trajectory from that attractor, may adequately represent it. The exact starting time and location of a train or stream of thought, and its exact spatio-temporal location is unimportant. I call this *insensitivity to initial conditions*. It is to be admitted that no one has specified exactly an attractor for a given memory (although Freeman, 1991 is coming close), or any other process of *mind* (see Basar, 1990; and Abraham, 1993 for discussions of neurophysiological attractors), or how different attractors need to be for discriminability.

Within a social organization, an analogous process takes place. It takes time for an organization to get a concept of self, to see patterns of change and bifurcations, to build up its own historic appraisal of its response diagram, to model itself, grasp an appreciation of its control parameters, forecast its potential futures, and manipulate its control parameters, or even its state space, if necessary.

Parenthetically, the dynamical systems view may benefit from a distinction between concepts of time that are nonlinear, Bergsonian, and irreversible (Greek's *chairos,* Henkel's event time, Loye's timeless and spatial times) and those that are linear, Newtonian, and reversible (Greek's *chronos,* Henkel's ordinary linear phase, Loye's serial time). Temporally linear motion along a trajectory obeys chronos, but the *mind,* integrating over periods of time, creates the saltatory evolutionary event time of chairos (Henkel, 1989; Loye, 1983; Wiener, 1948). Because they are self-organizational, *minds* and social organizations can navigate their response diagrams, that is, maneuver along the control parameters of the real and virtual realities of their complex dynamical structures. They can change state spaces, if necessary, and navigate to cause bifurcations in their own organization. Using a similar conception, Solow (1991) showed how the control parameters of greed, impersonalization, and quality control affected company profit—which, along with self-organization, pushed his firm to a highly unstable bifurcation point on the very threshold of an annihilation catastrophe.

The distinction between the linear time, from the view within the attractor, and simultaneously the nonlinear event integrated time of the view outside the attractor, is similar to Kugler's et al.'s (1990) excellent discussion from the dynamical systems point of view of the Gibsonian approach to "ecological physics," especially in their distinction between *holonomic* and *nonholonomic* constraints on intentional behavior:

Holonomic constraints. . .can be expressed functionally as a relationship among coordinates, and thus do not materially alter the system.

If intentions are holonomic constraints. . .through evolution or through learning organisms come to exploit existing laws very effectively in achieving their goals without necessary recourse to rules of behavior or "internalized" models of goal paths, etc.

Nonholonomic constraints are able to restrict trajectories in state space only because they. . . require some mechanism that materially alter the system.

. . . if intentions are nonholonomic, then something like cognitively internalized models of the environment and the actor's place in it would have to be assumed because rules require such mechanisms in order to be applied.

CONFLICT

Since the classic demonstrations of acquired aversive drives (Estes & Skinner, 1941; Miller, 1937a, 1937b, 1959), there has been an evolution of studies of the effects of classically conditioned drives (conditioned emotional responses [CERs]) on instrumental performance (Rescorla & Solomon, 1967), mostly based on Hullian–Spencian models. Some are quite mature in considering all the logical possibilities of aversive-appetitive interactions between the CER and the instrumental reward (Koerner, 1992). One of the most interesting is the model of approach–avoidance conflict (Dollard & Miller, 1950; Lewin, 1931, 1950; Miller, 1959).

Miller's Linear Model

On their famous trip, Jack and Jill went across the street and up the hill to fetch a pail of water and have a good time at the playground. They spied a snake and ran away scared. Jack fell down, and Jill came tumbling after. As a result of this classical conditioning trial and tribulation (and perhaps of other learned and innate fears of snakes), their positive–appetitive and negative–aversive CER gradients (the strength of the learned emotional responses to the stimuli of the playground and the route to the playground) were different for each of them as well as for their friend, Miss Piggy, who was away in space at the time of this fearsome incident (Fig. 11.3, upper parts). Jack, who was more frightened, had a high aversive gradient (Fig. 11.3a). Miss Piggy had a high appetitive gradient (Fig. 11.3b). Jill was in between, with the aversive gradient steeper than the appetitive gradient, the aversive gradient exceeding the appetitive gradient closer to the playground, and the appetitive gradient exceeding the aversive gradient closer to home (Fig. 11.3c).

The vectorfields for these hypothetical variables were considered a linear function of distance from the goal, and they were additive. The rate of change of locomotion to or from the goal was thus a linear function of distance from the goal; the vectorfield for this observable behavior was thus also a linear function of distance from the goal. The manifold, the state space, was thus all on a straight line (Fig. 11.3, lower parts), and reveal that Jack would have ended up at home, Miss Piggy on the playground, and Jill playing in the road in between— very different fixed point attractors. Note that space and motion are interactive variables; motion changes Jack and Jill's positions in space, which changes their CERs, which change their motion. Miller recognized this interaction under the title *dynamic relationships:*

> But it can also be seen that the Response of Approach or Avoidance on the consequent side of the diagram will change the Distance in centimeters from the Point of Reinforcement on the antecedent side. Because such changes in distance affect the strength of avoidance more than that of approach, the response of approaching tends to increase the relative strength of avoidance until approach is stopped, whereas the response of avoidance tends to decrease the relative strength of avoidance until it is stopped. It is this phenomenon (analogous to negative feedback) which leads to the deduction of a point of stable equilibrium represented diagrammatically by the point at which the two gradients cross. (Miller, 1959)

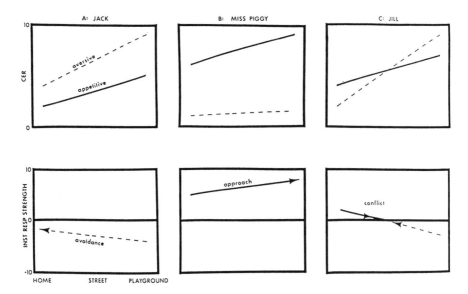

FIG. 11.3. Approach-avoidance conflict: Miller's linear dynamical model. Appetitive and aversive CERs (conditioned emotional responses, vertical axes of upper row of graphs) and distance to goal (horizontal axes) gradients, established by learning. These two gradients are additive to result in an instrumental response strength (vertical axes of lower row), resulting in the observed variables of rate and direction of motion in the space. Jack always avoids, Ms Piggy always approaches, but Jill's crossed gradients have her approach or flee the goal depending on where she starts out, but always ending up in the middle of the street because of the equality of aversion and desire there. Jill is exhibiting conflict; the two tendencies compete. Adapted from Abraham et al. (1990). Courtesy of Aerial Press.

We use the term *interaction instead of feedback,* reserving the latter for feedback to a control parameter—though there is a great deal of variability in the literature on this score—and because of the interactive nature, we don't use antecedent/consequent language for this continual mutual influence. Lewin's (1931, 1950) model was nonlinear, but still limited to fixed point attractors (Fig. 11.4).

The Nonlinear Model

To exhibit more complex behavior, the vectorfields (CER gradients) were made a function of not only distance from the goal, but also the direction and magnitude of velocity of the motion (Fig. 11.4 upper). Loosely, there is cognitive distortion—perceptual distortion in the stimulus sampling process—with a hysteresis effect in that, on approach to the goal, the aversive gradients are depressed

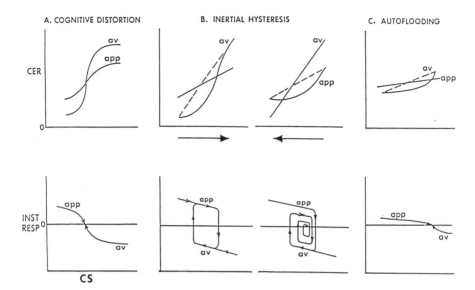

FIG. 11.4. Approach-avoidance conflict: Nonlinear dynamical model.
(A) Simple cognitive distortion, Lewin's model, fixed point attractors.
(B) Cognitive distotion with hysteresis. The gradients are a function of
the direction and velocity as well as the distance from the goal. They
are different during approach and avoidance. (C) Autoflooding, due to
slowness of motion, or deliberate self-exposure to the feared goal,
there is habituation, a lowering of the aversive gradient. Adapted from
Abraham et al. (1990). Courtesy of Aerial Press.

when Jill is far from the goal but come back to dominate near the goal where they
send her on fast retreat (Fig. 11.4, left). On retreat, the sampling of aversive cues
dominates, while the appetitive gradient is depressed until Jill finally realizes she
has reached safety. She slows down, resets the cognitive appraisal or sampling
process, and the appetitive gradient dominates and turns her around again (Fig.
11.4, right).

There may result a damped oscillation to a spiral (focal) fixed point attractor
(Fig. 11.4, lower right). Or there may be a continually undamped oscillation, a
periodic attractor (Fig. 11.4, lower left). Usually goals are also under the influence of other forces, often with near periodic features, such as eating, schedules,
school, sleep, and activity schedules, so that these attractors can become more
complicated, spreading over the surface of a torus whose phase is following these
other forces, and thus exhibit chaos. The response diagram is shown with a
general sensitivity to fear as a control parameter (Fig. 11.1). It shows a sequence
of subtle bifurcations, a Hopf going from fixed point to periodic, and excitation
to chaos going from periodic to chaotic. The chaotic is depicted as collapsed
from its torus to a plane. This is purely conjectural, though there are several

mathematical models capable of such sequences, like the Van der Pol and Brusselator oscillators.

Networking, Social Behavior, and Self-organization

We are beginning to explore how complex this behavior might become and how it might change itself, self-organize, when individual's behaviors, with respect to a common goal, become coupled to the behavior of others. Of course, an individual may self-control without the involvement of another. The first step in this program, just underway, is to observe the behavior of the model coupling two individuals displaying such conflict (This is a computer modeling effort with Peter Kugler and Xie Min). In place of two individuals, here, you may substitute two components of an organization or social structure, such as the parts and service department at your local auto repair shop, or the administrative and judicial branches of government during Watergate or the Rodney King affair, or substitute two organizations, such as two firms, or two nations negotiating contracts and treaties.

So far, we have coupled only two participants or "oscillators" together. The two-dimensional state spaces of each are combined into a four-dimensional state space. For a three-dimensional representation on a two-dimensional computer screen, Kugler and Xie have made the plane for one participant perpendicular to that of the other, and let the origin of it follow the trajectory of the other with a polar orientation, such that if they were uncoupled and each oscillated at a fixed frequency, their joint trajectory would approach and follow the surface of a torus (Fig. 11.5). I call their computer model the KX-4D torus. Next we coupled them, not via their control parameters as previously described, but by system variables. That is, in this first model the rate of change in position of each is a function of the position of the other. Future simulations will explore various types of such couplings where position can be coupled to position, velocity, and acceleration, and velocity can be coupled to velocity and acceleration, and acceleration to acceleration.

When thus coupled, good graphical computers like those of the IRIS family, used by the KX-4D torus, make it easy to explore the parameter space in real time. Such efforts reveal a rich variety of complex trajectories (Fig. 11.6). While these solutions are periodic, fixed point attractors can be generated by bifurcations caused by changing the amplitude parameter, a. And periodic complexity approaching chaotic, which we might call "practically chaos," can easily be achieved. (The graphic torus of Fig. 11.6 is a visual aid that can be toggled between a wire-ghost representation, a solid, or off, to better view the trajectory. The torus is not a manifold, that is, the trajectories are not restricted to it as the state space; it just helps visualize the state space, as normally drawn axes do for two- and three-dimensional spaces.) The orientation (rotation) of the state space, the scaling of the space, display parameters controlling trajectory length and

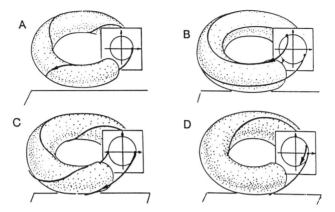

FIG. 11.5.   4D state space for two uncoupled individuals. The state space for one individual is velocity vs. position on the horizontal plane, for the other individual the state space is on the vertical plane. Here, to help visualize the space, a torus is shown for the two uncoupled individuals (1 = 0) each oscillating with constant amplitude, shown with winding ratios of (A) 3:1, (B) 1:3, (C) 3:2, and (D) irrational where the winding of the trajectory never repeats, that is, it is a chaotic attractor rather than a periodic attractor as with the others (some authors do not include this case as chaotic as it does not possess sensitivity to initial conditions, see Abraham in Abraham and Gilgen, 1995). Adapted from Abraham et al. (1990). Courtesy of Aerial Press.

thickness, and parameter of the model itself are made via screen-graphic slider switches that are controlled by the mouse, while the trajectories are evolving and in motion.

Figure 11.6 shows but one of four windows simultaneously displayed by the program, another shows the time series of each variable, and another the trajectories of each participant superimposed on the same two-dimensional plane, all evolving along with the joint four-dimensional trajectory. The fourth window displays the slider switches for parameter entry. (We would like someone to port this program to a PC so we wouldn't have to visit Jurassic Park to compute!)

Rössler (1986), allowing motion along two spatial variables, x and y, but with different equations for x and y, and coupling on the difference between the two positions along one of the spatial variables, obtains chaos for two individuals. The behavior, as with most low-dimensional dynamical systems studied by mathematicians, shows nearly periodic behavior, as can be seen in Fig. 11.7.

Another type of chaos we might see in such a system is that exhibited by a forced Van der Pol system (Fig. 11.8), and Ashwin and King showed chaos in three symmetrically coupled electronic oscillators (Fig. 11.9). Richardson (1991) stated the obvious, that "deterministic chaos is a phenomenon in mathematical models. We cannot prove perceived correspondences between models and real-

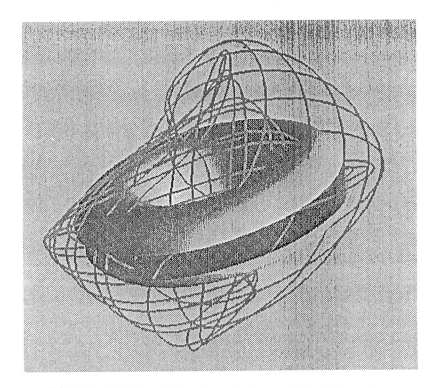

FIG. 11.6. Complex trajectory for mutually coupled individuals. Two individuals each with their own conflict schemes. There is quite a high frequency ratio of the individual of the horizontal plane of the torus to the individual whose state space is represented by the vertical plane. Computer-snapshot-technology freeze framed the video output of the animated/real-time model and transferred it in color to a transparency. © by Fred Abraham. Created with a program by Kugler and Xie, with the help of the staff of the EMBA computer facility at the University of Vermont.

FIG. 11.7. Chaos in coupled autonomous optimizers: Rossler's two mice. (Left) two coupled individuals each shown acting in 2D space with a trajectory for each. (Right) Time series of one of the dimensions. From Rössler (1986), courtesy of New York Academy of Science and Otto Rössler.

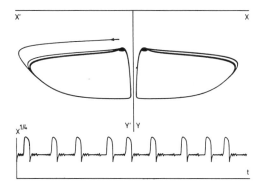

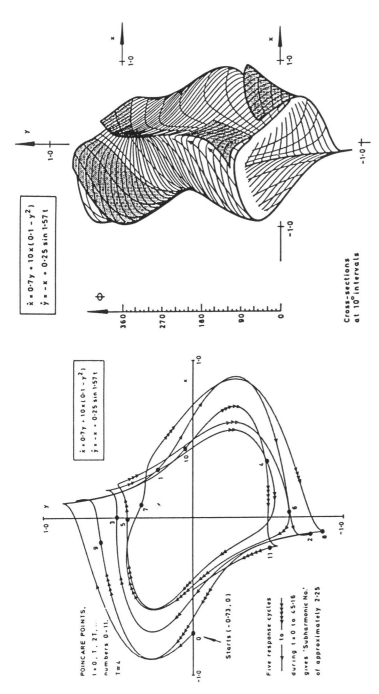

FIG. 11.8. Transient chaos in the forced Van der Pol oscillator. If one of the two individuals is like a clock uninfluenced by the other, then the other is a forced oscillator. The forcing is on the velocity term. These are summarized in Thompson and Stewart (1986) from the work of Guckenheimer and Holmes (1983) and others. The transient chaos eventually settles down to a periodic oscillation. The transient part collapsed onto 2D space is on the left, the 3D rendering is on the right. From Thompson and Stewart (1986). Reproduced by courtesy of Wiley.

A   B   Bifurcation

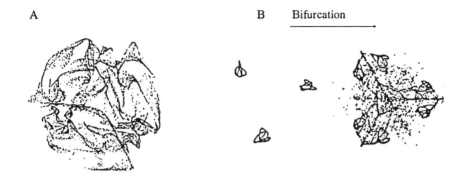

FIG. 11.9.   Three symmetrically coupled electronic oscillators in Poincaré section. On the left we see Symmetric chaos; on the right, a bifurcation where three "individual attractors . . . merge to create a strange [chaotic] attractor with more symmetry." Courtesy of Blackwell, based on work of Ashwin and King reported in Stewart (1989).

ity." It is obvious that our model is too simplified to be anything but a stepping stone to more realistic models.

Self-Organization by Enticement Coupling

We noted two types of coupling. In our coupled conflict model described by the equations just given and the simulations of Fig. 11.5 and 11.6, variables are directly coupled, creating a higher dimensional state space. This is in distinction to the network model described earlier (Fig. 11.2) where a control parameter of one system is a function of (under the influence of) the state of another. Either way, some of the couplings could be weak or eliminated—for example, if Miss Piggy doesn't care what Jack does. Another coupling might be strong such that one was completely entrained to the other—Jack may follow Miss Piggy completely. This would represent the extreme case of nonsymmetrical coupling. Intermediate couplings are more likely, but still quite asymmetrical. Jack might finally bolt when Miss Piggy gets him too close to where the snake was, and she might move away a bit if his flight was vigorous enough. Such feedback enables self-control. If they exert influence on each other, this influence feeds back to the originator. This is self-organization in the social system. They settle into playing in a region that depends on the nature of their own uncoupled tendencies plus the relative strengths of their coupling constants.

We just described Jack with his avoidance-dominated system, who is strongly coupled to Miss Piggy. He follows her even when he is afraid. She is a leader (weakly coupled to Jack) and in possession of a stronger approach-dominated system. But Miss Piggy could have been more of a follower, though we don't usually think of personality traits of leadership or assertiveness and conditioned fear being dissociated this way. We think of leaders as fearless, and followers as those who tend to follow to be protected from the imagined sources of their fears. But this is not necessarily the case. Network coupling may be more passive, operating in linear real time. The participants follow their gradients, influence each other, and themselves, by network feedback, without being particularly aware of their own control parameters.

A more active situation occurs when each individual learns to control a parameter of their own conflict system. They may do this directly. "I shouldn't be such a scaredy-cat. I'll grit my teeth and ignore my fear or habituate it." (Fig. 11.4C). Or they may try to influence the behavior of the other person, and condition their own fear parameter upon the response of the other. Jill knows the difference between hers and Miss Piggy's phase portrait, so she gets Miss Piggy into the space. "Let's go to the playground, Miss Piggy." She modifies her behavior by modifying Miss Piggy's. I'll call this "'enticement coupling."

But this actually implies yet a new, third type of coupling. Note that, in self-control and recruitment coupling, some learning has taken place. Remember what I said about two types of time perception when discussing *mind*? *Chairos*-event time is required to represent learned attractors, dynamical schemes, and complex dynamical systems (as represented by response and network diagrams). The response diagram of the approach-avoidance conflict portion of a developing cognitive concept of self is built up. *Mind* integrates over time and operates on that integrated image. This means that a full development of this third type should show not simply a coupling or feedback from the state spaces of the component approach-avoidance schemes to their control parameters, but should interpolate new boxes (additional dynamical schemes and their responses diagrams within the network diagram) of the complex system between the state spaces and the control parameters of the original approach-avoidance schemes (Fig. 11.10). One of these (the upper box or response diagram) represents Jill's enticement scheme, which listens most closely to her approach-avoidance conflict (left hand box). Another is the dynamical scheme where some parameters as well as variables of the system are integrated over time—the *mind*'s map of the whole network (lower box or response diagram). This represents the *mind*'s mouse with which it can zoom to an outer or self-reflective view of itself. We ignore the classic homunculus within the homunculus paradox, and boldly assert that *mind* is capable of this, can get outside of itself, and is not a formal system subject to Gödel's restrictions. It is capable of constructing a dynamical model of itself, of reading its past, projecting its future, making choices about those futures, and controlling them through not only manipulation of control parameters, but of creating new, novel spaces and solutions. This is similar to many hierarchical schemes of cognitive function, with a higher, more executive feature (the *chairos* map), the intermediate approach-avoidance gradients, and the enticement behavior as the lowest enabler of the approach behavior. Since they are

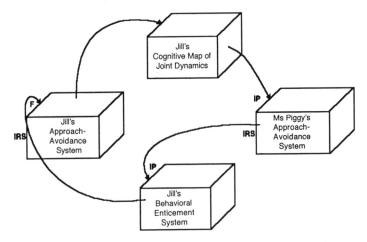

FIG. 11.10. Complex dynamical system of conflict, overseer, recruitment cognitive maps. Jill's event-time hierarchical cognitive map of
overall appraisal of complex system (upper box), her dynamical enticement scheme (lower box) and her conflict scheme (left response
diagram) and Ms Piggy's conflict scheme (right-hand response diagram; other controls and schemes could be added). F is the control for
sensitivity to fear, IP is a control for amount of interest in the playground, IRS is instrumental response strength, controls, and dimensions of the cognitive map are left to your imagination. © Fred
Abraham.

all interactive, one can play a variety of games with this hierarchical feature and
with the feedback controls, many left out of this discussion. All are very loosely
presented in this present preliminary sketch.

SOCIOLOGY AND RESPONSIBILITIES OF
PSYCHOLOGY

Within the field of Psychology there have been many recent areas of concern.
One is about over-diversificaiton, stemming from both its laboratory-
reductionist-few-variate myopia, and from a consequent proliferation of competent but idiosyncratic views of subject matter. A second concern is to give free
will a chance after a period of domination by reductionist causal explanations in
psychology. A third is about the social responsibilities of the profession, what I
call a need to improve its humanist mission. Dynamics can contribute to the
evolution of all three.

Unification

Leibniz (1669) argued for a universal mathematical language capable of unifying science, and of everything else for that matter. Dynamics, itself evolved from Leibniz's and Newton's calculus, is a visual geometry of complex interacting processes, applies to all areas of science, is very communicable, and is thus in a position to unify within and between all disciplines. Additionally, it gives a metaphorical perspective on the discipline by considering it as a chaotic attractor with self-organziational properties. Psychology has both convergent and divergent forces. When our super theories proved too inflexible, we correct toward divergence. Now, with diversification so great that we cannot synthesize it, we correct toward unification. Dynamics shows the value of both types of tendency and that there is a wide range of both types that could contribute to the maturity of our science. By providing a common language that improves communication among the isolated idiosyncratic islands, dynamics should allow a more natural evolution to a healthy balance between diversity and unity. A reasonably democratic environment also contributes to the good behavior of such a dynamical science.

Free Will

Dynamics as a mathematical enterprise is deterministic, but can be used to model probabilistic as well as deterministic systems. But as Basar (1990); Richardson (1991), as mentioned earlier; and many others have said, real systems (as apposed to the theoretical mathematical models of calculus) like the *mind* are finite (at least as observed and as observing; our knowledge is finite), and therefore indeterminate in the sense of incomplete understanding. Determinism versus indeterminism is therefore unprovable, and remains a matter of faith. Meanwhile the *mind,* we see, must operate as if it makes choices. It can make choices in two ways from the dynamical systems view. The first is by choosing initial conditions. It can place itself in a phase portrait in the basin leading to a desired attractor, that is pick a starting region for a trajectory. If a separatrix dominates the phase portrait, the actor may end up flipping a coin. The other mode involves self-control in terms of navigating the parameter space to create the desired system and then selecting a trajectory if more than one attractor survives there. This means hill climbing over some troubling bifurcation points and may involve some novel reconstructions of the response diagrams.

The Humanist Mission

The mission of psychology is twofold. The first is scientific, to understand mind and behavior. The second is to nurture conditions conducive to its enjoyment by the maximum number of people. That is, psychology should not only help people help themselves, but should help others to be sensitive to other people, for only by learning to respect the rights of all can we succeed in enabling the maximum well-being. That this should hold for social systems as well should be evident from the Harley-Davidson story mentioned previously (Solow, 1991), where loss of sensitivity to its labor force and its product quality nearly did in the company. But it is paradoxical for psychology, which is supposed to be a helping nurturing profession, that it has proved deficient in its own humanism. This failure has derived from its objectification of its subject matter and from some parameters of its own institutionalization, such as, just like the business world, its profit motive (research funding, academic funding, care delivery, etc.) and the usual impersonalization of large bureaucratic institutions. In the objectification of the subject matter, we have concentrated on scientific goals at the expense of social goals, ignoring the major humanitarian problems such as racism, sexism, handicapism, nationalism, etc.

Nevertheless, many have attempted to address these issues. Historically, Lewin led the way with his action psychology. But he did not recruit a large portion of the field. Probably leading the humanization of psychology is the feminist psychology movement. This movement has holistically fused its subject matter, women, with the humanist mission of empowering the participation of women, minorities, the impoverished. In the process, a new approach to psychology had to be undertaken, especially revealed in its critical review of the history of psychology, and in which the scientist and the subjects become involved as teams cooperating to find new ways of studying individuals and social processes. These teams found that subjects cannot be isolated form the multiple contextual situations in which they evolved as selves (Crawford & Maracek, 1989; Mednick, 1989; Murphy & Abraham, 1995). Now you see the relevance? While it is true that as mathematics was developing new tools for the study of complex cooperative processes, and many fields of science were beginning to chafe at the bit to have these tools to tackle their complex processes as they realized that the isolate-the-variable approach had yielded its limit of treasures, it took a commitment to a compelling social mission to focus on the need for the dynamical systems approach. On its side, the dynamical systems view, when it focuses on the real world, observes the obvious interrelatedness of virtually all phenomena, and thus highlights a responsibility toward a healthier planet and good will among all people (Abraham, 1994; Goerner, 1991; Loye & Eisler, 1987).

REFERENCES

Abraham, F. D. (1993). Book review: "Chaos in brain function" (E. Basar, Ed.). *World Futures, 37,* 41–58.

Abraham, F. D., Abraham, R. H., & Shaw, C. D. (1990). *A visual introduction to dynamical systems theory for psychology.* Santa Cruz, CA: Aerial.

Abraham, F. D., & Gilgen, A. R. (1995). *Chaos theory in psychology.* Westport, CT: Greenwood.

Abraham, R. H. (1994). *Chaos, gaia, eros: The orphic trinity in myth and science.* San Francisco: Harper & Row.

Barton, S. (1994). Chaos, self-organization, and psychology. *American Psychologist, 49,* 5–14.

Basar, E. (Ed.). (1990). *Chaos in brain function.* Berlin: Springer-Verlag.

Bay, J. S., & Hemami, H. (1987). Modeling of a neural pattern generator with coupled nonlinear oscillators. *IEEE Transactions on Biomedical Engineering, BME-34,* 297–306.

Crawford, M., & Maracek, J. (1989). Psychology reconstructs the female. *Psychology of Women Quarterly, 13,* 147–165.

Dollard, J., & Miller, N. E. (1950). *Personality and psychotherapy: an analysis in terms of learning, thinking, and culture.* New York: McGraw-Hill.

Estes, W. K., & Skinner, B. F. (1941). Some quantitative properties of anxiety. *Journal of Experimental Psychology, 29,* 390–400.

Freeman, W. J. (1991). The physiology of perception. *Scientific American, 264,* 78–85.

Goerner, S. J. (1991). The physics of evolution as a basis for understanding spirituality and evolutionary competence. *Proceedings of the International Society of the Systems Sciences, 35th Annual Meeting,* Ostersund, Sweden.

Henkel, J. (1989). Towards a Gaia philosophy: The dyadic realities picture. *The Gaia Review, 1,* 20–30.

Koerner, J. (1992). *Nonlinear dynamic systems in behavioral psychology* (Vols. 1 & 2). Unpublished Doctoral dissertation, University of Minnesota, Duluth.

Kugler, P. N., Shaw, R. E., Vincente, K. J., & Kinsella-Shaw, J. (1990). Inquiry into intentional systems I: Issues in ecological physics. *Psychological Research, 52,* 98–121.

Leibniz, G. W. F. von (1969). *On the general characteristic* (L. E. Loemmker, Ed. and Trans.). G. Wilhelm Leibniz: Philosophical papers and letters. Dordrecht/Boston: Reidel. (Original work published 1679)

Levine, R. L., & Fitzgerald, H. E. (1992). *Analysis of dynamic psychological systems* (Vols. 1 & 2). New York: Plenum.

Lewin, K. (1931). *A dynamic theory of personality: Selected papers* (D. K. Adams & K. E. Zener, Trans.). New York: McGraw-Hill.

Lewin, K. (1950). *Field theory in social science.* New York: Harper & Row.

Loye, D. (1983). *The sphinx and the rainbow: Brain, mind and future vision.* Boulder: Shambala.

Loye, D., & Eisler, R. (1987). Chaos and transformation: Implications of nonequilibrium theory for social science and society. *Behavioral Science, 27,* 53–65.

Mednick, M. T. (1989). On the politics of psychological constructs. *American Psychologist, 44,* 1118–1123.

Miller, N. E. (1937a). The analysis of the form of conflict reactions. *Psychological Bulletin, 34,* 720.

Miller, N. E. (1937b). Reaction formation in rats: An experimental analog for a Freudian phenomenon. *Psychological Bulletin, 34,* 724.

Miller, N. E. (1959). Liberalization of basic s-r concepts: Extensions to conflict behavior, motivation, and social learning. In S. Koch (Ed.), *Psychology: A study of a science, Vol 2, General systematic formulations, learning, and special processes.* New York: McGraw-Hill.

Murphy, P., & Abraham, F. D. (1995). Feminist psychology: Prototype of the dynamical revolution in psychology. In F. D. Abraham & A. R. Gilgen (Eds.), *Chaos theory in psychology.* Westport, CT: Greenwood.

Rescorla, R., & Solomon, R. A. (1967). Two-process learning theory: Relationships between Pavlovian conditioning and instrumental learning. *Psychological review, 74,* 151–182.

Richardson, G. (1991). Caveats about chaos. In M. Michaels (Ed.), *Proceedings of First Annual Chaos Network Conference.* Urbana-Champagne: People Technologies.

Rössler, O. (1986). Chaos in coupled optimizers. In S. H. Koslow, A. J. Mandell, & M. F.

Shlesinger (Eds.), *Perspectives in biological dynamics and theoretical medicine. Annals of the New York Academy of Science, 504,* New York: New York Academy of Sciences.

Solow, L. (1991). (R)evolution of employee involvement at Harley-Davidson, Inc. In M. Michaels (Ed.), *Proceedings of First Annual Chaos Network Conference.* Urbana-Champagne, IL: People Technologies.

Vandervert, L. (1993). Neurological positivism's evolution of mathematics. *Journal of Mind and Behavior, 13,* 277–288.

Weiner, N. (1948). *Cybernetics or control and communication in the animal and the machine.* New York/Paris: Wiley.

IV <div>EDUCATION, SOCIAL SCIENCE AND CHAOS THEORY</div>

When we examine applications of chaos theory in the life sciences, in general, we find such a proliferation of possibilities that it is impossible to give more than a taste in this volume. The three chapters here apply chaos theory to everything from a general theory of problem solving in education (Torre) to the application of the mathematics of chaos theory in the real-life world of emergency disaster response (Koehler), to a general examination of the foundations of future social science that draws on chaos theory (Young).

Over the last decade, Torre has developed a triadic model of problem solving that has has not only written about in a number of papers, but has applied in practical educational projects in both public and private sector institutions. His chapter provides a history of problem-solving models and the problems inherent in these older models in order to illustrate how his own model evolved. "Intuitively and through our daily experiences, we know that such linear or cyclical procedures are artificial and contrived. When faced with an unwanted or perplexing state of affairs, few individuals (if any) think in an assembly-line step-by-step manner, or even in an orderly cyclical fashion."

Torre emphasizes that all problem solving involves a dynamic balance between cognitive processes (i.e., thinking), affective-perceptive processes (i.e., feeling), and pragmatic processes (i.e., action). Each process in turn splits into three subprocesses, for example, affective-perceptive into prognosis, solution generation, and decision making. Chaos theory reveals that problem solving (or any other process drawing on the human brain) necessarily moves dynamically between these processes and subprocesses. Yet the overall structure of the problem-solving behavior is preserved through self-similarity at different levels of the process. What makes Torre's model significant is that it draws on this knowledge to more realistically represent real-life problem solving.

Few situations can affect our lives more drastically than experiencing a major disaster, such as a flood or a fire, an earthquake or a riot. Yet few of us have little more than a sketchy idea what goes into the civil response to such disasters. Koehler draws on years of experience of actually having to plan government responses to such disasters and uses the mathematics of chaos theory to demonstrate when and how such procedures break down. He shows that errors in emergency response during such crises follow the classic pattern we've seen over and over again in chaos theory: Initial stability yields to bifurcations, then finally to chaos. More particularly, "an emergency medical system (EMS) phase transition occurs because of a progressive or sudden break down of the day-to-day EMS. More and more decision errors are made, driving the EMS over the organizational edge into a second-order phase transition and on to chaos." He hopes to develop computer models to test his conclusions.

It has become a commonplace in social theory to split cultures into pre-modern, modern, and postmodern. Young's chapter demonstrates how chaos theory provides a scientific structure in which all three are seen as emerging from the normal structures of change in the natural world. As with Koehler, he uses the three classic stages of chaos theory (self-similar stable structure, sharp change through bifurcation, deterministic chaos) to illustrate progressively more complex social orders. The torus "embodies first order change by virtue of the self-similarity involved in its dynamics." It represents any recurring social structure, such as "'a baptism, a marriage, a funeral or a mass," in which no two instances are identical, yet all share a similar stable structure. Premodern societies largely embody such self-similar structure.

"Under specific conditions, a small change . . . can force a stable torus to break up into two or more tori." Modern society offers a multitude of examples of such change: "gender differentiations, occupational roles, and religious status roles are examples of normative bifurcations in outcome states between persons with but small differences in initial states."

It is the third order of change—deterministic chaos—that Young presents as offering a model for social science of how human beings can begin to take responsibility for the eventual structure of their postmodern society. "We cannot appeal to nature or to the gods for direction, nor may we assign blame to devils and genes when things go wrong. In that loss of innocence resides our dignity as architects of our own fate."

It is revealing that the underlying structural patterns revealed by chaos theory emerge not only in physics and chemistry and biology, where chaos theory has already been well-explored, but in human areas ranging from problem solving in the human mind, to the spread of errors in disaster response, to the wide variety of types of societal change. These three chapters thus point to the possibilities of applying chaos theory far beyond the examples they present.

12 Chaos, Creativity, and Innovation: Toward a Dynamical Model of Problem Solving

Carlos Antonio Torre

Recurrently, we think about chaos and, no doubt, we often say that our thinking is "chaotic." But is chaos a governing principle in the way we think, create, and solve problems? Is a healthy clear thinking or creative problem-solving process, by nature, a chaotic one? If so, how does chaos help the brain in the thinking and problem-solving role it was designed to perform? What are the processes of thinking and the tasks of problem solving and how do these interact? Finally, what is the nature of the mental dynamics or procedures through which a problem solver advances in the effort to understanding and bringing about purposeful change in a given situation?

It is well recognized that problem solving poses considerable difficulties even for people of normal and above average intelligence (Brightman, 1980; Hayes, 1981; Naisbitt, 1982; Robertshaw, Mecca, & Rerick 1978; Seif, 1981). Whether dealing with academic or real-world problems, many of us are often unable to distinguish among the various elements of a problem situation. Our thinking often lacks clarity and we tend to act in a confused, aimless manner. Disoriented, we often endeavor to merely persist hammering away, jumbling issues and information together without purpose or a sense of direction. Alternately, we may revert automatically to standard operating procedures, to a previously successful approach, or to some other pre-established formulae. We seem to learn little from riddles, accidents, and wars. . . only enough to continue stumbling from crisis to crisis.

Such muddling through is inadequate in today's complex world, characterized by rapid changes (such as the sudden disintegration of nations), as well as by gradual changes that are usually more threatening and dangerous (i.e., the contamination of our natural environment). Yet, the processes through which the human mind makes sense of and deals with difficult situations are poorly understood. Little is known about the role that cognitive, affective, perceptive, and pragmatic processes play in problem solving, about how these processes interact, or about how their optimal functioning can be tapped and encouraged.

This chapter examines these issues. A brief overview of problem-solving approaches provides a context for a model that delineates how problem solving comprises a combination of order and randomness among cognitive, affective perceptive, and pragmatic mental processes. Creativity and innovation are portrayed as qualities that emerge from the interaction of these mental processes. Our model demonstrates, further, that the interaction among these three kinds of mental processes involves an interplay in which each of the processes can randomly assume any of three roles: that of moving the problem solver toward a particular direction (activation), that of holding the problem solver back from moving in that direction (restraint), or that of serving as a mediator (integration) between the forces of activation and restraint. The model is generated from the triadic theory of mental functioning (Torre, 1984, 1987, 1989, 1994) and is congruent with chaos theory and fractal geometry. It places the chaotic dynamics inherent among cognitive, affective perceptive, and pragmatic mental processes at the heart of both effective and ineffective problem solving.

HOW DO GOOD PROBLEM SOLVERS PROCEED?

Many complex or vague definitions of the concept of problem have been offered (e.g., Davis, 1973, p.12; Webster's Dictionary, 1961). As with any other seemingly simple or implicitly understood idea, however, we can easily muddy the waters if we become too specific or complex with our definition. Therefore, a problem, for the purposes of this paper, is any situation in which something undesirable or unwanted exists in the opinion of the person calling it a problem (Agre, 1983, p.96).

Implicitly, we may not always be able to agree that there is a problem or what the real problem is. In fact, what constitutes a problem for one individual may be a solution for somebody else. For example, in the U.S. Revolutionary War, the rebelling of the Colonist was a grave problem for the British, yet, for the Colonist, it was the solution. Thus, the question of how good problem solvers proceed, must be prefaced by an understanding that both problem and solution are relative concepts determined by circumstance and individual perception and perspective. Herein lies the potential for problem-solving activity to become a problem in and of itself.

THE DYNAMICS OF PROBLEM SOLVING

For the most part, problem-solving models or sequences exhibit linear (step-by-step activity heading toward a fixed point) or cyclical (periodic) activity through which a problem solver advances when trying to understand and change an unwanted situation (Torre, 1984). On the one hand, linear sequences, tend to be rigid. They usually treat the problem in an assembly line fashion or as a static one-time procedure aimed at reaching a static fixed point known as *the* solution. Although none of the problem-solving procedures I examined are strictly linear, Vinacke and Kepner/Trego's models (Fig. 12.1, sequences 4 & 7 respectively) do come close. Kepner/Trego's model calls for an intricate rational thinking process and requires comparative sources of information in order to provide maximum results. Its procedures virtually eliminate user discretion and are so highly structured that they become awkward and difficult to use. Vinacke's model is closer to Lyles's definition of the traditional approach to problem solving. It lacks structure, specificity, and a rationale of the role that various kinds of thought processes play in problem solving.

Cyclical problem-solving models, on the other hand, provide for the recycling of problems not satisfactorily resolved during an initial attempt. They allow enough flexibility to render problem solving a recurrent activity. These models often treat problem solving as an ongoing process driven by feedback that may guide toward corrective action or reconsideration of the issues (Brightman, 1980; Robertshaw et al., 1978; Fig. 12.1, sequences 9 & 10). The cyclical nature of these models conjures up an image in which new problem situations are created with every cycling, requiring a new cycle of problem-solving activity. As a result, the problem is supposed to get smaller and smaller—as does the sine wave of a dying patient in a hospital—until it finally flat lines.

Such conceptualizations of how problem-solving activity occurs affect the way we organize problems as well as the way we formulate our working hypotheses about the search for solutions. The concern here is not to determine which problem-solving models are right and which ones are wrong. It is assumed that none of the sequences reviewed here is wrong, since any one of them can help to solve a problem. Instead, the concern is for their degree of clarity in helping us to understand the problem-solving process and for the degree of naturalness of the behavioral requirements called for in each model. The various suggested sequences are, therefore, viewed as strategic guidelines that aim us in approximately the right direction. They are analogous to the variety of directions a traveler may receive by asking several people along the way how to get to a particular destination. Presuming none of the directions received is misleading, our traveler will find some of them clearer, more specific and complete, or more veritable than others to the traveler's experiences while en route to the particular destination.

TAKING ANOTHER LOOK AT PROBLEM SOLVING

Intuitively and through our daily experiences, we know that such linear or cyclical procedures are artificial and contrived. When faced with an unwanted or

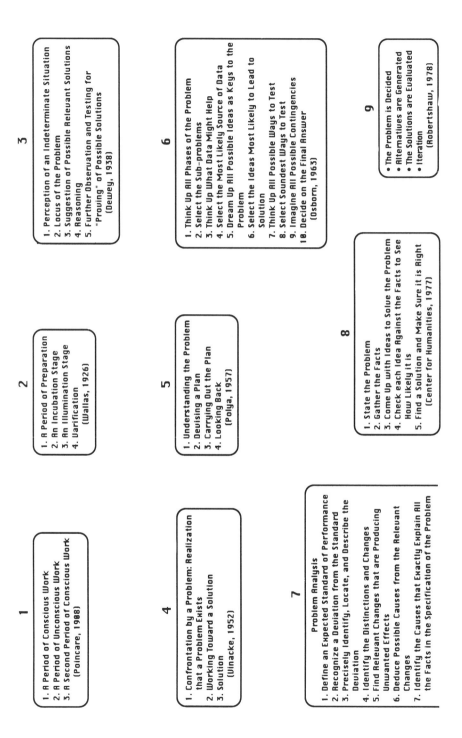

1

1. A Period of Conscious Work
2. A Period of Unconscious Work
3. A Second Period of Conscious Work
   (Poincaré, 1908)

2

1. A Period of Preparation
2. An Incubation Stage
3. An Illumination Stage
4. Varification
   (Wallas, 1926)

3

1. Perception of an Indeterminate Situation
2. Locus of the Problem
3. Suggestion of Possible Relevant Solutions
4. Reasoning
5. Further Observation and Testing for "Proving" of Possible Solutions
   (Dewey, 1938)

4

1. Confrontation by a Problem: Realization that a Problem Exists
2. Working Toward a Solution
3. Solution
   (Vinacke, 1952)

5

1. Understanding the Problem
2. Devising a Plan
3. Carrying Out the Plan
4. Looking Back
   (Polya, 1957)

6

1. Think Up All Phases of the Problem
2. Select the Sub-problems
3. Think Up What Data Might Help
4. Select the Most Likely Source of Data
5. Dream Up All Possible Ideas as Keys to the Problem
6. Select the Ideas Most Likely to Lead to Solution
7. Think Up All Possible Ways to Test
8. Select Soundest Ways to Test
9. Imagine All Possible Contingencies
10. Decide on the Final Answer
    (Osborn, 1963)

7

Problem Analysis

1. Define an Expected Standard of Performance
2. Recognize a Deviation from the Standard
3. Precisely Identify, Locate, and Describe the Deviation
4. Identify the Distinctions and Changes
5. Find Relevant Changes that are Producing Unwanted Effects
6. Deduce Possible Causes from the Relevant Changes
7. Identify the Causes that Exactly Explain All the Facts in the Specification of the Problem

8

1. State the Problem
2. Gather the Facts
3. Come Up with Ideas to Solve the Problem
4. Check each Idea Against the Facts to See How Likely it is
5. Find a Solution and Make Sure it is Right
   (Center for Humanities, 1977)

9

- The Problem is Decided
- Alternatives are Generated
- The Solutions are Evaluated
- Iteration
  (Robertshaw, 1978)

11

1. Finding the Problem
2. Represnting the Problem
3. Planning the Solution
4. Carrying Out the Plan
5. Evaluating the Solution
6. Consolidating Gains

(Hayes, 1981)

10

1. Problem Awareness. Detection
2. Problem Diagnsis
3. Define Decision Objectives
4. Design Alternative Actions
5. Predict Consequences of Actions
6. Judge Alternative Solutions
7. Acceptable Solution-Pre-implementation
8. Implement Action
9. Monitor Goal(s) Attainment
10. Goals Attained; or ...
11. Corrective Actions or Recycle Problem

(Brightman, 1988)

Decision Analysis

1. Establish the Objectives of the Decision
2. Classify the Objectives as to Importance
3. Develop Alternative Actions
4. Evaluate Alternatives Against Established Objectives
5. Tentatively Choose the Best Alternative
6. Explore Tentative Decision for Future Possible Adverse Consequences
7. Control Effects of the Final Decision by Taking Actions to Prevent Possible Adverse Consequences and by Making Sure Actions Decided on are Carried Out

(Kepner/Tregoe, 1965)

12

1. Define the Problem
2. Define the Objectives
3. Generate Alternatives
4. Develop Action Plan
5. Troubleshoot
6. Communicate
7. Implement

(Lyles, 1982)

13

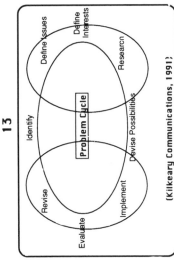

(Kilkeary Communications, 1991)

FIG. 12.1. Problem-solving sequences: 1908–1991.

perplexing state of affairs, few individuals, if any, think in an assembly-line, step-by-step manner or even in an orderly cyclical fashion. Further, no two people follow any given procedure in precisely the same manner or take the same problem-solving approach in similar situations the same way twice. People often overlap steps, double back, repeat an operation, and generally improvise along the way in a manner that can more accurately be described as nonlinear. Any number of more or less successful variations is, therefore, possible within any suggested problem-solving sequence. One could almost claim that there are as many problem-solving procedures as there are problem solvers or problem-solving situations.

A recognition of the discrepancy between academic renditions of problem solving and everyday manifestations of the same phenomenon was articulated, in a moment of some frustration, by a colleague who, in the middle of a class in which he was presenting his own theory of thinking, exclaimed, "Why do we keep devising schemes like these when nobody thinks that way?!" I believe this discrepancy tells us something. It is imperative and timely that we take another look at the working of the human mind and its activity during the problem-solving process, especially in light of the progress that has been made in chaos theory and nonlinear dynamics, the neural sciences, and fractal geometry (fractals are a recently discovered geometric form and mathematical modeling process that can describe and analyze the structured irregularity of nature (Mandelbrot, 1982).

CHAOS AND THE MIND

In all fairness, a limited number of existing models hint at recognition of non-linear activity during problem-solving activity. However, these are often so vague and inexplicable as to leave the problem solver to his or her own devices about how to do what the model calls for (e.g., Poincaré, 1908; Wallas, 1926; Fig. 12.1, sequences 1 & 2). Osborn's (1963) model (Fig. 12.1, sequence 6) is more explicit and explicable. It alternates linear and nonlinear activities. Its odd-numbered steps are divergent and nonlinear, while the even numbered steps are more convergent and linear. Although this is an interesting combination of linear and nonlinear modes of organization, the overall nonlinear structure of the model suffers because of its aspiration to come up with a final answer. The Kilkeary Communications' "Problem Cycle" (fig. 12.1, sequence 13) is appealing in that it provides for recycling of steps at various points along an overall problem-solving cycle (cycles within cycles, if you will). It is, thus, more vigorous than most other models and can serve as a closer approximation of the starts and stops, interruptions, and doubling back of everyday problem solving. Its cyclical nature, however, does not fully explain processes resemble the structurally irregular form of a random fractal (later, I argue that, as a chaotic dynamical system, such is the nature of the mind's problem-solving behavior. It is represented schematically in Fig. 12.2 & 12.3).

It is also important to acknowledge that Köhler (1925) and other Gestalt psychologists sought more natural problem-solving processes to study. Many of them criticized Thorndike on the unnaturalness of the behavior called for in his problem-solving tasks. Likewise, contemporary cognitive psychologists often

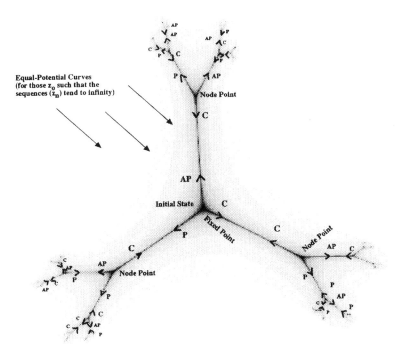

FIG. 12.2. Chaotic dynamics of the triadic theory of mental functioning. Cognitive, affective/perceptive, and pragmatic mental processes interact in ways that are concerted (activation), antagonistic (restraint), and reconciliatory (integration). Computer image generated by Yunping Jiang (CUNY/Queens College). Take formula: $z_n = z^2_{n-1} + b\bar{z}_{n-1} + c$ in which $b = 1 + .2i$ and $c > 0$ are complex parameters and z_n, z_{n-1} are complex numbers. For a complex number z_0, we have a sequence $\{z_n\}$, where $z_n = z^2_{n-1} + b\bar{z}_{n-1} + c$. Consider those z_0 in the complex plane such that $\{z_n\}$, are bounded. The set of those z_0 forms a triadic figure for parameters above $c = 0$, $b = 1 + .2i$. At each node point of the figure there are three choices: one is "C" (Cognitive); another is "AP" (Affective–Perceptive); and the third is "P" (Pragmatic). Then they form a random walk (with appropriate weights) on this triadic figure. By math theory, we know the limit set of this triadic figure will be the result of the experiment. But this limit set is a fractal set.

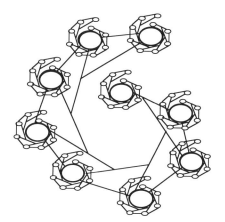

FIG. 12.3. The dynamical problem-solving model. The iterative self-similar nature of the problem-solving process is nonlinear and can occur in any order or sequence.

follow in the footsteps of the Gestaltists, applying dynamical approaches to their analyses. For example, the idea that mental functions are regulated by the laws of chaos is receiving strong support (Garfinkel, 1983; Gregson, Campbell, & Gates, 1992; and others). Researchers in this area posit that chaos not only serves as a useful framework for viewing the brain, but that chaos is perhaps the best model for comprehending the brain's functioning.

Applying dynamical principles to human mental functioning, Mandell (1980) claimed that we all oscillate between two brain stages. One stage is laminar, consisting of a smooth predictable flow of activity that can be described by fixed point or periodic attractors—pictures in space of the long-term behavior that a system settles down to (in this case, a single point or a closed-end loop, respectively). The other stage is an unpredictable, turbulent or chaotic diffusion of activity that can be described by a chaotic attractor (a picture of a system's unpredictable behavior that is nonetheless bound within definite parameters). In an interview with Hooper and Teresi, Mandell (1980, p. 373) claims that, from this perspective, the dynamics of the two hemispheres of the brain become evident. "The left brain is laminar, orderly. It gets home by saying, 'two blocks left, one block right, six blocks north.' The right brain just gets home by the geometry. It's a disorganized flow, a strange attractor."

One might further hypothesize that the brain needs to be chaotic in order to perform the problem-solving function for which it was designed. In other words, that the brain searches for the best solution to a problem through a unique combination of order and randomness that optimizes the scope of that search. Through such chaotic dynamics, problem-solving efforts can evolve into novelty and creativity or into abnormal ideas and emotions such as arrhythmic behavior and pathology.

In nature, randomness often results in irregular shapes and patterns and non-linearity in a system's behavior (and in its corresponding mathematical data).

Yet, such irregularities contain information. As a result of such information, this cacophony of irregular shapes and patterns can self-organize and create more complex patterns. The heating up of a fluid past a critical value (temperature) presents an excellent example of how this self-organizing phenomenon occurs. As the heat drives molecular activity to the critical level, millions of individual molecules organize themselves into hexagonal cells, as if they were being arranged by some unperceived force. Thus, the interaction among these various elements results in new relations, shapes, and patterns that respond more effectively to the demands of the situation and may produce purposeful outcomes (steam pressure for cooking or driving a locomotive). However, depending on the particular liquid (water or gasoline), if environmental conditions, the state of the system, or some other variables are not suitable to the task, the results could be disastrous (a scorching or an explosion).

Mental activity follows a similar pattern of behavior. When the thoughts or desires that activate us toward specific goals or directions are countered by barriers that hold us back from these goals or directions, tension, stress, frustration, and instability arise in our mental functioning. If unresolved, the situation heats up. These tensions, stresses, frustrations, and instabilities increase and can, if well orchestrated, serve to pull together essential elements of the forces that activate us with those of the forces that restrain us. In so doing, this type of interaction can, on the one hand, coordinate the organizing of the creative processes that give birth to new ideas, new knowledge, the emergence of new patterns of interaction or forms of organization, and so on. On the other hand, however, if the strength of the stresses or pressures are beyond the particular capabilities of the given individual, instead of creativity and innovation, the result could be disorientation, loss of cadence, or even pathology.

In brief, the new intuitions created by the dynamical sciences provide us with at least two major contributions for understanding how we think and solve problems. First, the brain appears to be regulated by the laws of chaos. Our individual and collective experiences and intuitions support this perspective, amply and consistently. One need only observe the sequence of thoughts that stream through our minds within a 30-second period. There seems to be no apparent string holding together all these pearls, nor do they seem to follow in any linear or cyclical order or pattern. Gregson, Campbell, and Gates' (1992) work with EEG data also demonstrates that problem-solving activity can increase the complexity of dynamical behavior. With a subject at rest, brain activity displays the smooth flow of a low-dimensional chaotic attractor. Increasing the complexity of a mental task increased the dimensionality of the EEG, indicating that it became more complex and chaotic.

Second, novelty and creativity are natural consequences of the chaotic dynamics of human mental functioning, and it is the orchestrating of these chaotic dynamics that shepherds problem-solving activity. We are led to think of mental functioning as an integrated process of processes and interactions. Thus, the success, or lack thereof, of our efforts to deal with unwanted situations depends sensitively on how well we orchestrate these dynamics toward novelty and creativity. Implicitly then, the above intuitions call attention to our need to reconceptualize the dynamics of problem solving and its inherent tasks.

The following section present a dynamical model of problem solving within the framework of the theory upon which it is based: the triadic theory of mental functioning.

THE TRIADIC THEORY OF MENTAL FUNCTIONING— A MODEL FOR DYNAMICAL PROBLEM SOLVING

Expanding on Bruner's (1986) observations of psychology's treatment of mind, we find that, historically, many psychological approaches to thinking, human intelligence, problem solving, and other functions of the mind have drawn formidable conceptual lines of demarcation among thought, emotion, and action. These same approaches often find themselves tunneling and trestling conceptually to reattach what is inherently inseparable. Instead of pursuing more useful explanations of reasoned thought, unreasoned or affective thought or emotion, and of the mental capabilities and processes necessary for doing, such approaches concentrated increasingly on formulating more exact principles of logical reasoning. Consequently and regrettably, any possible convergence among thought, emotion, and action is greatly reduced or, more commonly, approached in a piecemeal and fragmented manner.

The triadic theory of mental functioning, by contrast, includes the affective perceptive and action (pragmatic) domains within the realm of thinking and problem solving (see Torre, 1984, 1987, 1989, 1994). It suggests that the working of the mind and its various functions such as thinking, problem solving, creativity, and innovation emerge out of the interwoven chaotic interaction among cognitive, affective perceptive, and pragmatic mental processes. These mental processes behave as a team in a massive parallel manner rather than being sequential or occurring in isolation. Through their interaction, any one of the mental processes can activate us to move toward a particular goal or direction, restrain us from moving toward that goal or direction, or help us to reconcile unwanted situations through the integration of the opposing forces of activation and restraint. As such, the triadic theory suggests a model for problem solving that I believe is more concordant with our common experiences than are traditional models.

THE PROCESSES OF MENTAL FUNCTIONING

Thinking and problem solving involve a constant and inseparable flow of interaction among cognitive, affective-perceptive, and pragmatic mental processes (see

Fig. 12.2). Each process is associated with its own way of knowing and verifying what is learned.

Cognitive processes are analytic, linear, and rational. They represent the modes of thinking associated with the scientific method and with academic knowledge and skills. Knowledge is acquired through intervention (experiment, manipulation), observation, the application of logic and by reducing the whole to its parts. characteristically, these processes approach goal attainment through the designing of sequential step-by-step procedures. Before one actually feels that a particular object is understood, one may need to manipulate the various parts of the whole so as to consider them from different angles and be able to reassemble them again (Torre, 1987). The aim is to discover of what an object under consideration is composed, and how its parts relate to each other. To verify the validity of information or of what has been learned, cognitive processes call for the establishment of formal empirical proof. These are often preoccupied with such epistemological questions as, "how to know truth?" The aim of these processes is to conceptualize, categorize, idealize, and instantiate in an effort to formulate a system for explanation and description.

Cognitive problem-solving processes subsume three tasks: (a) statement of the problem—specifying purpose, goals, and objective in approaching the particular situation; (b) information gathering—selecting sources of information, gathering, classifying, and storing information, and assessing the quality and type of information gathered; and (c) diagnosis—analyzing and synthesizing information.

Affective-perceptive processes bring about emotional thinking (love, hate, fear, insecurity, doubt), as well as perceptivity (intuition, feelings, hunches, and keen insight). Through these processes we are able us to discern what can be considered intangible knowledge flowing from imperceptible sources of information. This unmediated awareness of truth may also arise when one places the object of consideration in context. Doing so allows us to appreciate the larger background of which the object is part. Following this way of thinking to its logical conclusion, we would want to comprehend the context of the context and so forth. To verify, the affective-perceptive processes require probability and likelihood—that is, verisimilitude. These processes are concerned more with how to endow experience with meaning.

For problem solving, the three main tasks of the affective-perceptive processes are: (a) prognosis—forecasting probable future courses or trajectories of the problem if nothing is done about it; (b) generation of solutions—proliferation of ways to deal with the unwanted situation; and (c) decision making—selecting what appear to be optimal responses to the unwanted situation.

Pragmatic processes constitute experiential, observational, and tacit modes of thought and learning. These processes entail understanding the utilitarian nature of the object or situation under consideration. That is to say, "For what can it be used?" "What can be achieved by dealing well with this situation?" "What's in it for me/us?" And so on. Pragmatic processes also involve the development of aptitude and capabilities (reading, writing, playing baseball, negotiation, or riding a bicycle). Such proficiencies can neither be taught solely through lectures nor written about in ways that the learner can develop mastery merely through reading or discussion—although attempts to do just this are constantly being made through how-to manuals.

Pragmatic processes require hands-on or indirect means of teaching and learning, such as rehearsal, orientation, and mentorship. Often, exposure to certain lifestyles or ways of doing something can implicitly and subconsciously fosters particular attitudes and behaviors. For a person raised in an academically inclined family, for example, or in a poverty-stricken ghetto, the chances are that one would not feel alien in a university or in a slum, respectively, and would probably be able to manage or orient oneself adequately in the given environment. Similarly, observation of those who have mastered a particular ability can be essential in one's own development. Learning to dance, not be taking formal lessons, but by observing others and eventually joining in, is a good example.

TO VERIFY, PRAGMATIC PROCESSES REQUIRE CONCRETE RESULTS AND EVALUATION OF THE DESIRABILITY OF OBTAINED OUTCOMES

In problem solving, pragmatic processes involve three kinds of tasks: (a) planning—delineation of desired outcomes, description of the process or procedures necessary for obtaining the desired outcomes, and stipulation of the capabilities required of the problem solver to undertake the described process or procedures successfully; (b) implementation—performance of tasks specified in the planning task; and (c) evaluation—consideration of feedback about how effectively one's problem solving efforts have addressed the issues involved or generated desired outcomes.

Cognitive, affective-perceptive, and pragmatic mental processes can each be used to convey and acquire knowledge (teach and learn), persuade others, inspire, and so on. However, what each helps you to teach or learn and what each persuades or inspires others to do is substantially different.

Cognitive processes can be used to teach and help one learn concepts and ideas, while persuading one of the truth of the arguments they help to establish. These deal with the establishment of general causes, consistency, and noncontradiction. Cognitive processes are facilitated by a variety of available tools, such as mathematics, science, logic, and others. They go from the particular to the general by continually increasing the level of abstraction.

Affective-perceptive processes can help one teach and learn of connections and similarities among things, awareness, and wisdom, while persuading of the possible-ness of the analogies, stories, creative solutions, or of the approaches and feelings they generate. These processes deal with the particulars of human experience (individual stores and anecdotes).

Pragmatic mental processes help one teach and learn skills, proficiencies, and dexterities, develop capabilities, acquire experiences and exposure, and so on while convincing one of the practicality of the proposed plans or procedures.

Because of these various ways of knowing, we experience the world in different ways and from different beliefs and points of view. We often place more credibility on one or another of these ways of knowing at the cost of others. For example (and for stereotyping), the sciences emphasize cognitive, logical, linear mental processes. The arts value affective-perceptive processes as sources of inspiration and creativity. Business invests heavily on the bottom-line approach of pragmatic processes.

The fractured symmetries of these various stances often bring about opposition, contradiction, or some other form of conflict that destablizes our mental functioning and creates the need to reconcile apparent opposites. Yet, in our daily experiences, the cognitive, affective-perceptive, and pragmatic ways of knowing come together to form what we perceive as reality. Thus, I suggest that a given situation may call for a heavier dose of one or more of the mental processes discussed here and that such distinction is often useful or even necessary. However, it is through the interaction of all three processes (cognitive; affective perceptive; and pragmatic) that transition, change, and good problem solving take place and that the working of the human mind can best be understood and optimized. For this reason, any reconceptualization of the problem solving process needs to subsume the activity of these three mental processes.

FORMS OF INTERACTION AMONG THE MENTAL PROCESSES

Cognitive, affective-perceptive, and pragmatic mental processes interact among themselves in three major ways: activation, restraint, and integration. In essence, two opposing forces (activation and restrain) are brought together into a working relationship by a third, reconciling force (integration). This relationship is analogous to one in which a fulcrum creates a relationship between the two ends of a wooden plank.

More specifically, activation is the kind of interaction among mental processes that induces motivation of thought and behavior toward a specific goal or direction. For example, when a young child is unable to walk as a result of a car accident, a social work student develops a deep (affective-perceptive) desire to raise the quarter of a million dollars necessary to pay for an operation that would allow her to walk again.

Restraint counteracts activation by holding one back from goal attainment (this is what creates the problem in the first place). In this manner, restraint can provide the stress or instability necessary to take us away from our stable but often stagnant ways of thinking or from our habitual patterns (attractors) of mental functioning. This type of instability is useful because systems (minds, people) are more amenable to change during such unstable transitionary states (Guess & Sailor, in press; Torre, 1994). Problem solving, then, is usually more successful when it is undertaken during transitions (bifurcations) between the strong attractors created by our ingrained or habitual ways of thinking. In our example, the social work student's practical (pragmatic) friends advise him that his goal is unrealistic in their town of only 125,000 mostly poor, adult inhabitants.

Integration can orchestrate activation and restrain into a working relationship through the reconciliation of their opposing forces. It can shift or perturb the problem solver's thinking toward mental transitions (bifurcation points) that can generate creative thinking and innovation (Torre, 1994). In this manner, integration processes can avert potential gridlock. In the example, again, our social work student decides that, before giving up his dream, he wants to do some calculations (cognitive). In the process he realizes that if every adult in the town was asked to contribute at least $4 toward this cause, even if only approximately 50% of them do so, the goal of a quarter of a million dollars could be closely approximated, met, or even surpassed.

However, if attempts to integrate the opposing forces of activation and restraint are not up to the task (misunderstanding of the problem; inadequate skills for coping with the given situation), problem solvers can be overwhelmed by the instabilities created by the forces holding them back. Their thinking can be incited toward higher-dimensional, more disordered chaos (Torre, 1984). Under such levels of stress, the range of things on which problem solvers can focus narrows considerably. Their intake of environmental cues that might help to orient them better to the issues at hand is reduced greatly, rendering them ineffective. Thus, insurmountable restraints without adequate integration, can turn into personal frustration or disorientation, apathy, blunder, oversight, wasted labor, or incapacitating pathology. Our student could have surrendered to the pragmatic realities of the situation, kept on hammering away at the situation without a plan or much hope of beating the odds, worked himself into a fanatic frenzy (and possibly into a psychiatric ward), or abandoned his future career in social work feeling that things are such that nothing can be done about the situations addressed by the profession.

A useful analogy for visualizing how cognitive, affective-perceptive, and pragmatic mental processes interact among themselves is offered by the interaction of a sailboat with wind and sea. The wind activates the boat (moves it in a particular direction), the sea's friction, the boat's inertia, and so on, restrain it (they resist the wind's efforts to move the boat), and the combination of rudder, movable sail, and helmsman can be employed to reconcile (integrate) these opposing forces into productive movement in a desired direction or toward a desired goal.

The interaction among cognitive, affective-perceptive, and pragmatic processes runs the gamut of behavior. It can range from static (fixed point) to cyclical (periodic), to chaotic attractors and may involve several bifurcation sequences. Any one of these mental processes can be in complementary opposition (restraint vs. activation or vice versa) to either of the remaining two. Likewise, any one of them can play the role of mediator (integration) between the other two.

DYNAMICAL PROBLEM SOLVING—A MODEL

In order to unfold, from the triadic theory, a dynamical model for understanding problem solving, we need to articulate the problem-solving tasks implicit in each of the theory's three mental processes (cognitive, affective perceptive, and pragmatic). As discussed previously, each of these three mental processes suggests three problem solving tasks. Integrating these three sets of tasks results in a nine-task model (three tasks in each set) of the problem-solving process: the dynamical problem solving model. This dynamical model encompasses statement of the problem, information gathering, diagnosis, prognosis, generating of solutions, decision making, planning, implementation, and evaluation.

These nine tasks may be seen as regions in an interactive state space. The paths of problem solving do not necessarily occur in a fixed linear order. They occur as a random walk with the purpose of bringing about the particular aim of the broader task of which it is part. For example, in order to state the problem, one may have to gather information about it or diagnose the information one already has. Therefore, a problem solver may visit any of these nine regions in a multiplicity of sequences. Driven by their dynamics, the trajectories wander as the three basic mental processes ebb and flow. Figure 12.3 depicts graphically how this complex behavior can take place. It is a simplified sketch of the numerous trajectories that might occur among the nine problem solving tasks in one iteration of the dynamical model.

As implied, the tasks of this model are recursive or iterative, that is, that each task is related by feedback processes to every other task in the model. Thus, each task, in and of itself, poses a problem: "What is this situation in which I find myself?"; "What specific information will help me understand this situation?"; "Where is it going if nothing is done about it?"; and so on. Accomplishing the aim of each task, therefore, may involve the application of any of the eight remaining problem-solving tasks. Moreover, if we were to magnify any of the tasks of our dynamical model, each would be, roughly, a tiny copy of the entire model. If we were to magnify further any part of this tiny copy, it would again turn out to be an even smaller reproduction of the entire model. The model is, therefore, fractal. Further, when seen in Lorenz's cross-section, our dynamical model is typical of low-dimensional chaotic attractors. Thus, the dynamical problem-solving model posits that thinking and problem solving are low-dimensional chaotic mental processes that, over time, take the form of a random fractal. Further, it holds that thinking and problem solving are fractal in nature because the structured irregularity of their processes and interactions exhibit statistically self-similar structure on all scales.

The fractal nature of the model provides a new visual language in which to describe the shape of the wide range of dynamical and chaotic behaviors characteristic of the human mind and its problem-solving processes. If translated into narrative, such a geometric description of the problem-solving process might resemble Ian Stewart's (1989, p.146) account of how progress is often made in mathematics.

A mathematician working on a problem will mess around with simple examples until he decides he's in a rut, and then he'll switch to a more general point of view and worry about that for a while, and then he'll go back to a slightly different set of examples and ask slightly different questions. Then he'll badger all other mathematicians within earshot. He'll telephone colleagues from Knoxville to Omsk. If he gets really stuck, he'll go off and do something else: tackle another problem, change the oil in the car, build a fish pond, climb a mountain. And, often at the least appropriate moment, inspiration will strike. It seldom solves everything, but it keeps the process going.

EDUCATIONAL IMPLICATIONS OF THE MODEL

Of all purposeful mental functions, problem solving is perhaps the one that we engage in from (at least) the moment of birth until the moment of death. A baby's first cry is an attempt to solve a problem: discomfort, hunger, and so on. Similarly, during their last moments of life, many people strive to achieve inner peace or to triumph over death. How well we deal with such unwanted situations underlies our degree of success in a given instance as well as our degree of life satisfaction as measured by the progressive realization of goals we deem important.

On a global scale today, as so often in the past, we find ourselves in a time of unprecedented human and societal conflict: from a world-wide resurgence of racism and ethnocentrism to a gradual yet wholesale depletion of our planet's life-support systems. The difference is that today our level of technology is such that we can now destroy civilization.

Presumably, if we can learn how the mind is structured to solve problems we can improve the ability to achieve more meaningful outcomes for ourselves and for others and avert human catastrophes by learning to act on that knowledge. Yet, as mentioned earlier, most of us perform poorly and experience great difficulty when it comes to solving problems. Additionally, most present models envision problems as static and the search for solutions as linear or cyclical procedures that most people recognize as unnatural. The urgency for problem-solving models that are more concordant with our experiences is, thus, under-scored.

We need to understand our problem-solving nature and teach it to our children in the early years of their education. Analogous to learning a second language, unaccented problem solving is best developed early. Without such orientation, students begin to develop fragmented strategies for coping with (more like mud-dling through) difficult or unwanted situations. Over time, these strategies may develop into strong and stable, though often maladaptive, behavior patterns (attractors) that are increasingly more difficult to transition (bifurcate) out of.

Continuing our second-language metaphor, some individuals seem to pick up languages by osmosis. Similarly, a small percentage of students develop ade-quate ways of approaching unwanted situations through seemingly effortless, unconscious absorption of ideas and influences from apparently trivial contacts with good problem solvers. Unfortunately, most students will not do so. If not oriented at an early age, by the time these unsuccessful problem solvers get to college (if they don't drop out along the way), their undeveloped savoir faire is usually no match for the level of academic demands placed on them by higher education. They develop fears and insecurities of being unable to cope or of being discovered as scholastically deficient. These fears and insecurities, in turn, create emotional restraints that result in stable, yet, maladaptive coping-behavior patterns (stable attractors). Consequently, educators then need to mitigate these emotional restraints before being able to help students improve their learning strategies. Such mitigation can perturb the stable coping-behavior patterns, cre-ated by students' fears and insecurities, toward less stable transitionary states (phase shifts) that are more responsive to change as a result of intervention (Torre, 1994). Nonetheless, while some of our students' ineffective or fragmen-tary problem-solivng behavior patterns can be redirected later in life, it is usually at a very high cost. Thus, it would seem advisable to minimize the need to deal with this ineffective behavior by starting to teach about the nature of human problem solving during the earliest years of education.

In this regard, the proposed dynamical problem-solving model is a useful way of conceptualizing the thinking and problem-solving processes. My expectation is that this model can provide enough understanding of how people solve prob-lems to encourage us to change our educational practices in ways that more conducively attend to the fundamental issues we need to address in today's intricately interdependent world.

Although no theory, dynamical or otherwise, can solve everything or do full justice to the complex working of the human mind, the proposed model can facilitate understanding of the nonlinear interaction among mental processes during thinking and problem-solving activity. It can also serve as an heuristic stimulus for encouraging and nurturing the optimal functioning of cognitive, affective-perceptive, and pragmatic mental processes toward creative and inte-grative thinking and away from thinking that fosters artificial dichotomies and conflict in problem resolution. In other words, it can facilitate understanding of how the solutions to an undesirable situation can be found, implicitly, within the situation itself.

If the various processes of the mind are innately indivisible and function as a whole, it could follow that the genesis of thoughts, ideas, and problem solutions happens as an incalculable complexity of interaction or movement among mental processes. Orchestrating the essential elements of the issues and circumstances that activate us with those of the forces that restrain us might then allow us to see the solutions implicit in the situation itself. This is what Bohm (1980) referred to as the implicate order—the order of the whole implied in the interaction or motion of each component part (or in this case, of each mental process).

These perceptions urge us, as educators, to create learning environments that exploit the chaotic nature of thinking and problem solving by stimulating interaction among students' cognitive, affective-perceptive, and pragmatic mental processes. Problems can be raised with few, if any, contingencies or stipulations that a right answer exists and that it is to be found. Instead of minimizing or eliminating uncertainties so as to precipitate instruction, problems can be introduced with all inherent uncertainties (or as Shakespeare might say, "with warts and all"). To do otherwise usually results in the creation of further uncertainties and more problems than solutions. By contrast, Peter Senge's (1985) work with corporate executives concludes that systems thinking implies a reverence for uncertainty. He believes that this reverence marks the difference between creative visionaries and fanatics: "A fanatic looks for something that will stamp out uncertainty. The creative person acknowledges the uncertainty. That person says, 'Here is what I'd really like to see happen. I'm not sure it's possible, but I'd really be willing to stick my neck out for this'" (Briggs & Peat, 1989, p.200).

In a similar fashion, we need to trust our students' mental and group interactive processes. Through such techniques as cooperative learning, the considering of ambiguous or controversial issues, and others, we encourage students to freely and openly bring logic, feelings, intuition, and experience to bear on given situations. Resultant class discussions and activities may appear to be irregular disarrays of contributions on the part of students. Yet, over time, patterns of ideas, assertions, confrontations, and new questions become evident. It could be said that the overall interaction among learners in the classroom echoes the chaotic trajectories of the mental processes (Fig. 12.3; Stewart, 1989).

Education, then, becomes a juggling act. Educators would continually induce mental or group interactions that are balanced precariously enough to cause students to move away from their usual comfortable patterns of thinking (stable attractors) and toward less comfortable ones (unstable transitionary states near points of bifurcation). Simultaneously, teachers need to make sure that the instabilities at these transitionary states are not so great as to preclude a meaningful transition (bifurcation) to useful attractors, that is, toward patterns of behavior or thinking that allow groups or individuals to prevail beyond their present capabilities. Implicitly, this perspective sees teaching and learning as chaotic experiences. The specifics of what chaos in the classroom looks like, however, are beyond the scope of the present chapter and shall be the topic of a future work.

We are in the fledgling stages of understanding the dynamical nature of problem solving. Much work still remains to be done in this area; however, pioneering efforts in closely related fields can cast new light on old educational issues and help educators discover uncontrived ways to approach educational effectiveness. Gregson, Campbell, and Gates' (1992) previously mentioned dimensionality analyses of EEG data and Redington and Reidbord's use of heart rate data to chart the flow of thoughts and emotions experienced by people under psychotherapy might be good initial models. Through a similar use of EEG and EKG data, educators might be able to characterize the specific configurations of problem-solving strategies exhibited by students, along with the sequences or trajectories followed. In this manner, chaos theory could provide a rigorous mathematical foundation for education and problem solving.

In any case, the role of the teacher takes on new implications. Rather then being a mere imparter of knowledge, the teacher could, more importantly, perform as a midwife who assists students bring forth the birth of new knowledge through creativity and innovation. In this role, teachers might focus on the disparity between what students state as their purposes for addressing given problems and what they in fact accomplish or practice. These disparities can be seen as control parameters that influence the students' problem-solving effectiveness. It becomes clear, then, that a passive process of instruction is not adequate to stimulate self-motivation to create knowledge and upgrade academic capabilities because a linear process of education cannot generate new knowledge. New knowledge, creativity, and innovation emerge from the kind of mental and group flux discussed above. It means approaching problems from a "let's see what I can learn" mode instead of a "let's see how I can fix it" mode. Thus, students need to learn to recognize their own disparities as problem solvers through the use of feedback. As educators, we need to mediate their learning processes as they navigate their way around their own disparities, looking to find meaningful transition points; as they learn to create response diagrams to inform future action or directions to be taken; as they develop self-intervention techniques to get to transition points; and as they generate the will to pass through these transition points into the educational world beyond.

REFERENCES

Agre, G. P. (1983). What does it mean to solve problems? *Journal of Thought, 18,* 96.

Bohm, D. (1980). *Wholeness and the implicate order.* London: Routledge & Kegan Paul.

Briggs, J., & Peat, F. D. (1989). *Turbulent mirror.* New York: Harper & Row.

Brightman, H. J. (1980). *Problem solving: A logical and creative approach.* Atlanta: Georgia State University, College of Business Administration.

Bruner, J. (1986). *Actual minds, possible worlds.* Cambridge, MA: Harvard University Press.

Davis, G. A. (1973). *Psychology of problem solving: Theory and practice.* New York: Basic Books.

Garfinkel, A. (1983). A mathematics for physiology. *American Journal of Physiology, 245,* 455–466.

Gregson, A. M., Campbell, E. A., & Gates, G. R. (1992). Cognitive load as a determinant of the dimensionality of the electroencephalogram: A replication story. *Biological Psychology, 35,* 165–178.

Guess, D., & Sailor, W. (in press). Chaos theory and the study of human behavior: Implications for special education and developmental disabilities. *Journal of Special Education.*

Hayes, J. R. (1981). *The complete problem solver.* Philadelphia, PA: The Franklin Institute Press.

Hooper, J., & Teresi, D. (1986). *The three pound universe.* New York: Macmillan.

Köhler, W. (1925). *The mentality of apes.* New York: Harcourt Brace.

Lyles, R. I. (1982). *Practical management problem solving and decision making.* New York: Petrocelli Books.

Mandelbrot, B. (1982). *The fractal geometry of nature.* San Francisco: Freeman.

Mandell, A. J. (1980). Statistical stability in random brain processes: Possible implications for polydrug abuse in the borderline syndrome. In N. K. Mello, *Advances in substance abuse: Behavioral and biological research* (vol. 2). Greenwich, CT: JAI Press.

Naisbitt, J. (1982). *Megatrends: Ten new directions transforming our lives.* New York: Warner Books.

Osborn A. F. (1963). *Applied imagination: Principles and procedures of creative problem solving.* New York: Scribner's.

Poincaré, H. (1908). *La science et l'hypothese* [Science and hypothesis]. Paris: E. Flammarion.

Robertshaw, J. E., Mecca S. J. & Rerick M. N. (1978). *Problem solving: A systems approach.* New York: Petrocelli Books.

Seif, E. (1981). Thinking and education: A futures approach. *Journal of Thought. 16.*

Senge, P. M. (1985, July). *Systems dynamics, mental models, and the development of management intuition.* Paper presented at the International System dynamics Conference.

Stewart, I. (1989). *Does God play dice?: The mathematics of chaos.* Cambridge, MA: Basil Blackwell.

Torre, C. A. (1984, August). *Problem solving and decision making: An integration of cognitive, affective, and pragmatic operations.* Paper presented at the second biennial International Conference on Thinking, Harvard University, Cambridge, MA.

Torre, C. A. (1987, January). *Thinking, culture, and education.* Paper presented at the third biennial International Conference on Thinking, University of Hawaii at Manoa.

Torre, C. A. (1989). *El Proyecto Cayey: Una Investigación Sobre la Calidad del Pensamiento* [The Cayey Project: A study on the quality of thinking]. Cayey, PR: University of Puerto Rico.

Torre, C. A. (1994). Chaos in the triadic theory and problem solving: Implications for educational psychology. In A. Gilgen, & F. Abraham (Eds.), *Chaos theory in psychology.* Westport, CT: Greenwood.

Wallas, G. (1926). *The art of thought.* New York: Harcourt Brace.

Webster's third new international dictionary of the English language, Unabridged. (1961). Springfield, MA: Merriam.

13

Fractals and Path-Dependent Processes: A Theoretical Approach for Characterizing Emergency Medical Responses to Major Disasters

Gus Koehler

Since the late 1980s, I helped manage the California state government's medical disaster response. Disasters that I responded to include earthquakes, fires, civil disturbances, massive explosions, and hazardous materials spills, both liquid and gas. As a state manager, I was to reinforce the city and county emergency medical response in the field and at hospitals with personnel and supplies so that injuries could be rapidly stabilized.

Managing a state's medical response to a major medical disaster involves tracking the relationships between various dynamical processes over a wide area involving many cities and counties. The trick is to "see" what is happening during an event that has occurred at a random moment in time, which generates an unknown number of casualties in unknown locations, and with many local emergency medical systems (EMS) responding that have damaged components. Having "seen" this, the disaster manager tries to influence the development of the multicounty EMS disaster response system such that more lives are saved.

In what follows, I show that fractal and path-dependent theories are useful for understanding such events, derive hypothesis that may predict the optimal size and cost of an efficient EMS disaster response system, and propose methods for testing them.

THE EMERGENCY MEDICAL RESPONSE TO MEDICAL DISASTERS

Day-to-Day Emergency Medical Systems

An EMS is "a coordinated arrangement of resources (including personnel, equipment, and facilities) which are organized to respond to medical emergencies, regardless of cause" (American Society for Testing Materials, 1988). Typically, an EMS has the following components:

A public emergency telephone call system (9–1-1).

A dispatch center that receives calls from the public, tracks emergency field responders, and dispatches them.

Emergency medical field responders, such as paramedics.

Hospital Emergency Department(s) that the injured person is transported to.

Emergency communications system that ties all the components together.

An emergency medical system must be tightly coordinated to save lives. A failure in any one of the components can cause life-threatening delays.

Medical Disasters

A medical disaster occurs when the local EMS's normal triage standards, transport, transport, medical care, and local mutual aid resources are severely damaged and/or overwhelmed by victims. These conditions, which are developed more fully later, require substantial changes in the way emergency medical care is delivered. They raise the following fundamental questions:

Macrolevel: How do I perceive and understand the emergence of the emergency medical response structure relative to the progression of the forces causing the disaster? That is, is there a pattern that emerges over the entire affected geographical area, including the state's various emergency response systems that feed personnel and material into it, that can be anticipated and used to mange the response?

Microlevel: How does the emergence of dynamic microstructures, such as the fire service establishing localized emergency operation centers, hospitals organizing their internal response, distribution of patients, and rapid spontaneous emergence of response structure, effect the macropattern, and what can be done to improve or direct this dynamic so that the most efficient emergency medical response macrostructure emerges?

MACROSTRUCTURE: EMS PHASE TRANSITION
AND PERCOLATION FRACTALS

EMS Phase Transitions

There are two types of phase transitions: first order and second order (Waldrop, 1992). A first-order phase transition involves a sharp change from one physical state to another. An example is the rapid transformation of water to ice. The change is very abrupt and well defined. A second-order phase transition takes more time to accomplish and is less precise. Once the transition starts no clear-cut structure remains or immediately emerges, but there are lots of little structures coming into and going out of existence. Later, a new structure forms but only after an extended period of time. Langton described such a second-order phase transition as: "order and chaos intertwine in a complex, ever-changing dance of submicroscopic arms and fractal filaments. The largest ordered structures propagate their fingers across the material for arbitrarily long distances and last for arbitrarily long times" (Waldrop, 1992, p. 230)

I believe that EMS systems go through a second-order phase transition immediately following a major medical disaster. The EMS phase transition occurs at the moment when the day-to-day EMS is struck by a disaster and just before it self-organizes to form a new "disaster" EMS (or fails to do so) to care for the injured. Experience shows that this process of establishing a new EMS disaster structure is not orderly and may take many days to accomplish. For example, an EMS phase transition would probably follow a Richter magnitude 7.5 earthquake on the Hayward fault in the San Francisco East Bay area. A report by the California Division of Mines and Geology makes some sobering predictions (1987):

> Deaths resulting from this scenario earthquake are estimated to range from 1,500–4,500 depending upon the time and day of occurrence. Hospitalized casualties are estimated to be 3 times the number of deaths (4,500–13,500); significant non-hospitalized casualties are estimated at 30 times the number of deaths (45,000–135,000). Eight of the 26 acute care hospitals (99 beds or more) in Alameda and Contra Costa Counties are located within one mile of the Hayward fault. This represents a bed capacity of 2,300 of a total of 6,200 available in these major facilities (about 35%). Almost all buildings at these 8 sites were constructed prior to adoption of more stringent hospital building requirements in 1972.

The proximity of the hospitals, fire stations, communications system, and population to the Hayward fault leads to the prediction that major portions of the EMS will be destroyed or severely impacted. Field responders will be scattered all over the area trying to deal with the injured, fires, and other problems. It will be difficult to link field responders with each other, to hospitals, or to emergency response management systems. Studies of medical disasters, such as the Bhopal chemical disaster in India and major earthquakes show that standing or damaged health care facilities are inundated by those who are least injured first, followed by those who are more injured (Jacobs, 1983). The vast majority of thousands of earthquake victims will be rescued and waiting for care, or being cared for, within the first 24 to 72 hours of the event. Hospitals will probably continue to see a considerable number of casualties for an additional 6 days (De Vill de Goyet, del Cid, Romero, Jeannee, & Lechat, 1976), and may continue to perform earthquake-related operative procedures for 4 or 5 weeks after the event.

The death toll for an earthquake peaks about the same time that the majority of injured have been rescued. Clearly, the elements of the EMS resemble a second-order phase transition as they try to reorganize.

EMS Phase Transition, Chaos, and Fractals

When we examine the organizational dynamics of this self-organizing process, we are talking about chaos theory. The structural forms that a chaotic process leaves in its wake are fractals. In summary, chaos is the process; fractals are the resulting structure (Peitgen, Jurgens, & Saupe, 1993).

Fractals are geometric objects that demonstrate self-similarity across several size scales. For example, a cauliflower head contains branches or parts, which, when removed and compared with the whole, are very much the same, only smaller. These clusters can be broken up into even smaller clusters and they too will appear to be similar to the original cluster. This concept of self-similarity can be applied to a geographical area such as that occupied by a mountain range or river system. Pictures taken from space show self-similarity across several scales (see Plates 4 and 14 in Peitgen, Jurgens, & Saupe, 1993).

Viewed from the macroperspective of the multicounty of the entire disaster, we see a large number of local EMS responders and organizations all reading out toward, across, and around one another. I propose that, at a certain point, a percolation fractal emerges, integrating all these components. This fractal is the macrostructure that links all the local EMS responders and organizations together into an EMS disaster response system. The fractal is self-similar in so far as the local EMS structure resembles the entire multicity and multicounty response structure.

The EMS Phase Transition and the Generation of Errors

According to Feigenbaum, a series of ever increasing self-reinforcing errors carries an organized system over the edge of order into a phase transition and on to chaos (Feigenbaum, 1993). Analogously, a medical disaster destroys a substantial portion of the EMS's predictability. From the everyday perspective, the decisions and actions that are being made following a disaster are an ever increasing series of errors. It is at the phase transition/chaos boundary that decision "errors" accumulate at a high and self-reinforcing rate. The decisions are driven by the immediate need to organize and face conditions at that particular moment in a particular geographic place within the larger disaster area. An EMS second-order phase transition occurs when the number of self-reinforcing errors are so great that the components of the day-to-day EMS are no longer effectively integrated.

Percolation Fractal: The EMS Macrostructure

According to Peitgen, Jurgens, and Saupe (1992):

> When a structure changes from a collection of many disconnected parts into ba-
> sically one big conglomeration, we say that percolation occurs. The name stems
> from an interpretation of the solid parts of the structure as open pores. . .Let us
> pick one of the open pores at random and try to inject a fluid at that point. What
> happens? If the formation is below the percolation threshold. . .we expect that the
> pore is part of a relatively small cluster of open pores. . .Below the threshold we
> can only inject some finite amount of fluid until the cluster is filled but no more.
> (p. 464)

The "collection of parts" are all of the existing and emergent elements of the
EMS disaster response. The EMS components of the "finite cluster" that are
traced out by "injecting a fluid" are a combination of the following "pores" and
"connections." EMS pores are defined as:

All geographical concentrations of the injured.

All hospitals or field hospitals.

All city, county, state, and private emergency operations centers.

All city, county, state, and private communications centers.

All supply and staging areas.

All means hospitals, staging areas, and any other entity involved in the disaster response, both in the geographic area of the disaster and outside of it.

The connections that extend out from and connect to other EMS pores over
time are:

Paths traveled and the fire trucks, police cars, military vehicles, ambulances,
and citizens that are delivering the injured to field and fixed hospitals.

Paths traveled and the transport vehicles carrying personnel and supplies from
staging areas.

Radio and telephone communication paths.

If fluid was injected into the center of an EMS pore it would reveal communications paths and the road or air corridors being taken to deliver the injured,
supplies, and personnel. This local pattern is defined as an *EMS cluster.*

Immediately following the disaster, the pattern of EMS clusters that emerges
across the area of the disaster would probably be highly localized to discreet
pores and their immediate connections. As time goes by, more and more connections are made between EMS pores, such as hospitals and communications

centers, with emergency operations centers and staging areas. Ideally, nearly all the EMS clusters connect to each other and a percolation fractal emerges.

Percolation Threshold

We have already observed that, at the moment when one overall structure emerges from all of these disconnected parts, percolation occurs. This event is called the *percolation threshold*. Figure 13.1 shows four triangles that clarify what a percolation threshold is. Each triangle is subdivided into a large number of smaller triangles, some shaded and some not. Each subtriangle is colored black or not, according to a random event. This random event occurs with a prescribed probability of not being colored at all (0.0) to a virtual certainty of being colored (1). The overall shape and connectedness of the individual triangles depends dramatically on the probability chosen. When the probability of a triangle being colored is around 0.3 (30%) very few of the triangles are filled, in contrast to when it is closer to 1, say 0.7 (70%; Fig. 13.1). At a critical value, the percolation threshold, the number of triangles, and their interconnectedness seem to become glued together into one big irregular lump. Peitgen, Jurgens, and Saupe tell us that, "Right at the percolation threshold this maximal cluster is a fractal!" (p.465)

Returning to our problem, how close the EMS is to the percolation threshold is defined by the probability of an EMS cluster being connected to another EMS cluster (the interconnection of the little triangles in Fig. 13.1). This probability has been measured experimentally using a simulation of probablistically determined points (not for an EMS). It is approximately 0.5928 (Peitgen, Jurgens, & Saupe, 1993, p.466). This suggests that each cluster throughout the disaster area must have almost a 60% chance of being connected to another for a percolation fractal (EMS disaster response system) covering the entire area of the disaster to emerge. At the percolation threshold, the probability for establishing an EMS is high since the maximum interconnectedness of the entire disaster area is achieved, as demonstrated by the emergence of a percolation fractal.

FIG. 13.1. Probability and percolation fractal creation. Subtriangles are chosen with a probability *P*. In the first large triangle many small clusters coexist. In the last, one major cluster exists along with only a few smaller clusters. (Estimates from Peitgen, Jurgens, and Saupe, 1993, p. 463).

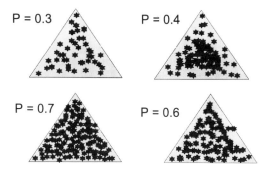

Mathematical simulations predict that this occurs very rapidly. The same studies predict, however, that the time it takes to get to this point will be longer for a large number of clusters, in fact exponentially longer, than the time it takes for a smaller number of clusters. For example, if it takes ten hours to reach the percolation point for a multicasualty incident with twenty clusters, it will take ten times as long for 100 clusters, and 100 times as long for 500 clusters (Peitgen et al., 1993, p. 466). I return to this point later.

MICROSTRUCTURE: EMS PORE- AND CONNECTION-BUILDING DYNAMICS

Our discussion has shown that the behavior of the underlying network and the emergence of a percolation fractal is determined almost entirely by the probability of connectedness of each pore, and of each EMS cluster with other EMS pores and EMS clusters. In this section I try to identify some major EMS factors that determine how an EMS pore develops and what determines its connection probability. The factors that account for this variation can be grouped into four categories:

1. Sensitivity to initial conditions.
2. Organizational structuration processes.
3. Time-delayed decision making.
4. Principal of increasing returns.

The first three factors define how an EMS pore evolves. The last one describes the connection process associated with reaching the percolation threshold. All four factors are interrelated; the rate at which the first set of factors change effects the last, which in turn feeds back to affect the first group.

Factors That Affect the Evolution of an EMS Pore

Sensitivity to Initial Conditions

How the day-to-day EMS is disrupted establishes the initial conditions that will govern the local self-organizing response (Jantsch, 1980). Many of these critical factors are listed in Table 13.1. Probably the most important are:

The distribution of the injured and their injuries.

The availability of communications equipment and transportation.

The physical condition of hospitals and emergency medical response equipment.

TABLE 13.1
Some Critical Factors Affecting EMS Rate of Response

Injuries in the Field:
—Rate of increase in number of injured expected
—Rate of casualties discovered
—Distribution of type of injuries (crush, gas, etc.)
—Waiting for evacuation/rate of evacuation

Rate of County/Community Response:
—Use of supplies
—Worker fatigue
—Number of hospital beds available
—Surgery rate
—Capacity and number of Casualty Collection Points (CCP)
—Food, water, fuel available
—Number at CCPs and hospitals waiting for transport

Rate of State Response in Disaster Area:
—Cot and bed capacity of airports
—Medical personnel at airports
—Supply arrival, management, and deliver
—Food, water, fuel
—Number waiting for transport/rate of transport

Rate of State/Federal Response Outside of Disaster Area:
—Hospital bed availability and transport time
—Supply identification, acquisition, warehousing and
   packaging
—Volunteer recruitment and processing
—Food, water, fuel identification, warehousing and
   packaging

Responders make decisions—or "errors"—based on the initial state these factors occupy following a disaster. This produces an ever increasing decision-making error rate leading the response over the day-to-day EMS organizational edge into a phase transition and on to chaos. These distinctions also establish the new EMS pores that may eventually aggregate into an EMS percolation fractal.

The Injured.   First, the rate at which the medical disaster itself unfolds depends on continuation of the mechanism of injury (after shocks, continuous release of a poisonous gas), the rate at which victims are being rescued, their injuries (crushing versus gas inhalation, for example), and the type of medical care required. The dynamical relationships of the conditions drive the response elements.

Unusual oscillatory relationships between injury groups may emerge due to the maldistribution or lack of medical resources. Individuals with life-threatening injuries may compete with less injured people, both represented by friends and relatives or directly with each other for care. The epidemiologist, May (1984), speaking about infectious diseases, noted that "it is widely accepted that non-seasonable fluctuations arise as a consequence of the dynamical interactions between two or more populations whether they be host and parasite, predator and prey, plant and herbivore, indeed any of these combinations" (p. 587). The differential rates at which the most injured and less injured arrive at a Casualty Collection Point or hospital could create such oscillations.

If there is unimpeded access to care the least injured get the most care. They quickly overload available resources and the more injured die from long waiting times. On the other hand, if care is restricted to the most injured, which is very personnel and supply intensive, the result may be fewer deaths but more morbidity. Thus, unusual oscillatory behavior in mortality/morbidity statistics could result from triage criteria, arrival rates and times of the two populations, and competition for scarce medical care.

Field Responders and Supplies.   A second group of rates is driven by how quickly responders can be mobilized, transported to where they are needed, fed, and be relieved by other staff. For example, following the start of the Los Angeles civil disturbance, fire fighters were able to quickly organize themselves but were delayed in getting into the field by a lack of law enforcement support. Once in the field, the logistical support structure for food, rest, and personal hygiene was terrible at best (Koehler, 1993). Thus, the rate that first responders become exhausted (24 hours is probably the maximum limit for most people) and can be replaced will have an important affect on the response. A third set of rates involves how quickly supplies are used relative to type of injury and the number requiring care. For example, inhalation injuries require different supplies than do crushing injuries. IV solutions must be available in large numbers. Again, oscillatory effects may result from the interaction of the availability of medical supplies, movement of medical personnel in and out of the area, and the rate that the injured arrive for care (Koehler, 1991).

Communications.   The ability of the managers to regulate the medical disaster response depends on availability and quality of communications. For example, the location, number of injured and their injuries must be effectively communicated to the county if personnel and supply needs are to be met. A runner would be quite slow and probably able to carry only relatively little updated information in contrast to digital radio communications. Thayer suspects that it is the blocking of communication and thus, the creation of nonequilibrium between critical response elements that leads to mutations and the emergence of new organizational forms (Thayer, 1972). I suspect that there is more to it than blocking communications; how timely and relevant the information is about how the disaster/response is going is equally important.

Following a disaster there is communications failure and information overload. For example:

Communications are not always quickly available where they are needed.

The day-to-day communications system is damaged, used for other purposes, or is overloaded with information.

It is often unclear who should receive a particular message or where they are located.

The volume of information is so high that it cannot be reduced in a timely and efficient manner into usable intelligence for decision making.

Transportation.   California state government exercises have shown that the availability of transport is a key variable that regulates how quickly the response system can be organized. Casualties will have to be moved from the site of their injury to emergency care field stations, hospitals, and evacuation areas. A significant percentage of the surface transportation in the disaster area, possibly more than half, will be carried out by the public. The remainder will require public and private agency assistance. Depending on the disaster, a very large number of casualties may have to be evacuated. For example, one plan calls for the evacuation of 60,000 casualties from seven counties in Southern California within 96 hours. Such an effort requires very rapid availability and proper configuration of a considerable number of CH-47 and UH-1 helicopters, and C5A and C-130 aircraft (see California Emergency Medical Services Authority, 1985, 1986, 1988, 1989, 1990). This evacuation rate, in turn, drives how quickly hospitals and other care centers use up their personnel and supplies.

The rate at which supplies are used must be matched by the combined rate of acquisition, volume, handling, and supply delivery systems (an estimated 700 tons of material will have to be acquired and moved to the disaster site within 72 hours for a major earthquake medical disaster).

Organizational Structuration

Organizational structuration is the second major factor that regulates EMS pore formation. Organizational structuration refers to the process that formal and informal organizations must go through to self-organize. The factors that regulate the speed of organizational structuration following a disaster are:

Spontaneous emergency of small-scale community organizations.

Forty-two different organizational structuration processes.

Different stress levels for each organization.

Spontaneous Emergence of Localized Small-Scale Community Organizations.   Immediately after a major disaster, many families and neighbors spontaneously organize themselves to rescue and care for victims. Within 30 minutes of a major disaster, 75% of the health survivors are actually engaged in efficient rescue operations (Drabek, 1986, p. 155). Sociologists have identified factors that influence emergent group formation:

Emergency demands exceed community capabilities.

Low interorganizational coordination of city and other day-to-day emergency resources.

Authority lapse.

Low community preparedness.

Lack of prior disaster experience.

Crises remains inadequately defined.

Local EMS field responders also begin to organize themselves. Typically, individual fire departments and ambulance companies assess the local damage and injuries and begin to act based on limited local information. Dispatching and interhospital communications are often spotty or overloaded. This limits the formation of response structures. If there had been a disaster exercise prior to the event, the established lines of authority don't break down. But, if authority is weak, it can completely disappear. Generally, the tendency is for overall authority not to be exercised (Drabek, 1986). In fact, old jurisdictional disputes between agencies may be exacerbated, as was the case in Los Angeles between the Los Angeles City Police Department and Los Angeles County Sheriffs Department (Webster, 1992).

Forty-Two Types of Organizational Structuration Process.   Established organizations such as hospitals and fire departments, are impacted in different ways by a disaster. Kreps and his colleges have demonstrated that any one of 42 different organizational types may emerge as these and emergent organizations self-organize (Kreps, 1989). This theory and its supporting empirical evidence is too extensive to review here. The point is that organizations will take a multitude of different paths as they go through their own structuration process depending on:

How they define their domains of authority.

Availability of resources.

When and how they initiate their activities.

How they organize their human resources.

Looking at the entire disaster area, many of the various EMS pores would be structurating differently.

Differential Stress Levels for Different Organizations.   Organizational stress can take different forms. Not all public and private organizations will experience the same level of stress. Those who respond to multicasualty events, such as fire and ambulance personnel, may experience less stress than health department personnel who have only conducted infrequent disaster drills.

Increased stress on organizations tends to increase the rate of decision making, particularly at lower levels. An emergency department nurse may make critical organizational decisions that, under normal circumstances, are made by the department chief. More autonomy and less coordinated decision making results in the rapid commitment of organizational personnel and resources. Such a commitment may be adaptive in the short run but lead to serious problems in the long run. For example, over commitment of staff quickly burns them out.

Delays Between Availability of Information, Decision Making, and Action

The third factor that regulate EMS pore formation is delays between when a decision is made and the time it is carried out. The basic premiss of time-delayed control theory, which addresses this phenomenon, is that the consequences of an action taken now tend to be delayed into the future (Waldrop, 1992). The process is analogous to trying to adjust the hot water in the shower. It takes a few moments for the effect of the adjustment to actually reach the spray hitting your skin.

Disaster management has similar problems. The delay between the availability of information, decision making, and the final action can take a number of forms. It can be:

Past time delayed: when decisions are made based on late information that is no longer accurate about what is going on in the field.

Future time delayed: the time between the making of the decision and the action being taken is delayed. For example, during the LA Civil Disturbance, Daniel Freeman Hospital was being overwhelmed by patients. The Lost Angeles EMS Agency directed ambulances to take the injured to St. Francis hospital. By the time the decision was fully implemented, Saint Francis Hospital was being overwhelmed (Koehler, 1993).

Policy lag: A decision is made based on assumptions about how a system of agreements that are no longer applicable (Kress, Koehler, & Springer, 1981). For example, it is assumed that the military will make airplanes and helicopters available for the disaster response; however, military base closures in the region may have removed all these resources.

These delays in turn affect the evacuation, supply, transportation, and other rates already identified. Delays in decision making can also create various unintended oscillations. Both increase the error rate driving the system even further into chaos.

Our brief discussion of organizational structuration shows that there will be considerable variation in how any one EMS pore connects. These dynamic variations are multidimensional and very hard to control.

Principle of Dependent Processes

Once an EMS pore begins to form it automatically reaches out for support. At the same time state, county, and city Emergency Operations Centers are reaching towards some of them. Brian Arthur's work helps understand this connecting up process.

Arthur developed the "principle of increasing returns" or path-dependent processes to account for the outcome of self-reinforcing structures that typically posses a multiplicity of possible outcomes (Arthur, Ermoliev, & Kaniovski, 1987). Basically, the theory holds that once a point begins to aggregate it is likely to aggregate further.

> What happens . . . where [business] firms' locational choices depend on part upon the numbers of firms in each region at the time of choosing? Here increments to the regions are not independent of previous locational choices... We now have a path-dependent process, where the probability...of an addition to a [particular region over another] becomes a function of the numbers of firms, or equivalently, of the proportions of the industry, in each region at each time of choice. (p.295)

Generally, more and more firms tend to come to the location where earlier arriving firms have already located (Arthur, 1990).

The principle of increasing returns also appears to describe the dynamic process of how a single EMS pore becomes an EMS cluster by connecting to the response structure through path-dependent processes. In our case, path-dependent processes are the factors that shape the creation of supply, communications, and other constantly reinforced paths that link EMS pores. The more EMS pores there are in a particular area, the greater the chance of their being connected.

Sociologists have identified various interorganizational linking behaviors that may regulate path-dependent processes (Drabek, 1986). Some of them include interorganizational relationships constrained by prior communication patterns, personal friendships, and decision-making needs. Each of these factors increases the probable connection for some pores and reduces it for others. This phenomenon was shown in the Los Angeles civil disturbance where hospitals that were virtually within blocks of each other received significantly different numbers of injured (Koehler, 1993).

The greater the number of interorganizational roles and personnel in an established organization, the more routine the organizational response and the more adaptive the organization is in arriving at solutions when demands exceed capabilities. Paths can be quickly established and reinforced where there are reciprocal staff relationships. If these relationships don't exist, the path-forming process will be slowed.

Organizational managers arrive at the perception that a disaster has occurred at different rates. Most see it as very localized and do not appreciate the extent of it. Thus, they are not inclined to quickly reach out and establish long-distance paths early on.

Centralization of authority is relatively rare during the first phase of a disaster. It is even less likely as the magnitude of the event increases. This suggests, along with the previous point, that connections will be localized and emerge from the bottom up in the disaster area.

Big cities with a large number of resources tend to cooperate badly with centralized authority. This suggests that there is a tendency toward fragmentation that will slow the connection process across the entire area of the disaster.

MACRO- AND MICRO-STRUCTURING PROCESSES: A SUMMARY

Theoretically, the steps that lead to the formation of an EMS disaster response percolation fractal are:

1. An EMS phase transition occurs because of a progressive or sudden break down of the day-to-day EMS. More and more decision errors are made, driving the EMS over the organizational edge into a second-order phase transition, and on to chaos.

2. Unpredictable initial conditions, organizational structuration processes, differential stress, and other factors provide and define seed points for the evolution of EMS pores.

3. The delay between decision making and actions creates unexpected variations and oscillations of critical rates that affect EMS pore formation and connections.

4. EMS pore connectedness varies because of sociological conditions and decision-making activities, and the principle of increasing returns. Decisions made very early on and the number of EMS pores and clusters in an area may have a decisive affect on whether or not the percolation threshold can be reached.

5. If the percolation threshold is reached, fractal percolation occurs, resulting in an area-wide EMS disaster system percolation fractal.

6. The percolation threshold may not be reached because the probability of connecting all of the EMS pores does not reach 60%. The result is a clumpy structure with a higher mortality and morbidity rate for the entire disaster area than would have been the case if a percolation fractal had emerged.

Some Implications for Managing the Formation of EMS Disaster Medical Systems

The discussion of EMS connection making has been very oversimplified. In reality, multiple connections have to be made to any one EMS pore for it to function. The connection probability of 60% applies to making a critical connection with multiple EMS clusters. We already know that the time it takes to make these connections increases exponentially with increased numbers of connections. This can be changed by increasing the number of hardened communications linkages that cannot be disrupted by the disaster and are capable of handling the information load. Satellite communications and geolocators for emergency response vehicles are critical. Procuring the number of transport vehicles, supplies, and personnel on very short notice poses a different and more challenging problem.

The experimental percolation threshold findings suggest that the number of ground and air transport, as well as materials and personnel needed to achieve the 60% connection rate must increase exponentially to significantly improve the probability of any one cluster being connected in a large medical disaster. This is a hard task for disaster managers who typically have few "connection" resources or large numbers of personnel and supplies at their immediate disposal.

If EMS cluster growth is determined by the principle of increasing returns, then the amount of resources must be very high indeed, since clusters that are close to many other clusters will have a much higher probability of being reinforced, while more isolated ones won't. This leads to the prediction that large, highly visible urban counties with good communication and low numbers of casualties will quickly receive aid, while small, rural counties with poor communications are more likely to be ignored, even if they have many casualties relative to their population and EMS's capacity. This occurred during the California Loma Prieta earthquake. San Francisco and Alameda Counties received the most attention early on, even though Santa Cruz and San Bonito Counties had relatively more damage.

The most interesting conclusion that this theory suggests is that it should be possible to determine how long it will take for a predicted number of EMS clusters for a particular disaster (e.g., earthquake on the Hayward fault) to reach the percolation threshold. This estimate of how long it will take to establish an EMS disaster response system can then be compared with the time available for saving the vast majority of lives, which, as noted earlier, is between 24 and 72 hours following an earthquake. (The length of this standard will probably vary by the profile of disaster-related injuries.) More optimal EMSs could be designed by reducing the number of clusters or increasing the connection rate. For example, this could be accomplished by improving communications and transportation and increasing hospital carrying capacity so that the percolation threshold can be quickly achieved. Data on system alternatives, in turn, could be used to estimate costs. To my knowledge, no means to estimate EMS response costs is currently available for large disasters.

Testing the Theory

Computer simulation is probably the most cost-effective method for testing the theory. EMS simulations already exist for field care, for hospitals, and for emergency medical systems (Fletcher & Delfosse, 1979; Fletcher, Delfosse, & Richards 1981). These simulations look at single units or a single path of interactions rather than at the entire disaster area, as would be required for a test of this theory. Some kind of connectionist model would have to be programmed that would tie all these elements together (Waldrop, 1992).

Key concepts and assertions that should be experimentally investigated are:

1. Demonstrate that if the day-to-day EMS goes through a second-order phase transition following a medical disaster and mathematically define it.
2. Prove that the EMS disaster system percolation threshold is approximately 0.5928.
3. Demonstrate that path-dependent processes do occur during a disaster response and show how the various rates, structuration processes, etc., effect when the paths are established, how they are reinforced, and how plastic they are in terms of redirecting the flow of supplies, communications, etc.
4. Conduct simulation experiments to determine how many clusters are likely to form after a Haward Fault Earthquake and the length of time it would take to cross the percolation threshold for an efficient EMS to emerge. Determine if this data can be used to estimate the cost of the Emergency Medical Services response.

The opinions and viewpoints expressed in this chapter are the authors' and should not be attributed to the California Research Bureau or the California State Library.

REFERENCES

American Society for Testing Materials (ASTM). (1988). *Standard terminology relating to emergency medical services* (Standard F117–90a). Philadelphia.
Arthur, B. (1990). (1990, February). Positive feedback in the economy. *Scientific American.*
Arthur, B., Ermoliev, Y., & Kaniovski, Y. (1987). Path-dependent processes and the emergence of macro-structure. *European Journal of Operational Research, 30.*
California Department of Conservation, Division of Mines & Geology. (1987). *Earthquake plan-*

ning scenario for a magnitude 7.5 Earthquake on the Hayward fault in the San Francisco bay area (Special Publication, 78).

California Emergency Medical Services Authority. (1985). *Quake '85 disaster exercise after action report.*

California Emergency Medical Services Authority. (1986). *Southern California earthquake response plan* (Medical and Health Annex).

California Emergency Medical Services Authority. (1988). *State emergency plan* (AnnexD). Emergency Medical Services.

California Emergency Medical Services Authority. (1989). *Unified Medical Operations Center.*

California Emergency Medical Services Authority. (1990). *Proposal for integrated medical response to a catastrophic earthquake.*

De Ville de Goyet, C., del Cid, E., Romero, A., Jeannee, E., & Lechat, M. (1976). Earthquake in Guatemal: Epidemiologic evaluation of the relief effort. *Pan American Health Organization, x*:95–109.

Drabek, T. (1986). *Human system response to disaster.* New York: Springer-Verlag.

Feigenbaum, M. (1993). Foreword in H. Peitgen, H. Jurgens, & D. Saupe *Chaos and fractals.* New York: Springer-Verlag.

Fletcher, J., & Delfosse, C. (1979). Computer model for simulation of emergency medical systems. *Military Medicine, 144*(4).

Fletcher, J., Delfosse, C. & Richards, P. (1981). *Predicting the effectiveness of concepts for future Marine Corps medical support systems.* Washington, DC: Naval Research Laboratory.

Jacobs, L. (1983, August). The role of a trauma center in disaster management. *The Journal of Trauma,.*

Jantsch, E. (1980). *The self-organizing universe.* New York: Pergamon Press.

Koehler, G. (1991, November). The emergency medical services response to the I-5 interstate highway multicasualty incident. In *Task Force Report to Governor Pete Wilson, Dust-Related Collisions, Interstate 5, Panoche Junction Overcrossing/Kamm Ave.*

Koelher, G. (1993). *Medical care for the injured: The emergency medical response to the April 1992 Los Angeles civil disturbance.* California Emergency Medical Services Authority.

Kreps, G. (1989). *Social structure and disaster.* Newark: University of Delaware Press.

Kress, G., Koehler, G., & Springer, F. (1981). Policy drift: An evaluation of the California Business Enterprise Program. In D. Palumbo & M. Harder, *Implementing public policy.* Toronto: Lexington Books.

May, R. (1984). Oscillatory fluctuations in the incidence of infectious disease and the impact of vaccination. *Journal of Hygiene, 93,* 587–608.

Peitgen, H., Jurgens, H., & Saupe, D. (1993). *Chaos and fractals.* New York: Springer-Verlag.

Thayer, L. (1972). Communication systems. In E. Laszlo (Ed.), *The relevance of general systems theory.* New York: Braziller.

Waldrop, M. (1992). *Complexity: The emerging science at the edge of order and chaos.* New York: Simon & Schuster.

Webster, W. (1992, October). *The city in crises.* Office of the Special Advisor to the Board of Police Commissioners City of Los Angeles.

14 Chaos Theory and Social Dynamics: Foundations of Postmodern Social Science

T. R. Young

Chaos is ubiquitous,
it is stable
and it has structure.
—Gleick (1987, p. 76)

The forms of social order and the sources of disorder have always been a central problematic in the behavioral sciences. For most of human history, the assumption has been that there is but one and only one natural way to organize social relations; a way sanctified by religion and reproduced with rough-hewn social skills over the centuries. With the modern concept of evolution, stability in social life worlds has given way to change, but, in most theories of social evolution, there is an "advanced" or final stage of social organization to which all change is directed. Chaos/complexity theory forces one to question both the normality of any given social order as well as the presumption of directionality and finality in social evolution. As theory and technology develop by which to explore the infinite variety of social life, even less may one offer privilege to given social forms as a product of the "iron laws" of nature, society, or the gods since human beings increasingly have the knowledge and the means to shape the world as they would have it.

In the pages that follow, I sketch out the larger transformations of the knowledge process as it wends its way through human history and through the many struggles within and between tribes, ethnic groups, nations, and empires. In doing so, I stress the complementarity of these many pathways to human knowledge and, in the same moment, place the differences between them in perspective. Each epoch in the forging of human knowledge is essential to the task of

217

building the elegant and fragile forms of social reality in which we all must, perforce, live out our lives. With skill, patience, and good will we just might be able to do a bit better in the 21st century than have we in the recent past.

PREMODERN KNOWLEDGE PROCESSES

Until the scientific revolution, most social philosophy presumed an enduring social life world centered in the present, unchanged from millennia past. The mission for premodern knowledge processes was to teach the folk methods by which a given social life world could be reproduced while the human interest that organized the knowledge process was sanctification of that social order. Out of the incredibly complex web of events and processes in human societies, premodern thinkers selected, created, and celebrated just those variables and just those truisms that helped do that. Premodern knowledge processes required belief, faith, trust, and shared engagement in the reality of creating process and thus serve as a permanent foundation for all modern sociological theories about the character of human societies.[1]

The language and practice of moral indignation used in the reality creating process, with its concepts of evil, sin, depravity, iniquity, corruption, error, and debauchery, bring along with them concepts of the good, right, correct, fair, pure, true, and upright life that served the human interest in sanctifying existing forms of social reality. In such societies, socialization and social control efforts tend to reproduce existing patterns of gender relations, political practices, economic forms, and religious understandings. Living at the edge of uncertainty and equipped with only the most basic of tools, such preoccupation with the reproduction of existing ways to do family, economics, and politics made and still makes good sense. To the extent humans embody belief, faith, and trust in their everyday activity, society does reflect a certain stability that defies change and the second law of thermodynamics. The incalculable improbability of even simple and brief social encounters still depends upon these premodern knowledge processes.

MODERN KNOWLEDGE PROCESSES

Modern science changed belief and faith in stable social relations with the idea that previous societies were flawed, primitive, or "underdeveloped." In this knowledge

---

[1]A word about terminology; I use the conventional categories of premodern, modern, and postmodern, but I want to make it very clear that I regard all these to be essential to the human condition and deeply interconnected in every human act including the most objective of scientific research. More than that, I would use the term, *ultramodern* instead of postmodern since I doubt much that the methods and missions of modernity will ever lose their values. What we see is rather a much more complex and more nuanced modernity that accepts and pursues variability and contrariety.

process, science and technology could find the path to truly modern social science and technology could find the path to truly modern social systems in family, education, economics, and transport. The mission of the knowledge process became a circling quest for a stable set of principles that could be welded into an eternally valid theoretical structure upon which to ground social policy and social practice. Modern methods of research set aside folk methods and folk beliefs in favor of a more objective and putatively value-free research design that, in turn, could generate knowledge apart from human interests and political agenda.

In the name of "modern science" and modernization, societies that had been stable for millennia were delegitimated and dismissed as part of a primitive past. Such delegitimation cleared the way for the impersonal, desanctified mass societies now emerging in the modern world. In place of a self-system anchored in the belief systems of premodern understandings, the problem of social order was given over to science and technology. In factories, workshops, schools, prisons, hospitals, and politics, interactively rich interpersonal dynamics were slowly displaced by unilateral application of regulations, rules, statues, laws, principles, and theories of scientific management. Thus, dry and impersonal rules of scientific method replaced wisdom, judgment, insight, and poetic genius as the foundation of human knowledge.

Out of the incredibly complex and interwoven fabric of social reality, the quest for certainty selected just those variables and findings that confirmed the use of rules, principles, laws, and regulations and included them in the body of knowledge called science and used them to guide behavior. As these scientific "principles" reentered the ever changing social life world from which they came, uniformity and universality displaced variety, creativity, surprise, and discontinuity as the tools of scientific management. Human beings, in the guise of scientists, worked assiduously to find and reproduce order in the same moment they disprized and tried to discard variety and disorder.

The very logic of the method of successive approximations presumes a stable set of natural and social laws to which all normal persons subscribe and all modern societies emulate. Modern science, more so even than premodern social philosophy, gives preference to stability and control as the natural and normal form of theory and research. In the lived experience of research subjects, deviance from a scientific principle is thought to mark pathology while refusal to accept the inexorable workings of social laws become grounds for therapy, confinement, or warfare. Concepts embedded in modern theoretical paradigms depersonalize sources of disorder, change, and diversity by attributing variations from putatively normal social relations to genetic inferiority, to birth defects, poor socialization, primitive cultural beliefs, inadequate controls and/or social disorganization. This was the rough beast lumbering toward Bethlehem to be born of which the poet warned; if human agency gave way to scientific fiat about how the world should work, then truly we live in an iron cage; truly freedom is but compliance to that which is written in the textbooks of experts.

In the laboratory, faced with research findings, each different from the last, modern epistemological paradigms dismissed variations among such findings with reference to faulty research design, inaccurate measurement, missing variables, observer error, poor instrumentation, observer bias, or just plain bad theory. This new science of complexity, often called chaos theory, makes it possible to accept that variety and disorder are a feature of the social life world itself rather than of bad behavior, imperfect social controls, or poor research technology. Self-similar findings are common; identical results rare. In this new philosophy of science upon us, even contrary but valid findings are possible. Variations in findings are dependent on the region studied in a complex outcome field, on the dynamical regime at hand, and the scale at which one chooses to do research. The use of replication, statistical inference, and falsification as epistemological tools are thus greatly limited. For point attractors and for limit attractors such tools suffice. When more complex dynamics are at hand, fractal truth values and semistable generalizations are the best we can do.

POSTMODERN SOCIAL SCIENCE

Chaos/complexity theory and research findings offer a view of the ontology and dynamics of social systems that promises to help build an entirely new paradigm for the understanding of order and disorder. In so doing, chaos/complexity theory provides intellectual and moral space for variety and contrariety. This new science of complexity offers support and direction for postmodern understandings that honor change, variety, and disorder. Dramatically changing rations between order and disorder, found as one moves along the bifurcation map shown in Fig. 14.1, resonate with premodern understandings of social change: Miracles, magic, and mystery once again become acceptable conceptualizations of the dynamics of social change, of healing, of interpersonal dynamics, and even of the evolution of life forms. Quantitative change transforms into qualita-

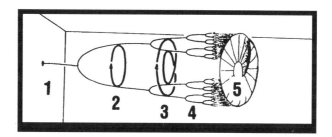

FIG. 14.1.   Cascading bifurcations. If one were to take a Poincaré section of Region 5, the grey and white area, one could see a very complex basin of outcomes; some of which are stable and others not.

tive change at each bifurcation. Uncertainty grows and prediction fails with the appearance of each new set of attractors in an exploding field of outcomes.

In contrast to both premodern and modern assumptions, chaos/complexity theory locates the source of social disorder in the nonlinear dynamics of the system itself rather than in evil, sin, error, or ignorance of particular persons or outside agents. It provides an elegant theoretical envelope for the grounding of postmodern social policy and social practice. It offers a reading of the change process that encompasses both structural determinism as well as, at special moments, human agency, since that which is process at one level of observation is structure at another scale. In chaos/complexity theory, most of the dramatic changes observed in nature and society accrue from small changes of system parameters, but there is ample room for individual or collective contributions for fundamental change at strategic points in the transformation from near-to-stable equilibria to full-blown chaos. Feigenbaum numbers, to which much attention is given in the literature, define those points.

In chaos/complexity theory, variation around a central tendency as well as qualitative change from one dynamical state to another is to be found in the *interactions* of systems in an eco-energy field.[2] One can account for first order change by reference to differences among persons. But second and third order change derive from interactions between two or more interacting variables in an outcome basin rather than from differences between members of a set per se. It is not that new variables intervene, but rather that small changes in existing variables produce qualitatively new patterns of behavior; some very different from those found in the previous attractor. Water molecules in one equilibrium state are not qualitatively different from water molecules in another, more chaotic state. The same is true of trout, hummingbirds, cicada, heart beats, or human beings. It is small changes in key parameters of a larger field that can produce qualitative change, not necessarily the appearance of an outside agent, a new pathogen. Without any change at all in the genetic or psychological organization of such organisms, they may take very different life courses depending upon dynamics of variables external to the individual organism.[3]

It is important to keep in mind that postmodern knowledge processes do not

---

[2]There are three kinds of interaction that are most important to the stability/ultrastability of a system or set of systems: linear positive feedback, linear negative feedback, and nonlinear feedback. Since only chaos can cope with chaos, nonlinear feedback processes become very important to an ultrastability in which the human need for order is matched by the human need for change and renewal. Space limitations preclude further discussion.

[3]I do not discount the role of physiological or psychological variables in differing social behaviors. I am certain that such differences do play an important part in nonnormative behavior. The operative question, not treated here, is how much of the variation in a torus accrues from enduring personal attributes and how much is a consequence of immediate factors. I tend to think that much of the variation in most social tori comes from psychological and/or physiological differences, while bifurcations in key parameters account for most of the transformations from a torus to a butterfly to a more richly detailed outcome basin.

replace premodern and modern missions or methods; they supplement them. Premodern knowledge processes are essential to human agency in the reality creating process; modern science and technology are essential to the expansion of human agency in the management of physical and natural systems; postmodern knowledge processes are essential to an increase in moral agency. We cannot appeal to natural or divine agency for the choices we now must make among outcome basins in a complex outcome field. With each increase in knowledge, we become less innocent and more responsible for the fates we meet. This is the lesson of the fruit from this tree of knowledge; we now know of the drama of social change and we become responsible.

CHAOS THEORY

Chaos theory has developed rapidly in the past 30 years to reorganize theory and research in a wide variety of disciplines.[4] The geometry of nonlinear dynamics came to be formalized in the work of Benoit Mandelbrot (1977). Mandelbrot worked at IBM's Thomas J. Watson Research Center and discovered that patterns of noise (disorder, in lay terms, and deviancy, in more sociological terms) has *fractal* geometry. More than that, in the study of daily, monthly, and yearly cycles of stock prices, he found that the stock market had similar patterns of disorder at any number of scales of analysis. Using the fractal model he found in stock prices and in bursts of noise in telephonic transmission, Mandelbrot produced a visual distribution of galaxies in the universe that astronomers have since confirmed. Galaxies are not distributed randomly over space but display patterns that have fractal geometries (Briggs & Peat, 1989, p.90).

In thinking through the implications of chaos/complexity theory for social dynamics, we want to focus upon three forms of *nonlinear* dynamics revealed by studies of natural systems. There are two linear forms that are common in simple mechanical systems, but these are seldom, if ever, observed in living systems. These three forms entail three different dynamics, each more nonlinear than the last. Figure 14.2 gives two views of both linear systems (boxes A and B) as well as two views of nonlinear systems (boxes C and D). Let us look at each form of order and together think about their implications for a postmodern social science.

We find first-order change in the torus attractor, Figure 14.2, box C (and Fig. 14.3 and 14.4, below). It embodies first-order change by virtue of the *self-similarity* involved in its dynamics rather than the precise sameness of simple dynamical systems. The butterfly attractor, Figure 14.2 box D (and Fig. 14.5)

---

[4]James Gleick (1987) has an engaging social history of chaos theory, while Briggs and Peat (1989) have a very accessible treatment of it. John Waldrop has a most engaging intellectual history of some of the more interesting contributors to nonlinear social dynamics. Mandelbrot's work (1977) is now a classic and is foundational reading. There are many fine videos that supplement printed treatments.

4 SEMI-STABLE ATTRACTORS

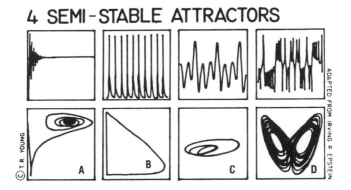

FIG. 14.2.   Linear and nonlinear dynamics-4 semi-stable attractors.
The torus [C] embodies 1st order change. The Butterfly Attractor [D]
displays 2nd order change. Courtesy of James Gleick.

displays second-order change; qualitatively different pathways arise for natural
and social systems that are otherwise very similar. Third-order change is found in
the last half of the bifurcation map shown in Fig. 14.1. Yet, even with the great
disorder found in third-order dynamics, pattern is found and new order emerges.
The Feigenbaum bifurcation numbers inform us when, if not why, such dramatic
social change occurs (see Fig. 14.1).

FIG. 14.3.   A torus after one cycle.

FIG. 14.4.   A torus consisting of five iterations.

FIG. 14.5.   A torus consisting of 20 iterations.

THE TORUS AND SELF-SIMILARITY

In generating postmodern understandings of self and society, of social change and human history, one begins by looking at the nature and sources of self-similarity in social systems. Self-similarity, as a concept, means that the behavior of any natural or social system, including individual human beings, may be similar from day to day, year to year, or generation to generation, but no one embodiment in any given cycle or iteration of any given system is precisely like a previous embodiment. Thus, variation is the natural state of social forms that take the geometry of a torus; self-similarity comprises first-order change found in all symbolic interactional processes, in all cases of crime, in all worship services, and in all forms of business activity.

The fractal geometry of a torus is seen in more detail in Fig. 14.3, 14.4, and 14.5; each succeeding cycle builds up a portrait of self-similarity in that there is a loose approximation of one cycle of behavior to the precious cycle. Thus, in a baptism, a marriage, a funeral, or a mass, however practiced is the priest, however formal is the ritual, however skilled are the communicants, still no given cycle of religious service is precisely like another. The same is true in any given social act one might wish to examine, even in the most stable and enduring of societies. In any given social role, in any given social occasion, or in any given embodiment of a classroom lecture, self-similarity displaces sameness. Whatever pattern is found in social life, it is there because sentient human beings work hard to create one iteration of an occasion in the image of a previous cycle. Human action entails variety.

It is here that individual judgment can cope with exigency; it is here that individual creativity can assert itself within the limits loosely defined by external parameters: food supply, cultural values, social controls, social esteem, and interpersonal dynamics. But do note that, while there is uncertainty about the life course of any given marriage in a simple agrarian political economy, all marriages will fall within the boundaries of the torus. . .in that, there is great certainty. If one doesn't respect the norms of food preparation and usage, hunger awaits. If one doesn't respect the norms of property holding and property transfer in settled agrarian society, poverty awaits. If one doesn't observe the norms of sharing and caring, mutual aid is foresworn.

If it is the life course of a single marriage that is modelled in phase space (Fig. 14.3), one can see process transforming into structure. Each marriage has a similar beginning, waves loosely around given norms: for example, norms about how to organize gender relations, child rearing practices, size of family, frequency of visiting kin, fidelity to the spouse, or whatever else is of interest to the researcher and found to be part of the ways of marriage in a culture. Variations outside the fractal boundaries of the torus are damped out by negative feedback in the larger environment. If several such marriages in the same culture are superimposed on each other (Fig. 14.4), one can begin to see a normative pattern emerge. This is the beginning of customary law. After thousands of iterations of marriage forms over dozens of generations, the idea of the normal and the abnormal emerge (Fig. 14.5). Together, the similar dynamics of a family in a given environment merge to produce structure, which in turn shapes the dynamics of other social forms in a field.[5]

Ordinarily, we do not think in terms of a torus since most research takes slices of the marriage form or of hundreds of marriages at one point in time (called a Poincaré section). Figure 14.6 shows this technique. This practice reduces a three-dimensional dynamical form to a two-dimensional static form. Ideas of normality and eternality thus come to be, in part, as artifacts of research tools one uses. In brief, self-similar systems, such as a torus, exhibit near to stable dynamics. In the observations of thousands and millions of iterations of natural and social systems, a structure emerges; that structure is a chain of small variations with infinite variety, infinite length, and infinite detail rather than a stable, natural pattern. Modern research designs can pick up distributions around a central norm but, in the sectioning of a much more dynamical process, lose the larger pattern of change and renewal. We will see that larger pattern in the graphics in Fig. 14.6.

Just as no two marriages are identical, no two meetings of a classroom or a conference are precise iterations of each other. This similarity, but not sameness, is of special interest to deviancy theory. It sets variation as the nature of the social process rather than conformity. These small and local variations, under some conditions, amplify and transform into much more complex patterns. I return to this point in the discussion of even stranger attractors next.[6]

Sources of Sameness: Feedback

Most sociological theories of order place great emphasis on socialization and social controls, as well as on a magical but quite human process in which things defined as true become true in the consequence: the self-fulfilling prophecy. Again, the process doesn't fulfill itself; sentient human beings do the necessary work of trusting, believing, and acting as if something quite problematic would indeed become real. Without denigrating these sources of sameness, we want to

---

[5]This point is fundamental for postmodern science; causality is fractal; it opens and closes. Causality is a function of the degree to which process transforms into structure. Causality is interaction more than action, while the concept of the independent variable is a poetic device made possible by ignoring the rich interaction between systems. This is the elusive understanding of causality and causal directionality for which Hubert Blalock, to whom this essay is dedicated, spent most of his career seeking.

[6]Such a form is called an attractor since a system tends to end up in a fairly small portion of a larger field in which it is found; that is, it is "attracted" to a basin but cycle around it. It is called strange since the pathways a system takes through time, space and its environment is marked by hops, jumps, and skips in ways not trackable by calculus and rational scaling systems.

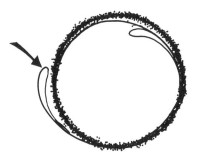

FIG. 14.6. A Poincaré section of a torus. This is a sample of 8,000 iterations. Note the tongue [arrow], beginning to form on the torus; this signals the advent of 2nd order change.

look at another very important source. Modern science uses the concept of causality in which one variable changes another; complexity theory makes great use of the concept of feedback to explain system of both stable and changing social dynamics.

The source of the semistable order of a social torus is to be found in nonlinear feedback. Unrestrained, positive linear feedback drives systems into deep chaos; negative linear feedback tends to restrict creativity and innovation. If we want to maintain the integrity of any given social form, then there must be some form of social response with which to defeat the transformation of the torus into a butterfly attractor. In human affairs, this requires forgiving, forgetting, and treating incompatible events as if they had never happened and, in general, a continuous and expert editing of the reality process as it unfolds. In everyday interaction burps, belches, grunts, sneers, and shrugs are treated as if they did not occur. More serious defects are registered on human consciousness but defined as "not really" there. Infidelity in marriage, dishonesty of employees, contempt of students, disobedience of soldiers, and heresy in the priesthood are usually defined nonlinearly . . . as noise in the system.

The curious thing is that, if we want to resist change, we must couple one kind of change with another (Briggs & Peat, 1989, p. 37). With recourse to nonlinear and qualitative change, it is possible to institute a stability that relies upon instability. This curious feature of ultrastable systems depends upon nonlinear change.

Ultrastability

The effort to conserve traditional structures in times of great uncertainty depends more heavily on change than on repressive social control tactics since, to paraphrase H. Ross Ashby, only chaos can cope with chaos. In a concrete case, if we want to maintain the integrity of the nuclear family in the social, cultural, and economic conditions of the 1990s, we must innovate. New ways of doing child care, new ways of doing food preparation, and new ways of organizing education and religion are required. Instead of health care, child care or housing apportioned to each family in terms linear to their income—poor families having poor housing, health care, or child care, while rich families have interactionally rich child care, informationally rich health care, or just plain rich housing—nonlinear processes of distribution must occur for the poor family, or else the family falls apart; children wander off, spouses separate, and landlords evict.

In similar fashion, if we want to design a low-crime society, then we may have to make qualitative changes in quite ordinary practices. Corporate crime, white-collar crime, organized crime, as well as street crime explode when key variables exceed given limits. In other work, I have suggested that the key variables include inequalities in class, race, and gender relations, which is discussed later. It may well be the case that some inequality in wealth is helpful to the economic life of a nation, Plato suggested a four to one ratio, but it is likely that larger ratios set the stage for a wide variety of corporate and political crime for those at the top of the pyramids of power, while street-crime and organized crime become attractive for those at the bottom of such pyramids. White-collar crime may begin to be interesting to rich and poor alike who live on the cusp of financial uncertainty.

There is any number of nonlinear ways to discourage the positive feedback found in laissez faire market societies that produce great inequalities and, thus, perchance, the potential for great crime. Progressive taxation is a well-known social policy. Programs of social justice by which access to education, health care, and decent housing are found in low-crime societies. Deuteronomic Law required the forgiveness of debts every seven years and forbade usury as a violation of God's Law. Indeed, the mercy, forgiveness, and charity found in many religious are exemplars of nonlinearity.

In modernist views of causality, globalization of the economy threatens to eliminate diverse cultures and religions. Some have looked at that process and have despaired of the possibility of diversity. They see one global culture marked by uniformity, rationality, and finality of social change. Chaos/complexity theory is more reassuring; mutually exclusive religions can exist side by side; rationality is reduced in importance as a social tool; the end of history is never, never near. Again, it is nonlinearity that makes such variety possible, even in the largest, most totalizing process one could imagine. The psychological processes of compartmentalization have their counterpart in nonlinear social processes.

Social controls work to minimize entropy of a social torus yet no set of social controls can generate that precise behavior favored by modern science and intrinsic to its assumptions of linear causality. And, as we shall see in the anatomy of a butterfly attractor, when a system parameter changes beyond a given value, that system goes from self-similarity to contrariety in outcomes and increase in uncertainty between the wings of such attractors. In each more chaotic dynamical regime, social controls lose efficacy; indeed, causality, prediction, and control become casualties to the knowledge process.

The Butterfly Attractor

Under specific conditions, a small change in a key parameter can force a stable torus to break up into two or more tori. Such change produces a tongue as in Fig. 14.6 (arrow), which expands to offer two quite different fates for a person, a family, a firm, or a society. It is very important to remember that it is a small change in *the same variable* that offers qualitatively different fates in either one of two wings, as in Fig. 14.7; the butterfly attractor.

The first such attractor was identified by Edward Lorenz in his modelling of a weather system with twelve variables in the early 1960s. Since then, butterfly attractors have been found in a wide variety of natural and social data sets.

In social terms, small differences in initial conditions between, for example, similarly situated children can be amplified to produce two entirely different life courses. Howard Becker (1963) picked up on this fact in his development of labelling theory. Small differences in processing and labelling inside the criminal justice system can produce large differences in the fate of children otherwise very similar in demographic conditions. One group of children in a city such as Chicago or Dallas might end up in college; one batch might end up in prison. The differences between members of both sets might be so small all would take pretty much the same pathway (that of a torus) were it not for the labelling process; a small change at a crucial point in the moral career of a child. Such labels become locked in for the child when school, police, court, and other authorities utter and publish such labels to peers, family, and neighbors.

Likewise, small reductions in income (or increases in expenses) can trigger qualitative change among white-collar professionals in tactics to generate income. In a given society, at one point in time, most if not all physicians might behave pretty much the same toward their patients in terms of diagnoses and prescriptions for tests, medications, and surgery. Given small changes in certain parameters of income and/or living expense, some number of physicians might begin to over-prescribe for patients and over-bill third party carriers. Of the

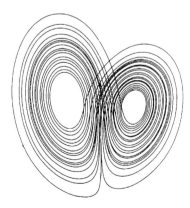

FIG. 14.7. A butterfly attractor with 2 outcome basins.

universe of doctors, each with very similar socialization, personalities, and life-styles, a small change at a change point might send one into embezzlement, stock fraud, medicare fraud, or income tax evasion, while the other might make adjustments in lifestyle (moving to a smaller house, selling a second home or third car, borrowing from family or friends). The operative point upon which to focus is that it would be impossible to predict which of that universe of doctors would engage in deviant behavior. All that the deviancy theorist could be certain of is that, given small changes in key parameters, even larger numbers of doctors will defraud or mistreat their patients.

The butterfly attractor can be viewed as comprised of two tori; each of which is a qualitatively different outcome basin for very similar systems. This is the essence of second-order change; similar systems will have different fates depending upon their journeys through uncertainty. Under some social conditions, an outcome basin in which each set of persons has a different fate could be, in human terms, desirable. In mapping the socialization of children, there comes a time when most societies track one set of children into one set of status roles and another set(s) into other status roles. Gender differentiations, occupational differentiation, ethnic and religious differentiations are examples of normative bifurcations in outcome states between persons with but small differences in initial states. Such differentiations serve as reservoirs of variety from which nonlinear transformations to new states are possible, thus, increasing survival chances in an ever-changing macroenvironment. Differentiations may be helpful also in that specialization occurs and experience is augmented. Yet the continuing subdivision of labor may be inimical to both quantity and quality of work. Stratification, as mentioned, also may have limits beyond which so much uncertainty accumulation for those at both the top and bottom that the pattern and predictability so essential to social processes fail.

Third Order Change

There is a third kind of change of interest to those in the social sciences. Chaos/complexity theory offers an explanation and description of the transformation of social tori and other strange attractors from quasi-stability toward deep chaos. The short version is that when the periods of a system bifurcate the third time, they are in a situation where another very small change can produce great numbers of possible endstates toward which a person, a group, a business, or a society might go. The operative point to keep in mind for a theory of deviancy is that this great increase in alternative ways to behave is a feature of the whole system not just the single, acting person; punishment of individuals for trying to cope with such emergent conditions is an exercise in folly if not in mean-spirited vengeance. And, for those in social philosophy generally, it is good to remember that, even in deep chaos, there is a great deal of order.

And, even in deep chaos, it is possible to obtain an uncertain stability. A.

Hübler (1992) of the University of Illinois, Urbana, has shown that, if one can model the key rhythms of chaotic displays, one can control chaos, even in the most uncertain regions of a bifurcation map. Figure 14.1 shows the cascade from very ordered behavior to very disordered, deep chaos. Even in deep chaos, careful, delicate intrusions can stabilize system dynamics. While this ability to control in deep chaos is now limited to very simple systems (in this case, a laser beam), we still see that, in principle, control of key parameters is possible. For those who like minimal intrusion by the state into public discourse, this fact is interesting.

In a great many different kinds of systems, a similar pathway toward full chaos is observed. As one can see in Fig. 14.1, the bifurcation map on page 220, after the first bifurcation (or forking), a system has but one loose endstate in which it might be found (Region 2); its dynamics describe a limit attractor. After the second forking (Region 3), it loops around and within that fractal geometric figure called the torus. After three bifurcations, there are two possible destinies that any normal system may take (Region 4). The pattern observed is called a butterfly attractor. Then there is a region in which several outcome states are routinely visited. After four bifurcations, however, the number of endstates possible for similar members of a set is progressively short lived (Region 5). Feigenbaum (1978) has found that a system with three bifurcations is fairly stable, but one with four quickly tumbles into full chaos. The Feigenbaum constant, 3.5699, gives us the possibility of making a prediction of the onset of full chaos when the first few period-doubling parameters are known.

There are many features of the sequence shown in the bifurcation map depicted in Fig. 14.1 that are of interest to the behavior scientist. In the first instance, the choice of which outcome basin to set as the normative and which others to define as abnormality, deviancy, error, sin, or crime is shown to be a human, thus a political, act. In all societies, in some fields of human endeavor, of some number of outcome basins, one such basin ordinarily, and quite reasonably, is set as normative.

In the pronunciation of a word, in the counting of bricks, in the naming of flowers, communication and interpersonal understanding depends upon pattern and consistency. In such matters as gender socialization, however, many societies set one and only one pair of gender orientations as normative. In other societies, three, four, or more genders are possible, each with varying patterns of sexuality and intimacy.[7]

---

[7]What is "'reasonable" in this context depends both on cultural preference and those parameters in the larger environment that sustain the human project. Sometimes one family form is preferable and useful, given food, climate, and political danger; sometimes a different family form is best for a given political economy; sometimes a plurality of family forms is possible even if not directly connected to key parameters in the environment. Current postmodern consensus aside, it is possible to ground social philosophy on the underlying ontos in which humans beings must live. There is much to do, however, in the way of perfecting the research tools and research designs and collecting data sets before one can do much more than state one's intuitive judgment.

Second, in the immediate vicinity of such change points, human agency is greatly augmented (Young, 1992, pp. 441–460.). Small adjustments of key parameters can prevent a great increase in the number of basins to which a system will go or, alternatively, facilitate change. It is a human choice to make and a human responsibility to make such choices. Social control tactics work fairly well until one gets to such points, but, without changes in the larger parameters, control fails (Briggs & Peat, 1989; Young & Deal, 1994).

Third, at the boundaries between any two outcome basins, small untrackable differences push a system into deep chaos. In the case of economic dynamics, well-run businesses might not survive a great depression, while other poorly run businesses might not fail (Young & Kiel, 1992). A small difference in location, in customer traffic, in profit margin might catapult even well-run businesses into bankruptcy. Nonlinear feedback from their failings might trigger other bankruptcies of well-run companies or, perchance, help other poorly run firms survive. In the boundaries between stable regions of such an outcome basin, the fate of any given business in quite unpredictable.

An important point to note is that, in a sea of disorder, there are pockets of order. The emergence of such pockets of order is entirely unpredictable. Ilya Prigogine (1984) won a Nobel prize for setting forth the principles by which new order emerges out of disorder. If we look at the left side of a bifurcation map, we see the order that warms the heart of a conservative. If we look at the right side of Fig. 14.6, it is easy to see the second law of thermodynamics at work; things do tend to their most probable state. But if we look more closely, we see pockets of order that ground the insight that new order is always emerging out of chaos. Such new forms do come; come what may. And they do come when linearity in feedback pushes system dynamics beyond the fourth bifurcation. For those in public policy as in social philosophy, the operative question becomes how and whether or not human agency can be deployed to provoke dramatically new forms of social life.

Postmodern Philosophy of Science: Conclusion

Chaos/Complexity theory reveals an ontological grounding for the knowledge process very different from that of modern science and strangely akin to some premodern presumptions. Prediction, replication and falsification lose efficacy as the tools of the knowledge process as physical, biological, and social systems move from stable to unstable dynamics along a bifurcation track. In the new science of complexity, order occupies a small niche, while the changing ratio between order and disorder fills the geography available to it with emergent macrostructures whose geometry becomes so complex that research designs cannot encompass them.

Chaos/complexity theory requires an entirely new way of thinking—one in which fractal geometries replace neat and tidy Euclidean forms; in which the excluded middle discarded by Aristotle is reclaimed; in which truth values of propositions change with region in a complex basin of outcomes; in which Newtonian physics is displaced by discontinuity and qualitative change; in which Newtonian calculus gives way to qualitative mathematics; and in which the second law of thermodynamics is seen to describe but half the fate of natural and social systems. Out of the other half emerges entirely new and unpredictable forms of social order. Most troubling to modern sensibility is that fact that two similar systems can meet very different fates; that contradictory results are found in the same complex causal basin; and that causal relationships change as a system leaves one dynamical field for another.

The geometry of social and natural systems seem bizarre in this new understanding; they turn, twist, fold, and occupy the same space–time continua as do other such systems. Even simple systems can display complex behavior. What is true at one scale of observation can be very wrong at another. What is true for the dynamics of natural and social systems in one region of phase space is not true in another. Truth values themselves are fractals in such a science. This opening in the truth table requires much thought while it permits more human intervention than modern science thought possible.

At the edges of a causal field, small differences in ways of acting, ways of thinking, and ways of feeling interact to propel a person or a set of persons into a very uncertain fate. In complex causal fields, those with 16 or more outcome basins toward which a member of a society might go, idiosyncratic interactions can create entirely new forms of order and certainty. The more complex the system, the more likely it is to become irrational in the technical sense. It is the story of this contest between order and disorder; between precision and pattern; between certainty and possibility; between fate and chance; between truth and fiction to which chaos/complexity findings speak so well.

Chaos/complexity theory offers a series of insights about the origins and patterns of variation and change most useful to theories of change and deviancy. As such it creates and defines a postmodern science in which disorder has equal standing to order as a feature of natural and social systems. Those who prefer order and view the bureaucracy as the central organizing tool in modernized society have much to consider. In decentering stability and monolithic social forms, it provides an elegant theoretical envelope with which to ground postmodern explorations in art, music, dance, drama, religion, health care, education, and other cultural forms heretofore deemed repugnant, unnatural or evidence of pathology.

Chaos/complexity theory thus forces a comprehensive review and an extensive revision of the basic assumptions that guide the knowledge process in research and theory. It retains and respects the many contributions made by premodern contributions to intersubjective understanding. Trust, belief, faith, hope, and love all increase the possibility that one human being will take the role of the other and, in the doing, the geometry of self expands to create a "we." Feeling, thinking, and acting then become shared processes. If such processes are wide and deep, the boundaries of the localized "we" can expand to create a more universal we. Thinking, feeling, and acting become a much more collective endeavor. The division of labor, as well as ancient divisions of gender, race, and ethnicity, tend to restrict the knowledge process, but knowing that, human beings have a moral choice in domains of life not possible in either premodern or modern knowledge processes.

Modern science continues to be basic to the knowledge process but is modified to be far more concerned with the entirety of the causal field in which a system is found. . .the epistemological utility of analysis is greatly augmented by that of totality and synthesis. Simple systems do exhibit the precision and predictability that the early founders of empirical science sought. Truth values of real existing dynamics, however, were subverted by research designs that isolated, controlled, and restricted the interaction to some two or three interacting variables. It little serves the knowledge process to find certainty unconnected to the practical interests in health, safety, economy, or efficiency that inform most research most of the time. Indeed, pure research is, for the most part, irrelevant research. It is real praxis that drives the modern knowledge process.

Chaos/complexity theory thus offers a version of the dynamics of nature and society in which there is room for human agency as never found in the God-hewn worlds of premodernity or in the iron-bound laws of modern science. What we do with the vast genius and the great knowledge that we inherit from premodern and modern knowledge processes is, in postmodern social science, our own responsibility. We cannot appeal to nature or to the gods for direction, and we cannot assign blame to devils and genes when things go wrong. In that loss of innocence resides our dignity as architects of our own fate.

REFERENCES

Becker, H. (1963). *Outsiders: Studies in the sociology of deviance*. New York: The Free Press.

Briggs, J., & Peat, F. D. (1989). *Turbulent mirror: An illustrated guide to chaos theory and the science of wholeness*. New York: Harper & Row.

Gleick, J. (1987). *Chaos: Making a new science*. New York: Penguin.

Hübler, A. (1992). Modelling and control of complex systems: Paradigms and applications. In L. Lam (Ed.), *Modeling complex phenomena*. New York: Springer.

Mandelbrot, B. (1977). *The fractal geometry of nature*. New York: Freeman.

Prigogine, I., & Stengers, I. (1984). *Order out of chaos: Man's new dialogue with nature*. New York: Bantam.

Young, T. R. (1992). Chaos theory and human agency. *Humanity and Society, 16*(4).

Young, T. R., & Kiel, L. D. (1992). *Chaos and management science*. (Under review).

Young, T. R., & Anthony Deal. (1994). *Law and social control in complex societies*. Copies available from the Red Feather Institute, 8085 Essex, Weidman, MI 48893.

V PSYCHOTHERAPY AND CHAOS THEORY

Marshall McLuhan first demonstrated that, as each new communications medium comes into existence, the previous medium recedes from the forefront of our consciousness to become an archetype. In first making use of the new medium, we draw on the archetype of the previous medium. Of course, this never fully fits, and eventually the new medium finds its characteristic voice.

This process is hardly limited to communications media; it holds true for every advance in human thought. As each of the sciences first differentiated itself from philosophy, it looked to the previous science for its theoretical underpinnings. Before psychology was a separate science, our view of the mind was colored by the metaphors implicit in each of the sciences successively: first physics, then chemistry, then finally biology at the point when psychology became an explicitly named branch of science. Most especially, psychology drew on the concept of equilibrium, which originated in the analysis of physical systems, such as pulleys and levers, became more complex in the study of chemical reactions, and even more complex in dealing with biological systems.

In his chapter, Goldstein carefully traces the history of the concept of equilibrium, which underlies, directly or indirectly, most models of psychotherapy. He points out that "equilibrium is inadequate for understanding the process of change" because "the mind is a nonlinear system that transforms into regions of more complex attractors under far-from-equilibrium conditions." Thus, chaos theory can provide an expanded model of reality in which equilibrium is a "limiting case."

Each of the psychotherapeutic theorists represented in this section can be seen as developing Goldstein's thesis in their individual ways, by selecting one or another central aspect of chaos theory. Probably because Francis deals with psychophysiological self-regulation rather than psychotherapeutic transformation, he comes closest to developing the general characteristics that any nonequilibrium model of the body/mind would have to include. For Francis, the key human ability that takes us beyond equilibrium models is our ability to look not only without for information, but within: a process called interoception. This involves a feed-back loop that is inherent in even the simplest nonlinear dynamical systems and that goes beyond equilibrium models.

Chamberlain discusses how family systems seem to exhibit similar structure to the "strange attractors" that are the media stars of chaos theory. Family systems naturally settle into complex patterns that cannot be analyzed solely in terms of the individual family members. These family systems, though dysfunctional, still remain inherently stable. At some point, however, the family system loses its structure and collapses into a point attractor around a single problem. In examining the family, there is no single causal chain the therapist can trace to identify why the system collapsed, and the system cannot be restored to stability by attacking the presenting problem. The structure of family systems looks much like that of the strange attractors presented in complex physical systems, except they are much more complex.

Since the structure of a single individual is still more complex than the structure of a family, individual therapy is forced to look to chaos theory even more for metaphorical model than for actual application. Marks-Tarlow points out that "such models display unusual power to crystallize an understanding of complicated, multidetermined realms, such as the psyche and the mind/body relationship." She selects four key aspects of fractal geometry (a branch of chaos theory) "relevant to the advancement of psychological theory": self-similarity, bounded infinity, ordered unpredictability, and fractional dimensionality.

For example, in considering bounded infinity, she points out that "with the psyche, just as with fractals, the closer you look, the more there is to see. One can start with any detail about a person, no matter how trivial seeming, and the more it is explored, the more richness and complexity is revealed. There is no limit to the depth of exploration possible, or the size of the scale of observation."

Lonie's chapter demonstrates exactly this point. She takes a single poignant dream she calls "The Princess and the Swineherd" and shows that "far from being able to be understood as a fragment, it requires a rich setting in order to have significance. The richer the setting, the more meaningful it becomes." The is because of the mental "mechanism of condensation, where a single idea comes to represent several different trains or thought and may be conceptualized as existing at their intersection." Her chapter develops at length this concept of the boundary between the known and the unknown, which characterizes therapy, and how therapy can draw on chaos theory for an underlying model.

Finally, by limiting herself to a single psychological topic—regression—Perna is able to present the most explicitly developed model of any of the papers. She turns the traditional view of regression as a "disruptive pathological state" on its head and instead presents it in terms of its "inherent creative potential for the development of new psychic structure. . . ."Regression is representative of a transformational process in psychic development of new integrative psychic structures." Her detailed development of how chaos theory describes this process might provide a model for how a new total theory of psychotherapy might evolve out of the combination of chaos theory and existing models.

Just as these theorists show how chaos theory can enrich psychotherapy, psychotherapists have the potential to enrich chaos theory in turn. As a single example, psychotherapists. by the very nature of their profession, deal with patients in a chaotic state that, hopefully, self-organizes into a new stable structure of more complexity and flexibility than their previous structure. Because of the patients' subjective ability to describe their experiences of that state, therapists drawing on chaos theory may eventually be able to provide more complex examples of self-organization than can the current physical descriptions, such as the transition of water to boiling or the Beluzhow-Zhabotinsky reaction.

Therapists should find much in this section to draw on in their own work. And nontherapists may be surprised at the extent to which putting chaos theory into clinical terms enriches their understanding of how nonlinear dynamical systems actually operate.

15 Unbalancing Psychoanalytic Theory: Moving Beyond the Equilibrium Model of Freud's Thought

Jeffrey Goldstein

Consider the following citations from psychoanalytic theorists, each of which employs the concept of equilibrium (italics added):

[Outline for a book draft] Mechanism of the Neuroses. The neuroses as disturbances of *equilibrium* owing to increased difficulty in discharge . . . (Freud, 1893/1955, Vol. 1, p. 187)

. . . [psychological drives are] mechanisms that tend toward final states of *equilibrium* that are relatively fixed, even though under varying circumstances the route by which the final *equilibrium* is reached may vary widely. (French, 1970, p. 165)

. . . the living functions are extremely flexible and mobile, their *equilibrium* being disturbed uninterruptedly, but being re-established by the organism equally uninterruptedly . . . the ultimate goal of all these equalization tendencies . . . [is] the aim of maintaining a certain level of tension characteristic for the organism. (Fenichel, 1945, p. 12)

Let us assume that what we call the drive-needs of the organism are *disequilibria* in energy-distribution. Let us assume that the principles of physics hold here and such *disequilibria* tend toward reestablishment of *equilibrium*. (Rapaport, 1951, p. 659)

The energy-transforming function of symbols (i.e., from primary to secondary process) is an absolute necessity for safeguarding the homeostatic *equilibrium* of the organism. (Deri, 1964, p. 529)

When circumstances arise which lead to a major disturbance in libido *equilibrium,* a pronounced diffusion of libido and aggression occurs . . . (Levin, 1970, quoted in Rosenblot & Thickstan 1978, p. 539)

In the attempt to maintain some form of psychic *equilibrium* under all circumstances every human being is capable of creating a neurosis, a psychosis, a pathological character pattern, a sexual perversion, a work of art, a dream, or a psychosomatic malady. (McDougall, 1974, p. 438)

. . . a particular type of relationship with an object alters and disturbs a previously held *balance,* then it is usually felt to be much more traumatic and violent. . .The methods which such patients have been using to maintain their *balance* show considerable variety—but they have in common the employment of their important objects to contain parts of the self. (Joseph, 1989, p. 89)

I believe that it is the volatility and the lability of the psychic energy function that preclude the establishment or maintenance of the ordinary psychic *equilibrium* between drive and defense, so that even the ordinary processes of symptom formation and pathogenesis are disrupted. (Ostow, 1990, pp. 148–149)

These quotations indicate the significant role played by the concept of equilibrium (and its synonym "balance") in psychoanalytic thought since Freud's first use of the concept. The idea of equilibrium is mainly utilized to explain regulatory mental mechanisms as equilibrium-seeking *systems:*

System referring to how the mind operates as an unified entity, not just an agglomeration of parts;

Equilibrium alluding to a basic condition of rest or constancy of some psychological/affective/libidinal quantity in the mental system.

Seeking having to do with the fundamental tendency of the mental system to either maintain equilibrium or restore it after it's been disturbed.

Normal psychological functioning is thought to be maintained by equilibrium-seeking processes, whereas psychopathology is the result of disturbances in equilibrium.

While most commentators on Freud's physicalist leanings have focussed their attention on the notion of "psychic energy," in a previous work (Goldstein, 1990), I emphasized the corollary development of the equilibrium idea in Freud's thought and how it could be supplanted with the recent concept of far-from-equilibrium conditions. My intention in this chapter, however, is to understand equilibrium as a limiting case of a more general nonequilibrium and nonlinear theory of psychodynamic change. Within this nonequilibrium perspective, equilibrium has a crucial role to play in identifying the "attractor" characterizing the initial "stuck" condition of patients in psychotherapy. But, because equilibrium is inadequate for understanding the process of change, there is a need for a theory that allows for a potential for change inherent in the psyche. Very briefly, the assumption being made is that the mind is a nonlinear system that transforms into regions of more complex attractors under far-from-equilibrium conditions. It is hoped that the resulting "unbalancing" of psychoanalytic theory can help shed light on how change is facilitated during the process of psychotherapy.

EQUILIBRIUM—FROM A DETERMINATE CONDITION
TO A TELEOLOGICAL EXPLANATION

Science and Mathematics

Psychoanalytic thought has not had a social science monopoly on the concept of equilibrium. Indeed, equilibrium-based ideas have had considerable influence on many key social science theories including those of Talcott Parsons, Laurence Henderson, Kurt Lewin, Leon Festinger, and Jean Piaget (Goldstein, 1993; Haroutunian, 1983; Russet, 1966). These theorists, following the trend of "physics-envy," have tried to put their ideas on a firm footing by borrowing heavily from the hard sciences. Thus, to get a clear grasp on the appeal of the equilibrium idea for the social sciences, we first need to examine the development of the idea in the sciences.

In early Greek mathematics and science, "equilibrium," as its etymology indicates, referred to a balance of weights on a lever, that is, a determinate condition of a simple mechanism (Boyer, 1968). Because of its extraordinary quality, the phenomenon of balance prompted further investigations, such as Archimedes' proofs about the relation of weights to distances from the fulcrum when a lever was in equilibrium. In the late Middle Ages, when modern science was in its formative stage, equilibrium as a determinate condition was again utilized in explaining the dynamics of pulleys, cords, and weights (Mach, 1960). But inquiry shifted to include motion in those simple systems. For example, Galileo (Boyer, 1968) proposed motion would result as a system attempted to restore its equilibrium when a state of disequilibrium had occurred. This was a critical shift for the equilibrium concept since it became more than a determinate condition; now it was an explanatory condition, a condition that a system tended toward.

This explanatory role of equilibrium was generalized and expanded in the eighteenth century using the newly discovered techniques of calculus. Thus, the great mathematician Euler interpreted "force" as any disturbing factor displacing a system from equilibrium (Jammer, 1957). Then, in the nineteenth century, the view of equilibrium as a determinate and explanatory condition was combined with earlier concepts of inertia and conservation that had been anticipated by Galileo, expounded on by Kepler and Descartes, and mathematically formulated by Newton (Cohen, 1985). For example, Hamilton's mathematical studies implied that the equilibrium-seeking tendency of a conservative system could explain its overall dynamics (D'Abro, 1951).

Similarly, the First Law of Thermodynamics was based in an equilibrium explanation. For instance, Helmholtz claimed natural processes would always proceed toward an equilibrium position at which the process stops (Elkana, 1974). Since for Helmholtz (1976), external forces disturb equilibrium and this disturbance consequently moves the system, the movement of a system was ultimately a matter of the action of external forces. Similarly, in Carnot's conception of the "equilibrium of caloric" or heat, motive power in a steam engine was produced by the system seeking to eliminate internal temperature differences, that is, heat being transferred or equalized from a warmer to a colder body (Elkana, 1974).

This equilibrium-based tendency to equalize differences was also connected to the Second Law of Thermodynamics, which Boltzmann understood in terms of a transition from less probably to more probable states, the latter being the equilibrium state (Broda, 1983). With Boltzmann's formulation, the concept of equilibrium had made full passage from a simple determinate condition to the final, sought-for state of a physical system. This is the form that equilibrium took as it was applied to chemical reactions by the great American physicist J. Willard Gibbs (1928) and in Germany by Ostwald (1976). In 1884, Le Chatelier proposed his influential Principle of Equilibrium: if a system in equilibrium is subjected to a change threatening the equilibrium, the system attempts to annul the change (Sorokin, 1941)[1].

Psychology

During the 19th century, the concept of equilibrium was not limited to physics and chemistry but also had an important role in psychology. To explain how ideas emerge into or out of consciousness, Herbart (1891), for example, turned to equilibrium seeking in explaining the process of thought as the result of mental representations in disequilibrium pressuring the mind to move.

According to Sands (1988), the establishment of mental equilibrium in Herbart's scheme was crucial to his theory of consciousness and unconsciousness, two ideas obviously of great concern to Freud later on. What remains after the arrest of an idea by its progressive "sinking" into unconsciousness was an equilibrium state. Since, for Herbart (Wolman, 1968), each idea involved a discharge of energy, and since energy was imperishable, no idea could completely disappear, just change form. Mental stability, therefore, was the result of ideas whose similarity, corresponding to equilibrium, form the basis of "apperceptive masses" that organize the mind.

Herbart's equilibrium-seeking concepts were carried forward by Eduard Beneke (Sands, 1988), who focused on the idea of tension-driven processes seeking fulfillment. In his model, equilibrium was the distribution of a certain element that flowed between mental structures, presumably the apperceptive masses. It is interesting to note that Beneke was a key person in turning psychology into a discipline demanding an empirical investigation on its own terms (Leary, 1978).

In the mid-19th century, Fechner (1966), one of the founders of psycho-

---

[1]Bernfeld and Feitelberg (1929) pointed out how similar Freud's view of equilibrium was to that of Le Chatelier.

physics, applied the conservation laws of physics to neurological matters and formulated that the nervous system sought to maintain a constancy of total energy. Theodore Lipps was another psychological theorist whose concepts of force and energy influenced Freud (Kanzer, 1981, 1983). Lipps's psychology also relied on the conservation of energy leading to a Herbartian doctrine of forces tending to equilibrium. The "unconscious" was equivalent to the equilibrium-seeking processes that underlie conscious thought similar to the heat underlying the light of a hot substance (Peters, 1962).

Psychology was closely linked to philosophy in nineteenth century, so it is not surprising to find late nineteenth century philosophical psychology was also imbued with an equilibrium-seeking system concept. Thus, Hermann Lotze (1886) explained various mental phenomena from the point of view of the nervous system, an equilibrium-seeking mechanism. Moreover, although Lotze had explicitly rejected Herbart's quantitative approach, Lotze's "feelings" accounted for mental activity by an equilibrium-seeking tendency (Peters, 1962).

Similarly, Eduard von Hartmann, another influential philosopher whose work has been said to foreshadow many of Freud's ideas on the unconscious, also used an equilibrium-based model in his physiological excursions to indicate an "unconscious teleological principle." In fact, von Hartmann raised the equilibrium principle to a metaphysical level.

Finally, the philosophy of Richard Avenarius at the end of the nineteenth century was deeply committed to an equilibrium-seeking system approach startlingly like Freud's[2]. His general goal was the systematization of all experience into the most general of concepts, a "centralvorstellung" or simple picture, which combined physiology with a Herbartian associationist psychology (Janik & Toulmin, 1973). His "centralvorstellung" was that the central nervous system strove to maintain a state of equilibrium when it was faced with change resulting from either stimuli from the external world or fluctuations in the internal metabolism (Austedo, 1967; Herrnstein & Boring, 1965). This recounting of the history of the idea of an equilibrium-seeking system shows that by the late 19th century, the equilibrium postulation had become taken for granted: As soon as you had any kind of system, you automatically had a system whose functioning could ultimately be explained by its tendency to seek equilibrium. To achieve the long-range goal of equilibrium, a system could take different paths: equalization or discharge (Shope, 1971). Equalization was the transfer of energy through the system to equalize internal differences, say, of temperature. Discharge implied that energy was somehow released out of the system. Moreover, the stability of a system was conceptualized in terms of its equilibrium-seeking purpose.

The concept of equilibrium was transformed from a mere determinate condi-

---

[2]Yet there is no mention of Avenarius in the biographies of Freud by Jones (1953) or Gay (1988), or, for that matter, in Freud's work itself (Freud, 1955, Index). Often compared to Mach's philosophy of science, Avenarius' thought hoped to supplant vitalistic teleology with the goal-directed activity of an equilibrium-seeking system (Peters, 1962).

tion to a teleological explanation of both a system at rest and a system undergoing change. This explanation of change was associated with the formulation of force as an external agent causing change in a system by disrupting its equilibrium. Moreover, the stability of a system was understood as its capacity for resisting the action of forces threatening the equilibrium.

This equilibrium-seeking explanation for systemic behavior had become so ubiquitous in nineteenth century science, psychology, and, philosophy that it was just about impossible to conceive of a system in any other fashion. For example, Russett (1966) recounted how Talcott Parsons exclaimed that the concept of equilibrium was a direct derivation of the concept of a system itself! By the time Freud appeared on the scene and began his psychoanalytic theorizing, the concept of an equilibrium-seeking system was so firmly entrenched in the sciences, psychology, and philosophy that it would have been greatly surprising if he hadn't resorted to it.

As stated earlier, in a previous work I discussed how Freud relied on the concept of an equilibrium-seeking system to explain the basic dynamics of the nervous system as well as psychological functioning. The concept can be seen in Freud's theories of neuronal inertia, the constancy and stability principles, the pleasure principle, the primary and secondary systems, the nature of instincts, the death instinct, the Nirvana principle, and resistance. Following in the tradition of psychophysics, Freud (1955, vol. 1) interpreted the equilibrium-seeking constancy demands of the nervous system as ". . . the most fundamental conditions of the psychical mechanism" (p. 221).

Freud was searching for a theoretical underpinning that would simultaneously accomplish several neuropsychological goals: (a) explain the dynamics of neuroses; (b) show why his and Breuer's therapy worked; (c) expound on why sexual tension and release were so intimately linked to neurological and psychological functioning; (d) account for the motive power and purpose as well as for stability of the nervous system; and (e) to do all the previous in the context of a physicalist and mechanistic model of the mind that would be congruent and acceptable to the scientific community. That his equilibrium-seeking systems model of mental functioning seems to have accomplished these goals in an acceptable mechanistic manner was confirmed by Freud's (1955, vol. 1 p. 285) own, almost ecstatic exclamation to his friend Fliess upon completion of the "Project": "Everything seemed to fit in together, the gears were in mesh, the thing gave one the impression that it was really a machine and would soon run of itself."

MOVING BEYOND THE EQUILIBRIUM-SEEKING SYSTEMS MODEL

A Clinical Role for Equilibrium

Serious problems with the entire energetic/economic underpinnings of psychoanalytic theory have been voiced ever since its inception. As a result, the equilibrium-seeking systems idea has often been thrown out with the bath water. For example, Roy Schafer (1976) chose to dump the metaphyschological edifice of Freudian theory in favor of an Wittgensteinian "action-language." Consequently, in Schafer's reformulation, there is no recourse to the equilibrium-seeking systems concept. Others simply reinterpret the metapsychology as *metaphor* and, thereby, side step the need to explain any actual equilibrium-seeking mechanisms at work in the metapsychology (Ricoeur, 1970).

But even in those who reject the explicit Freudian metapsychology, glimmers of the equilibrium-seeking system peek through. For example, Rosenblatt and Thickstun (1977 p. 549), in their information-theory approach to psychoanalysis, consciously abandon the "power-engineering model" (*sic*) and associated equilibrium-seeking principles but, nevertheless, resort to mental mechanisms of goal seeking and negative-feedback loops that are really nothing more than a different language expressing the same concept of an equilibrium-seeking system: "If the appraisal process of a particular system reflects a mismatch between goal and current input, especially a discrepancy that increases over an interval of time, the felt phase of the process (if attained) will be experienced as unpleasurable; if the reverse occurs, the feeling will be pleasurable in quality."

Here, the discrepancy between goal and input, felt as unpleasurable, is a departure from equilibrium that the mind as a system seeks to eliminate because of its tendency to seek pleasure and get rid of unpleasure. This, of course, is simply a modern restatement of Freud's equilibrium-seeking pleasure principle. Similarly, Galatzer-Levy (1983) avoided the term *equilibrium* in his sophisticated mathematical rendering of Freud's regulatory precepts, but the equilibrium-seeking systems idea is implicit in Galatzer-Levy's resort to the calculus of maxima and minima.

Even those theorists wanting to retain the equilibrium-seeking systems basis of Freud's regulatory principles have realized modifications were needed in order to account for the delay of discharge characterizing the build-up of tension during pleasurable activities like sex. For example, Rappaport (1960, pp. 29–30) turned to the psychic "structures" of ego defenses to explain the delay of discharge, ". . . .full discharge of drive tension gives way to discharge compatible with maintenance of tension which is made inevitable by structure formation." Yet, no matter what additional accouterments are added to make the theory more palatable, the equilibrium-seeking basis of the pleasure principle has remained the fundamental law of the psyche for those staying within the economic/energetic framework.

From the principle of Occam's razor alone one should probably disassemble the complicated edifice that has been erected to save the energetic model in psychoanalysis. However, there is a crucial role for the idea of an equilibrium-seeking system in psychoanalytic theory, albeit a role that must be reinterpreted within the context of nonlinear and nonequilibrium dynamics. This role for the concept takes into consideration its clinical and heuristic value. As Horowitz (1977, p. 577) pointed out:

> The theories that have grown out of the psychoanalytic method, the metapsychological viewpoints and their quantitative assumptions, have proved useful in the exegetical work of analysis. The explanation of symptom formation and the interpretation of dreams have been illuminated by those viewpoints. However, the psychoanalytic method cannot answer our questions about the functioning of the nervous system. . .The theory holds for a narrow segment of stylized reality and may be retained for clinical work.

An important clinical role for the equilibrium-seeking systems idea has to do with how this concept phenomenologically reflects the "stuck" emotional place in which patients often find themselves when entering therapy. The concept of a system being dominated by a tendency to remain at or to restore a state of equilibrium corresponds well with this experience of being "stuck." For example, even Schafer (1976, p. 258) referred to the phenomenological condition of being "stuck": ". . .for this analysand there is no conceiving of change in the future just because there is no envisaging any variety of experience, and so there is only living timelessly in a closed phenomenal world."

Toward a Nonequilibrium and Nonlinear Context

A problem arises, however, when this phenomenological experience is used as the basis for an entire theory of psychodynamics. Remember the point made earlier how, during its long historical development, the concept of equilibrium was transformed from determinate conditions to a teleological explanation. Freud and later psychoanalytic theorists accepted the equilibrium concept in its explanatory, teleological form because it was the only thing available to them for understanding the dynamics of systems as systems. But what I am recommending here is putting equilibrium back in its original role as a determinate condition and not viewing it as the whole picture, only a limited part of it—an initial phase.

Such a way of conceiving equilibrium as a limited, initial phase of a system's development is found in nonlinear and nonequilibrium theory. A nonlinear system, under nonequilibrium conditions, passes through different attractor regimes with equilibrium dominance being only an initial attractor (Mayer-Kress, 1991). One of the truly remarkable discoveries in these new sciences is that certain types of nonlinearity have built right into them this transformative, evolutionary transition into more and more complex attractors (Berge, Pomeau, & Vidal, 1984).

Therefore, the equilibrium-seeking systems concept is not rejected en masse; it is simply put in its proper place as a limiting case of a much wider, more general theory. Unlike an equilibrium-based approach that cannot account for change and development, a more general nonlinear and nonequilibrium theory includes change and development as a natural process of system evolution. Understanding a psychotherapy patient's "stuck" condition, then, as an initial equilibrium-dominated phase of a wider nonequilibrium evolutionary trajectory would do greater justice to the developmental potential of psychotherapeutic treatment, while, at the same time, remaining true to a patient's experience.

Adopting a nonlinear and nonequilibrium understanding of psychotherapeutic change would include the following assumptions:

> Change that occurs during psychotherapy can be conceived as system transformation according to the model of self-organization.
>
> As self-organization, therapy consists of a nonlinear system under a nonequilibrium condition.
>
> What undergoes development or transformation is the psychological/mental/emotional self as a nonlinear system.
>
> This nonlinear system of the self has a developmental or growth capacity purely as a result of its nonlinearity.
>
> Therapeutic change can either be a change within the initial equilibrium attractor or it can be change as a transition into new attractors.
>
> Therefore, therapy can coincide with either an equilibrium or a nonequilibrium condition, depending on whether change is within or between attractors.
>
> Deep-rooted therapeutic change as the transition into more complex attractors could be understood as the generation of a nonequilibrium condition.
>
> Therapeutic treatment as the generation of a nonequilibrium condition could utilize diverse types of methods as long as these methods facilitated a nonequilibrium condition.

Advantages of a Nonequilibrium Model

Besides being able to more adequately understand the processes of change, development, and growth in psychotherapy, a nonequilibrium approach would also be able to account for the following therapeutic phenomena that elude an equilibrium-based theroy:

1. *Taking advantage of the unexpected.* As I have demonstrated elsewhere (Goldstein, 1994), an equilibrium-based approach to change is primarily linear and, therefore, assumes processes and outcomes are predictable. However, nonlinear and nonequilibrium research has shown unpredictability in the evolution of systems (Nicolis, 1989). For example, in self-organization, random, and, hence, unpredictable, departures from equilibrium are recognized and utilized by the system in its reorganization. Similarly, psychoanalysis in its many guises has long recognized the potential efficacy of unexpected crises, fortuitous events, accidents, and so on during treatment. Thus, Fenichel (1941, p. 48) could write:

"Freud once warned us against attempting too often in the course of an analysis to sketch a picture of the case. We must always be ready to let ourselves be led by the patient to something quite different from what we had expected." In the equilibrium model of psychotherapeutic change, there is no place for allowing the unexpected to guide treatment.

2. *Insight into resistance reveals its affirmative core.* Schafer (1976) and Kohut (1984) in psychoanalysis, Erickson (Dolan, 1985) in strategic therapy, and Hoffman (1981) in the family systems school have amply demonstrated that, clinically, the phenomenon of a patient's resisting change is about the affirmation of a sense of dignity, self-integrity, and adherence to ideals. Resistance has an affirmative core, and, therefore consists of a great deal more than simply a manifestation of equilibrium-seeking or a stubborn opposition of wills (Goldstein, 1989). Therefore, its resistance can be better characterized by what the patient is attracted to rather than what the patient is opposing. The analysis of the affirmative core of resistance then may facilitate therapeutic change by acting as a nonequilibrium condition freeing up energies for self-organization by.

3. *The importance of boundary work in therapy.* In equilibrium models there is an implicit assumption of a closed system. For example, Freud's equilibrium understanding of the regulatory principles of the nervous system presume this system is closed and that all the important dynamics are internal to the system. The connection to the environment is thereby disregarded. Later object relations theorists, of course, tried to remedy this oversight, but if they continue to use an equilibrium-based model, they have to resort to fancy foot work to get around the assumption of an isolated system.

Yet, psychotherapeutic work has much to do with differentiating the boundaries between client and therapist and the firming up of weak boundaries in the patient. This, of course, is possible by way of the "holding environment" created in the therapeutic situation. There is a paradoxical nature to boundary work in therapy that remains mysterious to an equilibrium-based theory. First, self-organization occurs only in systems with clear and firm boundaries that act as containers of the nonlinear processes taking place. But self-organization is also only possible when boundaries are crossed between a system and its environment. Therapy has to do with a traversing of boundaries between therapist and client, getting across the dysfunctional defense keeping the other person out or confined to a narrow sector of relationship. A nonequilibrium approach is concerned with connecting a system to its environment so that a vital exchange can take place.

4. *Sex and sexual issues in the therapeutic relationship.* In Freud's interpretation of sexuality, an equilibrium-seeking model lends itself to sex a build-up and discharge of tension. Yet, Freud (1955, pp. 160–161; emphasis added) himself recognized sex was much more than tension discharge: "Pleasure and unpleasure, therefore, cannot be referred to an increase or decrease of a quantity. . .It

appears that they depend, not on this quantitative factor, but on some characteristic of it which we can only describe as a *qualitative* one.

Moreover, sexual issues that arise in analysis certainly have a lot to do with boundary issues (e.g., having to do with a sense of being "violated" or "penetrated").

Thus, a nonequilibrium view could offer a more appropriate understanding of how therapy can deal with the complex dynamics of sexuality as more than the discharge of tension. This might include understanding sexual fixations as attraction to attractors.

5. *Integrating incremental and revolutionary change.* As mentioned earlier, change can be of at least two types: within an equilibrium attractor or a shift to new attractors. These two kinds of psychotherapeutic change would correspond to what Watzlawick, Weakland, and Fisch (1974) called first-order versus second-order change. A nonequilibrium framework could thus account for both types of change. For example, certain types of behavior modification could be seen as change within an attractor, whereas deep rooted change that occurs might be better conceived as a transition into a more complex attractor. As a host of psychotherapeutic modalities by understanding them in the light of their ability for either causing incremental change within an equilibrium attractor or for generating a nonequilibrium condition.

Conclusion

Freud (Jones, 1953, vol. 1, p. 374) once stated his theoretical goal: "My life has aimed at only one goal: to deduce or to guess how the psychic apparatus is constructed and what forces interplay and control it." What has been suggested in this chapter is that the concept of an equilibrium-seeking systems concept be retained, not for understanding the "psychic apparatus," but, instead, for it's usefulness in shedding light on the "stuck" emotional condition of a patient in psychotherapy. This clinical use of equilibrium would be only a phase of a wider, nonequilibrium and nonlinear understanding of psychotherapeutic change as self-organization. This shifts the focus to ascertaining what type of change is required and then designing appropriate methods that work by either changing within an attractor or transiting to a more complex attractor.

REFERENCES

Austedo, F. (1967). Richard Avenarius (A. E. Blumberg, Trans.). *Encyclopedia of philosophy* (Vol. 1). New York: MacMillan.

Berge, P., Pomeau, Y., & Vidal, C. (1984). *Order within chaos: Towards a deterministic approach to turbulence.* New York: Wiley.

Bernfeld, S., & Feitelberg, S. (1929). Das Prinzip von Le Chatelier und der Selbstverhaltungsstrieb [The Principle of Le Chatelier and the Survival Instinct]. *Imago, 16,* 200–289.

Boyer, C. (1968). *A history of mathematics*. Princeton, NJ: Princeton University Press.

Broda, E. (1983). *Ludwig Boltzmann: Man, physicist, philosopher* (L. Gay, Trans.). Woodbridge, CT: Ox Bow Press.

Cohen, I. B. (1985). *The birth of the new physics*. New York: Norton.

D'Abro, A. (1951). *The rise of the new physics* (Vol. 1). New York: Dover.

Deri, S. (1990). The Homeostatic and the representational function of the symbolic process; with reference to the "Rat Man's" obsessive ideation. *Psychoanalytic Review, 77*(4), 525–534. (Original work published 1964)

Dolan, Y. (1985). *A path with heart: Ericksonian utilization with resistant and chronic clients*. New York: Brunner/Mazel.

Elkana, Y. (1974). *The discovery of the conservation of energy*. Cambridge, MA: Harvard University Press.

Fechner, G. (1966). *Elements of psychophysics* (Vol. 1). (H. Adler, Trans. D. Howes & E. Boring, Eds. New York: Holt, Rinehart & Winston. (Original work published 1860)

Fenichel, O. (1941). *Problems of psychoanalytic technique,* (D. Brunswick, Trans.). New York: The Psychoanalytic Quarterly.

Fenichel, O. (1945). *The psychoanalytic theory of neurosis*. New York: Norton.

French, T. (1970). Goal, mechanism, and integrated field. In *Psychoanalytic interpretations: The selected papers of Thomas French, M.D.* Chicago: Quadrangle Books. (Original work published 1941)

Freud, S. (1955). *Standard edition of the complete psychological works of Sigmund Freud*. (J. Strachey, Trans. & Ed.). London: Hogarth Press. (Original work published 1893)

Galatzer-Levy, R. (1983). Perspective on the regulatory principles of mental functioning. *Psychoanalysis and Contemporary Thought, 6, 255–289.*

Gay, P. (1988). *Freud: A life for our time*. New York: Norton.

Gibbs, J. W. (1928). The equilibrium of heterogeneous substances. In *Collected works*. London: Longmans, Green.

Goldstein, J. (1989). The affirmative core of resistance to change. *The Organization Development Journal, 7*(1), 32–39.

Goldstein, J. (1990). Freud's theories in the light of far-from-equilibrium research. In *System dynamics '90, vol. 1: Proceedings of the 1990 international system dynamics conference*. Cambridge, MA: The System Dynamics Society, MIT, 440–454.

Goldstein, J. (1993). Beyond Lewin's force-field: A new model for organizational change interventions. In F. Massarik (Ed.), *Advances in organization development* (Vol. 2, pp. 72–88). Norwood, NJ: Ablex.

Goldstein, J. (1994). *The unshackled organization: Facing the challenge of unpredictability through spontaneous reorganization*. Portland, OR: Productivity Press.

Haroutunian, S. (1983). *Equilibrium in the balance: A study of psychological explanation*. New York: Springer-Verlag.

Helmholtz, H. (1976). On the conservation of energy. In R. B. Lindsay (Ed.), *Applications of energy in the nineteenth century*. Stroudsburg, PA: Dowden, Hutchinson, & Ross.

Herbart, J. F. (1891). *A textbook in psychology: An attempt to found the science of psychology on experience, metaphysics, and mathematics* (M. K. Smith, Trans.) New York: D. Appleton. (Original work published 1816)

Herrnstein, R., & Boring, E. (Eds.) (1965). *A source book in the history of psychology*. Cambridge, MA: Harvard University Press.

Hoffman, L. (1981). *Foundations of family therapy: A conceptual framework for systems change*. New York: Basic Books.

Horowitz, M. H. (1977). The quantitative line of approach in psychoanalysis: A clinical assessment of its current status. *The Journal of the American Psychoanalytic Association, 25, 559–578.*

Jammer, M. (1957). *Concepts of force: A study in the foundation of dynamics*. Cambridge, MA: Harvard University Press.

Janik, A., & Toulmin, S. (1973). *Wittgenstein's Vienna.* New York: Simon & Schuster.

Jones, E. (1953). *The life and work of Sigmund Freud.* New York: Basic Books.

Joseph, B. (1989). *Psychic equilibrium and psychic change: Selected papers of Betty Joseph* (M. Felman & E. B. Spilius, Eds.). London: Tavistock/Routledge.

Kanzer, M. (1981). Freud, Theodor Lipps, and "Scientific psychology." *Psychoanalytic Quarterly, L,* 393–409.

Kanzer, M. (1983). The inconstant "Principle of constancy." *The Journal of the American Psychoanalytic Association, 31,* 847–858.

Kohut, H. (1984). *How does analysis cure?* (A. Goldberg & P. Stepansky, Eds.). Chicago: University of Chicago Press.

Leary, D. (1978). The philosophical development of the conception of psychology in Germany, 1780–1850. *Journal of the History of the Behavioral Sciences, 14,* 115–128.

Levin, S., (1970, December). *The depressive core in schizophrenia.* Paper presented at a Meeting of the American Psychoanalytic Association, New York.

Lotze, H. (1886). *Outlines of psychology.* (G. Ladd, Trans. and Ed.). In D. Robinson (Ed.), *Significant contributions to the history of psychology, 1750–1920* (Vol. 6). Washington, DC: University Publishers of America.

Mach, E. (1883, 1960). *The science of mechanics: A critical and historical account of its development* (J. McCormack, Trans.). LaSalle, IL: Open Court Publishing.

Mayer-Kress, G. (1991). *Role of nonlinear dynamics and chaos in international relations.* Paper presented at First Annual Chaos Conference, Washington, DC.

McDougall, J. (1974). The psychosoma and the psychoanalytic process. *International Review of Psychoanalysis, 1*(4),437–459.

Nicolis, G. (1989). Physics of far-from-equilibrium systems and self-organization. In P. Davies (Ed.), *The new physics.* Cambridge, England: Cambridge University Press.

Ostow, M. (1990). Comments on the Pathogenesis and Psychopharmacological management of the Borderline Disorder. *The Journal of the American Academy of Psychoanalysis, 18*(1)145–151.

Ostwald, W. (1976). Studies in energetics. In R. B. Lindsay (Ed.), *Applications of energy in the nineteenth century.* Stroudsburg, PA: Dowden, Hutchinson, & Ross.

Peters, R. S. (Ed.). (1962). *Brett's history of psychology.* London: George Allen & Unwin.

Rappaport, D. (1951). *Organization and pathology of thought: Selected sources.* New York: Colombia University Press.

Rappaport, D. (1960). *The structure of psychoanalytic theory.* (Psychological Issues, Monograph 6). New York: International Universities Press.

Ricoeur, P. (1970). *Freud and philosophy: An essay on interpretation.* New Haven, CT: Yale University Press.

Rosenblatt, A. D., & Thickstun, J. T. (1977). Energy, information, and motivation: A revision of psychoanalytic theory. *Journal of the American Psychoanalytic Association, 25,* 537–558.

Russett, C. (1966). *The concept of equilibrium in American social thought.* New Haven, CT: Yale University Press.

Sands, R. (1988). Early nineteenth century anticipation of Freudian theory. *Review of psychoanalysis, 15,* 465–479.

Schafer, R. (1976). *A new language for psychoanalysis.* New Haven, CT: Yale University Press.

Shope, R. (1971). Physical and psychic energy. *Philosophy of Science,* March, 1–12.

Sorokin, P. (1941). *Social and cultural dynamics* (Vol. 4). New York: American Book.

Watzlawick, P., Weakland, J., & Fisch, R. (1974). *Change: Principles of problem formation and problem resolution.* New York: Norton.

Wolman, B. (1968). The historical role of Johann Friedrich Herbart. In B. Wolman (Ed.), *Historical roots of contemporary psychology.* New York: Harper & Row.

16 Chaotic Phenomena in Psychophysiological Self-Regulation

Stephen E. Francis

The study of the behavior of complex, nonlinear dynamical systems or chaos theory has gained in popularity across scientific disciplines and has recently been applied to the areas of physiology (Freeman 1991, 1987; Goldberger, 1990; Redington & Reidbord, 1992) and psychological development (Bütz, 1992a, 1992b). This chapter falls somewhere in the middle of that continuum and draws from each end for support in developing a new model for understanding human psychophysiological self-regulation and biofeedback in nonlinear dynamical terms.

Freeman (1992 p. 1080) commented that model builders "are prone to dig intellectual holes into which they disappear." I tried to keep his comment in mind in developing a new model of human psychophysiological self-regulation. My goal is to develop a model that will improve diagnosis and treatment in the area of chronic illness, particularly chronic pain, and stress-related disorders. In my own estimation, an understanding of chaos theory and the behavior of complex nonlinear dynamical systems would allow psychophysiologists to understand the patterns and unpredictability inherent in an individual's healing process. There is a need for a model that can capture humans not only as open systems but as capable of self-regulation, self-organization, and personal transformation. Keeping this orientation in mind will prevent any sort of intellectual holes of the kind that Freeman spoke of earlier.

The language and concepts of chaos theory could prove useful in developing a more comprehensive model of human psychophysiological self-regulation. Elsewhere (Abraham, 1989; Bütz, 1992a, 1992b), models of the human psyche have been developed utilizing Jungian concepts combined with the language and concepts of chaos theory. In a similar vein, I use some of the chaos theory language to speak about health and illness as *attractors* and to conceptualize an individual's experience as dynamical and speak about the movement of that system through its *phase space*.

Earlier models of psychophysiological self-regulation have failed to consider the biofeedback training state as an altered state of consciousness (ASC). As outlined later, shifting attention from outside of the body to sensations within the body is often such a dramatic shift of consciousness that an altered state of consciousness automatically results. This chapter argues that such an altered state of consciousness is the proper ground state from which states of health can emerge.

First, I review previous models of psychophysiological self-regulation, highlighting the limitations of these models. Next, I present the advantages of applying the concepts and language of chaos theory to a model of psychophysiological self-regulation. This leads to a discussion of health and illness as attractors, followed by a comprehensive treatment of interoception and flexibility. Finally, a new model of health is presented, which includes the significance of chaos theory on psychophysiological self-regulation training.

GENERAL SYSTEMS THEORY AND CYBERNETICS

General systems theory is an approach to understanding the behavior of systems by studying the interaction within and between different levels of a system. Furthermore, a system cannot be understood by being reduced to its constituent parts and each of the parts studied in isolation (von Bertalanffy, 1967). Instead the behavior needs to be considered as a whole, and in its interaction with other whole systems.

For much of this century, biological systems have been considered to be steady-state systems. In his famous work, *The Wisdom of the Body* (1932 p. 25), Walter B. Canon studied the "fundamental condition of stability, . . .[and] the various physiological arrangements which serve to restore the normal state when it has been disturbed. . ." Thus, the body's natural, resting state was described in terms of stability and of a steady state. When perturbations occurred, the system entered a state of flux and then normalized itself by returning to the steady state. The models that we look at later are steady-state models that utilize the concepts of homeostasis. In contrast, I suggest that the resting state of the psychophysiological makeup is actually filled with low-level chaotic variability. Interestingly, near the end *The Wisdom of the Body,* Canon admitted the extreme instability of the human organism but presented it not in terms of flexible adaptivity, but rather as an extreme perturbation. Von Bertalanffy (1967) also made reference to processes that seem extreme and unpredictable—such as creativity—and admits the possibility that sensory overload can have positive consequences.

Both the early models of psychophysiological self-regulation and the model presented in this chapter consider the human organism as an open system. An open system is open to its environment; that is, the internal aspects of the system can affect its external environment, and the outside environment can affect the internal processes of the system. This concept was a major contribution of all of the models developed this century. Von Bertalanffy (1968 p. 150) made several distinctions between open systems and steady-state models. He conceived the steady state as essentially a closed system, while the "open system may *actively* tend toward a state of higher organization, i.e., it may pass from a lower to a higher state of order owing to conditions in the system." Earlier he stated:

[T]he basis of the open-system model is the dynamic interaction of its components. The basis of the cybernetic model is the feedback cycle in which, by way of feedback of information, a desired value is maintained, a target is reached, etc. The theory of open systems is a generalized kinetics and thermodynamics. Cybernetic theory is based on feedback and information. (Von Bertalanffy, 1968, p. 156)

The concepts of homeostasis, feedback, and open systems have been central to the models of biofeedback developed thus far. The models by Green and Green (1977) and Schwartz (1979, 1980), which are presented later, made significant contributions to the field of biofeedback and charted new territory for those of us who have followed them. Rather than discrediting them, the model I present in this chapter attempts to build on their models by incorporating the recent advances in nonlinear dynamical systems theory.

Both Green and Green (1977) and Schwartz (1979, 1980) draw cybernetic models describing biofeedback as a new source of information in the organism's system. According to Schwartz (1979, p. 558), "Biofeedback (Stage 5) is a parallel feedback loop to Stage 4 (Negative Feedback), detecting the activity of the peripheral organs (Stage 3) and converting it into environmental input (Stage 1) that can be used by the brain (Stage 2) to increase self-regulation." Prior to the introduction of the feedback of biological activity, the individual had only unconscious negative feedback loops within the body to regulate its activity. Green and Green (1977) emphasized that the addition of "inside the skin events" provides a new cybernetic loop of information that can be used by an individual to learn self-regulation skills. Both of these models emphasize that a return to a homeostatic balance is necessary for the optimal maintenance of the organism.

Elmer Green's background was in guided missile systems in the 1950s (1977). It was a natural step for him to use the cybernetic model to develop a theory of human psychophysiological self-regulation. Central to his model was what he termed dynamic equilibrium or homeostasis. The use of the word *dynamic* hints at the transformative dimensions of humans as open systems, but it is undercut by the homeostatic notion of a return to a steady state.

Schwartz also applied general systems theory to the process of psychophysiological self-regulation and health maintenance. Schwartz (1979) developed a model based on a systems disregulation to explain feedback and psychophysiological self-regulation. The starting point in disregulation is *disattention*. This consists of an individual no longer attending to internal bodily cues, continues onward to *disconnection*, to *disregulation*, to *disorder*, and, finally, to *disease*. The introduction of biofeedback to an individual, according to this model, will aid the individual in finding the path from *attention* to *connection* to *self-regulation* to *order* to *"ease"* or *health*. From the perspective of this chapter, several problems emerge with Schwartz's model. The starting point of attention in his process is in accord with this chapter and is addressed later. The process from connection to self-regulation to order to health is overly optimistic and reflects the linearity of traditional general systems theory. As is shown later, the process toward health is not a linear one. The theory also does not have an intrinsic clinical reality. It implies that all individuals will start at the same point and progress in a similar fashion. In the language of nonlinear dynamical theory, Schwartz's model does not account for sensitivity to initial conditions.

Foss and Rothenberg (1988, pp. 42–43, 46) developed a cybernetic model of health that they termed *infomedicine*. In their words "the patient-as-decoder-of-information can gain (in some areas) cybernetic control to achieve a state of health through reestablishing either systemic stability or systemic reorganization." And further they continue "message-program interactions within a feedback loop are reciprocal influences. They are capable of triggering either stabilizing (healthy) or destabilizing (diseased) processes. In the first case they are therapeutic agents, in the second pathological agents." It can be seen from these remarks that there is a disdain for a lack of order and nonlinearity in an individual's healing process. Interestingly, Foss and Rothenberg do state that "the system itself, as defined by the state of its interactive parts, may be far from equilibrium. In such a system, a small change in one of its parameters can result in a qualitatively redefined system."

It seems that, in these areas of cybernetics and general systems theory, an awareness of nonlinearity was alluded to but never closely examined. So the question arises: What is the next step for a theory that can account for more of the dimensions of psychophysiological self-regulation training and change? In the next section evidence is presented for developing a new model that will incorporate findings from nonlinear dynamics.

THE CASE FOR A NEW MODEL

Chaos as a concept has roots in many ancient mythologies (Briggs & Peat, 1989). Unfortunately, in the English language, chaos has been falsely derived to mean "a confused and unorganized mass of elements" (Krippner, 1991, p. 1). Chaos theory has its mathematical roots in several problems that had developed at the turn of the century in physics and mathematics. The linear mathematics developed by Newton and Leibniz several centuries earlier was too limited for the modeling of certain problems such as aperiodic flow and turbulence (Briggs & Peat, 1989; Gleick, 1987; Krippner, 1991). To be properly understood, the behavior of chaotic systems required the development of nonlinear and qualitative mathematics. Whenever more than two variables are to be accounted for, a system becomes complex enough to be considered a potentially chaotic system.

Chaos theory offers two advantages in developing a comprehensive theory for psychophysiological self-regulation. First, the language and concepts of chaos theory better describe the potential for transformation possible during self-regulation training. Second, chaos theory enriches the concept of health by describing it as a complex set of behaviors rather than as an end state or steady state. This is addressed later in this chapter.

Many people associate chaos with randomness and unpredictability. As Bütz (1992a) illustrated, chaos should not be seen as something ugly or undesirable but as a part of a healing process. Evidence has been presented for chaotic processes in both psychological development (Abraham, 1989; Bütz, 1992a, 1992b), and biological systems. According to Skarda and Freeman (1987):

> [Brains] rely on mechanisms not found in other models; we propose four such mechanisms that may be necessary to solve problems critical to the efficient functioning and survival of any system that has to behave adaptively in an environment subject to unpredictable and often violent fluctuations. . .Chaos constitutes the basic form of collective neural activity for all perceptual processes and functions as a controlled source of noise, as a means to ensure continual access to previously learned sensory patterns, and as the means for learning new sensory patterns. (p. 161)

In cardiology, Goldberger (1990; Goldberger, Rigney, & West, 1990; Pool, 1990) presented evidence that chaotic variability in heart activity is necessary for flexibility and adaptability in a changing environment. I suggest that there is an emergent property of chaotic variability in the brain states and heart activity that continues on up to the level of mind states for humans. We should consider the possibility that chaotic processes are healthy and normal and help us deal with the demands of a changing environment without always having to return to a steady state, as the cybernetic model would posit.

HEALTH AND ILLNESS AS ATTRACTORS

I would like to consider health and illness as strange attractors. In chaos theory, "phase space [is] composed of many dimensions that describe a system" (Briggs & Peat, 1989, p. 32). Chaos occurs in an orderly system when "simple and limited motion breaks down so that nature begins to explore all the implications of the much larger phase space at its disposal" (Briggs & Peat, 1989, p. 33). In the same way that water finds its way down a hillside to the lowest point in the terrain, a system will move toward certain regions of a phase space that seem to pull on it. In chaos theory terms, these regions are called *attractors*. In isolated systems, equilibrium appears as an attractor of nonequilibrium states (Prigogine & Stengers, 1984). Instability will cause a system to seek an attractor.

Chaos theory identifies several types of attractors (Abraham, 1989; Tsonis & Tsonis, 1989). First is a point attractor, where the system returns to a steady state or a fixed point after each perturbation. A common example of a point attractor would be a pendulum. The second type of attractor is a cyclic attractor, in which the system visits two different points periodically but never breaks out of that cycle. Acute illness is an example of a cyclic attractor with health as the other region of the cyclic attractor. The third type of attractor is a strange attractor, which moves a system into unpredictable behavior creating the possibilities of a bifurcation of the system's previous behavior, and allowing for a new way of being to emerge.

In the clinical realm of psychophysiology, acute pains and illness often trace the paths of point attractors and cyclic attractors. When an individual comes for biofeedback therapy, however, the presenting symptoms have often become chronic and are causing a bifurcation in the person's experience such that chronic illness has become a strange attractor. In other words, the behavior of the person on all levels from molecular to mental and emotional are attracted to the region of illness. Often previously successful treatments in the presence of acute problems are unsuccessful because the dimensions of illness as an attractor are exerting a powerful influence on the person. The challenge to the psychophysiologist is to facilitate the person's possibilities of exploring health as an attractor.

In this model, illness is no longer viewed from the traditional western medical model as something to be eradicated, but as an opportunity for the individual to explore fuller dimensions of their being (Bütz, 1992a). This emerging model's reconception of health and illness recalls the tradition of the wounded healer commonly described in preindustrialized societies. In those societies, a life-threatening or chronic illness can become a transitional point of development for an individual who will later become a shaman (Achterberg, 1987).

Previous models of psychophysiological self-regulation have not placed enough emphasis on the process and properties of the biofeedback setting that could enable an individual to explore these dimensions of their experience. Next, I elaborate on what I consider some of these factors to be and how they fit into my model.

INTEROCEPTION AND ALTERED STATES
OF CONSCIOUSNESS

Humans are unique as systems because they contain the capacity for behavior shaped by will, intention, and purpose. They are not merely shaped by the environment as the behavioral paradigm of stimulus–response conditioning has asserted. We also have the ability for interoception; that is, we can turn our attention inward and reflect on internal processes. Tart (1980) defined interoception as "sensory reception for perceiving what is happening in our bodies—position, muscle tension, internal discomfort, pain, etc." (p. 280). The output signals from our interoceptors are usually excluded form our awareness; however, some signals can be perceived by turning one's attentional awareness inward (Tart, 1975). Interoception can become an informational source completing a feedback loop in psychophysiological self-regulation. According to Granger (1987), "awareness [of] somatic process establishes a critical feedback link to cortical processes which may initiate self-regulation" (pp. 75–76). Tart (1975) stated that a "loss of contact with our actual body sensations puts us out of contact with ourselves" (p. 95).

Tart (1980) emphasized that, in this culture, we often make the assumption that our ordinary state of waking consciousness is "normal." Consequently, we have come to regard "altered states" as inferior or pathological. Examples of this include the familiar statements of "I must have been out of my mind" and "I felt as if someone else was doing it." Tart (1980) made an important point by clarifying that *state* is not identical to the momentary content of consciousness, but that "states are temporal clusterings of the content and organization of consciousness" (p. 251). He continued: "We may formally define a discrete state of consciousness for a given individual as a unique system or configuration of psychological structures or substructures" (p. 255). For the model I am proposing, I would amend that statement by saying that a discrete state of consciousness is defined by the configuration of physiological *and* psychological structures or substructures *and* their interactions.

For the induction of a discrete altered state of consciousness, Tart (1980) stated that several factors are necessary. First, the stabilization of one's current discrete state of consciousness, most likely one of ordinary consciousness, must be disrupted through means such as "anomalous stimuli that can't be processed in habitual ways or [by] deliberately withdrawing attentional awareness form them as a way of de-energizing them" (p. 262). Second, it is important to alter the patterning forces, the psychological or physiological pressures to restructure consciousness. There needs to be a transitional period before the new contents of consciousness constellate into a discrete new state of consciousness.

Techniques that have developed to enhance psychophysiological self-regulation use interoception as a means to shift an individual's state of consciousness. These systems include, but are not limited to, meditation, biofeedback, and autogenic training. There are many forms of meditation, some of which use a form of "mindfulness," whereas others incorporate concentrative exercises that emphasize turning attentional awareness to internal body processes, such as breathing patterns. This is an attempt to repattern awareness, partly achieved by a reduction in the attention paid to external sensory stimuli. Meditation is often misrepresented as a form of relaxation (Benson, 1975; Brown, 1986). Granger

(1986) considered these three practices, meditation, biofeedback, and autogenic training, as well as yoga, not as relaxation techniques per se, but awareness repatterning techniques. So, perhaps it is through the repatterning of awareness that optimum psychophysiological self-regulation is restored and maintained in the behavior of the complex nonlinear dynamical system of the human.

Biofeedback uses instruments to measure internal bodily processes and then provides the individual with the information about these internal states such as heart rate, muscle tension, and peripheral skin temperature (Brown, 1977; Green & Green, 1977). In the 1960s and early 1970s there was popular interest in altered states of consciousness. EEG biofeedback was touted as an electronic meditation and the other modalities of biofeedback did not receive as much popular interest. Because our "normal" waking state of consciousness is outwardly focused on the world around us, directing our attention inward to sensations within the body, coupled with the information provided by biofeedback instrumentation, can represent such a dramatic shift in one's state of consciousness, that alterations in sense of time, space, or self could occur. In this way the biofeedback training experience utilizing any of the training modalities could be considered an induction to an altered state of consciousness. Self-organization has been described in dynamical terms as having the capacity to influence control parameters (Abraham, 1989). It could be said that the process of acquiring psychophysiological self-regulation skills is a process which enables an individual to self-organize at a higher developmental level.

In terms of the behavior of complex nonlinear dynamical systems, the interoceptive process and the subsequent altered state of consciousness, combined with the information provided by the biofeedback instrumentation, can provide sufficient energy to the individual so that he or she can now begin exploring other basins of attraction. Normal waking consciousness imposes constraints on the psychophysiological system. By shifting attentional awareness to events inside the body, we change the constraints on the system, thereby allowing the system to explore other areas in the space of possible psychophysiological states. According to Schuman (1980), "meditation can be viewed as a methodology for destabilizing the structures of normal waking consciousness, thus allowing altered patterns of activity to emerge" (p. 372). To reiterate, the altered state of consciousness allows for the possibility of new patterns of self-organization to emerge.

A necessary condition for a successful experience achieving self-regulatory abilities, whether through meditation, autogenic training, or in biofeedback is the cultivation of passive awareness (Green & Green, 1977; Peper, 1979; Schuman, 1980). "Passive awareness. . .involves a fundamental shift in the frame of reference of experience" (Schuman, 1980, p. 336). Passive awareness can facilitate the reduction of sympathetic nervous system output, thereby enabling more presence of the parasympathetic nervous system. Parasympathetic dominance can be characterized by a slowed breathing rate, lowered heartrate, reduction of muscle tension, an increase in peripheral skin temperature, and a lowered skin conductance (Olton & Noonberg, 1980).

Ikegami (cited in Brown, 1986) made some interesting observations by noting that his meditation subjects did not show a decrease in muscle tone, but an even distribution of muscle nerve firing. This suggests that focused interoceptive awareness can be said to create an energy-efficient state rather than merely a relaxed one. This would be consistent with the notion that the physiological constraints are changed during these states of consciousness. Autogenic training has been noted to cause a diminution of hypothalamus-cortical discharges producing a dominance of the trophotropic (parasympathetic) system (Gellhorn & Keily, 1972). Although Gellhorn (1969) addressed autogenic training and meditation in homeostatic terms, his comments are relevant to our concept of psychophysiological change through interoceptive means. He stated that the "lessening of the proprioceptive bombardment of the diencephalon through relaxation restores the physiological level of ergotropic activity and through the reciprocal relations between ergotropic and trophotropic systems" (p. 101). Broader models of psychophysiology have been developed that include a variety of techniques for induction of altered states of consciousness (ASC); some of the physiological aspects of ASCs as discussed earlier seem to have inherent therapeutic effects (Winkelman, 1990).

This indicates that passive awareness and interoception in most cases provide a necessary step toward the creation of an altered state of consciousness that changes physiological constraints to health. Thus, an individual undergoing some form of self-regulation training, such as biofeedback, meditation, or autogenic training can begin to explore other areas of possible psychophysiological states. Psychophysiological feedback instrumentation can aid in this process. The individual's experiences can be profound enough that they can shift from an illness attractor to a health attractor.

FLEXIBILITY

One critical fact was omitted from the earlier discussion: Why do some people get better during biofeedback or other forms of self-regulation therapy and others do not? And possibly a larger question needs to be asked: Why do some people seem to get worse during such therapy? Aside from the obvious answer that some organic pathology prevented them from improving, we are left to speculate.

Wickramasekera (1987, 1988, 1991) developed a model for predicting the development of chronic stress-related symptoms. His multidimensional model states that individuals who are in the upper 10% or lowest 10% on a hypnotic susceptibility scale and score high on neuroticism and catastrophizing self-report measures are more likely to develop stress-related symptoms. The high and low hypnotic dimensions are extreme examples of attentional functioning. The highly hypnotizable individuals easily produce psychophysiological shifts; unfortunately it is usually to their detriment because it is not under their conscious control. The lease hypnotizable individuals, on the other hand, are so cut off from perception of their internal states, that they often attribute physiological feelings to external events (Wickramasekera, 1991). In this model of psychophysiological psychotherapy, a person can discover "the secrets that they keep from themselves." These secrets are often unveiled during deep interoceptive processes involving psychotherapy in combination with either biofeedback or hypnosis. During the process of uncovering the secrets, there can be a heightening of sweat gland activity and/or heart rate activity, which is normalized as the secrets are resolved in the therapy.

This is again an example of a complex dynamical system exhibiting what would seem to be chaotic behavior as it bifurcates, then finds an attractor region and moves toward it, but in a relatively unpredictable fashion. In other words, the individual seems to get worse before he or she get better. If we pick any place in the process and examine it, we perceive disorder, possibly disease. But when we examine the system dynamically and observe the shifts of the whole system in its process, the apparent disorder becomes chaotic as it moves toward a more integrated mode of being. We can say that the introduction of the ASC associated with the biofeedback therapy caused a bifurcation for the individual and a larger phase space was explored before health was established as an attractor.

Green and Green (1977) described a woman who had migraines; during her biofeedback training she began to cry as she increased her peripheral skin temperature. At that moment she was able to recall past memories that were associated with the onset of her migraine headaches. Through the process of learning the self-regulaton skills, she began to recover more such hidden parts of herself. From the psychophysiological perspective, stress-related disorders often represent a lack of ability to respond in healthy, adaptive ways to challenging or potentially threatening situations. At this point, illness is often established as an attractor.

To return to the question of what allows some people to get better, it appears that it is necessary for them to be able to examine their own characteristics and how easily they can be influenced. As stated earlier in this chapter, there is chaotic variability in the healthy brain and heart, but the less healthy ones display an inability to respond to novel stimuli and challenging situations (Freeman, 1991; Goldberger et al., 1990; Skarda & Freeman, 1987). It seems that the more dynamic variability an individual's physiology exhibits, the healthier he or she will appear to be. Redington and Reidbord (1992) demonstrated that flexibility in a person's psychological style and process can be reflected in that individual's heartrate. Redington (1991) later replicated his study with four other individuals. In the first study, they measured an individual's heartrate activity during a psychotherapy session. The individual had been in psychotherapy in this setting for several years. He found that during a moment of insight, the individual's heartrate produced dimensional changes different from other periods of the session. This type of behavior could be graphed as a trajectory in the individual's phase space. In his research Redington and Reidbord found several types of trajectories. A Type I trajectory consisted of a "regular path within a tight or moderately loose cluster with no apparent perturbations or transitions" (p. 1000). This style exhibited no flexibility. A Type IV trajectory was characterized by increased and novel exploration. This is the style of adaptivity and flexibility that we hope to achieve in psychophysiological self-regulation training. In this way, the individual becomes better suited to coping with the unexpected challenges and stresses that are common elements of living and becomes capable of insight.

CONCLUSIONS: REDEFINING HEALTH

Previous models of psychophysiological self-regulation have defined health as a steady state and a return to homeostasis. Similarly, our culture defines health as an end state or goal. Deviations are considered indications of disease or illness; being "sick" is considered a weakness. We have seen that the language and concepts of complex, nonlinear dynamical systems, coupled with existing models of psychophysiological self-regulation training and health, lead us toward a new definition of health.

Striving toward health in this new model is analogous to a mountain climber choosing to climb a peak he or she deems to be the tallest peak in the area. As the ascent is made, the surrounding landscape takes on a different look. And to the climber's surprise, on successfully making it to the top, there are actually other taller peaks that the climber can access. In the same way, for an individual undergoing psychophysiological self-regulation training, states of health give way to more complex states of health. Sometimes in the process, valleys are encountered. This can come in the form of memories recovered that elevate skin conductance and heartrate, or it can come in the form of a return of pain because the person—now able to explore more of their world—"overdid it," causing a relapse.

When an individual is first referred for psychophysiological self-regulation training, it can be said that he or she is conducting too much stress. The first phase of training often consists of teaching them to be stress resistant. But that only gets them to the point of symptom reduction. To allow them to explore true health and high-level wellness, it is necessary to go further so that they can comfortably conduct more stress in their lives, thereby living more fully and being in contact with more of themselves physically and psychologically.

In order for Western self-regulatory techniques, such as biofeedback and autogenic training, to be endorsed by Western medical science, they have become narrowly focused on symptom reduction. This narrowing has been further encouraged by the medical insurance reimbursement industry and the current socioeconomic climate, which impose linear constraints on the notion of healing. As a result, much clinical psychophysiological self-regulation training never advances beyond the realm of symptom reduction, into the frontier of authentic, high-level wellness.

As we accept the concept of the human as a open, complex, nonlinear, dynamical system interacting in the context of larger and larger dynamical systems, such as families and societies, we can begin to appreciate the need for a model of psychophysiological self-regulation that is composed of nonlinear feedback loops. This chapter has been a modest first step in developing such a model. Looking at interoception as an induction to an altered state of consciousness that pushes the human as a system to explore its phase space, and possibly becoming capable of flexibility and adaptivity and at health and illness as attractors in nonlinear chaotic systems could, in fact, help us move further along in our understanding of health and illness. It can also deepen our appreciation for the human experience and the spontaneity, intention, and will of humans as dynamical systems.

REFERENCES

Abraham, F. D. (1989). Toward a dynamical theory of the psyche. *Psychological Perspectives,* 156–167.

Achterberg, J. (1987). The wounded healer. In G. Doore (Ed.), *Shaman's path.* Boston: Shambhala.

Benson, H. (1975). *The relaxation response.* New York: Morrow.

Briggs, J., & Peat, F. D. (1989). *Turbulent mirror.* New York: Harper & Row.

Brown, B. (1977). *Stress and the art of biofeedback.* New York: Bantam.

Brown, D. P. (1986). The stages of meditation in a cross-cultural perspective. In K. Wilber, J. Engler, & D. P. Brown (Eds.), *Transformations of consciousness.* Boston: Shambhala.

Bütz, M. R. (1992a). Chaos, an omen of transcendence in the psychotherapeutic process. *Psychological Reports, 71,* 827–843.

Bütz, M. R. (1992b). The fractal nature of the development of the self. *Psychological Reports, 71,* 1043–1063.

Canon, W. B. (1932). *The wisdom of the body.* New York: Norton.

Foss, L. & Rothenberg, K. (1988). An infomedical model: A cybernetics approach. *Advances, 5*(3), 38–49.

Freeman, W. J. (1991, February). The physiology of perception. *Scientific American,* pp. 78–85.

Freeman, W. J. (1992). Chaos in psychiatry. (Editorial). *Biological Psychiatry, 31,* 1079–1081.

Gellhorn, E. (1969). Further studies on the physiology and pathophysiology of the tuning of the central nervous system. *Psychosomatics, 10,* 94–104.

Gellhorn, E., & Keily, W. F. (1972). Mystical states of consciousness: Neurophysiological and clinical aspects. *Journal of Nervous and Mental Disease, 154*(6), 399–405.

Gleick, J. (1987). *Chaos.* New York: Viking.

Goldberger, A. L. (1990). Nonlinear dynamics, fractals and chaos: Applications to cardiac electrophysiology. *Annals of Biomedical Engineering, 18,* 195–198.

Goldberger, A. L., Rigney, D. R., & West, B. J. (1990, February). Chaos and fractals in human physiology. *Scientific American,* pp. 42–49.

Granger, D. L. (1986). The psychophysiological role of awareness in the cortical mediation of autonomic and somatic manifestations of anxiety. *Dissertation Abstracts International, 46,* 12B.

Green, E., & Green, A. (1977). *Beyond biofeedback.* New York: Dell.

Krippner, S. (1991). *Chaos theory and humanistic psychology: The third revolution and the third force.* Keynote address presented at the inaugural conference for a Society for Chaos Theory in Psychology, Saybrook Institute, San Francisco.

Olton, D. S., & Noonberg, A. R. (1980). *Biofeedback: Clinical applications in behavioral medicine.* Englewood Cliffs, NJ: Prentice-Hall.

Peper, E. (1979). Passive attention: The gateway to consciousness and autonomic control. In E. Peper, S. Ancoli, & M. Quinn (Eds.), *Mind/body integration: Essential readings in biofeedback.* New York: Plenum.

Pool, R. (1990). Is it healthy to be chaotic? *Science, 243,* 604–607.

Prigogine, I., & Stengers, I. (1984). *Order out of chaos: Man's new dialogue with nature.* New York: Bantam.

Redington, D. J. (1991). Nonlinear dynamics in autonomic nervous system activity: Bridging mind and body phenomena. (Abstract). *Psychophysiology, 28*(3A), S7.

Redington, D. J. & Reidbord, S. P. (1992). Chaotic dynamics in autonomic nervous system activity of a patient during a psychotherapy session. *Biological Psychiatry, 31,* 993–1007.

Schuman, M. (1980). The psychophysiological model of meditation and altered states of consciousness: A critical review. In J. M. Davidson & R. J. Davidson (Eds.), *The psychobiology of consciousness.* New York: Plenum.

Schwartz, G. E. (1979). The brain as a Health Care System. In G. C. Stone, F. Cohen, & N. Adler (Eds.), *Health psychology.* San Francisco: Jossey-Bass.

Schwartz, G. E. (1980). Biofeedback and Patterning of autonomic and central processes: CNS-cardiovascular interactions. In N. E. Miller, T. X. Barber, L. V. DiCara, J. Kamiya, D. Shapiro, & J. Stoyva (Eds.) *Biofeedback and behavioral medicine* (pp. 183–219). Chicago: Aldine-Atherton.

Skarda, C. A., & Freeman, W. J. (1987). How brains make chaos in order to make sense of the world. *Behavioral and brain sciences, 10,* 161–195.

Tart, C. (1975). *States of consciousness.* New York: E. P. Dutton.

Tart, C. (1980). A systems approach to altered states of consciousness. In J. M. Davidson & R. J. Davidson (Eds.), *The psychobiology of consciousness.* New York: Plenum.

Tsonis, P. A., & Tsonis, A. A. (1989). Chaos: Principles and implications in biology. *Computer Applications in Biology, 5*(1), 27–32.

von Bertalanffy, L. (1967, May). *General systems theory in psychology and psychiatry.* Paper presented at the 123rd annual meeting of the American Psychiatric Association, Detroit, MI.

von Bertalanffy, L. (1968). *General system theory.* New York: Braziller.

Wickramesekera, I. (1987). Risk factors leading to chronic stress-related symptoms. *Advances, 4*(1), 9–35.

Wickramasekera, I. E. (1988). *Clinical behavioral medicine.* New York: Plenum.

Wickramasekera, I. (1991, November). *Psychophysiological psychotherapy: The unconsciousness and somatization.* Keynote address presented at the 17th annual meeting of the Biofeedback Society of California, Los Angeles, CA.

Winkelman, M. (1990). Physiological and therapeutic aspects of shamanistic healing. *Subtle energies, 1*(2), 1–18.

17 Strange Attractors in Patterns of Family Interaction

Linda Chamberlain

SO WHAT IS A STRANGE ATTRACTOR?

Initially, defining a *strange attractor* is like trying to grasp Jell-O®. It's easy to see that there is some substance there, that the substance has some specific form, and that it appears solid. When one tries to actually pick some up, however, it quickly becomes a challenge to manage and is transformed into a very different substance than it appeared to be while sitting on a plate. This may be typical of the cognitive experience many have on first encountering the new concepts of chaos theory, such as the strange attractor.

Strange attractors began their existence as mathematical terms that helped explain why smoke from a cigarette finds a patterned swirl as it curls up from the first puff and why flooding water finds its point of ebb and flow. The attractors are defined as strange because they "describe systems that are neither static nor periodic" (Stevens, 1991, p.23). Briggs and Peat (1989, p.31) eloquently described attractors as "creatures that live in a curious abstract place called *phase space*." They are beasts that exist at the juncture between turbulence and order. Later in their book, they define strange attractors as turbulence; the turbulence that "breaks up orderly systems and causes disorder to boil across our landscape" (Briggs & Peat, 1989, p. 45). It is difficult even for mathematicians like David Ruelle (1980, p.126) not to sound poetic when describing strange attractors "I have not (yet) spoken of the esthetic appeal of strange attractors. These systems of curves, these clouds of points, suggest sometimes fireworks or galaxies, sometimes strange and disquieting vegetal proliferations. A realm lies here to be explored and harmonies to be discovered."

Think of strange attractors as an idealized state toward which an unpredictable or dynamical system is attracted. Essentially, a strange attractor is the process that unfolds through the complex interactions between elements in a system. Some think strange attractors are the foundation for the hidden order in natural systems. Although chaotic systems vacillate erratically, they stay within a particular range or norm. When the data points of strange attractors are mapped, they often resemble a complicated infinity sign.

Although there is apparent order in the pattern, the system is chaotic because there is never an exact repetition in any of the "orbits" around the attractor points. This phenomena is common to systems that function according to chaotic principles: as data accumulates over time, they appear ordered, but they are unpredictable from one moment to the next. Chaos is a science of pattern, not predictability.

The attractor's apparent function is to limit the range of behavior in a system. DiBello, (1990, p.1) noted, "The strange attractor acts like a magnet constraining systemic variables to lie within (these) given ranges." Bütz (1992, p.10) helped to simplify the concept by stating that, "an attractor simply is what it sound like, something that attracts this or that." He described strange attractors as nonlinear and fractal in nature. This differentiates them from other types of attractors (e.g., higher and lower frequencies on an oscillator) that are fixed point, limit-cycle attractors. Patterns in strange attractors are never repeated exactly, but they do exert some limits on the activity in a system.

Strange attractors exist in a mysterious place called *phase space*. Phase space is a mathematical term that allows physicists to visualize many numbers simultaneously. "They take the situation of the system at an instant as a point in what they call a 'phase space' so that in phase space the complete state of knowledge about a dynamical system at a single instant in time collapses to a point. That point is a dynamical system–at that instant" (Albert, 1990, p. 109).

Gleick (1987) considered the concept of phase space one of the most powerful inventions of modern science. It gave scientists a way of mapping information by turning data points into pictures that "abstracted every bit of essential information from a system of moving parts, mechanical or fluid, and making a flexible road map to all its possibilities." (Gleick, 1987, p.134). According to the theory, all of the information about a complicated system can be stored in any point in the phase space. Empty spaces on the map indicate areas into which the system does not venture, changes in the direction of the loop indicate changes in behavior, the pattern of loops show periodicity and the limits of the system.

STRANGE ATTRACTORS MEET HUMAN BEINGS

What happens when the concept of a strange attractor is used to study human dynamical systems? The theory has been applied to many areas of social science including changes in patients' mental states during psychotherapy (Pendick, 1993), daily mood fluctuations (Hannah, 1990), the study of personality (Di-Bello, 1990), societal transformation (Loye & Eisler, 1987), and the autogenesis of the self (Schwalbe, 1990). I noted elsewhere that the fit between chaos and family systems theory seems inescapable (Chamberlain, 1989). As Stevens (1991, p.24) stated, "Even in the most chaotic of family situations there may be organizing principles." It is the patterns of organizing principles or behaviors that constitute the strange attractors in families and provide stability when the family is in danger of moving outside the limits.

The concept of the strange attractor is beginning to make inroads into the realm of human relationships in general. For example, Gampel (1990) wrote that "when we are drawn to another—perhaps as being drawn to another attractor—with great intensity, we transform as we fall in love and risk the dissolution of our boundaries in the merger." She describes the pull of the strange attractor as the familiar conflict between solitude and intimacy in a relationship. Strange attractors are even appearing in popular literature. In the story entitled *Ten Laws of Lasting Love,* Paul Pearsall (1992) introduced his readers to the world of strange attractors. He described love as the product of two personal "strange attractors" drawn to each other to make windows through the chaos of living. He hypothesized that most couples view life's chaos as an obstacle in their quest for self-fulfillment; for them, the necessary turmoil of life is a barrier. But those who have reached the level of "high monogamy" see chaos as a necessary and natural life process. Most family therapists have certainly experienced the phenomena described by Stevens (1991) of the inability to predict from one session to the next how a conflicted couple will behave and the ability to discern certain patterns over time. Despite the appearance of chaos in relationships, there are certain boundaries that limit behaviors.

Although the concept of duality is inexorably embedded in the definition, strange attractors are not simply bidimensional (e.g., solitude versus intimacy). Particularly in the realm of human relationships, even the most basic two-person relationship includes the two as a couple, each as individual, and each as a product of his or her own family and social experience. In the case of a couple, there is not just the conflict between the partners with regard to intimacy and distance, but also within each partner at any given time. The desire for greater closeness or separateness is experienced on both an individual and relational level and is further complicated by the unremitting influence of environmental factors that enter the pattern. Chubb (1990, p.172) noted "The fact that chaotic interactions occur between individuals while other interactions, nonlinear and therefore also chaotic, are occurring within the organisms, adds an extra measure of complexity to the study of social systems. This also contributes to the inherent unpredictability of human relationships. It is the interaction of diverse attractors at different levels of organization that gives us the richness and diversity seen both in strange attractor patterns and in family relationships.

WHO LET THAT STRANGE ATTRACTOR INTO THE
FAMILY THERAPY SESSION?

Why do families come to therapy? What gives people the impression that something can occur in a therapist's office that will change their relationships? It may be that when the fluctuation in the patterns around attractor points becomes too erratic, out of sync, or far from equilibrium in families, entering therapy becomes a way to establish a new strange attractor point that can restore order to the increasingly chaotic interactions in the system. To some degree, there is an agreement to bring in an agent (represented by the therapist) of stability and positive change. Dell and Goolishian (1981, p.179) noted:

> ...as the system becomes sufficiently nonequilibrium and approaches instability, a variety of different paths become available to the system. Which path is "chosen" is determined randomly by the particular fluctuation that is amplified to the critical value—that is, "order through fluctuation."

The path of entering therapy is an attempt to create order from the increasingly chaotic fluctuations in the family's pattern of interactions. We can hypothesize that, at the point the family enters therapy, the information in the system will have "collapsed" around the identified problem. The complex web of interactions that define the parameters of the strange attractor pattern have become too unstable, unpredictable, or unworkable. Identified problems often involve the need for the couple or family to make a complicated decision that has generated several differing opinions or options. Clinicians often meet with couples who enter therapy when there has been a unresolvable disagreement about how to parent a child or whether to pursue a divorce. Family members are in a period of indecision that has many chaotic features. "By necessity, the system needs to become more complex to move into a more stable condition and yet there are many directions in which it could move" (Gibney, 1987, p. 79). They are at that point in the strange attractor process that determines the next trajectory or loop in the pattern.

The experience of immobility, impasse, or helplessness imposed by the problem can be seen as restricting the normal fluctuation from problem to solution. The solution patterns in the attractor are absent or not functioning as well as they have in the past. From this perspective, the therapist serves as an attractor point focused on solution and positive change. Clinicians who are mindful of chaotic process know that, as soon as some understanding of what is happening in the family is obtained, something else happens that changes the picture. The relationships between family members are processes, not events. Also, Chubb (1990, p.174) stated: "two structurally coupled organisms can perturb each other but they cannot make each other do anything." An important part of the therapist's job is to "perturb" family members to act differently in order to complete the loop from chaos to a new order. Although families entering therapy are already operating at far-from-equilibrium conditions, "in forming a therapeutic system with the therapists, the family no doubt incurs greater fluctuations in functioning due to input of information" (Gibney, 1987, p. 79).

The following case will help to illustrate the far-from-equilibrium conditions that generally exist for persons seeking help. A young couple came in seeking therapy. The woman, "Molly," was 24 years old, very attractive, and dangerous with both her fists and projectile objects when perturbed. The man, "Desmond," was 23, tattooed, charming, and good at taking punches and ducking dishes. They had dated for 6 months and were planning to move in together when a fight "got out of control" and he slapped her after she repeatedly kicked him as he was trying to get out the door. His slap was nothing new for her; just a reintroduction of a pattern she had experienced with other partners. Slapping a woman was, however, a new experience for him. Instead of apologies, he made appointments.

Much to Molly's surprise, Desmond wanted to decrease the level of fighting rather than escalate the battles until he could overwhelm her as other boyfriends had done. The hurling of kitchenware ended almost immediately. New information was introduced in the therapy sessions that gave them options for expressing their differences and verbalizing anger. They went for 2 months without an argument that escalated into a physical confrontation. Especially for Molly, stating her displeasure rather than internalizing anger until she became explosive was a new loop in the pattern. The changes arose out of the complexity introduced by both parties. When Desmond didn't follow the familiar pattern of escalation and both agreed to search for a different route, the shifts began to occur. Their interactions became increasingly unpredictable until some new information about "fair fighting" helped them to establish a variant order in the relationship. It is highly likely that the newly established "attractor" may compete with the pull for the couple to physically battle when distressed. As the alternative behaviors are repeated, however, the strength of their pull is increased. The couple then has a greater range of choice when they experience discomfort with each other. A new pattern of interactive behavior has emerged; the strange attractor evolves as data points accumulate from the change in the process. Depending on the properties of this couple system and the other attractor processes that exert an influence, the couple will eventually settle into some different but stable patterns of behavior when they argue.

PHRASE SPACE

Instead of "phase space," I think of relationships as existing in "phrase space." Phrase space can be defined as the patterns of communication that establish both problems and solutions in families. In theory, relationships are maintained through the balance of energy between the two attractor points of fear and love.

In intimate relationships, the crucial communications between parties are expressions of fear or love, of closeness or distance, of desire or despair. Ongoing relationships are maintained through the expression and acceptance of the dual aspects of our own and our partner's inner and relational life. The process of relating to another over time is the weaving of separateness and togetherness so that the complex pattern of intimacy emerges.

The repeated patterns of holding and letting go, of pulling together and pushing apart, are the rhythm and breath of intimacy. As Gampel (1990, p.1) noted, when we risk the dissolution of our individual identity in intimate relationships, "it is not long before the arguments ensue, with the result that the boundaries defining identity are regained in the solitude. Intimate relationships generally reverberate between these two limiting conditions." Perhaps the definitive strange attractor pattern in relationships is the fluctuation between fear (loss of the other) and love (loss of self). The strange attractor reflects the complex interaction of these elements within and between individuals.

In order to begin mapping the phrase space in a problematic relationship, the clinician needs to equally examine what is being said and what is not being said. To break the immobility and collapse of a family system, there must be a solution point established that the members can revolve around that is as compelling to them as the problem point. The metaphor of a waltz may help to illustrate the idea. In any ongoing relationship, patterns of interacting, or steps in the dance, become established. The movements are never repeated exactly, but the pattern of moving around each other and the sense of where the next step will fall is generally predictable. There is some sense of order. When a familiar dance partner takes a new step, however, the entire balance and pattern changes. Toes are stepped on, momentum is slowed or speeded up, predictability is gone and there is the threat that the dancers will stumble and be unable to continue. Unlike the sensation of a waltz where the body learns to adjust, learning a new step in a relationship occurs in the phrase space between the partners. In the process of the relationship over time, the steps and perhaps even the nature of the dance must be redefined. The dance of romance and seduction is very different from the dance of raising young children. The patterns of interchange, the timing and tone of approaches and responses, the meanings attached to behaviors, and the established expectations are challenged and changed. As DeShazer and Molnar (1984, p.482) noted "change, or difference, or something new can often best be produced when there is some source of random within a system."

CONCLUSION

In terms of providing a broad application of strange attractor dynamics to family functioning and pattern change, clinicians could begin by examining where the information or energy in the family has collapsed. What issue or problem appears to pull the family like a vortex and limit the flexibility and mobility of the system? Has the process been immobilized by too much love or too much fear? Essentially, when there is too strong a pull exerted by an attractor, the degree of randomness needed for balance and stability is unavailable to the system. Moving the "turbulence" or energy from the attractor point where the family dynamics have collapsed to another source of turbulence is the job of the clinician. If the fear of conflict in the family is avoided and too much energy is being consumed by the attractor of harmony and togetherness, the therapist becomes an advocate for confrontation, appreciation of differences, and increased individuality. Simply stated, if there is an imbalance in the expression of love or fear in the family, the task is to assist the family in redirecting their energy and attention to the attractor point that is being avoided or denied in order to allow the family to shift to a different level of functioning.

REFERENCES

Albert, M. (1990). *Chaos: A new order.* Unpublished manuscript.

Briggs, J., & Peat, F. (1989). *Turbulent mirror.* New York: Harper & Row.

Bütz, M. (1992). *Chaos theory, psychology's new friend?* Unpublished manuscript.

Chamberlain, L. (1989). *Chaos and change in systems: A model for understanding suicidal behavior in families.* Unpublished manuscript.

Chubb, H. (1990). Looking at systems as process. *Family Process, 29,* 169–175.

Dell, P., & Goolishian, H. (1981, July). Order through fluctuation: An evolutionary epistemology for human systems. *Australian Journal of Family Therapy,* 175–184.

DeShazer, S., & Molnar, A. (1984). Changing teams/changing families. *Family Process, 23,* 481–486.

DiBello, R. (1990, December 31). Personality as a strange attractor. *The social Dynamicist.*

Gampel, D. (1990, August). *Fractal selves, the fragility of relationships, and chaos theory.* Paper presented at meeting of the Society for Chaos Theory in Psychology, San Francisco, CA.

Gibney, P. (1987). Co-evolving with anorectic families: Difference is a singular moment. *Australia & New Zealand Journal of Family Therapy, 8*(2), 71–80.

Gleick, J. (1987). *Chaos.* New York: Viking.

Hannah, T. (1990, Fall). Does chaos theory have application to psychology?: The example of daily mood fluctuations. *Network,* 13–14.

Loye, D., & Eisler, R. (1987). Chaos and transformation: Implications of nonequilibrium theory for social science and society. *Behavioral Science, 32,* 53–65.

Pearsall, P. (1992). *Ten laws of lasting love.* New York: Simon & Schuster.

Pendick, D. (1993). Chaos of the mind. *Science News, 143,* 138–139.

Ruelle, D. (1980). Strange attractors. *Mathematical Intelligencer, 2,* 126–137.

Schwalbe, M. (1990, March). *The autogenesis of the self.* Paper presented at the meeting of the Southern Sociological Society, Louisville, KY.

Stevens, B. A. (1991). Chaos: A challenge to refine systems theory. *Australia & New Zealand Journal of Family Therapy, 12*(1), 23–26.

18 The Fractal Geometry of Human Nature

Terry Marks-Tarlow

Psychological theories frequently attempt to visualize invisible universes of the psyche. They use metaphors to concretize thinking, often by supplying with visual images drawn from current scientific observation and experimentation. Such models exhibit unusual power to crystallize an understanding of complicated, multidetermined realms, such as the psyche and mind/body relationship.

In ancient China, irrigation technology formed the basis for the healer's model of Chi, the life-force energy believed to flow through meridians like aqueducts. In the last century, Freud's conceptualization of emotion utilized a hydraulic model, one based on steam engine technology. In this century, the computer's software and hardware have helped us understand human information processing and its neurological underpinnings. Laser technology and holography has prompted the neurological investigation of memory.

Theories drawn from hydraulic, computer, and laser technologies each provide a metaphor that fits a different facet of the human condition. This chapter introduces a new scientific metaphor to tickle the psychology for the imagination. This model derives from fractal geometry, a branch of mathematics whose applications cut across the physical, biological, and social sciences. The thesis of the chapter is that hitherto unarticulated facets of psychology may be revealed using this new metaphor. Four properties of fractals are set forth, each relevant to the dynamic structure of the psyche and its principles of operation. First, a general description of fractal geometry and its broad utility is presented.

HISTORY AND APPLICATIONS

The term *fractal* was coined by Benoit Mandelbrot in 1975 and popularized 2 years later (Mandelbrot, 1977). Mandelbrot discovered the computer's ability to visually display what had previously been abstract, mathematical equations. The math is simple, consisting of a single equation, the output of which is fed back into that equation as its next input, forming a recursive loop. The seed, or initial input, is a complex number involving both a real and an imaginary component. The equation is run over and over again. With each iteration, numbers and corresponding computer graphics change, while the underlying equation always stays the same. The process shows how a very simple pattern generator can produce a complicated, unpredictable, yet internally consistent result.

Although the numbers and equations have been around for a very long time, it is only with the advent of modern high-speed computers that corresponding images could be generated. The resulting graphics are compellingly beautiful and universally appealing.

Fractal geometry falls in an area of mathematics popularly called chaos theory (Briggs & Peat, 1980; Gleick, 1987; Peterson, 1988; Stewart, 1989), which is the study of nonlinear system dynamics. The utility of chaos theory is in its ability to disclose hidden order underlying nonlinear events that appear random or chaotic on the surface, like eddies in a stream or patterns of weather.

An important discovery of chaos theory is that it does not take a large number of variables for a system to generate complex behavior. Even a system with a few variables may, under certain conditions, display highly complex, erratic behavior (Taubes, 1989). Fractals are closely linked to chaos theory. The geometry of chaotic systems over time reveals a fractal structure in space.

A Blueprint for Nature

Fractal images are so highly complex as to actually simulate the forms and functions of natural objects in the world around us. Computer graphics with simple fractal programs produce clouds, mountains, coastlines, and trees that look strikingly realistic. Fractal patterns exist in the flow of a liquid through a solid matrix, such as water seeping through soil or ground coffee beans. Fractals occur in the motion of air bubbles in oil, the growth of crystals, and lightning bolt patterns of electrical discharges (Sander, 1987). Physiologists and physicians (Abraham, 1983; Garfinkel, 1983; Goldberger, Rigney, & West, 1990; Skarda & Freeman, 1987) discovered fractal architecture in the trachea branches of the lunges and in the blood vessels of the heart. Further, they have found chaotic dynamics in patterns of neuron firing and heartbeats. Ironically—and perhaps counterintuitively—chaos in the body often signals health while strictly periodic behavior can foreshadow disease, as seen in the entrainment of brain waves during an epileptic attack.

Fractal Geometry and Human Nature

Fractal geometry offers an extremely compact algorithm for representing complex natural objects and processes (Jurgens, Peitgen, & Saupe, 1990). It provides a language for broadly describing the complexity of nature that transacts time frame and spatial scale. The language of fractal geometry cuts across media as well, with the same shapes often seen in objects and processes composed of radically different materials. If such a universal language applies to physical structures and to the processes in our environment, as well as to the physiological structures and processes of our bodies, it is reasonable to suspect that the language of fractal geometry might apply to psychological events as well.

In the remainder of this chapter, four properties of fractals are outlined, each potentially relevant to psychological theory: self-similarity, ordered unpredictability, bounded infinity, and fractional dimensionality.

Self-Similarity

As mentioned previously, fractals are produced using simple, recursive equations where each result becomes the new input for the next iteration. The subsequent computer graphics exhibit a curious feature; if a small section of a fractal is isolated and enlarged the product often looks strikingly like the original. This is termed *self-similarity*. This procedure can be performed any number of times, either moving toward a smaller or larger scale. This means that the self-similar shape of a fractal is invariant across scale size.

An example of self-similarity is found in clouds. Within a certain range of distance, clouds appear to have the same global shapes. This sometimes causes accidents, when a pilot misjudges distances due to perceptual confusion. Mountains, coastlines, branches of trees, and of the circulatory system, all display self-similarity that, within several orders of magnitude, are independent of the scale of observation.

The property of self-similarity has a perfect parallel in the study of chaotic events over time, where maps of nonlinear dynamics, such as turbulence in fluids or gas, reveal similar patterns of variation across different time scales. This corresponds precisely to the self-similarity of structural patterns on different spatial scales. This is not surprising since, as mentioned, fractal geometry is the geometry of chaos (Jurgens, Peitgen, & Saupe, 1990).

Turning to psychology, perhaps intrapsychic structure is fractally organized, manifesting dynamic self-similar patterns of behavior. People tend to resemble themselves in fundamental ways that are independent of spatial, temporal, or situational scales of observation. When they possess a certain psychological characteristic, they tend to exhibit that characteristic at many, if not all, levels. An aggressive person demonstrates this trait over and over, whether at the verbal level of hogging air space in a conversation, the behavioral level of pushing to the front of a line, or the tactical level of pushing a colleague aside to get a promotion at work. Each is different in kind, with its own set of temporal, spatial, and situational parameters, and each reflects the same underlying tendency.

Self-similarity may be responsible for something clinicians see again and again in their offices, when the structure, or form, of a therapy session mirrors the content under discussion. An example is the patient who complains he has difficulty dealing with authority and deadlines and who demonstrates this by consistently arriving late for sessions. One might argue that some people are less predictable than others and, for that reason, do not demonstrate self-similarity. However, if we jump up to the next level of observation, their unpredictability is equally as predictable.

The differences between relatively predictable and relatively unpredictable people resemble those between a pristine, or perfectly self-similar fractal, in which each level of observation perfectly matches the last, and a statistically self-similar one, where a degree of randomness is programmed into its construction.

People are so self-similar ("Isn't that just like Him!") that it is almost difficult to grasp the significance of the point. Yet, the point is crucial. Perhaps one's degree and kind of self-similarity is the hallmark of identity. Self-similarity in psychological processes may allow for the emergent and invariant patterns we perceive as a "self" across iteration after iteration of experience. In other words, perhaps it is due to the operation of self-similarity and scale invariance that we are able to recognize ourselves from minute to minute, from circumstance to circumstance, throughout the kaleidoscope of a lifetime.

Ordered Unpredictability

The hallmark of chaotic phenomena is *sensitive dependence on initial conditions,* described originally by Poincare (1952). This means that a tiny difference in the initial condition of a chaotic system will be amplified over time into an enormous difference. A useful visual representation is the unpredictable relationship between two dots of vanilla as they are folded into the rest of the batter. Both dots will stray in the bowl; that is their ordered, bounded nature. Beyond that, whether they will remain side by side and how much they will separate is, in effect, unpredictable, and depends not on their relationship to one another, but on the churning movements of the baker's arm.

This idea was applied to the analysis of weather patterns by a meteorologist named Lorenz (1963). Lorenz noted how tiny differences could cause hugely disproportionate effects over time. He quipped that the fluttering of a butterfly's wings in Sydney, today, might change the weather in Peking tomorrow. For this reason, he declared weather to be unpredictable. Translated into the language of fractal geometry, fractals are ordered, in the sense that they are generated from a simple mathematical equation, yet the sequence of their numbers is fundamentally unpredictable.

Perhaps people display ordered unpredictability as well. They retain an identity and continuity over time. They exhibit patterns that can be isolated, identified, and that fall within limited bounds. And their present situation can be understood in terms of their past. And yet people are also unpredictable. Their behavior is determined by tiny, unknowable processes, including interaction with the random events in their immediate environment. Tiny differences in circumstances may lead to huge differences over time. Moreover, while behavior is bound within certain knowable parameters, details are quite unpredictable. This may explain why social scientists have always relied on statistical prediction, which is able to define the outer parameters of the aggregate but fails to predict the behavior of individuals.

The unpredictability of human behavior is well known to the clinician who, for instance, attempts to assess the risk of a suicide, or to the expert witness who is asked, based on past performance, to predict the likelihood that a person will commit a particular crime in the future. Just as in human physiology where chaotic processes are often a sign of healthy functioning, unpredictability in human behavior may indicate an optimal responsiveness to a subtle, ever-shifting environment. Often times pathology is most evident when human behavior or thought become calcified, as in obsessions, compulsions, or addictions, which assert themselves regardless of the situation.

Finally, this property of ordered unpredictability may allow, without contradiction, the coexistence of free will and determinism. Just as the behavior of a chaotic system is globally stable but locally unpredictable, so too, patterns of human behavior belie underlying order, according to physical, biological, social and psychological constraints, while within these constraints individuals enjoy the possibility of infinite variation according to free will.

Bounded Infinity

Another apparently contradictory quality that fractals possess is that of bounded infinity. Within the constraint of a bounded shape, fractals possess infinite depth and complexity. This is similar to the trajectory traced by a chaotic system in phase space; it never repeats itself exactly. Theoretically, one could infinitely magnify a section of a fractal and still produce another self-similar variation of the original pattern. Because of this, the closer one looks at a fractal, the more there is to see.

This kind of bounded infinity may be visualized by returning to the example of the cake batter. The shape of the bowl provides the outer bounds and the infinite part is inside the bowl. It is represented by the endless possibilities for patterns of vanilla swirls according to how the cake batter is enfolded.

A second way to conceptualize the property of bounded infinity derives from Mandelbrot's (1977) classic example of a coastline. Coastlines are fractal in nature. Their jagged edges are self-similar in shape and evident at any size scale. Because a coastline exhibits so many subtle changes of direction at any and every scale of observation, the length that one obtains upon measuring it depends on the size of the yardstick. The smaller the yardstick, the longer the coastline. At the very smallest scale of measurement the coastline is infinitely long.

Perhaps this property of bounded infinity holds for people as well. With the psyche, just as with fractals, the closer you look, the more there is to see. One can start with any detail about a person, no matter how trivial seeming, and the more it is explored, the more richness and complexity is revealed. There is no limit to the depth of exploration possible, or the size of the scale observation. In true fractallike fashion, any part one examines reflects and is intimately connected with the whole. How much one sees depends on how close one looks; the closer one examines an individual, the more information becomes available. No wonder the process of self-examination in psychotherapy can sometimes feel endless. It is. As long as one has the energy for self-examination, there will be something new about the self to examine.

Perhaps the property of bounded infinity elucidates the power and utility of the psychoanalytic method of free-association. Any aspect of a person, no matter how large or small, can be zoomed into, expanded, and explored in an infinite number of possible directions. Theoretically, any bit, no matter how seemingly insignificant or arbitrary, will ultimately lead to the same larger picture, if the exploration is unhampered.

Herein lies part of the utility of fractal images to the therapeutic process. In Freud's other famous metaphor, the unconscious is pictured as an iceberg, with consciousness residing at its tip. This metaphor is very cold and analytical. It encourages one to feel out of control, with important aspects of the self inaccessible and very scary. The iceberg model has been abused by some who have turned it into a manipulative weapon. This is not uncommon in institutional settings where practitioners work with captive resistant populations. Sometimes, in cases where behavior control is the goal, the practitioner may vie for control of the patient's psyche by giving the following unnerving message: "Your consciousness is only one tenth of what you can know. Nine tenths of yourself is unknown to you, but it is known to me."

In contrast to the iceberg model, fractal images are warm and fuzzy. They are beautiful to look at and intrinsically interesting. They show how the macrolevel reflects the microlevel and how, regardless of where you start, you will always wind up in the same place. This can be very reassuring to someone who is not confident that he or she is going about therapy correctly. Unlike the iceberg metaphor, where exploration involves going under the surface by piercing a repression barrier that is dangerous and scary, exploring the fractal world is painless, interesting and can be effortless. The emphasis is not on the barriers to self-knowledge, but on the freedom and treasures produced by the exploration process.

In the fractal universe, one goes where one chooses by selecting one's own scale of observation. Although we are not in control of the patterns that emerge, we do control the rate and scale of the exploration process. This satisfies our need for safety and control in the process of self-examination. It also allows for the meaningfulness of even the smallest scale, since the same patterns are often seen as on the large scale. Meanwhile, the intrinsic interest and beauty of the fractal world demonstrates how the process of self-examination can be self-fulfilling and self-perpetuating in and of itself. The beauty and awe inspired by the emergence of an endless variety of patterns generates interest in yet further exploration.

This property of bounded infinity may also be relevant to human spirituality. Perhaps it is the infinite aspect of ourselves, internal rather than external in nature, which enables such earth and time-bound creatures as ourselves to contemplate the infinity that surrounds us. There is uncanny resemblance between fractals and the shapes seen in Hindu and Moslem religious art. Indian cosmology includes the visual unfolding of thousands of minor, self-similar deities. Likewise, in a typical Moslem temple one sees the large pattern of the temple reflected in the smaller pattern of a room, which looks like the individual shape of a tile, reflected at a smaller level still in the brush stroke pattern tucked away in one corner. The hierarchical unfolding of deities and architectural patterns through many levels, from large to small, seems an example of ancient, intuitive understanding of an infinitely self-similar world across scales of observation.

Fractional Dimensionality

Fractals are numbers that occur in the fascinating twilight zone between ordinary Euclidean dimensions. We ordinarily think of the shapes of the world as composed of one- and two- or, three-dimensional objects, or simply as lines, planes, or solids. Fractals, however, exist between these dimensions, possessing fractured dimensionalities of, for example, 1.685 or 2.342.

Here is a way to visualize this quality. A squiggly line, like a scribble drawn on a sheet of paper, is a one-dimensional shape whose meanderings (or degree of complexity) occupies a two-dimensional surface. So, a squiggly line exists between one and two dimensions. The more complex the line, the higher the dimensionality. A lace doily also exists between one and two dimensions. A piece of Swiss cheese exists between two and three dimensions. Fractal images called *quaternions* have even been generated for four-dimensional space.

How does fractional dimensionality relate to psychology? The author can only hint at possible implications, using metaphor as a guide. Perhaps, the relation between Euclidean and fractional dimensionality resembles that between a person's basic psychological structures and his or her modes of functioning. The Euclidean dimension represents the basic or primary structures of the psyche. The fractional dimensionality represents how they fit together, reflected in one's coping style or potential, or the tendency of the system towards growth or disintegration.

Here are some examples. The first relates to the notion of regression. Under stress, individuals tend to regress to earlier forms of coping. This is a kind of self-similar behavior that bears the scar of past history. What is known as repetition compulsion is self-similar as well. It, too, is modeled on past circumstances and indicates a block in sensitivity to current ones. Perhaps the potential to regress and repeat the past rather than experience the present and move towards the future, can be represented by a fractional dimensionality rating. Ordinary coping may possess the integrity of integers; behavior under stress may possesses the disintegrity of fractional dimensionality. Perhaps obsessions, compulsions, and phobias are all evidence of the fractional dimensionality of a fragmented self.

It is possible that expressions, such as "crack up" or "fall to pieces" imply internal divisiveness likewise descriptive of fractional dimensionality. It is also possible that certain individuals, such as the borderline personality, exhibit greater complexity of higher fractional dimensionality than other diagnostic categories. The borderline's dilemma of where the limits of self leave off and those of another begin can grow infinitely complex, with self-recursive dilemmas that are confusing to both patient and therapist.

Another type of fractional dimensionality is illustrated by people who appear to operate at a higher level than their basic psychological structure would suggest. An example is the "as if" personality, or the narcissist, who often looks good on the outside but actually is fractionated on the inside. Such a person may do the "right" thing, but for the "wrong" reasons. In this case, the fractional dimensionality of the functioning is higher than the basic structure of the psyche, unlike the regressive borderline described earlier.

The possibility of translating the notion of fractional dimensionality into a language of description for psychological self-structures seems potentially fruitful. Fractals tend to occur at boundary zones between materials and processes. So, too, our psychological make-up is formed at the dynamic boundary zones between biological, social and environmental processes. The application of fractional dimensionality to the psyche carries possibilities for a qualitative system of description that is precise, yet nonpejorative.

SUMMARY

Each of the four properties outlined above appears to illuminate a slightly different aspect of the psyche than captured by previous metaphors. Self-similarity provides a handle on consistency of behavior, no matter how erratic, across different scales of observation. Ordered unpredictability helps illuminate the patterned, yet fundamentally unpredictable element of behavior, even when influenced by only a few significant variables. Ordered unpredictability also illuminates the necessity for a statistical level of analysis for social and psychological events. Bounded infinity attests to the infinite depth and variety we each possess, no matter how empty we may feel. Finally, fractional dimensionality may help us derive a precise qualitative method for delineating the shape of self-structures. Because of the newness of this enterprise, at least for now, each property appears to raise more questions than it answers. Hopefully, in true fractal fashion, enough interest may be generated by this chapter to stimulate further development, articulation, and revision of its concepts.

REFERENCES

Abraham, R. (1983). Dynamical models for physiology. *American Journal of Physiology, 245,* 467–472.

Briggs, J. P., & Peat, F. D. (1989). *Turbulent mirror: An illustrated guide to chaos theory and the science of wholeness.* New York: Harper & Row.

Garfinkel, A. (1983). A mathematics for physiology. *American Journal of Physiology, 245,* 455–466.

Gleick, J. (1987). *Chaos: Making a new science.* New York: Penguin.

Goldberger, A. L., Rigney, D. R., & West, B. J. (1990, February). Chaos and fractals in human physiology. *Scientific American,* 43–49.

Jurgens, H., Peitgen, H., & Saupe, D. (1990, August). The language of fractals. *Scientific American,* 60–67.

Lorenze, E. N. (1963). Deterministic nonperiodic flow. *Journal of the Atmospheric Sciences, 20,* 130–141.

Mandelbrot, B. (1977). *The fractal geometry of nature.* New York: Freeman.

Peterson, I. (1988). *The mathematical tourist: Snapshots of modern mathematics.* New York: Freeman.

Poincare, H. (1952). *Science and method.* New York: Dover.

Sander, L. M. (1987, January). Fractal growth. *Scientific American,* 1987.

Skarda, C. A., & Freeman, W. J. (1987). How brains make chaos in order to make sense of the world. *Behavioral and Brain Sciences, 10,* 161–195.

Stewart, I. (1989). *Does God play dice? The mathematics of chaos.* New York: Basil Blackwell.

Taubes, G. (1989, May). The body chaotic. *Discover,* 62–67.

19

The Princess and the Swineherd: Applications of Chaos Theory to Psychodynamics

Isla E. Lonie

It is out of silence and uncertainty that new knowledge and ways of being in the world emerge.

—John Cage

A man has a dream that his lover is dreaming she is a princess. It is as if he has entered her mind and can see the long dress, and the spiky crown, and the dragon that must be vanquished so that she can be rescued. This is the first dream that he has ever brought to his therapy, which has lasted now for some 30 sessions. He explains this by saying that although he had known he had been dreaming on other occasions, those dreams had slipped out of his grasp, just as all his relationships do, sooner or later. All that remained then was something like the shadow of where a dream might have been—a sense of something almost grasped, but inevitably lost. It was a vague and shadowy sense, like his mother who seemed always not to really be thee for him, distracted by other demands on her attention. His associations to the dream fragment then run on to a fairy tale about the adventures of a prince, which his lover was reading to her infant son the evening before, and to his feelings of exclusion from the charmed circle of mother and child. Referring to previous sessions in which an emotional reaction had been provoked by the thought of the therapist's other patients, he wonders if he might also have felt like this when observing his own mother spending time with his younger brother.

The therapist contributes the thought that by creating a princess, as it were, a gap seems to appear. If he makes a princess of his lover, aught not he himself have been a prince? He ponders this for a while and then responds that he cannot think of himself as a prince, but rather as the swineherd—who also figured in the tale. This was a loutish character who displayed a greedy lust for the princess's golden hair and who was soon sent about his proper business. This time though, says the therapist, he has managed to catch for himself something like a strand of golden hair—a fragment of his own dreaming. He is silent then for some time before he says he finds this a disturbing thought. Even a single golden hair ought to have been something quite out of his reach, for he is, he says firmly, only the swineherd. Just as his dreams have been quite out of reach, the therapist answers—like his mother who was not there for him emotionally; like a dreaming place or a breast that he feels as a lack rather than as a presence. Usually, she adds, the mother has a dream about her baby: perhaps something about how he will grow up one day to become a prince; perhaps like the dream that he may have sensed his lover could be having about her own infant son.

Again there is silence, but when he speaks, it is not in his usual somewhat businesslike manner, but in a tone of reverie. He says he has just remembered how his mother told him once that his name, which is John, means "beloved." He sees then that this could have been the dream she dreamed for him and that it has many implications for the way his life has progressed so far. In particular, his insistence that he is the swineherd may have been his way of not letting himself know about her passionate feelings for him. In the dream, his lover's long dress, the spiky crown, and the threatening dragon, perhaps represent barriers he has erected so as to keep her, too, at a safer distance and do much to explain the inhibitions he has experienced in making love.

The material just presented may serve to illustrate the complexity of the process of psychotherapy and how, within a single dream fragment, a wealth of associations is condensed in an image of incredible evocative power. Here is the day's residue, of the fairy tale actually read to the child, with its many layers of meaning in our culture. An overwhelming sense of exclusion is expressed in the man's recognition of his jealousy of the attention given to the infant, as well as numerous references made in the course of the therapy to his mother's distracted care of him during the years of his own childhood. Here is the sense of a gap, or a missing breast, or a lack of attention that permeates his life, and that finds expression in the dream fragment by the placing of the creativity within the image of his lover, while his own existence seems to be in doubt. And for the first time, here is the dawning realization of erected defense against a deeper recognition of the dream of his mother, that he is her beloved.

In the transference, too, the same effect may be seen. The man who dreams that his lover is dreaming she is a princess, maintains towards his therapist an attitude of immense respect, as if she, too, were a princess. If he ever has occasion to be critical, he offers his views with humility and the greatest of tact, apologizing for causing her any hurt. This contrasts, of course, with the savagery with which he attacks himself. His insistence that he is the swineherd in the fairy tale rather than the prince, echoes his conviction of his own essentially denigrated status, a condition that he has attempted to convince his therapist in almost every session so far as being the true expression of his black soul. Again, any notion of his being a prince with legitimate desires of his own is absent.

This magical ability of the human mind to play with images and to represent extremely complex ideas in condensed form is the stuff and fabric of psychotherapy and psychoanalysis. It is, therefore, small wonder that researchers have found these processes resistant to study, especially when the usual methods of enquiry seek to reduce the subject to its component parts, rather than to understand its complexity. As those who study physics have found, division of matter into subatomic particles, far from revealing some infinitely small component of the atom as the basic building block, has unveiled instead glimpses into a world of awe-inspiring complexity.

Not only does matter seem to consist of parcels of energy that must be considered as processes rather than objects, but it can also be shown mathematically that they seem to exist only when there is somebody present to observe them (e.g., Capra, 1975; Davies, 1980). In the same fashion, analysis of the structure of this fragment of dreaming gives rise to an extraordinarily complex interweaving web, with components from many phases of the individual's life, including the observation and participation of the therapist. This interdependence of the individual and his environment might be likened to the image of the miraculous net of pearls cast over the heavens by the Hindu god Indra, where, if one gazed into a single jewel one could see there reflected each and every other (Lonie, 1985).

Traditional research models assume that everything has a defined nature, that events are fully predictable and predetermined, and that an event can be considered separately from its agent. In the example of the man who dreams his lover is dreaming she is a princess, the dream fragment cannot be said to have a defined nature, for it can only be understood in terms of the whole history of his life, taking this back to the moment when his mother found his name. While the act of naming a child may have some predictive and determining power, it is certainly not the case that every person named John has a life trajectory such as that of this man, for this was shaped by his unique circumstances, the presence of a younger brother being merely one factor among many others. And neither can it be said that the man would have realized the importance of his naming without the thirty or so sessions that had led up to this particular encounter, nor without the interactions with the therapist in the course of the session described. The fragment of dream achieves meaning from the various associations the dreamer was able to assign to it. Far from being understandable as a fragment, it requires a rich setting to have significance. The richer the setting, the more meaningful it becomes.

These observations find an echo in the words of the famous French mathematician, Poincaré (1908, p.30), who wrote of the process of creation of a mathematical formulation:

If a new result is to have any value, it must unite elements long since known, but till then scattered and seemingly foreign to each other, and suddenly introduce order where the appearance of disorder reigned. Then it enables us to see at a glance each of these elements in the place it occupies in the whole. Not only is the new fact valuable on its own account, but it alone gives a value to the old facts it unites.

In the last few decades Poincaré's insights have come to be appreciated as basic to the new understandings of complex phenomena generally considered now under the rubric of "chaos." The word here retains its ancient meaning of the formless void from which matter was created, in contrast to later usage indicating "randomness." Despite efforts to speak rather of "nonlinearity," or "complex dynamical systems," the word "chaos" persists, perhaps because of its many cultural links, and its ability to summon up a sense of unfathomed mystery. Indeed it might be suggested that the enormous public interest generated by that amazing and magical figure, the Mandelbröt set, may be attributed to its capacity to present us with a visual representation of infinity. For instance, Penrose (1990, p.124), a physicist, in considering the question of whether the Mandelbröt set is an invention or a discovery, remarked:

Mathematical objects are just concepts. . . .Can they be other than mere arbitrary constructions of the human mind? At the same time there often does appear to be some quite profound reality about [them]. . . .It is as though human thought is. . .being guided towards some external truth—a truth which has a reality of its own, and which is revealed only partially to any one of us.

The revolutionary discoveries being made concerning the structure of chaos have involved many events previously dismissed as too complex to understand by Newtonian laws—phenomena such as weather patterns, cloud forms, turbulence, the behavior of subatomic particles, or the essential uncertainty about the length of coastlines. It has been shown that, despite incredible complexity, these phenomena nevertheless possess pattern and form and that these can be shown to follow rules, now defined as follows (Gleick, 1988):

1. They form deterministic dynamical systems, as compared with probabilistic systems.
2. They display sensitive dependence on initial conditions.
3. Their motion is bounded within a representational field.

These concepts may be represented for instance by a pegboard, where two balls may start off at the same position, but by taking a slightly different direction at some point, may end up far apart at the end of their course (see Fig. 19.1). In the case of complex dynamical systems, very small differences initially become magnified by feedback to produce major effects. Since the initial differences may

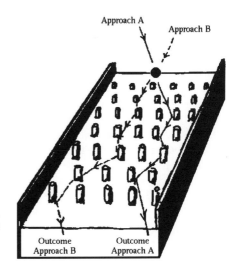

FIG. 19.1. Experiment to illustrate the chaotic principle of sensitive dependence on initial conditions.

be so small as to be unable to be measured, even with the most accurate instruments, it is not possible to predict the course of an event governed by these factors, although it may be understood retrospectively. Where the activity is chaotic, meaning that it never repeats its trajectory exactly, it does occupy a particular area in what is known as "phase space," which may be thought of as a representation of all the possible paths along which a system may evolve. The field that bounds these phenomena is referred to as a "strange attractor," and allows for complex motion that jumps back and forth between two centers of activity.

Relating the concepts of chaos theory to the complex of ideas obtained from the man's dream may increase the power of our description. In the first place, it is then possible to understand something of the chains of causality that have operated for him in retrospect, but knowledge of the outcome of the session—the recovery of information about the meaning of his name—could scarcely have been predicted. The branch points that shaped his life may be understood in part from these insights concerning his naming, the birth of a younger brother, experiences of his mother as not being focused on him, his relationship with his lover and the child who is not clearly his son, his recognition of jealous feelings concerning him, his overhearing the reading of a fairy story, and so on. Any individual person also has only one history. Equally, in psychotherapy, it is not possible to understand events in terms of statistical probabilities, standardized for large populations, because the discipline concerns itself especially with the unique experience of the individual.

It is characteristic that psychotherapists look for patterns in the material that patients present. Here we have a recurring pattern of behavior appropriate to that between a princess and a swineherd, and self-defeating in terms of healthy narcissism. The condensation of many layers of meaning into a single image is useful in conceptualizing this man's difficulty in living creatively.

In the unfolding process of psychotherapy information is generated and retained. The information that the man's self-concept is not that of a prince but a swineherd, with no legitimate claim on the princess, can be linked with experiences of his mother's distracted care, and provides an immediately accessible image that will be fed back into the therapy when appropriate in future sessions. Similarly, the knowledge of the importance of his naming can be used to further understanding of his difficulty in seeing himself as a prince and the rival of his father, the king.

In considering the fragment of his dream, the therapist's observation of a gap instead of a prince led to recovery of knowledge of the meaning of the man's name and could be considered a branch point, similar to that with the pegboard, where there is a "choice" as to which direction is taken. An expectation of a therapy is that such "moments" should be of significance in influencing the future evolution of the person's life. As has been noted, it was at this point that the tone of the man's voice changed, and we would say there was a deepening of rapport. Peterfreund (1983) suggested the concept of the "good hour," where "the patient, the therapist and competent observers would agree that something important happened, something true, real and meaningful, both cognitively and affectively." He spoke of the possibility of taking a cross-section of the optimal process at a given moment and proposed the vignette, as developed for presentation in the psychiatric literature, as such a sample.

In terms of chaos theory, this might be compared with the Poincaré map, which takes a cross-sectional observation of chaotic motion at regular intervals. By this means, a dimension is removed from a strange attractor, and a continuous line may be turned into a collection of points, making complex data more manageable. The fragment of dream presented here, together with some of its many associations, by uniting elements and introducing order, fills the criteria given earlier by Poincaré as essential to the creation of a mathematical formulation.

One of the outcomes of the advent of the computer has been the possibility of studying intensive iteration, that is, the calculation of a huge series of different values for one equation, which can then be represented graphically. In effect, it permits the visual representation of feedback. The difference between linear and nonlinear mathematics is perhaps nowhere more vividly expressed than in comparing the familiar shapes of Euclidian geometry with the forms of the Mandelbröt set (Peitgen & Richter, 1986). By focusing on the edges of the figure at ever-increasing degrees of magnitude, one may obtain an infinite series of complex patterns, endlessly repeated, similar but never the same, and in which the original "gingerbread man" may be found over and over again. In thinking of the figure as a visual representation of the transition from order to chaos, we may consider its edge as the interface between two areas of attraction—that of the interior of the black figure, and infinity somewhere outside it.

This incredible complexity is often enhanced still further by the use of colored computer graphics, where the colors represent the relative tendency of a particular point on the computer graph to run off to infinity or to return to the heart of the figure. This may strike a chord of recognition for the therapist, who may often be concerned with whether the material of the session tends to focus on external events or to concern itself with the inner world. It certainly offers the possibility of a graphic representation of the complexity of the space between the therapist and patient.

The effects of feedback are apparent when we consider that the Mandelbröt set is derived from an extremely simple equation that takes a complex number, multiplies it by itself, adds the original number, squares the result, and so on, repeatedly,

$$z = z^2 + c$$

where c is a complex number. A complex number is essentially a mathematical device that permits an extra dimension to be represented on a two-dimensional plane. By means of an activity such as this, an equation becomes a dynamic process, rather than a static description. This formula could be applied perhaps to the case of the man who dreams his lover is dreaming that she is a princess, where, if we take z as representing a complex pattern of behavior—in this example the leitmotif of this man's life, that he is a swineherd who cannot expect much good for himself—we can think of it as multiplied by itself countless times in a myriad of different circumstances, as represented by c. Also included might be a recognition that the therapist must also be represented by a value of c, and that this c is by no means always the same. Finally, the dream might be taken as a verbal equivalent of the ever-recurring image of the "gingerbread man" in the Mandelbröt set.

It is well known that Freud considered his monumental work on the interpretation of dreams as his major contribution to human knowledge. It was here that he first recognized the importance of the mechanism of condensation, in which a single idea comes to represent several different trains of thought and may be conceptualized as existing at their intersection. As in a metaphor, or in Poincaré's mathematical formula, there is a uniting of elements, with a consequent increase in depth. It may be useful to think of condensation as represented by an image such as the Mandelbröt set, particularly since the complex number that makes up the basic equation for the figure might be thought of as a mathematical means of compressing an extra dimension onto the computer graph. Just as the effects of condensation and plastic representation in dreaming result in images that often have extraordinary power to summarize numerous disparate ideas, so the computer graphic charts of nonlinearity, by providing visual representation of complex phenomena, offer the immediate possibility of an understanding that is intuitive rather than intellectual. It is perhaps an especially human ability to perceive patterns and to create them, and indeed intelligence tests now make use of this ability to assess basic intelligence (e.g., Hofstadter, 1979).

Winnicott (1971), in his paper, *On the Location of Cultural Experience,* took as his metaphor an image of the seashore "where children play." He noted that it belongs neither to the ocean nor to the land, but is situated at the interface between the two. In defining this "transitional space," he drew attention to the interaction between the mother and baby and the importance of the space between them for the development of play and later, cultural activity. This he saw as crucial in the development of individual identity, or sense of self. Like Winnicott, Mandelbröt (1978) also pondered the nature of coastlines, pointing out that the more accurate their measurement, the greater their length. Moreover, he noticed that for any coastline, the overall pattern, at whatever scale of magnification, remained essentially the same—a phenomenon he named "self-similarity."

The complex boundary of the Mandelbröt set also demonstrates the features of scaling and self-similarity. The basic forms here can be recognized as being based on a series of figures known to mathematicians as Julia sets. These are created by "play" around various deformations of a circle. Their general feature is again, self-similarity, with the quality that the entire boundary can be regenerated from a small piece of it be performing a number of iterations. Careful observation of the boundary of the Mandelbröt set reveals that the structure is made up of various combinations and permutations of these more basic forms that are strangely reminiscent of elaborate pieces of jewelry. An important aspect of the concept of self-similarity is that the similarity is within the system, so that the material and understanding is unique to each individual example. In like fashion, psychodynamic theory attempts to make generalizations from events that are essentially singular.

Meditation over the forms of the Mandelbröt set, as with the example of the seashore, leads the observer to find ever-increasing degrees of "meaning," much as is demonstrated by the dream fragment. Part of the sense of finding a "truth" seems to come from the discovery of recognizable patterns and the sense of personal creativity, as we have seen also in the example of the dream fragment. This process of waiting for a pattern to emerge, the "negative capability," that the poet Keats considered an essential condition for the activity of the creative process, was linked by Bion (1970) to the process of psychoanalysis.

The concepts of scaling and self-similarity bring us to the question of repetition, both in terms of the manner in which a theme may insist in the course of a session, and also in terms of how it may reverberate throughout the course of a therapy. Patterns of behavior begin to unfold and can begin to be related to events that occurred earlier in the individual's development, often enough, early in childhood, even before the development of speech with its power to communicate with others concerning the contents of the inner world. The theme of the man who dreams that his lover is dreaming she is a princess, for instance, may be seen to permeate every area of his life. Harry Stack Sullivan (e.g., Mullahy, 1970) is credited with having said that all the major themes and preoccupations and defensive maneuvers of the patient are present in microcosm, in the very first session, and in every other session.

Commentary on the philosophy of science has included the work of Kuhn (1970) who suggested that, although stages of prescientific endeavor may present a bewildering array of theories, a mature science is governed by a single paradigm. He observes that, while a paradigm may defy precise description, it is possible to recognize several of its component parts: explicitly stated laws, theoretical assumptions, and standard ways of applying fundamental laws to a variety of types of situation. Certainly one of the problems facing the psychotherapist, but also all those who study complex behavioral interactions, is the lack of a paradigm with which to represent their activities. A major difficulty is that, in disciplines that emphasize the unique experience of the individual in the development of personality or symptomatology, methods that employ statistical values to verify validity must sacrifice the concept of personal meaning. There is, therefore, an impasse over the question of scientific validation of the efficacy of psychotherapy. It rages with particular vehemence over questions as to what constitutes a satisfactory outcome and how treatment may be assessed as potentially effective, or ineffective, before its termination.

It may be that chaos theory will be able to provide a paradigm that can permit a greater degree of understanding of these complex interactions, especially in that it provides a basis for demanding recognition that Newtonian science is unequal to the task. As has been observed, the tenets of nonlinearity provide satisfying recognition of many of the features of the phenomena with which the psychotherapist is familiar. concepts such as these might be relevant in considering ways of generating significant research that does not address symptom relief as much as the individual's capacity to lead a meaningful existence. An enhanced ability to dream, with increased richness of dream imagery, for instance, would be thought by some to be a reliable indicator of progress in a therapy. In this context, it is not relevant that the only human interaction currently capable of being convincingly represented by a computer is that of a person ill with paranoia (Hofstadter & Dennett, 1981). The reason for this is that such a person's thought is highly predictable and incapable of flexible adaptation. A movement in the direction of psychic health would demonstrate more complex and creative responses.

Perhaps, just as the normal distribution curve has become the emblem of the epidemiologist, so the Mandelbröt set might come to represent the belief system of the psychotherapist. Not only might it provide a graphic representation of the concept of the dyadic relationship, but it might also represent the possibility of complex change. Its unique value, however, could be that, as well as providing a form within which phenomenal events might be placed, its representation of the infinite might capture the noumenal quality of the human psyche.

REFERENCES

Bion, W. R. (1970). *Attention and interpretation*. London: Tavistock.

Capra, F. (1975). *The Tao of physics*. New York: Bantam.

Davies, P. (1980). *Other worlds*. London: Penguin Books.

Gleick, J. (1988). *Chaos*. London: Sphere Books.

Hofstadter, D. R. (1979). *Gödel, Escher, Bach: An eternal golden braid*. New York: Basic Books.

Hofstadter, D. R., & Dennett, D. C. (Eds.) (1981). *The mind's I*. Middlesex: Penguin Books.

Kuhn, T. S. (1970). *The structure of scientific revolutions*. Chicago: Chicago University Press.

Lonie, I. E. (1985). *Indra's net. Australian Journal of Psychotherapy, 4*(1), 36–42.

Mandelbröt, B. (1978). *The fractal geometry of nature*. Oxford: Freeman.

Mullahy, P. (1970). *Psychoanalysis and interpersonal psychiatry: The contributions of Harry Stack Sullivan*. New York: Science House.

Peitgen, H., & Richter, P. H. (1986). *The beauty of fractals*. New York: Springer-Verlag.

Penrose, R. (1990). *The emperor's new mind*. London: Vintage Books.

Peterfreund, E. (1983). *The process of psychoanalytic therapy*. Hillsdale, NJ: The Analytic Press.

Poincaré, H. (1908). *Science and method*. New York: Dover Publications.

Winnicott, D. W. (Ed.). (1971). The location of cultural experience. In *Playing and reality*. London: Tavistock.

294

20 Regression as Chaotic Uncertainty and Transformation

Phyllis Ann Perna

Historically, regression has been considered a disruptive pathological state representative of a psyche that is disintegrated, disordered, and in need of reparative work. Put the pieces back together again (often pharmaceutically) according to the medical model of health and disease and the linear assumptions on which it rests. Classical psychoanalytic thought, while recognizing the defensive and reparative nature of certain aspects of regressive states (Fenichel, 1945; Freud, 1955), did not consider them, holistically, as adaptive evolutionary processes that occur throughout the life span. To view regression within an evolutionary perspective is to acknowledge its inherent creative potential for the development of new psychic structure. It also substantiates the clinical work that self-psychologists and analyst—following the lead of D. W. Winnicott in particular—are doing, especially with severely regressed patients.

The hypothesis presented here is that regression is a transformational process in psychic development and that its function is to establish the conditions for the development of new, integrative, psychic structures. As such, it is an evolutionary process. It is further suggested that regression produces psychological and behavioral chaos in the self system, equivalent to turbulence and chaos in far-from-equilibrium nonlinear dynamical systems. To understand it as such is to enhance the ability of clinicians to respond to its expressions, and to interact with it so that we, as system parameters and constraints, may facilitate and enhance its creative potential rather than, through short-term and static methods, threaten the self system with "fossilization." For it is precisely these chaotic, stochastic processes that are the main source of the adaptive possibilities that allow organisms "to survive in the long term, to innovate of themselves, and to produce originality" (Nicolis & Prigogine, 1989, p. 242).

Three questions might be asked from the above. First, is there global evidence of turbulent, chaotic, transformation in psychological development? Second, what is the specific nature, or morphology, of regression in psychological terms, and what are the underlying processes which produce the form observed? And third, can an equivalence be demonstrated between regressive morphology and chaotic phenomena in model nonlinear systems? Alternatively, what might be the most appropriate nonlinear models from other fields of science to apply to psychological data?

METHODOLOGY

Vygotsky (1978) spoke of the importance of analyzing process rather than objects. This must be kept in mind when looking at regression, for it would be too easy to mistake behavioral expressions or symbols for the processes underlying them. Hans Werner (1978), for instance, stressed the importance of measuring development in terms of the processes underlying achievements, not solely by the achievements themselves. He used the term, *microgenesis,* to specify the "unfolding process" resulting in any cognitive act. It is precisely to the understanding of regression as an unfolding process, replicative of that in any mental act, demonstrating variable and fluid symbolic behavior, and resulting in new psychic structure, that attention is now turned.

Evidence for this view can be is drawn from theories representing, until recently, a spectrum of isolated fields of study concerned with psychological processes. These include classical psychoanalytic theory and its myriad offspring, including object relations and self-psychology; the dialectics of development emerging form infant research; cognitive psychology with its constructivist perspective; and developmental psychology, particularly the organismic-developmental conceptualization of development. Such disciplines have provided a merger of perspectives on developmental and identity systems. V. F. Guidano (1988, p. 311) stated:

> From a systems, process-oriented approach, knowledge development is regarded as a progressive construction, influenced from the very beginning by the self-organizing capabilities of human mental processing. Indeed, far from being an "impersonal" construction, human knowledge is imbued with and biased by all the invariant aspects (evolutionary and cultural constraints) that define human nature and consequently determine the human way of knowing reality.
>
> Thus the elaboration of a full sense of personal identity—and the inherent feeling of uniqueness and historical continuity—seems to be a hallmark of a human knowing system. From the earliest stages this sense is intertwined with the parallel process of cognitive growth and emotional development. Put another way, the mechanisms of identity are interwoven with the mechanisms of knowledge, and this interdependence unfolds during the development of an individual by means of

the progressive construction of selfhood structures along increasingly complex and integrated levels of knowledge.

Similarly, thinking, feeling, and self-systems include regressive processes. With the assumption of self-simiilarity in the psyche's fractal geometrical nature, it may be possible that a model of one system's functioning (e.g., the thinking system) can be an appropriate analogy for the others, either alone as subsystems or for the whole interactively.

The Historical Recognition of Nonlinearity and Autopoeisis in Psychological Processes of Development and Thought

Although chaos theory has been presented as a new scientific perspective, in fact, the *essence* of nonlinearity, of chaotic transformations to produce higher-level functional systems in developmental processes, had been recognized by certain luminaries in our field for many years. Note the words of Vygotsky (1978, p. 73, italics added):

> Our concept of development implies a rejection of the frequently held view that cognitive development results from the gradual accumulation of separate changes. We believe that child development is a complex dialectical process characterized by periodicity, unevenness in the development of different functions, metamorphosis or qualitative transformation of one form into another, intertwining of external and internal factors, and adaptive processes which overcome impediments that the child encounters. Steeped in the notion of evolutionary change, most workers in child psychology ignore those turning points, those spasmodic and revolutionary changes that are so frequent in the history of child development. To the naive mind, revolution and evolution seem incompatible and historic development continues only so long as it follows a straight line. *Where upheavals occur, where the historical fabric is ruptured, the naive mind sees only catastrophe, gaps, and discontinuity.* History seems to stop dead, until it once again takes the direct, linear path of development.

Scientific thought, on the contrary, sees revolution and evolution as two forms of development that are mutually related and mutually presuppose each other. Vygotsky, writing in the 1920s and 1930s, sounded like the harbinger of chaos theory. He recognized both linear and nonlinear, deterministic and probabalistic processes in human development.

David Rapaport (1951, p. 315), discussing N. Ach's "determining tendencies," defined them as "a regulative directional principle or dynamic organizing force." He further stated, "The crucial task of the science of thinking is to discover how in the present, which is a product of the past, this directedness by and orientation toward the future are effected." Rapaport surely sensed the autopoeitic and stochastic nature of the development of thinking. It is unfortunate that, at that time, modern mathematical models, systems theory, and computer technology were not yet available.

Piaget (1951, p. 186) spoke of the self-organizing functions of the organism—the *synthetic* as opposed to analytic functions—*being the functions of coherence.* In particular, the "dual functional invariant of adaptation and organization" expresses itself in " 'accord of thoughts and objects' and in the 'accord of thought with itself'. . . .These two aspects of thought are inseparable: thought organizes itself in adapting to objects, and *thought structures objects in organizing itself.*" Here is recognition that adaptation is related to the dialectical interaction of the external world and the self-organizing processes of the internal world, that is, processes that are both alloplastic and autoplastic.

Not only is there historical recognition of nonlinear and autopoeitic processes in development but also suggestions that transitions to higher levels of development demonstrate regressive trends prior to the achievement of higher order integration. Werner (1978) pointed out that one usually observes a decrease in accomplishment during the developmental move toward the use of more refined mental tools. Anna Freud (1965, p. 99) viewed regression as a principle in normal development, one that serves the function of both adaptation and defense. "According to experience, the slow method of trial and error, progression and temporary reversal is more appropriate to healthy psychic growth." While, traditionally, the symptoms of regression are interpreted as reversal in time, or return to more primitive levels of functioning, it is nevertheless known from the study of nonlinearity that reversal is not necessarily a reality (Prigogine & Stengers, 1984). Therefore, it becomes necessary to understand regressive processes from a new perspective. As seen previously, early psychological thinking considered regressive processes as involving psychological change and structural development. As such it may serve the same function as the chaotic behavior underlying evolutionary transformations in nonlinear complex systems.

THE NATURE OF REGRESSION

Structural Relations

Freud (1955) characterized the psychic apparatus as a compound instrument, the component parts of which he called systems that maintain a partial orientation to each other. Though he suggested no actual spatial arrangement of the psychic system, he assumed a definite temporal and directional order for psychic processes, describing them as usually proceeding from perceptive to motor events. He characterized the psyche as a reflex apparatus.

Freud was probably the first to discuss regression extensively and did so in 1900 in *The Interpretation of Dreams.* He distinguished three forms of regression, which he held to be basically the same and usually coincide. These are (a) *topical,* based on his hierarchical system of psychic processes that proceeds in the direction from perception to motility; (b) *temporal,* or a regression to older psychic formations; and (c) *formal,* "when primitive modes of expression and representation take the place of the customary (secondary process) modes." They, in fact, coincide because, "that which is older in point of time is at the same time formally primitive and, in the psychic topography, nearer to the perception-end" (Freud, 1955, p. 404). Breaking through the constraint of linear thinking exemplified in this representation, however, one can conceive of the psychic "apparatus" as a system with fractal dimensions, displaying self-similar processes on multilevels, and incorporating a dialectical dynamic rather than a reflexive mode. Then it is possible to recognize that it is not that some processes are older or more primitive than others, but rather only are their symbolic representations. That is, primary and secondary process, assimilation and accommodation, associative and directed/ordered processes, occur in every mental act. Furthermore, accepting the tenet of irreversibility in dissipative structures, temporal reversal to "earlier" modes of functioning is no longer an entirely accurate description of regression.

Giovacchini (1990) stated that regression is not simply a return to an earlier ego state and earlier modes of functioning. It is a much more complex process in which various parts of the psyche participate in a disproportionate manner. Zigler and Glick (1986, p. 37) stated it this way: "Regression involves not the abandonment of higher modes of operation, but a weakening of the structural ties whereby earlier forms are integrated with, and function in the service of, higher modes of operation." Freud (1955, p. 403) stated simply, "In regression the structure of the dream-thoughts breaks up into its raw material."

Freud talked of the power of dreams to recast their idea content in visual images (which he considered primitive psychological representations—the perceptual system as opposed to the motility system.)

> We may not have explained this character of the dreamwork by referring it to the known laws of psychology, but we have singled it out as pointing to *unknown relations,* and have given it the name of the regressive character. Whenever such regression has occurred, we have regarded it as an effect of the resistance which opposes the *progress of thought on its normal way to consciousness,* i.e. to ordered thinking, and of the simultaneous attraction exerted upon it by vivid memories. The regression in dreams is perhaps facilitated by the cessation of the progressive stream flowing from the sense-organs during the day. (Freud, 1955, p. 403)

That is, when regression occurs, there is no externally derived energy flow (at least it is minimal) or *reality constraint* impinging on the system's dynamics and to which the system must accommodate. There are only self-generated impulses unmodulated by external systems. Thus, "thoughts" or visual images, are allowed more free play and looser associations than when they are required to accommodate to incoming perturbations, or externally originated constraints.

This is the equivalence of that undifferentiated "matrix of primitive, syncretic mental processes," from which differentiated mental activity emerges (Freeman, Cameron, & McGhie, 1966) when subjected to external reality constraints.

It would seem from studies of cognition that in the psychic system there is a continuous and interactive operation of essentially two basic processes, those known as primary, assimilative, associative, synthetic, syncretic processes, which I am suggesting are *chaotic probabilistic* processes, and those known as secondary, accommodating, directed, formal, logical, or ordered deterministic processes. What establishes different forms or states of cognition is the prevailing relationship between these two processes and the level of the psychic system being observed.

Energic Relations

Rapaport (1951) suggested "that there develops within the ego a series of thresholds which impose limits upon the expression of the instinct drives, their mental representations, and the affects." This hierarchy of thresholds permits,

> a fine regulation of energy expenditure, in contrast with the "all-or-nothing" reaction of the id cathexes. It is this delicate control that underlies the capacity for environmental adaptation and finds expression in the mental processes of conceptual thought, perceptual constancy, memory schemata, and control of motility. These thresholds are essentially counter-cathexes operating with neutralized energy. Defects in their function may be the cause of the characteristic form which schizophrenic symptoms assume. (Rapaport, 1951, p. 31)

Rapaport's all-or-nothing characterization of id cathexes implies a far-from-equilibrium state in contrast to the delicately controlled, near-equilibrium energy transformations within the hierarchy of thresholds.

Freud (1955) posited that in pathological regressions there must be some equivalent process to the cutoff of energy flow from the sense organs during sleep, that is, a "strengthening of the other regressive motives," or, we might say, of self-generated energy flow. Psychoanalytic theory holds that it is the "endopsychic (unconscious) reaction to object relationships that initiates the pathological process. These unconscious complexes provoke anxiety and guilt which in turn leads to the primitivization (regression) of the mental functioning" (Freeman et al., 1966, p. 4). "It is this [primary process] form of mentation, with its condensations, displacements, and preference for concrete, pictorial representation, {is there a relationship here to the bias toward visual imagery in chaos theory?} which leads to the disruption of conceptual thinking and of perceiving and to an inability to selectively attend" (Freeman et al., 1966, p. 30) or to order. Thus, clinical data, including the symptomatology of the schizophrenic patient, is seen as dependent upon the vicissitudes of object relationships. "They [the symptoms] will increase or decrease in extent according to the pressure exerted by such anxiety. From a psychotherapeutic standpoint, all psychoanalytic authors are agreed that fundamentally the symptomatology of the schizophrenic patient represents a *means of avoiding anxiety* and guilt" (Freeman et al., 1966, p. 30).

We can easily see anxiety as analogous to externally or internally generated system perturbations, or the equivalent of heat transfers or energy flow in physical systems, or related conceptually to autocatalytic processes in chemical systems. But what else might the symptomatology represent when viewed from a nonlinear dynamical systems perspective? The experience of anxiety may be the experience of dedifferentiation, a sense of apparent (if not real) loss of structure in a normally near-equilibrium system of hierarchical subsystems, or thresholds. When under intensified energy pressure from both external and internal sources, amplified by positive feedback processes, the system is no longer able to adequately dissipate the "heat," it moves to a far-from-equilibrium position and evolves into turbulence, a chaotic phase with loss of hierarchical structure and maximum entropy.

How can this attenuated chaos, or regression that is the behavioral response to the internal psychological experience of maximum entropy chaos, be adaptive when what is *observed* from an ordered world is deemed so pathological? Conrad (1986) provided us with the motivations for chaotic system dynamics that allow us to consider the regressive process as a system in chaotic transformation—an evolutionary adaptive process. He considers chaotic processes as the most effective mechanism for dissipating disturbances in a system. "If the dynamics of one level of organization is to be very stable, it is necessary for disturbances to be absorbed by instabilities at some other level" (Conrad, 1986, p. 9). Uncertainty serves to absorb the disturbance. Conrad classifies the chaotic mechanisms of adaptability (or possible functional roles of chaos). Those most relevant to the present discussion of regressively functioning psychological systems are, "*Search* (diversity generation) with genetic and behavioral effects, [i.e., seeking alternative modes of response when typical modes have not been effective, allowing for new formations from the raw material of the old, as represented by the fluidity of behavior observed in psychosis]; *Defense* (diversity preservation) with immunological, behavioral and populational effects; and *Dissipation of disturbance* (qualitative insensitivity to initial conditions)" (Conrad, 1986, p. 10).

Finally, in line with the evolutionary adaptive argument, the following quotation provides some stimulating food for thought:

> While schizophrenic and creative thought may reflect a common propensity to rapidly shifting associations, the distinguishing feature appears to be the degree to which these earlier genetically predetermined forms are integrated within higher conceptual operations. In light of the assumption that adaptive forms tend to be perpetuated in the evolutionary process, why has schizophrenia, which seems so clearly maladaptive, continued to be so prevalent? If the genetic underpinnings are

not for a specific disorder but rather ones that permit highly creative thought and expression, what has been perpetuated is not a maladaptive form but a characteristic that has been central to the development of the species. (Zigler & Glick, 1986, p. 41)

My argument is that the essential difference between schizophrenic and creative thinking lies in two primary areas. First is in the level of the system undergoing the chaotic transformation. In schizophrenia, the experience of maximum entropy chaos has reached the level of the whole self system. Second is in the environmental response to the self experience. The experience of maximum entropy chaos at the level of the self could be interpreted, at least in part, as a trauma, that is, as the loss of self. It then becomes, in a large part, an environmental response that influences whether the trauma becomes self-perpetuating in a positive feedback loop or reconceptualized as the self, evolving to a higher level of integration.

As a final emphasis toward the integration of thinking processes, regression, the sense of self, and self-in-relation, are the observations by Giovacchini (1990) of patients with fragmented ego structures whose complaint is an absence of a real sense of self. In a regressed state *in the therapeutic situation,* however, these patients feel less fragmented and more integrated. Giovacchini called this paradoxical situation "amorphous integration and chaotic unity." I suggest that he is speaking of the psychological experience of the strange attractor in the regressed chaotic state. "The regressed state, besides bringing about a cohesion of disparate fragmented isolated parts of the self [as in Piaget's synthetic functions of coherence], also leads to the creation of transitional spaces" (Giovacchini, pp. 257–258). These transitional spaces (in Winnicott's terms) then, *in the context of a therapeutic relationship,* form the basis for connections and cohesiveness within the ego and the beginning of object relationships with the therapist representing the primary object. Thus, the possibility is created for the development of a psychic structure of object relating—*order out of chaos.*

REFERENCES

Conrad, M. (1986). What is the use of chaos?. In A. V. Holden (Ed.), *Chaos* (pp. 3–14). Princeton, NJ: Princeton University Press.

Fenichel, Otto. (1945). *Psychoanalytic theory of neurosis.* New York: Norton.

Freeman, T., Cameron, J. L., & McGhie, A. (1966). *Studies on psychosis: Descriptive, psychoanalytic, and psychological aspects.* New York: International Universities Press.

Freud, A. (1965). *Normality and pathology in childhood: Assessments of development.* Madison, WI: International Universities Press, Inc.

Freud, S. (1955). *The interpretation of dreams.* New York: Basic Books.

Giovacchini, P. L. (1990). Regression, reconstruction, and resolution: Containment and holding. In P. L. Giovacchini (Ed.), *Tactics and techniques in psychoanalytic therapy, Volume III: The implications of Winnicott's contributions* (pp. 226–264). Northvale, NJ: Aronson.

Guidano, V. F. (1988). A systems, process-oriented approach to cognitive therapy. In K. S. Dobson (Ed.), *Handbook of cognitive-behavioral therapies* (pp. 307–356). New York: Guilford.

Nicolis, G., & Prigogine, I. (1989). *Exploring complexity: An introduction.* New York: Freeman.

Piaget, J. (1951). The biological problem of intelligence. In Rapaport (Ed.), *Organization and pathology of thought* (pp. 176–194). New York: Columbia University Press.

Prigogine, I., & Stengers, I. (1984). *Order out of chaos: Man's new dialogue with nature.* New York: Bantam.

Rapaport, D. (1951). *Organization and pathology of thought.* New York: Columbia University Press.

Vygotsky, L. S. (1978). In M. Cole, V. John-Steiner, S. Scribner, & E. Soubrman (Eds.), *L. S. Vygotsky; Mind in society: The development of higher psychological processes.* Cambridge: Harvard University Press.

Werner, H. (1978). Process and achievement: A basic problem of education and developmental psychology. In S. S. Barten & M. B. Franklin (Eds.), *Developmental processes* (Vol. 1, pp. 23–40). New York: International Universities Press.

Zigler, E. & Glick, G. (1986). *A developmental approach to adult psychopathology.* New York: Wiley.

VI PHILOSOPHY AND CHAOS THEORY

Because chaos theory affects our view of reality at such a deep and fundamental level, it inevitably impinges on philosophy. In this section, we consider the relationship between philosophy and chaos theory in at least three distinct ways: the philosophic precursors of chaos theory, chaos theory's implications for philosophy, and philosophy's implications for chaos theory. We have already encountered this mix of philosophy and chaos theory in several earlier chapters, but here the connections are more explicit.

The first two chapters trace earlier views of chaos, either in religious and spiritual traditions (Ainslie), or in non-Western cultures (Bütz, Duran, Tong). In Bütz's second chapter, he goes into very different territory: exploring chaos theory's epistemological underpinnings from both bottom-up and top-down points of view. Loye then questions the limits chaos theory seems to impose on nature, when human consciousness is involved. Finally, Peat, in a wide-ranging philosophical discussion, arrives back at the point where Ainslie begins: where chaos theory comes to meet deeper spiritual issues.

Both Bütz and Ainslie argue that much of the appeal of chaos theory is "due to the universal mythological images it conjures up" (Bütz, Duran, Tong), and that "the most appropriate response to chaos is wonder" (Ainslie).

Ainslie's chapter is devoted to the inner experience of chaos within the spiritual quest, perhaps best known in the Western tradition through the "dark night of the soul" described by

St. John of the Cross. The details of this experience know no boundaries of dogma because they lie at a deeper level than dogma. These details can, in turn, shed light on the deeper aspects of modern chaos theory as it comes to encompass ever more areas of human thought and feeling.

Bütz, Duran, and Tong examine ancient precursors of chaos theory, centering on Taoism and Mayan creation myths. "The Taoists declare that life is 'radically contingent,' characterized by both steady and abrupt states of change." The Mayan creation myths reveal a deep and only newly discovered secret of nature: that chaos lies at the core of all creation. This Mayan recognition continues in the healing traditions of most Native Americans, in which "chaos is merely part of the totality which is part of ongoing creation, rather than a static, content-ladened idea." This is called "Coyote's Howl."

Chaos theory enthusiasts tend to split into two camps: those most interested in the way existing order gives way to chaos and those who emphasize how new order emerges out of chaos. In their already classic book *The Turbulent Mirror,* Briggs and Peat split their book in exactly that way, using the metaphor of Alice going into the looking glass, then emerging from it once more. The shortest section of that book is the single chapter that describes the point where chaos and order meet in the mirror.

Bütz tries to shed further light on this magical place by examining two very different approaches to the human psyche: the top-down approach of Jung's psychology, and the bottom-up presentation of Vandervert's neurological Positivism. He presents each of their models of reality along a continuum: in Jung's case, progressing downward from the emotional expression of wholeness, to mandalas, to symbols, to the archetypes that lie beyond the symbols, and finally to the numerical algorithms that are beyond even the archetypes. In Vandervert's case, he builds up from a biological expression of wholeness, to the Mandelbröt set, to the human neurological order, and again finally to the algorithm. Bütz' argument has philosophic implications that extend beyond chaos theory itself.

Loye's chapter presents evidence that human beings, especially humans working in concert, are able to predict events that cross the threshold between order and chaos to the new order that emerges on the other side. That is, while standing in front of Alice's mirror, they can already see what lies on the other side. This evidence provides a needed corrective for psychologists more enamored of the mathematical tools of chaos theory than of its deeper implications. As Loye says, "a vast—and very much underappreciated—sea change occurs when we must deal with the data of the human brain and mind that both rises out of and *can transform* (his emphasis) the data of the pre-human level."

Finally, Peat provides an embarrassment of riches in the closing chapter of our volume. It totally captivated an audience of chaos enthusiasts when delivered as a speech at the annual meeting of the Society for Chaos Theory in Psychology in 1993. He ranges across physics, mathematics, philosophy, and spiritual traditions in an attempt to push beyond chaos theory itself to "the great work" that underlies all deep human endeavors, whether scientific or spiritual. In his words, "chaos theory suggests that it is still possible to hold on to a certain sort of rationality even within the breakdown of all order. It suggests that when we are forced to give up control over our lives we may be giving ourselves to a deeper form of wisdom and guiding principle."

21 Chaos, Psychology, and Spirituality

Peter Ainslie

> *Life is a river that wanders and flows.*
> *Sometimes it's high, sometimes it's low.*
> *Sometimes it's rough and thrilling, sometimes it's smooth and easy,*
> *And though it may toss you around, it always carries you.*
> > *Life's always changing, so ride with the flow.*
> *Learn to master its ways and go where you want to go.*
> *Life is a river that wanders and flows,*
> *And though it may toss you around, it always carries you.*
> *So hold on, ride it through.*
> > > —Abby Endicott (nd)

The song was written by Abby Endicott, who is wife of Bill Endicott, the former coach of the Olympic kayak team. The kayakers know what chaos is like on the rivers, but they "hold on and ride it through." Stewart (1989) defined *chaos* as "stochastic (random) behavior occurring in a deterministic (ruled by exact and unbreakable laws) system" (p. 17). Chaos is like part of the flowing waters, injecting the innovative in the midst of certainty.

Chaos is an important subject to consider, because it recognizes the unknowing quality of life. There are levels of understandings and linkages that are simply beyond human comprehension. Chaos points to what Rudolph Otto (1958) defined as the "mysterium tremendum that at the same time exercises a supreme 'fascination'" (Otto, 1958, p. 41). The most appropiate response to chaos is wonder (Heschel, 1987, p. 43)—to be amazed at the mystery of creation from the whirlpool to the rumblings of neurotic impulses.

Chaos is defined in the Bible in two ways. It comes from the Greek word meaning "gap" or "yawning chasm." Greek spirituality has a strong contemplative base that lends itself easily to chaos, a searching into the often numinous inner reaches of the soul. Its Hebrew derivation is "'formlessness." Both understandings imply a state of no boundaries or definition. The Christian Gnostic writings claim that chaos comes from the "shadow" or darkness (Rudolph, 1984, p. 72). It is important to realize, therefore, that the Bible does not think of chaos as the current colloquial meaning of disheveled surroundings or frenzied behavior, although it may result in this. The antonym of chaos is order. The latter is derived from the Latin word that means "structured" or "'measured." Western spirituality, especially the Roman Catholic Church, is quite linear, ordered, and hierarchial. Chaos finds less familiar ground in western Christianity, than in its eastern counterpart. These two words—chaos and order—balance each other. They cannot be defined apart from each other. Tillich has stated that we cannot separate order and chaos anymore than we can "freedom from destiny" (Tillich, 1957, pp. 182–186). They are, maintained Whitehead, correlative terms, each completing the other (Whitehead, 1971, p. 94). In order to understand chaos, we need to be familiar with order and conversely. This is analogous to up–down, inside–outside, hot–cold, and similiar distinctions. Knowledge of one is based on familiarity with the other.

The arts portray the interplay of order and chaos in graphic ways. The painting, "The Black Signature," by Rene Magritte, shows a woman riding a horse through a forest where the interplay of chaos and order is portrayed. The trees, woman, and horse slip into each other. Chaos reigns, yet order is there, too. Also, in Maurice Ravel's "La Valse," "a waltz is evolved from an embryo into a vibrant living organism. Out of an orchestral haze (chaos), the hint of the waltz appears, first in the bassoons, then in the other woodwinds, slowly acquiring shape in the strings and oboe. The waltz unfolds, grows, and expands until the full orchestra becomes a delirium in three-quarter time. Dissonant chords bring the mad whirling (chaos) to a sudden end" (Cross & Ewen, 1953, p. 619). The arts reflect this lively and mutual interaction of chaos and order in a way that can lead into a reflection about spirituality in our midst.

Spirituality is defined as the "experience of God." This does not mean that we just receive God into our lives; it is more that we *know* God (Holmes, 1981, p. 1). It is neither doctrine oriented nor centered on any particular creed or liturgy. Rather it is a term that explicitly refers to one's relation with God. The *process* of relating to God experientially is significant. In this sense, spirituality can refer to the Jew, Muslim, or Christian. This study, however, will center on spirituality from the Christian perspective.

How do we think of God in a universe that contains chaos? Christian theology classically has always maintained that God is beyond definition. This has grounding in the Bible, where God addresses Moses, "You shall see my back (where I have been), but my face (who I am) shall not be seen" (Exodus 33:22). In fact, some of the most diligent attempts to define God have been in negative terms. Pseudo-Dionysius in the fifth century wrote, "It [God] is not sonship or fatherhood and it is nothing known to us or to any other being. We make assertions and denials of what is next to it, but never of it. . .for it is beyond every limitation; it is also beyond every denial" (Psuedodionysius, 1987, p. 141). In a world that contains chaos, all we can say from our experience is that God is ubiquitous, holistic, numinous, and contains compassion. Words leave us empty before the grand mystery.

In chaos theory, God can be thought of as an "attractor." Rasband has defined an attractor as "a set of points (or a point) in the space of variables for a dissipative system to which orbits or trajections tend in the course of dynamic evolution" (Rasband, 1990, p. 217). Stewart said that "an attractor is defined to be. . .whatever it settles down to. . . .Its essence is that it is some portion of the phase space such that any point which starts nearby get closer and closer to it." Perhaps God can be all dimensions of attractors (Briggs & Peat, 1989, pp. 31–44). At times, God may appear as a pointed attractor, at other times as limited-cycle attractor, torus attractor, and then as a strange attractor. As a pointed attractor, God can be addressed as an obvious stabilizing influence in times of great upheaval in the spiritual life. As a limited-cycle attractor, God appears as a more circuitous reference in the midst of change. As torus, God has more latitude than the two former attractors. God as a strange attractor is beyond our comprehension, but God is present. Gleick (1987) noted that with a strange attractor "the point is the dynamical system—at that instant. At the next instant, though, the system will have changed, ever so slight and so the point moves" (p. 124). Another way to think of God is as a "numinous attractor," which completes and goes beyond the "strange attractor." Admitting that we cannot see the face (what God is like) directly and live (Exodus 33:20), God, as an attractor of whatever shade, can still provide us a reference in the midst of chaos.

The imagination, rather than linearity, may be the most helpful basis for a theology in chaos theory. Much of systematic theology is based upon an ordered, Cartesian–Newtonian way of speaking about God. However, a theology of the imagination encapsules chaos, takes it into itself, and emerges with a creative and always flexible approach to God. One of the most helpful approaches comes from what Sallie McFague defines as "metaphoric theology" (McFague, 1987, pp. 29–57). This is a theology that is empirical and is derived from images similar, but not identical, to that which is described. Consequently, a metaphorical theology or what I call "a theology of imagination" is flexible, highly individualistic, and tranformative through the power of image. McFague (1987) applied this approach to her definition of God. The world is the body of God (pp. 59–87). This means that we commune with a God who is all pervasive—a panentheistic approach. God is identical with the world (pantheism), but transcends it (inclusion of "en"). The emphasis is on a holistic, integrative view of God. Since we are part of the world, we are constantly in interaction with God. It is a participatory relationship. It is a theology derived out of metaphor. God can be compared to mother, lover, and friend (McFague, 1987, pp. 97–180). These are metaphors, rather than descriptive analyses, to define our sense of God in a world that combines a lot of chaos.

Images of God change. Creation is continually going on. The Bible reads that "In the beginning, God Created heaven and earth" (Genesis 1:1), but the Hebrew word for "created" can also be translated simultaneously in the present tense. It can more accurately read that God "created and continues to create." Chaos is still going on. Our reactions to God as image vacilate. Blake expressed this seeming confusion, framing it around the drama within our souls.

> *God appears and God is light.*
> *To those poor souls who dwell in Night,*
> *But does a Human Form display*
> *To those who dwell in realms of day.* (Blake, 1985, p. 92)

The paradox of God's nature is proffered, not externally, but in the mind of the observer.

Evidence of chaos in spirituality is, therefore, experienced within. One of the most explicit evidences of chaos on the spiritual journey is exemplified by what the mystics term "the dark night of the soul." All the spiritual supports fall away, God is eclipsed or absent, and one is starkly alone. Chaos reigns in the soul. The "dark night" was defined by John of the Cross, a 16th century Carmelite, who wrote:

> *One dark night,*
> *Fired with love's urgent longings*
> *—Ah, the sheer grace!—*
> *I went out unseen,*
> *My house being now all stilled;*
> *In darkness and secure,*
> *By the secret ladder, disguised,*
> *—Ah, the sheer grace!—*
> *In darkness and concealment,*
> *My house being now all stilled:*
> *On that glad night,*
> *In secret, for no one saw me,*
> *Nor did I look at anything,*
> *With no other light or guide*
> *Than the one that burned in my heart;*
> *This guided me*
> *More surely than the light of noon. . .*(St. John of the Cross, 1973,
> pp. 295–296)

Through the darkness or chaos in his soul, John journeyed with no support other than the "light that burned in (his) heart." Fakhruddin 'Iraqi, a Sufi poet, had a similar experience, but he compared it to being lost in the sea,

I have tumbled into a sea whose shores are uncharted.
Indeed,
I am a match
for the Seven Seas
though in myself weak
as a speck of foam.
      And if I seem to repeat myself, forgive me, for whichever way I swim,
hoping to cast myself out of this boundless ocean, I cannot find the shore.
Sometimes I glimpse it, but the waves steal me away again and hurl me to the
abyss.
Praise be to God
I live in the sea like a frog:
If I open my mouth I get
a mouthful of water;
If I remain silent
I die of grief!
I blame myself, for
There where the waves
of the endless sea are crashing
how should the Ocean hobnob
with a little dewdrop?
      But Spiritual Resolve admonishes me: "Hopelessness is by no means
obligatory."
O frog in the unbounded waters,
struggle on, keep swimming.
Who knows? Perhaps. . .
      The heart swims through the sea of hope, and to the soul which has
drawn near its shores it will say,
"when shall we
divorce ourselves?
You and I gone
and only God remain?" (Fakhruddin 'Iraqi, 1982, pp. 126–127)

The chaos within the soul is like being lost at sea. There is no direction. One is adrift. Swami Rama defined this experience of darkness or being adrift to going to a movie theater on a sunny afternoon. When one first enters the theater, before the eyes have adjusted to the interior, it is as if one is suddenly blind. Slowly the eyes adjust, and the contours of the theater inside take shape. The darkness has created a momentary "chaos" within the person that soon dissipates. Rama explained this as a shift of awareness from a more familiar terrain to the unfamiliarity of the theater interior (Swami Rami, 1974). As the soul shifts to new levels of consciousness, it may experience a "darkness" or "lostness at sea" before it adjusts to a new state. Often spiritual masters mention this shift of spiritual orientation with its resultant chaotic orientation.

The requisites for struggling through the chaos are faith as the perception of meaningfulness. Faith in this sense does not imply subscription to a creed or theological posture. Rather it is a willingness to stay with the process and be personally engaged in the resultant chaos. Often prayer, or communion with God, is empty, and the spirit, listless. "My tears have been with me day and night, while people continually say to me, Where is your God?" (Psalm 42:2) All has collapsed. This makes the journey especially perilous.

Chaos on the spiritual path is so traumatic that it can stultify the soul. The anxiety of participating in chaos on the spiritual path is graphically portrayed by Edvard Munch's painting entitled "Geschrei" ("The Scream"). Munch shows a women with her hands to her ears, screaming in the starkness of a bleak landscape, all alone and without any support. Two people are even walking away from her. It is as the writer of Deuteronomy put it, "The skies above you are brass, the earth beneath you, iron" (Deuteronomy 28:23). Rather than face the horrific wrestling, lostness, and lack of meaning, it may appear more safe to retreat from the night of the soul. The spiritual seeker may want to slam the door on chaos, much like the musical piece, "The Door Is Ajar" (Kronos Quartet, 1988), in which a strong wind (chaos) is heard. Then a baritone voice says firmly, "The door is ajar," and one hears the sound of a heavy door slam soundly shut. Here is the temptation. The ultimate sorrow is to "shut the door." One must enter chaos to attain a new being. One can retreat, however, to the safety of order.

Rather than chaos, one may slip into theological fundamentalism. All the answers are given. There is a security in "knowing for sure." One need only subscribe to a prescribed set of beliefs; any deviance is heresy. This may not be limited to the more obvious rigid Calvinist or "right-wing" Christians but can also develop with the fundamentalist type mentality of some "left-wing" Unitarian types. Structured theology provides a safety net from chaos.

The other way to evade chaos is through morphological fundamentalism. This is rigidity in structures of worship, building architecture, denominational hierarchy, and clerical vestments. These forms provide a sense of well-being and apparent easy escape in the midst of spiritual disorder. This can apply just as readily to a highly liturgical church, such as the Catholic Church, as to one less so, like the Quakers or "free Baptists." Theological and morphological fundamentalism can become mutually informative. For instance, usually a theological fundamentalist is sectarian. Fundamentalism, no matter what shape it takes, offers a way, albeit not constructive, out of chaos.

In order to deal with chaos, one needs an open and participatory manner. Taylor (1984), a deconstructionist theologian, has defined the way as "erring." This literally means "to wander." One is to be like the Japanese sketch of a happy man with a frog on his head jumping along the way. This is a humorous and iconoclastic way to deal with chaos. The little fellow in the sketch does not appear to be tied down to any rigid structures. He is dancing along, moving freely in his world. A helpful theological posture for chaos is "erring," the searcher on the path with no road map. This is very much like God's call to

Abraham, who left the security of the known to go out into the unknown (Genesis 12:1–4). Chaos can elicit existential courage.

The implications of chaos theory for the spiritual life are far reaching. First of all, the sense of time changes. One goes from chronos (linear and, hence, measurable and somewhat controllable) time to kairos (nonlinear or existential) time. While one must measure the hours, days, and years to adapt to life, the emphasis is now on the here and now. Chaos does not pay credence to the linear dimension of reality. To the contrary, it shatters it and plunges one into the void. Chaos thrives in the moment. It promises nothing for the future, and the past is submerged into the morass of what has been. In order to appreciate chaos, one needs to shift the emphasis to the moment. This has deep connections with the perception of the Kingdom of God.

The Kingdom is not, as some Christians maintain, primarily a future phenomenon. Chaos theory leads to an experience of the Kingdom as powerfully present, too. It is here now. It emerges out of the chaos. Thomas Traherne, the English poet of the seventeenth-century, expressed it,

> Your enjoyment of the world is never right, till every morning you awake in Heaven; see yourself in your Father's Palace: and look upon the skies, the earth, and the air as Celestial Joys: having such a reverend esteem of all, as if you were among the Angels. The bride of a monarch, in her husband's chamber, hath no such delights as you. (Traherne, 1960, p. 14)

This is commonly defined as a "realized or initiated eschatology." God is present now, to be fully manifested beyond the dimensions of chronos.

Chaos brings the resurrection into the present. Resurrection is commonly relegated to the future (again thinking in linear time), but it is now a present experience. The Christian Gnostics had an awareness of this. The Gospel of Phillip wrote, "Those who say that the lord first died and arose are mistaken, for he first arose and then died. If one does not first get resurrection, one will die" (Gospel of Philip, 1987, p. 332). Resurrection, like the Kingdom of God, becomes much more existentially rooted. It is more a present experience, to be fulfilled beyond measured time.

Salvation is not based on some theological claim but is a holistic claim. It includes the relation of the body, mind, and spirit to the present moment. One exists in the balance within oneself between chaos and order. it is a perilous posture, but one that must be maintained. In fact, Rogers found that the more healthy (holy) one is, the more that chaos is allowed in the personality. Conversely, the more that order represses chaos, the more the person may be subjected to neurotic patterns of behavior (Rogers 1968, pp. 249–262). The ability to live with and balance chaos and order is much like the interplay of yin and yang in Chinese philosophy. Salvation includes a coming to terms with (acceptance of) chaos within the soul.

Chaos precludes outer direction. The emphasis shifts from group (church) control to the individual quest. One of the reasons that the early Christian hierarchy persecuted the Christian Gnostic community is that it did not adhere to outer direction. Pagels maintains that they were persecuted largely because "they all resisted accepting the authority of the clergy, the creed, and New Testament canon" (Pagels, 1981, p. 145). The individual has ultimate responsibility. In this spirit, George Fox, the founder of Quakerism, once remarked, "I know what Jesus and Paul said, but what do you say?" He understood chaos. . .and used it creatively.

Chaos implies a nonlinear world, where order is not dominant, but complementary. One can look not just for an evolution of the spirit, but for covolution (a creative and open interconnection with all of creation now). Every personal act impacts on every other act in the universe. All things interact with each other. Covolution implies an interaction of all created things in the immediate present. This changes one's perspective of the universe, of life evolving. We now know that what we do effects even the farthest star (Briggs & Peat, 1989, p. 166). There is a vast network in the universe of which we all are an intimate part. Teilhard de Chardin expressed this innate unity in "The Mass on the World,"

> You, my God, are the inmost depths, the stability of that eternal *milieu,* without duration or space, in which our cosmos emerges gradually into being and grows gradually to its final completeness, as it loses those boundaries which to our eyes seem so immense. Everything is being; everywhere there is being and nothing but being. . .(de Chardin, 1978, p. 122)

This interconnectedness allows the constant play of chaos and order in the present. It is well illustrated by the Jewish saying that the prayers of twelve people are holding the universe together, and no one know who those twelve are. We all are interrelated on the animate and inanimate levels.

There is a balance between chaos and order. It is like the interchange between Apollo (order) and Dionysius (spontaneity). Each dimension needs the other. Each is part of the other. One cannot be overly oriented toward Apollo or Dionysius. Both are part of the creative process. Isaiah wrote of a time when

> . . .the wolf shall live with the sheep,
> and the leopard lie down with the kid;
> the calf and the young lion shall grow up together,
> and a little child shall lead them;
> the cow and the bear shall be friends,
> and their young shall lie down together.
> The lion shall eat straw like cattle;
> the infant shall play over the hole of the cobra,
> and the young child dance over the viper's nest.
> They shall not hurt or destroy in all my holy mountain;

for as the waters fill the sea,
so shall the land be filled with the knowledge of the Lord. (Isaiah 11:5–9)

Edward Hicks graphically portrayed this scene in a painting called *The Peaceable Kingdom*. It shows a reconciliation of opposites where the lion and cow, the child and snake all dwell peaceably together. As we journey on the spiritual road, we encounter a status of ambiguity and direction. The balance is tenuous. Chaos is part of the path. The authenticity of the spiritual journey is measured by how well chaos and order are integrated. As Abby Endicott wrote, "Life is a river, it wanders and flows." How could a river be what it is without the integration of order and chaos!

REFERENCES

Blake, W. (1985). Auguries of innocence. In H. F. Bellin & D. Ruhl (Eds.). *Blake and Swedenborg*. New York: Swedenborg Foundation, Inc.

Briggs, J., & Peat, F. D. (1989). *Turbulent mirror*. New York: Perennial Library.

Cross, M., & Ewen, D. (1953). *Milton Cross' encyclopedia of the great composers and their music* (new rev. ed., Vol. II). Garden City, NY: Doubleday.

de Chardin, T. (1978). *The heart of matter* (R. Hague, Trans.). New York: Harcourt Brace.

Endicott, A. (n.d.). Life is a River. From *River Songs* (Record). Bethesda, MD: LOP Records.

Fakhruddin 'Iraqi. (1982). *Divine flashes* (W. C. Chittick & P. L. Wilson, Trans. and Introduction). New York: Paulist Press.

Gleick, J. (1987). *Chaos: Making a new science*. New york: Viking.

Gospel of Philip. (1987). *The Gnostic scriptures* (B. Layton, Trans.). Garden City, NY: Doubleday.

Heschel, A. J. (1987). *God in search of man*, Northvale, NJ: Aronson.

Holmes, U. T. (1981). *A history of christian spirituality: An analyticial Introduction*. New York: Seabury Press.

Kronos Quartet. (1988). A door is ajar. In Kronos Quartet, *Winter is hard* (Record). Nonesuch Records.

McFague, S. (1987). *Models of God: Theology for an ecological, nuclear age*. Philadelphia: Fortress Press.

Otto, R. (1958). *The idea of the holy*. New York: Oxford University Press.

Pagels, E. (1981). *The gnostic gospels*. New York: Vintage Books.

Pseudodionysius. (1987). *Pseudodionvsius: The complete works* (C. Luibheid & P. Rorem, Trans.). New York: Paulist Press.

Rasband, S. N. (1990). *Chaotic dynamics of nonlinear systems*. New York: Wiley.

Rogers, W. R. (1968). Order and chaos in psychopathology and ontology. In P. Homans (Ed.), *The dialogue between theology and psychology*. Chicago: University of Chicago Press.

Rudolph, K. (1984). *Gnosis, the nature and history of gnosticism*. San Francisco: Harper.

St. John of the Cross. (1973). *The collected works of St. John of the cross* (K. Kavanaugh & O. Rodriquez, Trans.). Washington, DC: Institute of Carmelite Studies.

Stewart, I. (1989). *Does God play dice? The mathematics of chaos*. New York: Basil Blackwell.

Swami Rama. (1974, Fall). (Lecture). Sewickly, Pennsylvania.

Taylor, M. C. (1984). *Erring: A postmodern A/Theology*. Chicago: University of Chicago Press.

Tillich, P. (1957). *Systematic theology* (Vol. 1). Chicago: University of Chicago Press.

Traherne, T. (1960). *Centuries*. London: The Faith Press.

Whitehead, A. N. (1971). God and the world. In E. H. Cousins (Ed.), *Process theology*. New York: Newman Press.

22 Cross-Cultural Chaos

Michael R. Bütz,
Eduardo Duran,
Benjamin R. Tong

The ideas encapsulated under the term *chaos theory* have engendered a great deal of attention not only in what are called the "hard" sciences, but also more recently in "soft" sciences such as psychology (Abraham, 1992; Bütz, 1992a, 1992b, 1992c, 1992d; Freeman, 1992; McCown, 1992; Vandervert, 1992; De Angelis, 1993). Here we find ideas such as dynamical systems (Abraham, Abraham, & Shaw, 1990; Freeman, 1991), fractal geometry (Vandervert, 1991), and self-organization (Bütz, 1992d, 1993) used to describe psychological phenomena, such as self-confidence, perception, brain organization, and therapeutic dynamics. More recently still, the cross-cultural meaning of chaos theory has been considered in a more ancient context (Bütz, 1992c; Bütz, Duran, Tong, & Tung, 1991; Duran, 1992; Tong, 1992). There, certain philosophical ideas about chaos theory are described as nothing truly new in the history of ideas. In this chapter, we explore the cross-cultural implications of chaos theory further by offering ideas about why chaos theory has become so popular, where the idea of chaos originated, what chaos has meant in ancient traditions such as Taoism, and how it might be used as a reference point for therapy with Native American clients.

CHAOS THEORY, AND CHAOS PLAIN AND SIMPLE

We begin our discussion with a few pertinent questions. First, what is chaos theory? To clarify our own position, we begin by observing that chaos theory appears to be a group of ideas that describes systems, individual or collective, which behave in a largely nonlinear fashion. Examples of this description are found in the Freeman's work on perception (1991) and Prigogine and Stenger's (1984) and Jantsch's (1980) ideas on self-organization. In each set of ideas offered by these theorists, the behavior of systems is best described by models that emphasize nonlinear dynamics.

This leads us to the second question. How did *chaos theory* gain acceptance as a term? It appears to have its roots in those scientists' perceptions of nonlinear dynamics as "chaotic." The term *chaos,* however, was not ascribed to this group of ideas until 1975, when James Yorke used it to describe Lorenz's work (1963) on weather patterns. Although we must be cautious in qualifying our observations on how the term *chaos* came into use, it is clear that once this group of ideas was given the name "chaos theory," the field started to attract greater numbers of scientists and laymen. This is probably best illustrated by the tremendous success of Gleick's book entitled simply *Chaos* (1987). A national best seller, *Chaos* made these theories accessible to both the scientist and the non-scientist alike.[1]

Once accessible, chaos theory quickly gained popularity, particularly in the psychological community. This was evident at the American Psychological Association centennial convention, where standing room only crowds attended several sessions on the subject (Abraham, 1992; Bütz, 1992c; McCown, 1992; Vandervert, 1992). Subsequently, an article appeared on the cover of the American Psychological Association's newsletter, *The APA Monitor,* entitled "Chaos, Chaos Everywhere is what the Theorists Think" (De Angelis, 1993). This leaves us to ponder what it is about chaos theory that has caught the attention of so many.

Currently, several chaos theorists describe what we might call "scientific chaos," associated with what scientists' properly consider chaos. Skarda and Freeman's (1987, p. 78) description may typify how these scientists describe this type of chaos: "Chaotic behavior serves as the essential ground state for the neural perceptual apparatus, and we propose a mechanism for acquiring new forms of patterned activity."

For them, chaos is "complex behavior that seems random but actually has some hidden order" (Freeman, 1991, p. 78). In psychiatry, Grotstein (1990, p. 274) has offered a possible explanation for why the this type of seemingly random behavior is described as chaos: "It is my belief that emotional turbulence constitutes chaos but is experienced as randomness."

Skarda and Freeman's scientific chaos and Grotstein's emotional chaos[2] sound in many ways similar to descriptions of chaos as a universal mythical concept. This is summarized in the Euramerican mythologies through the Biblical refer-

---

[1]The citations of this book in the social sciences are too numerous to mention in the scope of this essay.

[2]This type of idea has also been described by others (Bütz, 1992a, 1992b, 1993; Moran, 1991).

ence, "Before all things there was chaos." So, one possible explanation for chaos theory's popularity is the name itself, along with its mythological representation.

Our contention here is that one reason chaos theory has attracted so much attention is that it conjures up universal mythological images. In many mythologies, chaos is used to describe any sweeping unpredictable change out of which new and more complex forms arise (Bütz, 1992c).

CHAOS AS A MYTHOLOGICAL TOOL

Examining the mythologies of just a few cultures may bear out the universal significance of chaos. In Greek mythology, Hesiod described this scenario of creation: "Verily first of all did Chaos come into being, and then broad-bosomed Gaia, a first seat of all things for ever. . .Out of Chaos, Erebos and black Night came into being" (Kirk & Raven, 1957, pp. 24, 27).

While those of us in the Euramerican culture most commonly draw on Greek mythology for our representation of chaos, it can be found far earlier in ancient African and Asian mythologies. For example, chaos was discovered in the Pyramid Texts written by Heliopolitan priests in roughly 2500 BC (Guirand, 1965). According to these texts, the first creative process was the result of the "chaotic waste" from the flood waters of the ocean called Nun. This linked view of chaos and creation may have come about because the Egyptians routinely "witnessed the apparently miraculous way in which as the floodwaters subside the pools they leave behind soon swarm with animal life" (Guirand, 1965, p. 28). In his account, it is not clear why creation happened at that particular moment in time. Nevertheless, out of the "chaotic wastes," Atum, the complete one, later identified with the sun god Ra, emerged on the primeval hill to bring "light and disperse the chaotic darkness of Nun" (Guirand, 1965, p. 27).[3] According to one account given by Guirand (1965), Atum had to return to the chaotic waters of Nun to create his son and daughter. It appears clear that the idea of chaos was central to the early Egyptian mythologies found in Africa.

We can also see chaos in the ancient mythological context of Taoism. The existence of chaos in such ancient mythologies also appears to reinforce our contention that in the world of ideas, "chaos theory" is nothing really new.

---

[3]Guirand (1965) also makes reference to some different interpretations, as we are sure there must be. Our almost exclusive reference to Guirand is because of the fact that among the readings of Egyptian mythology available to us, his description seemed the clearest. Another point to be mentioned here is that Briggs and Peat (1989) likewise mention Ra's birth (p. 19) but state that he was born out of a formless abyss called "Nut?" We believe this must be a typographical error, or it is possible that they simply got it wrong.

TAOIST THOUGHT AND CHAOS AS THE NATURE
OF CHANGE[4]

> The substance of the great Life completely follows Tao. Tao brings about all things so chaotically, so darkly. Chaotic and dark are images, unfathomable and obscure in it is the seed. This seed is wholly true. In it dwells reliability. From ancient times to this day we cannot make do without names in order to view all things. Whence do I know the nature of things? Just through them. (Wilhelm, 1985, p. 35)

At roughly the same time as the Egyptian text, the Taoists,[5] held to the notion that there is only one unchanging, permanent "law" in the universe, the law of continuous change and impermanence. Like their European intellectual first cousins, the existentialists, the Taoists believed that life is "radically contingent," characterized by both steady and abrupt states of change. Accordingly, everything and everyone is in perpetual flux, perpetual birth, and perpetual decay. Those who would operate as though reality were otherwise, essentially anchor their very existence on a bedrock of massive illusion, if not outright delusion. In the language of chaos theory, "dynamical systems" move through the basic states of stability, bifurcation, and chaos. "The course of nature is similar to the curve of a bow. That which is at the top is pulled down. That which is at the bottom is pulled up. That which is overfull is reduced; That which is deficient is supplemented" (Chang, 1975, chapter 77, p. 201).

The "chaos" inherent in this universal state of affairs means that unpredictability and spontaneity reign supreme as "natural" constants. In this view, conceptual distinctions or "names" represent human contrivance designed to sustain the illusion that discrete boundaries exist between states of being; that such empirical demarcations as true beginnings and true endings exist. Or that, like a waterfall, the life span of a human being "begins" at point A and "ends" and point B. From ancient times to this day we cannot make do without names in order to view all things: "The Tao is forever undefined. Small though it is in the unformed state, it cannot be grasped. . . .Once the whole is divided, the parts need names. One must know when to stop. Knowing when to stop averts trouble. Tao in the world is like a river flowing home to the sea" (Feng & English, 1972, chapter 32).

Yet is it not the case that one who insists that "I began my existence in the year so-and-so and will probably die seventy-five years or so later" just might have an unexpected encounter, a few short hours or days later, with AIDS or a head-on highway auto collision? As such chaos theorists as Prigogine might put it, a system very often moves in a "dissipative" fashion, from order through a chaotic period to a new, unprecedented, more complex form of order. The forces that

---

[4]This section of the essay was largely the work of Benjamin R. Tong.

[5]Who continue to be misunderstood, not to mention misappropriated by European-influenced cultures.

trigger such movement are not always readily discernible. "Attractors. . .are nonlinear in nature with a more complicated set of rules. . .[their] behavior [is]. . .more similar to patterns of behavior one finds in nature" (Gleick, 1987, p. 43).

At the same time, both chaos theory and Taoism claim that change, no matter how "chaotic," can also proceed toward self-organization, that is, producing a new, more complex, order out of apparent disorder. We are also reminded of the "self-similar" internal logic of growth in fractal geometry represented by branching and bifurcating geometric structures, as well as the action of trees, lungs, and snowflakes. In the *tai chi* circle, the famous Taoist symbol of the fundamental energies of yin and yang—the opposing yet joined expressions of the universal force, Tao—we see that the seeds of disorder reside within the very heart or center of order and vice versa.

Compare this with the Mandelbröt set, which illustrates a system's movement through a sequence of local and global regimes of order and chaos: "Indeed, the hidden and the manifest give birth to each other. Difficult and easy complement each other. Long and short exhibit each other. High and low set measure to each other. Back and front follow each other" (Wu, 1990, p. 2).

Furthermore, chaos in the human realm is affirmed by the Taoist notion of the unity of opposites; situations, events, and things are, by their very nature, not of a readily discernible either-or character. There is not a steady state between what is mind and what is body. Likewise, life is neither simply good nor bad, contrary to the Euramerican perspective of the world.

In chaos theory terms, dynamical systems are both inherently stable and unstable at the same time. To be able to hold or contain opposing ideas is to experience one's existence as authentically chaotic or, put another way, on the thin edge separating art from madness. F. Scott Fitzgerald, sounding Taoist, once wrote: "The test of a first rate intelligence is the ability to hold two opposed ideas in the mind at the same time, and still retain the ability to function. One should. . .be able to see that things are hopeless and yet be determined to make them otherwise" (Toffler, 1943, p.7).

Chaos theory is, to be sure, something new. It is not identical to Taoism, or any other historical mythology. And yet, like everything else that emanates from the universal force, it is not entirely new. Accordingly, the Taoist may be perceived as the ancient link to existential thought in psychology today.

LINKING MYTHOLOGICAL CHAOS WITH PSYCHOTHERAPY

It is quite possible that the mythologies of ancient cultures provided the roots from which the new science of chaos theory found its nourishment. At this point, one may ask: How do these ancient perspectives translate into modern psychology? Let's begin by examining one influential mythology, that of the Mayan culture.

In the *Popul Vuh,* the ancient record of the Chichen Itza culture, we find a record of the Mayan creation myths (Recinos, Goetz, & Morley, 1950). According to it, in the beginning there is no form, no chaos, only darkness and the first creators, Tepeu and Cucumatz. But then a third personality called Huracan appears who will figure prominently in the creation of human beings. Tepeu and Cucumatz order Huracan to arrange for the creation of mankind. First comes water, that is, chaos, to fill the void. Then mountains materialize from the water (the emergence of form). But humanity does not yet appear.

McClear (1973) notes that, since this initial sequence of nothingness, then chaos, then order is unsuccessful in producing humanity, it is followed by further sequences of chaos and order. Each time that Tepeu and Cucumatz attempt to make mankind they must call in Huracan. It is well known that the Mayans would periodically destroy or abandon their cities and then rebuild them again.[6] This tradition seems to be a continuation of the chaos-order sequence of their creation myths, and might even be seen as a death-rebirth sequence.

This Mayan mythology of chaos could well represent the roots of the current therapeutic approaches of the Native American culture in general. The description in the following section borrows from the concepts found in ancient American myths to present a modern approach to psychotherapy from a Native American perspective. In order to provide an alternative context more comfortable for the Euramerican influenced mind, Jung's Analytical Psychology is used as a therapeutic framework. Hopefully, from these two contexts, we may find our way into perceiving the chaos of Coyote's Howl presented in Duran's (1992) therapeutic approach.

COYOTE'S HOWL—CHAOS IN THE LIFEWORLD OF NATIVE AMERICANS[7]

It may be argued that some of the theories in psychology are undergoing a new reductionistic hammering in order to be forged into the shape of chaos theory. it seems that the very process used in trying to fit psychological theories into the confines of chaos theory is incongruent with the paradigm of chaos. Since the only way that we can communicate ideas in this forum is through language,[8] are we doomed to be unable to communicate chaos to each other? Perhaps, but, it is possible that, through using words to create images, we may be able to get close to communicating the irrational with rationality. The affective changes that may

---

[6]Chichen Itza is just one example.

[7]This section of the essay was largely the work of Eduardo F. Duran.

[8]Reminiscent of our Taoist complaint above.

occur through this process will also help convey the essence of the irrational notion of chaos. Irrationality via rationality is made possible through Coyote's Howl (Duran, 1992). At this point, we ask the reader to begin this process by sitting back and howling in a way that will bring in the Sacred Creative Process of Coyote into our immediate lifeworld.

Coyote's Howl in the Native American culture is a process that encompasses harmony, unity, beauty, masculinity, femininity, and the mirror shadow counterparts of these ideas. Consequently, within the idea of aesthetic beauty, which encompasses all that is or has potential of becoming, also exists the concept of chaos. Chaos is merely part of the totality that is part of ongoing creation rather than a static, content-ladened idea. In some indigenous American cosmologies, a similar notion exists with the idea of the Seventh Sacred Direction. The Seventh Sacred Direction consists of the unity or center of the six cardinal points. The Seventh direction provides for ongoing creative potential as well as a point of harmony that transcends the six cardinal directions.

It is not expected that Euramerican readers will immerse themselves in either of those cosmologies in order to understand chaos or the Howl, since that may take a lifetime. Fortunately, in the psychology of Carl Jung, some of the notions of the Howl, and the Seventh Direction are alluded to in a way that makes sense to European-influenced cultures. The paradigm in Analytical Psychology that allows for chaos to be understood can be found in the psychological types integrated with the notions of anima and animus.

One of the most interesting ideas that has emerged out of the chaos camp has been that of bifurcations. The interesting theme emergent out of bifurcation theory is the number of bifurcations possible before the system first goes into chaos, or is taken over by chaos. Some systems bifurcate sixteen times[9] before chaos occurs. The number sixteen is of interest since it is a number that is regarded as sacred by different tribal groups and the number is critical in ceremony.

Sixteen is the fourth number taken four times. According to Jungian thought, the quaternity is the completion of the trinity, although the opposites are still in effect. As long as the field of opposites is in operation we are still in the spatiotemporal world that is interpreted by ego consciousness. This is the place at which the readers find themselves presently. Once the field of opposites is transcended, then we are without the restraints of space-time. The image that best represents the lack of opposites is the circle.

The typology of Jung (1971) provides a good bridge into the realm of understanding chaos and creative processes form a Native American perspective. Briefly stated, our personalities are made up of a combination of two different

---

[9]In Bütz (1992b), and more specifically, this means that the limit of repeated period-doubling behavior or bifurcations has reached a point that is infinite, this "limit" "is synonymous with chaos" (Coveney & Highfield, 1990).

prevailing attitudes toward life—extraversion and introversion—and four different psychological functions—thinking, feeling, sensation, and intuition. Further, these basic attitudes are directly affected by the archetypal energy of the anima and animus. The anima and animus are not to be confused with simple masculine and feminine sexuality. Instead, the anima and animus are the creative forces— pure energy forms—that mirror one another. They are called masculine and feminine only because our spatiotemporal egos need a framework for reference. When we take the two psychological attitudes, the four functions, and combine them with the anima and animus, we come up with sixteen combinations. That is, any of the four functions (e.g., thinking), can be extraverted or introverted, and expressed through either the anima or the animus energy.

When comparing the typology of Jung with Coyote's Howl and the Seventh Sacred Direction, we began to see common themes emerging. Once we bring the number 16 into the ritual of therapy from either a European or a tribal strategy, we are on very common archetypal turf. Euramericans are just beginning to incorporate the notion of chaos into their therapeutic ceremony, and perhaps, through some of the commonalities that exist in other cosmologies, chaos can also be incorporated into the paradigm of psychotherapy.

In Jungian therapy, the typology of the client is important because it determines the course therapy should take. For example, therapists often focus on developing the inferior function of the client, thus bringing a more balanced attitude. This means that if the client is primarily a thinking-extraverted type that the balance can be obtained in helping the client move toward a feeling-introverted attitude. (This is greatly simplified and the reader is referred to volume six of Jung's collected works for more depth.) Similarly, in many tribal therapies, the doctor also tells the client that she is out of balance and needs to move closer to the center. If the client is too spiritual, she is helped to become more earthly or vise versa.

A therapist deals with a psyche that is out of balance. This lack of balance is expressed through some type of symptom. The belief of the largest number of people on the planet is that we are born to learn certain lessons and then to transcend into some higher spiritual realm. We are born with the capability to have all of the types and to be in balance with the center of all the types. Imagine our personalities as a wheel, with the sixteen combinations equally spaced around the circumference. At the hub in the middle, things are always quiet and still, no matter how fast the wheel is turning. We should be able to respond to any challenge by moving to that center of peace and balance, choosing the appropriate way to respond, and stepping back onto the wheel. Instead, we normally become attached to one or two of the types. We excel in those directions and feel extreme discomfort when we are in a situation that demands an opposite response. Most people end up avoiding discomfort by staying where they are comfortable and, consequently, are unable to develop an integral personality.

According to Jung, the undeveloped part of the personality remains unconscious (shadow) and continues to live a life of its own in the unconscious. Some indigenous people call this the Black World. It is from the Black World that the undeveloped type demands recognition from the ego and puts pressure on the ego through symptoms, dreams, synchronistic events, and other signs. The pressure being put on the ego is merely the manifestation of Coyote's Howl. In mythology, Coyote is the trickster who will stop at nothing to teach his lessons that ultimately invoke harmony and the creative process.

The Howl from the Black World stuns the ego and breaks it apart into its 16 combinations of typology, thus cresting psychological chaos. Since chaos is by definition unpredictable, this is where therapeutic intervention becomes crucial. What is needed is a balancing Howl from a healer who is in balance, a Howl that can literally shadow the client's unconscious howl, and start the movement toward centering. Unfortunately, rationality persists in asking, how can one intervene with irrational chaotic events?

In the tribal healing ceremony, the healer is viewed as a psycho-pomp who guides the client through chaos toward healing. By symbolically acting out the client's imbalance, the shaman restores balance. The shaman uses a variety of trance techniques in a ritual that makes no sense to the ego. This is done to reach into the chaos emerging out of the Black World and communicate with it in its own language of irrationality. In essence, the shaman gives his own Howl from a mirror shadow. This Howl fuses, in an acausal fashion, with the chaos in the client, creating a bridge between client and healer. In this view, the client's psyche is an extension of the healer's, the healer's psyche an extension of the client's. That is Coyote's Howl.

Fortunately, Jung's psychology of types provides European-influenced therapists with a way to work within the chaotic world without having to become completely irrational.[10] During the therapeutic session, the therapist must be centered in order to be able to use a shadow mirror reflecting the psyche of the client. If the client is out of balance in a certain direction, the therapist should be able to mirror the inferior function of the client in such a way as to bring the client closer to the center of the Seventh Sacred Direction. If the client is an extroverted-thinking type, the therapist should be able to take on an introverted-feeling attitude in the session, therefore offering the opposite. In this therapy, the words spoken by the therapist are important but not nearly as important as the role of psycho-pomp that the therapist can mirror to the client.

When a therapist can become a shadow mirror for the client, he or she is able to directly touch the client's chaotic psyche. In Aztec mythology, this *smoking*

---

[10]In European-informed psychotherapy, the opposite usually holds true. The therapist attempts to deal with the chaos through a linear system centered in her ego through the use of consciously produced language. The European-influenced therapist is literally using rationality to communicate with the irrational—is this rational? Except for therapies like Ericksonian Hypnosis or R. D. Laing's work with people diagnosed with schizophrenia, most European-informed therapies are rational.

mirror is personified by Tetzcatlipoca, who is also closely related to the trickster or Coyote. The therapist must use the cunning, psycho-pomp abilities that belong to the archetype of the shaman or Coyote. The realm of Tetzcatlipoca is one that must be approached with caution by therapists. Without proper instruction and initiation this realm can prove to be disastrous to both the client and the therapist. Unsuspecting therapists can become caught in a bifurcation cascade during the therapeutic exchange, sucked in by the primordial chaos of Huracan (Recinos, Goetz, & Morley, 1950). Therapists who do not approach the chaos with respect and knowledge are risking their own psyches to the many pathologies that afflict therapists, the end result being burnout or suicide.

When therapists fall into their own chaos, they must undergo healing similar to the client. Therapists must undergo their own process of continuous balancing, in order to maintain harmony at the center of the therapeutic lifeworld. It is imperative that therapists who attempt healing in the realm of Coyote live in a manner that acknowledge the Seventh Sacred Direction in their lives. They must maintain a relationship with the Sacred. Additionally, they must consult with those who have been Howling and know the way out of the chaotic world of Coyote. We must never forget that one side of the Howl leads to awareness and the other to madness, which in the world of Coyote are one and the same.

CHAOS—IS IT REALLY NEW?

So now we may ask, is the scientific chaos we discussed earlier much different from the ancient idea of primordial chaos found in many mythologies throughout the world? The answer appears to be both yes and no. Yes, scientific chaos has an operational definition that ties it into physical and biological events. This definition, however, may vary to a greater or lesser extent depending on which scientist one would address. On the other hand, it appears that, no, these types of chaos are not that much different. Both types of chaos were used to describe what appeared to be a random process that, from a global perspective, revealed an underlying order. Both chaos and order are essentially complementary states, necessary to create new and more complex forms (Bütz, 1992c). It does not seem to be either a mistake or a coincidence that the term chaos was chosen. In both cases it was used to describe apparently random behavior that, if carefully examined, revealed an underlying or emergent order. Chaos has deep philosophic roots, perhaps archetypal roots,[11] in our world. We dare not lose sight of its ancient and universal heritage as we come to once again accept the idea of chaos after its long absence.[12]

---

[11]Prigogine and Stengers (1984, p. 169), as well as elsewhere in Prigogine's work.
[12]This absence is discussed further in Bütz (1992c, 1992d).

REFERENCES

Abraham, F. D., Abraham, R. H., & Shaw, C. D. (1990). *A visual introduction to dynamical systems theory for psychology.* Santa Cruz, CA: Aerial.

Abraham, F. D. (1992, August). *Chaos and bifurcations-a metamodeling strategy for psychology.* Paper presented to the American Psychological Association National Convention, Washington, DC.

Briggs, J., & Peat, F. D. (1989). *Turbulent mirror.* New York: Harper & Row.

Bütz, M. R., Duran, E. F., Tong, B. R., & Tung, M. (1991). Older civilizations and chaos theory: concern about horses, tigers and their relations to Heraclitus. *The Social Dynamicist, 2*(4), commentary section.

Bütz, M. R. (1992a). Chaos, an omen of transcendence in the psychotherapy process. *Psychological Reports, 71,* 827–843.

Bütz, M. R. (1992b). The fractal nature of the development of the Self, *Psychological Reports, 71,* 1043–1063.

Bütz, M. R. (1992c). *Chaos theory, philosophically old, scientifically new.* Paper presented to the American Psychological Association National Convention, Washington, DC.

Bütz, M. R. (1992d). *The necessary chaos of development: Chaos theory, and a new symbolic developmental paradigm.* Unpublished doctoral dissertation, Wright Institute, Berkeley, CA.

Bütz, M. R. (1993). Family therapy and symbolic chaos. *Humanity and Society, 17*(5).

Coveney, P., & Highfield, R. (1990). *The arrow of time, a voyage through science to solve time's greatest mystery.* New York: Fawcett Columbine.

De Angelis, T. (1993). Chaos, chaos everywhere is what the theorists think. *APA Monitor, 24*(1), 1 & 41.

Duran, E. F. (1992). Chaos realized through Coyote's howl. *The Social Dynamicist, 4.*

Feng, G. F., & English, J. (1972). *Lao Tsu, Tao Te Ching.* New York: Vintage Books.

Freeman, W. (1991, February). The physiology of perception. *Scientific American,* 78–85.

Freeman, W. J. (1992, August). *The kiss of chaos and the sleeping beauty of psychology.* Paper presented to the second annual meeting of the Society for Chaos Theory in Psychology, Washington, DC.

Gleick, J. (1987). *Chaos: Making a new science.* New York: Viking-Penguin.

Grotstein, J. S. (1990). Nothingness, meaninglessness, chaos, and the "black hole" I: The importance of nothingness, meaninglessness and chaos in psychoanalysis. *Contemporary Psychoanalysis, 26*(2), 257–290.

Guirand, F. (1965). *Egyptian mythology.* New York: Tudor.

Jantsch, E. (1980). *The self-organizing universe: Scientific and human implications of the emerging paradigm of evolution.* New York: Pergamon.

Jung, C. G. (1971). *Psychological types* (R. F. C. Hull, Trans.). Princeton, NJ: Princeton University Press.

Lorenz, E. N. (1963). Deterministic nonperiodic flow. *Journal of Atmospheric Sciences, 20,* 130–141.

McClear, M. (1973). *Popul Vuh: Structure and meaning.* Madrid: Plaza Maya.

McCown, W. (1992, August). *Chaos theory and family therapy: A new unifying paradigm?* Paper presented to the American Psychological Association National Convention, Washington, DC.

Moran, M. G. (1991). Chaos theory and psychoanalysis: The fluidic nature of the mind. *International Review of Psychoanalysis, 18,* 211–221.

Prigogine, I., & Stengers, I. (1984). *Order out of chaos.* New York: Bantam.

Recinos, A., Goetz, D., & Morley, S. G. (1950). *Popul Vuh: The sacred book of the ancient Quiche Maya.* Norman: University of Oklahoma.

Skarda, C., & Freeman, W. J. (1987). How brains make chaos into order to make sense of the world. *Behavioral and Brain Sciences, 10*(2), 161–195.

Toffler, A. (1943). *Previews and premises*. New York: Morrow.

Tong, B. R. (1992). Taoism: A precursor of "chaos theory." *The Social Dynamicist, 3*(4), 9–10.

Vandervert, L. (1992, August). *Why bother with chaos theory?* Paper presented to the American Psychological Association National Convention, Washington, DC.

Wilhelm, R. (1985). *Tao Te Ching*. London: Routledge & Kegan Paul.

Wu, J. C. H. (1990). *Lao Tsu: Tao Te Ching*. Boston: Shambhala.

23

Emergence in Neurological Positivism and the Algorithm of Number in Analytical Psychology

Michael R. Bütz

Chaos theory and other nonequilibrium dynamics orientations are providing important insights into the process of change. These views differ greatly from the commonly held belief that change occurs as an incremental linear process. Instead, this nonlinear paradigm holds that change is at times necessarily turbulent and chaotic (Bohm, 1980; Briggs & Peat, 1989; Jantsch, 1980; Gleick, 1987; Levy, 1992; Waldrop, 1992). The lion's share of work in what has popularly been called *chaos theory* has been done in mathematics, physics, and biology. Only recently, have psychologists attempted to apply these ideas to their field. Many of these initial papers describe what systems look like from the perspective of chaos theory (e.g., Barton, 1994).

Although these endeavors are significant, it is also important to understand how a nonlinear process of change is experienced by an individual or group. How can we describe psychological experience in chaos theory terms when we haven't yet even established what underlying constructs are involved? While with weather systems (Gleick, 1987) or chemical reactions (Prigogine & Stengers, 1984) we can only watch the process occur, human beings are able to articulate the experience of change from within. It has been my opinion, as well as others (Grotstein, 1990; Lonie, 1991; May & Groder, 1989; Moran, 1991; Pendick, 1993; Perna, 1992; Redington & Reidbord, 1992; Reidbord & Redington, 1992; Schmid, 1991; Singer, 1990; Stern, 1983; Van Eenwyk, 1991), that this experience of psychological change does feel like chaos—"a confused unorganized state of primordial matter" (Webster's Ninth New Collegiate Dictionary, 1989). Yet, although it feels like chaos in the primordial sense (Grotstein, 1990, p. 274, fn. 6), this change process is also chaos in our current usage of the word, where one describes "unpredictable and apparently random behavior" (Coveney & Highfield, 1990, p. 362). The emphasis should be placed on "apparently random," since chaos in this sense connotes self-organization out of chaos, and is often regarded as a step toward more adaptive and complex levels of functioning.

In humans this process of change inevitably expresses itself in part through internal symbolic representations, in effect capturing the experience of the passage through chaos. I argue that these symbolic representations of human change may offer clues not only to the direction and magnitude of change a person might experience, but perhaps to the process of change in nonhuman processes.

Symbols are visual representations of human emotional experience. As such they have both an emotional nature and a rational nature. This chapter concerns symbol formation, emphasizing the positions of two very different thinkers, psychiatrist Carl Jung and contemporary psychologist Larry Vandervert. Jung's work is used to emphasize the use of symbols as dynamic emotional expressions, whereas Vandervert's concept of *Neurological Positivism* is used to focus on symbols as algorithmic expressions of a new order, forming deep in the mind. While these authors seem to take markedly different positions, this chapter attempts to show that they are really discussing two sides of the same coin. We find that their work overlaps at a critical point—the algorithm.

Larry Vandervert's Neurological positivism (1988) is a theory that holds promise for describing a vast array of phenomena in biology and psychology (Vandervert, 1990a, 1991a, 1991b, 1992). Neurological Positivism's (NP) most fundamental concept is "the underlying algorithmic organization of the brain" (Vandervert, 1992). Although NP centers on the mathematical algorithmic properties of the brain-mind system, Vandervert's most recent descriptions of NP (1992, 1993) bring to mind concepts from Jung's analytical psychology, such as archetypes, symbols, and the relation between the personal and collective unconscious, all in relation to the idea of algorithmic organization. Jung's work argues that experience is filtered through collective organizational principles called archetypes, which are without content until actualized in the individual through symbol formation. He also argues that the most primitive expression of order in the human psyche is through the archetype or number (Bütz, 1992a, 1992b, Robertson, 1989). Therefore, it appears that there is something to be gained from a concurrent consideration of NP and Analytical Psychology.

Jung's model of the psyche emerged at roughly the same time as modern physics, and he turned often to modern physics for correspondences with his own work. He stressed the idea that psychology shares with subatomic physics the difficulty that the observer cannot be separated from the object under observation. Hence, there is no *Archimedean point* on which either could stand and observe. He suggested that each could turn to the other for an objective stance outside itself. Or perhaps that, when such a point was found, it would serve both (Jung, 1954, pp. 88–89).[1] Consider this in light of the algorithmic explanation

---

[1]In fact, there have been several conferences on this relationship in the summer of 1992. The most recent ,ne to my knowledge was titled "Philosophical Thought of Wolfgang Pauli" conducted at the

offered by Vandervert (1992), which seems to address what one might call an underlying[2] mathematical matrix residing in the unconscious. This matrix is represented by symbols that express both the unconscious contents of the personal unconscious, and its archetypal foundations in the collective unconscious. Reflecting on the two theories, it appears that the seeds of an integration point may lie between the more structuralistic ideas of Vandervert and the mentalistic concepts of Jung.

Before we describe some of the divergent points of view expressed by the structuralist and mentalist positions, it seems useful to briefly consider the Cartesian split between body and mind. While this split appears to exist, self-similarly at many dimensions of science (Bütz, 1991, 1992c), the recent debate in Cognitive Psychology between structuralist antirepresentationist models such as that of Maturana and Varela (1987/1992), and the mentalist-representationist models such as that of Baars (1988), seem to exemplify this problem. One model describes change through the felt experience of mind in representations (Baars, 1988), the other through structural transformation in the body (Maturana & Varela, 1987/1992).[3] Although each theory has its merits, our purpose here is not to add more weight to either view, but to attempt to integrate both. In this light, Vandervert's NP—which centers on the body—appears to have the potential to deal with mind, while Jung's Analytical Psychology—which centers on mind—equally has the potential to deal with body.

NEUROLOGICAL POSITIVISM

What are the main tenets of NP? According to Vandervert (1990a, p. 2) NP is a "system's view of world, brain, and mind relationships." He states that it is "an epistemological position which places the emergent algorithms of the neurological order at the top of the organizational hierarchy of all experience and inquiry." Vandervert (1990a, p. 2) described four postulates of NP in this manner:

1. Homological unity among world, brain, and mind is emergent in the algorithmic organization of the neurological order.
2. Transformational rules connect world, brain, and mind, and they are discoverable for everything in experience.

---

university of Helsinki, August, 1992. There, papers were presented entitled *Remarks on physics and the psyche* by K. V. Laurikainen; *Mind, matter and Pauli* by H. P. Stapp; *Modern physics and the symbols of the Self and The unus mundus as meeting point between modern physics, Depth Psychology and religion* by H. van Erkelens.

[2]Jung used the term *underlying* specifically in attempting to describe the type of relationship illustrated herein (Jung, 1969, pp. 515–516, par. 965)

[3]Moreover, Baars' idea of the Global Workspace appears to be a psychodynamic solution to cognitive psychology, where Maturana and Varela's Autopoiesis seems to be a type of biological behaviorism.

3. All experience is the result of the homological *projection* of the neurological order. (This is the element of neurological positivism which underlies recursion, and it is the epistemological basis for the ubiquitous appearance of the notion of copy.)

4. The world emerges and becomes encapsulated in the mind-brain through the processes of Darwinian evolution.[4] The paths taken by these processes (the course of human knowing) can be described by the interplay of fractal self-similarity and fractal dynamics (chaos).

ANALYTICAL PSYCHOLOGY

NP remains open to further clarification through mentalist explanations in a continuum of experience, with its base as an algorithm, and its emergence as a symbol. In comparison, Jung's Analytical Psychology has the potential to be expanded through further openness to bodily explanations. I only discuss those aspects of Analytical Psychology that are pertinent to the issue here, such as how archetypes are made conscious through symbol formation.[5] I impose these limitations because as a theoretical perspective, Jung's theory is so massive in the complexity and breadth of concepts. This approach entails a limited discussion of the personal unconscious, the symbol, the collective unconscious and the archetype. For brevity, Robertson (1992) brought theses concepts together in this manner:[6]

> According to Jung, consciousness, seemingly the *sine qua non* of humanity, is just the tip of the iceberg. Beneath consciousness lies a much larger substratum of forgotten or repressed personal memories, feelings and behaviors, which Jung termed the personal unconscious. And beneath that lies the deep sea of the collective unconscious, huge and ancient, filled with all the images and behaviors that have been repeated over and over throughout the history of not only mankind, but life itself. As Jung said ". . .the deeper you go, the broader the base becomes. (p. 15)

---

[4]Some may feel that ideas held by certain theorists such as Prigogine and Stengers (1984) and Gould (in Briggs & Peat, 1984, pp. 184–192) may play havoc with this Darwinian idea. Vandervert pointed out that his meaning here is simply "form out of pre-existing form" (personal conversation, November 1992). He also indicated to me that the "emergence" he referred to is consistent with the "emergence" that Gould indicated (1992, p. 48) in the second footnote of the cited article.

[5]Currently, the play with vernacular removes emphasis from those who originally developed some of these ideas. Symbols are now referred to as representations in mentalist cognitive psychology, or designations in structuralist cognitive psychology or isomorphisms in the theory of Vandervert.

It also seems important to mention that in the text that follows the extensive use of quotations is not due to the author's inability to describe the topics presented, rather these quotations are utilized to stress that these constructs have been in place starting in the early 1920s with Jung, and still earlier with other theorists such as Freud.

[6]See also Jung (1967, pp. xxv; 1976, pp. 8–10)

Thus, we see a continuum of unconscious contents expressed via conscious representation. Jacobi (1959), an early collaborator and student of Jung's, described this continuum by contrasting Jung's model of the unconscious with the Freud's more limited model.

> Jung had come to draw a sharp distinction between a "personal unconscious" (corresponding to the Freudian concept of the unconscious, whose contents consist exclusively of discarded or repressed material deriving from individual experience) and a "collective unconscious" (consisting of the typical patterns of human experience and behavior, i.e., of the "inherited potentiality of psychic functioning pure and simple"). (pp. 19–20)

According to Jung, the unconscious has two dimensions, personal and collective.[7] In the collective, we find archetypal constellations that act as a ground plan for symbolic expression by the unconscious. Jacobi (1959) explained the relationship between the archetype and the symbol in this manner:

> When the archetype manifests itself in the here and now of space and time, it can be perceived in some form by the conscious mind. Then we speak of a *symbol*. This means that every symbol is at the same time an archetype, that it is determined by a nonperceptible "archetype *per se*." In order to appear as a symbol it must, in other words, have "an archetypal ground plan." But an archetype is not necessarily identical with a symbol. . . .it is, nevertheless, always a potential symbol, and whenever a general psychic constellation, a suitable situation of consciousness, is present, its "dynamic nucleus" is ready to *actualize itself and manifest itself as a symbol*. (p. 74)

Thus, the archetype itself is not able to reach conscious expression alone, and must do so through the facility of the symbol. Often, there is confusion over what a symbol actually is in relation to psychological experience. It is frequently taken for a sign or an allegory. Von Franz (1980) made the differentiation clear:

> Within the context of his work on the hypothesis of the collective unconscious, the word *symbol* acquired for Jung an entirely new meaning. *Symbolikos,* in antiquity, meant "figurative, not literal." . . .Jung uses the concepts "symbol," "allegory," and "sign" in rather different ways. A sign for him, is a mark or token of something of a concrete or psychic nature that is generally known; this also applies to allegory, with the difference that half-unconscious mythical associations often surround and cling to allegorical images. Both allegory and sign are to a large extent consciously created or developed. . . .A symbol is an image that *expresses an essential unconscious factor* and therefore refers to something essentially unconscious, unknown, indeed something that is never *quite* knowable. (pp. 81–82)

---

[7]Analytical Psychologists such as Von Franz (1980) may disagree with what they may view as a simplification, since they conceptualize a community unconscious, etc.

Our "quasi continuum" is now complete, where we have two continua, one addressing the unconscious itself (collective-personal), and another addressing manifestations of the unconscious (archetype-allegory-symbol-sign).

ALGORITHMS

One may ask what such continua have in common with Vandervert's NP? NP emphasizes an emergent projection of an algorithm. I would suggest that the continuum of emergence that Vandervert describes, and the continuum presented here are analogous. Webster defines an *algorithm* as "a procedure for solving a mathematical problem in a finite number of steps that frequently involves repetition of an operation" (Webster's Ninth New Collegiate Dictionary, 1989). Most mathematicians would agree that an algorithm put into operation involves the application of numerical values.

But that leads us to ask what number itself is, and where it comes from.[8] Jung (1976, pp. 497–498) stated that numbers, like archetypes, were as much found as invented, that "they possess a relative autonomy analogous to that of the archetypes. . . .the quality of being pre-existent to consciousness." Jung's research on this and related topics spanned many cultures and included roughly 67,000 dreams. In his later work, Jung came to the conclusion that number was the most primitive archetype of order in the human psyche. In particular, he considered that the small counting numbers had both quantitative and qualitative archetypal aspects. Specifically, let us address the numerical values 1–4 in Jung's work to illustrate. Robertson (1989) summarized Jung's position this way:

> *one* is undifferentiated, unity, the point, and by extension the circle;
> *two* splits one apart; it demonstrates polarity, opposition, thesis and antithesis, a cross, an "X";
> *three* is movement away from the stasis of opposition, the possibility of reconciliation between two polarities, the new synthesis contained with thesis and antithesis, the Christian Trinity, a triangle;
> *four* is stability, a constructed unity, the Christian Trinity plus Mary, a square. (p. 130)[9]

---

[8]Robertson, R. (1989). The evolution of number: self-reflection and the archetype of order. *Psychological Perspectives, 20*(1), p 128–141.

[9]Robertson also made very clear that throughout Jung's *Collected Works* there are numerous examples of mini-essays on natural numbers and that "Jung discovered that these numbers (especially the smaller ones) were true symbols; that is, each was an endlessly inexhaustible metaphor." Examples of these mini-essays are *A psychological approach to the dogma of the Trinity*, specifically par. 179–184 (Jung, 1969); *On the significance of number dreams* (Jung, 1961); *Synchronicity: an acausal connecting principle*, specifically par. 870–871 (Jung, 1968); *An astrological experiment*, specifically par. 1182–1184 (Jung, 1968); *The mercurial fountain*, specifically par. 404 (Jung, 1966).

Jung (1966) presented his own thoughts on the topic as follows:

If we set aside the numerous "chemical"[10] explanations we come to the following symbolic ground-plan: the initial state of wholeness is marked by four mutually antagonistic tendencies—4 being the minimum number by which a circle can be naturally and visibly defined. The reduction of the number aims at final unity. The first to appear in the progression is the number 3, a masculine number, and out of it comes the feminine number 2. Male and female inevitably constellate the idea of sexual union as the means of production of the 1, which is then consistently called the *filius regius* or *filius philosophorum*. (p. 207)

These descriptions of these small counting numbers begin to sound like algorithms, in which the succession of numbers describes a successive pattern of logical operations upon the natural world.

Archetypes, Primordial Algorithms

Like Jung (1968, p. 376; 1969, p. 43), Vandervert indicated that ancient algorithms exist in the neurological order (1992, p. 270). Jung stated that the archetypes and the collective unconscious were passed on through our biology, "a deposit of world-processes embedded in the structure of the brain and the sympathetic nervous system" (Jung, 1969, p. 376). Here we find Jung's openness to a biological explanation, actually using biology as the facility through which this receptacle of experience is passed on to future generations: "The collective unconscious is in no sense an obscure corner of the mind, but the mighty deposit of ancestral experience accumulated over millions of years, the echo of prehistoric happenings to which each century adds an infinitesimally small amount of variation and differentiation (Jung, 1969, p. 376).

Vandervert's position is that there is an ever modifiable ontogeny in which all experience is the result of a homological projection. This appears very close to Jung's concept of the evolution and dynamics of the archetypes of the collective unconscious. For Jung, the archetype is the place at which phylogeny and ontogeny meet. The archetypes are themselves the result of phylogenic evolution. They emerge in the personal experience of an individual through the projection of the archetypes onto the world as symbols. Vandervert expresses the relationship between symbols and algorithms in the following excerpts:

The system does not win algorithmic properties from symbols, however; algorithms already exist isomorphically in neurological circuitry. (Vandervert, 1992, p. 270)
    Further, this intuitive discovery process is guided, in accordance with

---

[10]Meaning, alchemical explanations which are integral throughout these particular passages of Jung's work.

maximum-power evolution, toward the energy efficiency of the algorithmic organization of the brain. (Vandervert, 1992, p. 271)

There emerges a general model of a continual thought-governed "mining" of the mostly unconscious algorithmic organization of the brain for increasingly powerful mental models (in accordance with the maximum-power principle). (Vandervert, 1991b)

Vandervert seems to be arguing that there is an algorithm that precedes the symbol, that biology selects for evolutionarily efficient algorithms that later emerge as symbols. Here, one may find that, while Vandervert places his emergent hierarchy's "foundation" upon the structural algorithm and optimal efficiency evolutionarily, what Jung has stated about the same issue is not so different:

Number helps more than anything else to bring order into the chaos of appearances. It is the predestined instrument for creating order, or for apprehending an already existing, but still unknown, regular arrangement or "orderedness." It may well be the most primitive element of order in the human mind, seeing that the numbers 1 to 4 occur with the greatest frequency and have the widest incidence. In other words, primitive patterns of order are mostly triads or tetrads. That numbers have an archetypal foundation is not, by the way, a conjecture of mine but of certain mathematician, as we shall see in due course. Hence it is not such an audacious conclusion after all if we define number psychologically as an *archetype of order* which has become conscious. Remarkably enough, the psychic images of wholeness which are spontaneously produced by the unconscious, the symbols of the self in mandala form, also have a mathematical structure. They are as a rule quaternities (or their multiples). These structures not only express order, they also create it. That is why they generally appear in times of psychic disorientation in order to compensate a chaotic state or as formulations of numinous experiences. (Jung, 1968, pp. 456–457)

Starting from very different places, we appear to have agreement. Where Vandervert emphasized the biological, evolutionary aspects, Jung emphasized the psychical, symbolic view.[11] Stated another way, Vandervert emphasized a bottom–up approach to the problem, while Jung took a top–down approach. The hinge-pin is in the importance and placement of the algorithm. This algorithm exists both in Vandervert's neurological order and in Jung's archetypes in the collective unconscious. In a different way, the algorithm also appears to be of central importance in studies on cognition represented by the similar, and yet, dichotomous views offered by Baars (1988) and Maturana and Varela (1987/1992).

---

[11]Jung stated "the archetype is the introspectively recognizable form of an *a priori* psychic orderedness" (1969, p 516).

Cognitive Algorithms for Doing and Knowing

Maturana and Varela (1987/1992) described the process of cognition as "all doing is knowing, and all knowing is doing" (p. 27). Put another way, they seem to mean that in the process of doing something you begin to know it cognitively; conversely, knowing implies that in order to directly do something you must already know the cognitive strategy. This knowing seems to be an algorithm embedded in the ontogeny of a biological unity. This accords well with Vandervert's approach to knowing. Maturana and Varela's approach is bottom–up, and focuses upon the biology of cognition through the concept of autopoiesis. Autopoiesis emphasizes the ability of a biological unity to couple with differing environments as well as to be recursively self-producing.

An autopoietic unity's modifiable ontogeny may find its counterpart in Baars' (1988) concept, the Global Workspace, where representations are emphasized as constructions for novel situations. Baars based his theory on the ability of the mind to detect matched and mismatched representations. In familiar situations, there is a match with previously existing representations, whereas in novel situations there is no existing representational structure, and consequently, the novel situation is a mismatch cognitively. Baars' approach may be seen as a top–down solution to cognition.

In either case, we have an overlap in how each theory describes change, where Maturana and Varela described the difference between an autopoietic unity's doing and knowing, Baars described matches and mismatches with a person's existing representational system, suggesting that new representations must be constructed to deal with novel situations. Where Maturana and Varela emphasized a structural approach, Baars emphasized a mentalist approach in describing the operations inherent in our functioning.

The Archimedean point we have in all these ideas concerns structure as the foundation of consciousness. Vandervert and Jung's ideas seem to agree that there is an algorithm of some sort engraved in our neurological order. Next, we focus briefly on how this algorithm may be expressed in the present day Mandelbröt set in fractal geometry or in the ancient form of a mandala.

Expression of an Algorithm?

Vandervert focused on the emergent quality of NP, whereas Jung focused on an archetype's ability to emerge as a personal symbol. These two different approaches might be visualized by comparing the Mandelbröt set—which is produced from a simple recursive algorithmic formula—and a mandala, which, according to Jung, is produced by the human psyche as an expression of emotional wholeness. Both structures rely on self-similarity of design and geometric symmetry. In the Mandelbröt set, we might see what Vandervert called the

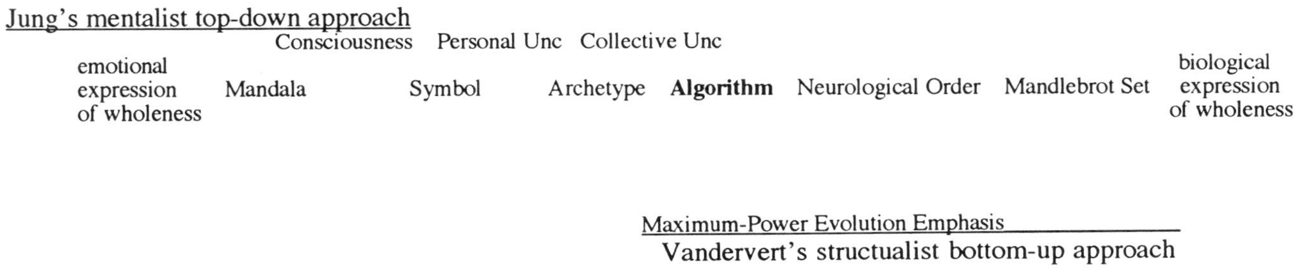

Jung's mentalist top-down approach

	Consciousness	Personal Unc	Collective Unc				biological
emotional				Archetype	**Algorithm**	Neurological Order	expression
expression	Mandala	Symbol				Mandlebrot Set	of wholeness
of wholeness							

Maximum-Power Evolution Emphasis

Vandervert's structualist bottom-up approach

FIG. 23.1. Continua of the algorithmic expression.

projection of the neurological order; in the mandala, what Jung described as a symbol of the wholeness of the Self. He stated, "symbols of the Self in mandala form, also have a mathematical structure. . . .as a rule quaternities (or their multiples)" (1968, p. 457).[12] Described from another vantage point, these types of images may at the same time act as multicomplex attractors that we gravitate toward to bring about wholeness in ourselves.[13] From either perspective, projection or attraction, these symbols appear to be representations of an universal algorithm of wholeness. Of course, this attempt to describe the purpose of the underlying algorithm, is at this point only speculation. It seems we still have much to learn about the nature of this algorithm we are attempting to describe.

A Continuum?

In comparing the relative emphasis of these ideas we find the type of overlap depicted in a continuum (Fig. 23.1). This continuum clearly shows the centrality of the algorithm in linking mentalist and structuralist approaches. Both Vandervert and Jung emphasize the algorithm's central importance in describing the nature of mind, and together it seems that their ideas mold into a unity that may satisfy both mentalist and structuralist. Perhaps there is no need to take either a mentalist or a structuralist position on these issues. Perhaps both are saying the same thing from a different perspective (Combs, 1992). with respect to Vandervert's and Jung's approaches, we close with some cautious words from Robertson (1992):

> Though we don't fully understand how this mechanism operates, it is clearly highly efficient, as it means that a given archetype (say the archetype of the mother) can operate over a wide variety of cultures in a wide variety of times and places. (Since the archetype seems essentially formless, one possibility is that an archetype is stored as some sort of numeric algorithm, but that is no more than speculation at this early point in understanding the nature of mind.) (p. 49)

REFERENCES

Baars, B. J. (1988). *A cognitive theory of consciousness*. New York: Cambridge.

Barton, S. (1994). Chaos, self-organization and psychology. *American Psychologist, 49*(1), 5–14.

Bohm, D. (1980). *Wholeness and the implicate order*. New York: Ark.

Briggs, J., & Peat, F. D. (1989). *Turbulent mirror*. New York: Harper & Row.

Briggs, J., & Peat, F. D. (1984). *Looking glass universe, the emerging science of wholeness*. New York: Simon & Schuster.

---

[12]Jung's concept of the *Self* is addressed at greater length in another essay (Bütz, 1992b).

[13]This wholeness is also described in greater detail in another essay (Bütz, 1992b).

Bütz, M. R. (1991). Fractal dimensionality and paradigms. *The Social Dynamicist, 2*(4), 4–7.

Bütz, M. R. (1992a). Chaos, an omen of transcendence in the psychotherapy process. *Psychological Reports, 71,* 827–843.

Bütz, M. R. (1992b). The fractal nature of the development of the Self. *Psychological Reports, 71,* 1043–1063.

Bütz, M. R. (1992c). *Paradigms afoot in science and psychology: beyond explication of fractal dimensionalty.* Paper presented at the annual conference of the Society for Chaos Theory in Psychology, Washington, DC.

Combs, A. (1992). Mind, brain, neural complexity and evolution: A progress report. *WESScomm, 2*(1), 12–15.

Coveney, P., & Highfield, R. (1990). *The arrow of time, a voyage through science to solve time's greatest mystery.* New York: Fawcett Columbine.

Gleick, J. (1987). *Chaos making a new science.* New York: Viking-Penguin.

Gould, S. J. (1992, November). The confusion over evolution. *The New York Review,* p. 47–52.

Grotstein, J. S. (1990). Nothingness, meaninglessness, chaos, and the "black hole" I: The importance of nothingness, meaninglessness and chaos in psychoanalysis. *Contemporary Psychoanalysis, 26*(2), 257–290.

Jacobi, J. (1959). *Complex/Archetype/Symbol in the psychology of C. G. Jung.* Princeton, NJ: Princeton University Press.

Jantsch, E. (1980). *The self-organizing universe, scientific and human implications of the emerging paradigm of evolution.* New York: Pergamon.

Jung, C. G. (1954). *The development of personality* (R. F. C. Hull, Trans.). Princeton, NJ: Princeton University Press.

Jung, C. G. (1961). *Freud and psychoanalysis* (R. F. C. Hull, Trans.). Princeton, NJ: Princeton University Press.

Jung, C. G. (1966). *The practice of psychotherapy* (2nd ed., R. F. C. Hull, Trans.). Princeton, NJ: Princeton University Press.

Jung, C. G. (1967). *Symbols of transformation* (2nd ed., R. F. C. Hull, Trans.). Princeton, NJ: Princeton University Press.

Jung, C. G. (1968). *The structure and dynamics of the psyche* (2nd ed., R. F. C. Hull, Trans.). Princeton, NJ: Princeton University Press.

Jung, C. G. (1969). *Psychology and religion: West and East* (2nd ed., R. F. C. Hull, Trans.). Princeton, NJ: Princeton University Press.

Laurikainen, K. V. (1992, August). Remarks on physics and the psyche. In Philosophical thought of Wolfgang Pauli. Helsinki, Finland: University of Helsinki.

Levy, S. (1992). *Artificial Life, the quest for a new creation.* New York: Pantheon.

Lonie, I. (1991). Chaos theory: A new paradigm for psychotherapy? *Australian and New Zealand Journal of Psychiatry, 25*(4), 548–560.

Maturana, H. R. & Varela, F. J. (1987). *The tree of knowledge, biological roots of human understanding* (2nd ed.). Boston, MA: Shambhala.

May, J., Groder, M. (1989). Jungian thought and dynamical systems, a new science of archetypal psychology. *Psychological Perspectives, 20*(1), 142–155.

Moran, M. G. (1991). Chaos theory and psychioanalysis: The fludic nature of the mind. *International Review of Psychoanalysis, 18,* 211–221.

Pendick, D. (1993). Chaos of the mind. *Science News, 143,* 138–139.

Prigogine, I., & Stengers, I. (1984). *Order out of chaos.* New York: Bantam.

Redington, D. J., Reidbord, S. P. (1992). Chaotic dynamics in autonomic nervous system activity of a patient during a psychotherapy session. *Biological Psychiatry, 31,* 993–1007.

Reidbord, S. P., & Redington, D. J. (1992). Psychophysiological processes during insight-oriented therapy, further investigations into nonlinear psychodynamics. *The Journal of Nervous and Mental Disease, 180,* 649–657.

Robertson, R. (1989). The evolution of number. *Psychological Perspectives, 20*(1), 128–141.

Robertson, R. (1992). *Beginner's guide to Jungian psychology.* York Beach, ME: Nicolas-Hays.

Schmid, G. B. (1991). Chaos theory and schizophrenia: Elementary aspects. *Psychopathology, 24,* 185–198.

Singer, J. (1990). *Seeing through the visible world: Jung, gnosis and chaos.* New York: Harper & Row.

Stern, D. B. (1983). Unformulated experience: From familiar chaos to creative disorder. *Contemporary Psychoanalysis, 19*(1), 71–99.

Van Eenwyk, J. R. (1991). Archetypes: The strange attractors of the psyche. *Journal of Analytical Psychology, 36,* 1–25.

van Erkelens, H. (1992, August). Modern physics and symbols of the self. In Philosophical thought of Wolfgang Pauli. Helsinki, Finland: University of Helsinki.

Vandervert, L. (1988). Systems thinking and a proposal for a Neurological Positivism. *Systems Research, 5*(4), 313–321.

Vandervert, L. (1990a). Systems thinking and Neurological Positivism: Further elucidation's and implications. *Systems Research, 7*(1), 1–17.

Vandervert, L. (1990b). From the Editor's desk. *Network, 8*(3), 11–12.

Vandervert, L. (1991a). On the modeling of emergent interaction: Which will it be, the laws of thermodynamics, or Sperry's "wheel" in the subcircuitry? *The Journal of Mind and Behavior, 12*(4), 535–540.

Vandervert, L. (1991b). A measurable and testable brain-based emergent interactionism: An alternative to Sperry's mentalist emergent interactionism. *The Journal of Mind and Behavior, 12*(2), 201–219.

Vandervert, L. (1992). The emergence of brain and mind amid chaos through maximum-power evolution. *World Futures, 33*(4), 253–273.

Vandervert, L. (1993, August). *Chaos theory and the evolution of consciousness.* Paper given at the American Psychological Association National Convention, Toronto, Ontario, Canada.

Von Franz, M. L. (1980). *Projection and re-collection in Jungian Psychology.* La Salle, IL: Open Court.

Waldrop, M. M. (1992). *Complexity, the emerging science at the edge of order and chaos.* New York: Simon & Schuster.

Webster's 9th New Collegiate Dictionary. (1989). Springfield, MA: Merriam-Webster.

24
How Predictable Is the Future? The Conflict Between Traditional Chaos Theory and the Psychology of Prediction, and the Challenge for Chaos Psychology

David Loye

The rise of modern chaos theory opens the prospect of an immense new stage of growth and challenge for psychology as well as all the other social sciences. In the fascinating mating of chaos theory with psychology now underway, however, a problem of critical importance for both parties emerges. It comes from the fact that the concepts and mindset for "traditional" chaos theory arise from the thinking of natural scientists and mathematicians accustomed to working with data at mainly prehuman levels of evolution. But a vast—and very much underappreciated—change occurs when we must deal with the data of the human brain and mind that both rises out of *and can transform* the data of the prehuman level.

I believe this disjunction of data and mind-sets—and the need for it to be resolved for the advancement of both disciplines—will be found in many areas of concern during the growth of the child of this mating, which can most economically be called *chaos psychology*. Here I focus on an example that may be useful to others in resolving this problem of disjunction over the years ahead. Out of work over 20 years (Loye, 1977, 1978, 1980a, 1980b, 1983a, 1983b, 1994a, 1994b), I have found the problem emerges if, from the perspectives of all three parties involved—that is, established chaos theory, the psychology of prediction, and the new chaos psychology—we take a new look at the central concept for all science of *prediction,* or the question of how reliably can we predict what is going to happen in any area of interest to us.

CHAOS THEORY AND THE CASE FOR A MAINLY UNPREDICTABLE WORLD

Widely popularized is the view that chaos theory shows us that prediction of the future is impossible. This conclusion is the end result of the progressive chipping away of a belief in ultimate predictability that, as sketched by physicist Joseph Ford (1989), began with Einstein's theory of relativity, accelerated with quantum physics, and now apparently has been given the coup de grace by chaos theory. The scientific actuality, however, is more finely differentiated. As we see in the case of Poincaré, Prigogine, Lorenz, Abraham, Bohm, Laszlo, and others, their position is that predictability disappears in far-from-equilibrium or chaotic conditions.

This position, surprisingly, is far more cloudy than one would think. Indeed, considering the centrality of prediction to science, it is startling to find how little comprehensive attention has been given to the concept and operational reality of prediction in chaos theory. To ground ourselves properly for what follows, we must take a careful look at prediction in terms of the three main facets to chaos theory: "how order gives way to 'chaos,' order is discovered within 'chaos,' and order is again created out of 'chaos'" (Loye & Eisler, 1987, p. 53).

How order gives way to chaos has been explored by Ralph Abraham (Abraham & Shaw, 1992) and other chaos theorists in terms of the increasing levels of instability in systems indicated by the familiar concepts of the "static," the "periodic," and the "strange" or "chaotic" attractor. In the first situation, as in a whirlpool, activity within a system is largely controlled by a single, centering "vortex" toward which everything is drawn. In the second situation, a second "vortex" appears, with activity within the system alternating between these two periodic attractors, as in a pendulum, back and forth. As becomes apparent if we think about what is happening in terms of these images, so far we have systems conditions in which there can exist a reasonable degree of predictability. But with the third situation, in which there is a rapid rise in forces de-stabilizing a system and/or with the appearance of the strange or chaotic attractor, we find a sharp rise in unpredictability. For now we are confronted with a phenomenon that may appear as no more than, so to speak, a tiny blip on the screen; then disappear—to never reappear, or to reappear and, with an astonishing rapidity, take over predominating control of the affected system.

We see, then, how as order gives way to chaos, predictability gives way to unpredictability. But do we move into states of complete unpredictability, as chaos theory at present tends to claim? Or under certain circumstances, using underexplored capabilities of the human brain and mind (as well as an improved linking of human and computer), is it possible to predict far into states of chaos—and even through chaos to the new order that lies beyond?

A gleam of hope in this direction emerged with the most publicized work of chaos theorists. This was the second type of chaos-order relationship: the discovery of new forms of order within chaos. Here, for example, we have the saga of how Cornel physicist Mitchell Feigenbaum (1980), working initially with only a hand calculator, discovered that many different equations could give exactly the same "renormalization" result, or what is now called Feignebaum mapping. In essence, through a variety of ways of exploring chaos, he showed how new patterns, new order, new predictabilities emerge (for details, see Gleick, 1987, or Stewart, 1989).

The third type of order-chaos relationship—that of how chaos gives way to order again—is perhaps best illustrated by the well-known "dissipative structures" work of Ilya Prigogine (Prigogine & Stengers, 1984). Here we see the dynamics defined whereby order forms out of chaos through "autocatalysis" and "cross-catalysis." Also of great usefulness in this regard is Prigogine's concept of "nucleation" as the gathering together of seemingly disparate elements into the "seed" of a new form. Running through this aspect of chaotic theorizing, expanding insight, has been the powerful influence of "self-organization" concepts, such as "autopoesis" (Maturana & Varela, 1980), and "autogenesis" (Csanyi & Kampis, 1985; Schwalbe, 1991). In terms of predictability, all this work may be characterized as a glimpsing of the reemergence of predictability.

So, throughout all three aspects of chaos theory, we have this interplay of predictability with unpredictability. But now let's once again focus on what seems to be the ultimate test of predictability: whether or not it is possible to predict the future within situations of extreme instability, which occur near or at bifurcation points, or more generally, within far-from-equilibrium and chaotic conditions. Here the classic, and seemingly unassailable, case in point is the dilemma mathematician Edward Lorenz faced in 1962 through his use of computer modeling to see if he could improve weather forecasting.

Lorenz (1984) had succeeded in programming the computer to simulate air movement above the earth with considerable realism and predictability. But then he noticed that predictions starting from nearly identical points diverged after a while, which led to the discovery of a strange new pattern that was both fascinating and greatly disturbing. The odd, three-fingered pattern he was later to project through computer graphics he named the strange attractor, also to become known as the chaotic attractor. To Lorenz this seemed proof that beyond a minimal point one came up against a complete breakdown in predictability, and that anything one might believe beyond this was nothing but illusion.

There was, he believed, a potential for "two week forecasts as good as today's four-day forecasts" (Lorenz, 1984, p. 109). But beyond this lay the unbridgeable chasm. "Accurate long-range prediction of global weather patterns," said Lorenz, "is impossible."

Similarly, from the perspective of chemistry and thermodynamics, Prigogine noted, "We cannot predict the details of temporal evolution. . .only a statistical description is possible" (Prigogine & Stengers, 1984, pp. 177–178). Likewise, physicist David bohm noted in his well-known analysis of the nature of order that predictability rapidly breaks down. It is, he observed, limited to "a special kind of order such that a few steps determine the whole order (i.e., as in curves of low degree. . ." (Bohm, 1980, p. 118) Similar limits for predictability have been noted by Laszlo (1987). All this is in keeping with the great mathematician Henri Poincaré's original insight, around 1900, that "it may happen that small differences in the initial conditions produce very great ones in the final phenomena. A small error in the former will produce an enormous error in the latter. Prediction becomes impossible. . ." (quoted by Gleick, 1987, p. 321).

THE PSYCHOLOGY OF PREDICTION AND THE CASE FOR CHAOS-TRANSCENDENT PREDICTABILITY

As detailed elsewhere (Abraham, Abraham, & Shaw, 1990; Loye, 1994a; Loye & Eisler, 1987), the work of a surprising number of psychologists bears on chaos theory—for example, Berlyne, Crutchfield, Dollard, Estes, Freud, Fromm, Hamden-Turner, Harlow, Hebb, Heider, Hull, James, Jung, Kohler, Lashley, Lewin, Loye, MacCorquodale, Miller, Mowrer, Osgood, Pavlov, Sanford, Skinner, Stevens, Sullivan, Tolman, and Tomkins. Also, directly bearing on questions that chaos theory presents of predictability versus unpredictability are works by Allport, Atkinson, Bogen, Bolles, Cantril, Erikson, Eysenck, Festinger, Freidman, Gallanter, Hull, Kelly, Kendler and Kendler, Koffka, Lippit and White, Luria, McClelland, McGregor, Meehl, Miller, Pribram, Riegel, Rokeach, Solomon, Sperry, Watson, Wertheimer, and others.

A direct contradiction of the chaos theoretical view of the limits for predictability shows up as early as 1930 in leading behaviorist theorist Clark Hull's careful analysis of prediction in stimulus–response (S–R) theory terms (Hull, 1930). Hull made the case that we predict the future through *generalizing* from what we already know to what we don't yet know.

Generalization, it is important to point out here, is a concept based on hundreds of experimental studies that show how we use a concept formed through an experienced event to explain events that have not been experienced, or even may only hypothetically exist. In other words, we detect metaphoric or analogic similarities in the experienced event (e.g., the death of a parent, which throws us into a far-from-equilibrium emotional condition) and the nonexperienced or hypothetical event (the death of a friend), and through *generalizing* meaning from one to the other we are able to predict how we would feel in the nonexperienced or hypothetical situation. Thus, if we reconsider Hull's careful analysis, we may project a forecasting tool of mind that can move through chaos to new order.

Moreover, a central point in this instance runs through all the other studies I note in this section. It is that here we see, in the case of generalization, a fundamental concept for the psychology of learning that operates at the data transformational level of the human mind but not at the evolutionarily prehuman data level of observed phenomena that chaos theory primarily models and on which it is primarily based. In other words, to comprehend the operation of generalization requires the more complex, more evolutionarily advanced viewpoint of the human agent—that is, ourselves, each one of us, perceiving and acting within the surrounding world of evolutionarily prior developmental phenomenon out of which the human body, brain, and mind emerges. It is not something that openly presents itself at the atomic, molecular, or chemical level.

But is this difference between the data and mindset of traditional chaos theory and a psychology of prediction only theroetical? Hardly, for the most impressive thing about the psychology of prediction is the amount of empirical data revealing a chaos-theoretical-transcendent range of predictability. Two of the most impressive studies of this type—striking in how they reveal a track of predictability across intervening times of maximal disequilibrium—are David McClelland's studies of the prediction of war and peace (1975) and economic expansion and decline (1961). In his classic *The Achieving Society* (1961), McClelland's goal was to see to what degree evidence of increases or decreases in *need for achievement* (n Ach) could serve as a predictor of rising or falling economies. To measure need for achievement, McClelland analyzed cultural artifacts of ancient Greece, feudal Spain, Tudor England, and pre-Incan Peru. He also conducted field studies of business entrepreneurs in Germany, Italy, Turkey, Poland, Japan, and Brazil, as well as field experiments with entire villages in India and Mexico. Need for achievement ratings were then compared with maps and other historical and contemporary measures of economic expansion and decline.

What McClelland found—crossculturally and over vast stretches of history involving every conceivable kind of social and cultural upheaval—was that a rise in need for achievement in a society or group or individual at an earlier point in time did indeed predict later economic success. Likewise, he found the reverse— that an earlier drop in need for achievement predicted later economic decline.

A pivotal work in the development of the mind-brain-computer link-up underlying the computer revolution in social science was Miller, Gallanter, and Pribram's *Plans and the Structure of Behavior* (1960). Here, through a wedding of S–R thinking with brain research and systems and cybernetic feedback theory, they were able to show how prediction functions in a chain-linked fashion with *intervention*—that is, as the forward-driving, feedback-modified, dialectical interaction of prediction and intervention. Similarly, in regard to the human-computer link-up, the pioneering work of Herbert Simon and Peter Newell (1962) in developing the grandaddy of artificial intelligence, The General Problem Solver, and the pioneering work of Oliver Selfridge and Ulric Neisser (1960) in computerized pattern recognition, opened vistas for the improvement of computerized prediction that chaos theorists, notably through the ingenious computer modeling of Ralph Abraham (1989), and Doyne Farmer and Norman Packard (Berreby, 1993), are currently exploring.

But let us now examine a striking sequence of studies over a 50-year period— the first two for some time now dropped almost entirely from the literature, the last for the first time reported here. As explored in detail in *The Knowable Future* (Loye, 1978), in 1936 a central figure in the development of management theory, psychologist Douglas McGregor (1938), asked 400 students at Dartmouth, Bennington, and Columbia, as well as faculty at MIT, to predict the outcomes of nine events then in process—Franklin Roosevelt's campaign for reelection, the rise to power of Hitler, and so on. By chance these short-term predictions should have been half right, half wrong, but majorities correctly predicted the outcomes for all nine events!

A curiosity, a fluke, one might say. But then a short time later, a central figure in the development of opinion polling and humanistic psychology, Hadley Cantril, published a complementary study, this time of long-term as well as short-term predictive ability (Cantril, 1938). His sample of 205 was older and more representative of the U.S. middle class as a whole. I came across these "lost" works forty years later, in 1976. Noticing that sufficient time had elapsed to allow one to check on the predictive ability of Cantril's group, I did so. Despite the obviously much greater difficulties of long-term versus short-term prediction —and despite the fact predictions for Cantril's group dealt with events during the exceptionally chaotic and far-from-equilibrium historical conditions preceding and during World War II—I found that the Cantril group had successfully predicted the future in 16 out of 25 rateable instances, or 64% of the time.

Deciding to extend this line of exploration, in the spring of 1983 I surveyed 1,500 people with a new set of prediction questions. Them sample, drawn from 33 U.S. states, fairly evenly balanced for gender, ranging in age from 16 to 70, was of students in a variety of majors in 18 colleges and universities and older adults in a wide variety of occupations ranging from violin-making to banking. Out of this sample, making use of a new measure I developed for use in a new "brain hemispheric consensus" method of prediction, the HCP Profile (Loye, 1983b, 1994a), I selected a data subset of those scoring high in brain "hemispheric equipotentiality," or the ability to switch with ease between left and right brain half modes of cognition. An 11-question prediction test was given at this time and a single, follow-up question in the following spring. The period for these tests of prediction was toward the end of U.S. President Reagan's first term, during which the economic and political situation was far more fluid than we assume in retrospect. With stretches of from 4 to 6 months between predictions and rateable outcomes, predictions for 12 questions (11 for 1983 and 1 for 1984) showed a ratio of 8 correct to 4 incorrect, or a successful prediction rate of 66%.

The thrust to this track of investigation is further strengthened, I believe, by a prior series of prediction studies, reported in *The Knowable Future* (Loye, 1978). Making use of the new IMP method of "ideological matrix" prediction I had developed, the first study was of how a use of the IMP approach in colonial times might have predicted changes in U.S. racial attitudes over a 100-year span leading to the U.S. Civil War. Spanning chaotic as well as relatively stable times in U.S. history, the results were uncannily successful. A second IMP study in 1972 with Princeton student leaders of campus liberal, conservative, left wing, and right wing groups—with the volatile years in American history involving the Watergate scandal intervening—successfully predicted national political trends emerging four years later during the 1976 presidential campaign. During that campaign, the IMP method with small samples fairly consistently outpredicted the established polls with large samples. And in 1980, during a time of considerable upheaval and a decrying of the loss of all predictability within the entertainment industry, my "HCP Profile" and "IMP Profile" approaches generated startling predictions of successful types for movie "hits" 2 and 3 years ahead in time (Loye, 1994b).

So, overall we have this pattern of an arresting consistency for human predictive abilities that seems to defy the limits and cutoff points dictated by chaos theory. But to show that this is true is only half the task. Beyond this, we must try to answer the questions of how and why.

HOW DO WE BEAT THE CHAOS ODDS? FOUR-DIMENSIONAL VERSUS MULTIDIMENSIONAL POTENTIALITIES

So far, we have explored the difference between established chaos theorizing and the findings of a psychology of prediction in terms of, on one side, observations, theory and mathematical modeling mainly based on the phenomena of earlier developmental stages in evolution (e.g., the atomic, molecular, chemical, biological levels) and what happens in evolution with the emergence of the human body, brain, and mind. Another way of looking at this difference, which I can do no more than identify here, seems to be the difference of theorizing within the constraints of the four well-known perceptual dimensions of physics (height, width, depth, and space–time) and what seems to be the entry of a multidimensionality going beyond these four when we try to understand the nature and operation of human consciousness (Combs, 1995; Laszlo, 1994; Loye, 1983a).

At this stage in our evolution, we can only theorize how consciousness works. I have been able to identify, however, at least four types of empirical data bearing on the operation of consciousness in prediction.

Individual Differences in Predictive Abilities

Within psychology there is considerable evidence of personality correlates that cluster within people who seem to have more of a capacity to "beat the chaos odds" than others. Explored in Loye (1980) as well as in Loye (1978, 1983a, 1994a), these qualities include such traits as open-mindedness, creativity, imagination, tolerance for ambiguity, brain hemispheric equipotentiality, and systems sensitivity. These findings, however, only barely tap the range of relevant differences that emerge from studies, at this point in our history and evolution, still considered beyond the pale for science—that is, studies of so-called PSI phenomena (Loye, 1983a).

Group Versus Individual Prediction

By far the most striking change in our capacities for prediction against the odds emerges when we shift from individual to group prediction. This is the uncanny power we see emerge in the McGregor–Cantril tradition. One may find an abysmal record for one individual versus an "intriguing" or "suggestive" record for another individual, but within groups there is the significant margin we have seen for predictive hits over misses.

Ideological Matrixing

Behind the development of the Ideological Matrix Prediction mentioned earlier (Loye, 1978, 1980a, 1994a) lies my finding that, aside from technology, the most significant complex of forces shaping group life at all levels over hundreds of years is ideological. Specifically, the "engine" of change seems to run according to the interaction and alternation of the contending mind-sets and actions of those whom we generally think of as liberal or conservative, progressive or reactionary, or left or right. Those who "soak" in these phenomena, such as extremely gifted politicians, historians, or political forecasters, can in a sense "read" the patterns that emerge through ideological dialectics. Thereby, sometimes at critical times, they can in vision plunge through times and conditions of maximal instability to the new order that will emerge out of chaos on the other side.

Predictability-Relevant Discoveries of Modern Brain Research

As outlined in Loye (1983a, 1983b, 1994a), three areas of comparatively recent brain research have uncovered findings that greatly help us understand our grossly under-utilized predictive powers. One is the highly publicized area of left–right brain hemispheric research (e.g., Cohen, 1973; Geschwind & Galaburda, 1984; Tucker, 1981). A second is the even more important—and beyond the ranks of neurologists and neuropsychologists, astoundingly little known—area of frontal brain research (e.g., Luria, 1973; MacLean, 1990; Pribram, 1973). Third is the still controversial area of holographic and holonomic brain research pioneered by Pribram (1991), which bears on precognition studies (Loye, 1983a).

Based on these kinds of brain research, I have developed a theory of how frontal brain "executive" processes work in partnership with right brain "gestalt," left brain "analytic," and whole brain "holographic" processes in prediction (Loye, 1983a, 1983b, 1994a, 1994b).

LEVEL 1 PREDICTION INTO CHAOS, LEVEL 2 PREDICTION FROM WITHIN CHAOS, AND THE CHALLENGE FOR CHAOS PSYCHOLOGY

While it now seems apparent we may push the limits of predictability far beyond what has hitherto seemed possible, there remains this gap—at times most certainly a chasm—between our far limits and what may emerge out of chaos in the way of order on the other side. Can we go still further in bridging this gap? Again the answer seems to be yes.

In individual differences in predictive ability, group versus individual prediction, ideological matrixing, and advanced predictive capacities of the human brain, we have been looking at what may be called Level 1 prediction, or *prediction into chaotic conditions* (or prediction that goes just so far and then no more). But now let's look at evidence for Level 2 prediction, or *prediction from within chaotic conditions.*

At the heart of all situations calling for prediction is the perspective of the human not simply as passive observer but as active *agent* at the grounding point for all human and human-impacted activity.

"The assumption that a process that is unpredictable is also uncontrollable is often made, but it is false," noted evolutionary theorist Ervin Laszlo (1987, p. 129). "Unpredictability means only that an external observer, even if he controls certain parameters of the system, is unable to decide which of several. . .alternative states will be realized in the system." But the *human agent,* the protagonist in life, can "critically influence the choice of its future states" (p. 127). More specifically, "the goals and ideals projected by the activist could become the attractors of society's next systemic state pulling it out of chaos and onto the next plateau of order" (p. 127).

How this would work is indicated by the nature of the prediction-intervention dialectic I touched on earlier, which emerged from cybernetic theory and brain research (Miller, Gallanter, & Pribram, 1960). We predict, then test this prediction through feedforward intervention in process. Through feedback, this reality test reveals a gap between prediction and reality. We adjust the prediction and intervene again, and thus—alternating prediction with intervention, again and again retesting, reintervening—we advance into the future.

Within the chaos, psychological perspective, what this observable pattern to the life processes of the human agent indicates is that we can attain predictability in far-from-equilibrium—that is, maximally unstable, chaotic—conditions by a strategy for survival somewhat like that of a hypothetical logger in a raging river filled with logs. Sustained for the split-second predictability of the log underfoot, the logger leaps across an unpredictable stretch of river to another such log of split-second predictability, in this way leapfrogging from log to log across the river.

But is this picture I have projected of prediction from within chaotic conditions in terms of hypothetical loggers reasonably close to the mark? Can we understand what is going on here more specifically in terms of the concepts and mathematics of chaos theory? Here the theoretical surmises of Fred Abraham and associates (1994) and the experimental work of Allen Neuringer and Cheryl Voss (1993) indicate corroboration for my theorizing as well as possibilities for some exceptionally meaningful pioneering for the new chaos psychologists.

Mind "can get outside of itself, and is not a formal system subject to Gödel's restrictions," Abraham (this volume, chap. 11) writes. "It is capable of constructing a dynamical model of itself, of reading its past, projecting its future, making choices about those futures, and controlling them through not only manipulation of control parameters, but creating new, novel spaces and solutions."

Of our capacity for detecting patterns within chaotic conditions—or in my theoretical projection, the log the logger leaps to—Abraham makes a though-provoking case, contrary to the chaos theoretical dictum of "sensitivity to initial conditions," for "*insensitivity* to initial conditions." He observes that "many trajectories from very diverse locations approach the attractive surface of a chaotic attractor, and while neighboring trajectories diverge along the attractive surface as they progress in time, they all obey the same laws (vectorfields), *and make for very similar patterns,* despite being at different places within the attractor at any given time." (Abraham, 1994 p. 4, italics added).

But how then can we in mind leapfrog in the right direction, past the seemingly incalculable bifurcation point? Or how, when jolted by an unexpected wave, does the logger calculate where the next log will be. Abraham makes a carefully reasoned case for what happens in terms of the imagery and language we use in constructing a self-organizing, self-sustaining, reasonably autonomous consciousness. Factors involved include "the MIND's view of the response diagram, that is, the system, its past and its potential futures" (p. 10); the self-control of bifurcations to novel attractors; extrapolation from the familiar to the unfamiliar (as Hull, 1930, projected); and the "waxing and waning of the balance between linear and nonlinear time" (p. 11).

Turning from theory to the vital empirical probe, we find the ingenious set of experiments by Neuringer and Voss, whereby they tested 11 participants, 9 females and 2 males, for their ability to predict the future in chaotic conditions. Their methodology involved the use of a well-known logistic equation for generating fixed, periodic, and chaotic attractors on the computer screen from the iterative (or repeating) inputting of results. At each iteration, participants were asked to predict the locations or numerical values that would show up next.

The result was a surprisingly close correspondence between predicted and actual outcomes. In part, this seems experimental confirmation of my logger in the raging river analysis. For here, through a human interface with computer generation, we see a scientific tracking of the operation of the human ability to detect the unfolding "gestalt" or pattern for movement through chaotic states that my long-time research has convinced me of. Mindful of the enormous impact on the field of psychology of the Asch (1952) conformity experiment design or Witkin's (1972) field–dependence–independence experimental designs, I feel the Neuringer and Voss experimental approach opens the way for themselves and other psychologists to comparably map the territory for a chaos psychology of prediction.

The central idea for my interpretation of Abraham's and Neuringer and Voss's work, as well as for other prediction-relevant chaos theorizing, is that, through dissipative structuring, self-organizing, autopoetic, and autogenetic processes, there rise out of the turbulent river of chaotic activity these "logs" of order we apprehend through prediction, on or within which "logs" we regain a new level of predictability.

PROSPECTS FOR A BETTER UNDERSTANDING OF AND AN INCREASE IN PREDICTABILITY THROUGH CHAOS PSYCHOLOGY

So have we at last pushed predictability in far-from-equilibrium states to its ultimate limits? No, actually we have not. For within an area of research still denied inclusion and respectability by social science—but paradoxically of increasing interest and acceptability within areas of natural science—lie findings that reveal a human capability not only for prediction in varying degrees of probabilities but also for the prediction of the future in nonprobabilistic, precise detail!

As I detail elsewhere (Loye, 1983a, 1994a, 1994b), this is in the area of so-called PSI phenomena, specifically precognition studies. To many investigating precognition, it is apparent that ultimately this line of investigation will radically transform all science, but at the present rate of acceptance and absorption, it will take well beyond the middle of the 21st century for this work to gain a significant place within scientific thinking and funding. As this is far too large and problematic a body of work to bring in here, I close by dealing with what we are left with on our plate at this point.

Are there then *no* limits to predictability? Of course not. Natural scientific and mathematical chaos theorists are essentially right in pointing to the implacable general fact of limits. In doing so, they are restating in mathematical terms what philosophers going back at least to Immanuel Kant in *The Critique of Pure Reason* (1781, 1958) have concluded about impenetrable limits to the reach of "reason."

So on one hand, we have the assessment of mathematics and natural science of limits that come up soon. On the other, we have the evidence of psychology, brain research, and practical experience that the limits of predictability lie much farther off and are much more flexible than chaos theorists—as well as many physicists—presently believe.

As prediction remains central to scientific endeavor as well as to social, economic, political, and personal advancement, the resolution of this disjunction must become a high priority. This is a task for which chaos psychology, building on the still fresh eruption of chaos theoretical findings and the "lost" findings of a psychology of prediction, seems ideally suited. It has been my intention in this chapter to show feisty younger chaos psychologists the territory and take them down a number of trails as far as I have been able to go in the hope they may be enticed to pick up where I leave off.

And what can be the practical benefits of tackling this challenge? What I have set forth in this chapter, as well as in *The Psychology of Prediction* to be completed within this year, is the result of what has been to this point a surprisingly lonely journey. If younger psychologists, forecasters, and other social and management scientists can extend this exploration, we can expect to see an increase in both the accuracy of forecasts and the prediction-guided tailoring of action affecting the marketplace, economies more generally, politics, governance, health, education, and indeed every other area of our lives.

And so where does all this leave us in regard to that benchmark for the prediction aficionado, Isaac Asimov's (1951) famous predictor Hari Seldon— who could, with pinpoint accuracy, forecast events over a 30,000-year span into the future? While arresting and suggestive, it is clear that Hari Seldon and his grasp of what is to come can never be anything more than science fiction. We are, however, left with the aspirational grounds for real-life mini-Hari's, who can greatly benefit humanity over much shorter and more realistic looks ahead.

REFERENCES

Abraham, F., Abraham, R., & Shaw, C. (1990). *A visual introduction to dynamical systems theory for psychology.* Santa Cruz, CA: Aerial Press.

Abraham, R. (1989). Political weather reports. *World Futures: The Journal of General Evolution, 27*, 2–4, 125–130.

Abraham, R., & Shaw, C. (1992) *Dynamics: The geometry of behavior* (2nd ed.) Reading, MA: Addison-Wesley.

Asch, S. E. (1952). *Social psychology.* Englewood Cliffs, NJ: Prentice-Hall.

Asimov, I. (1951). *The foundation trilogy.* New York: Doubleday.

Berreby, D. (1993). Chaos hits wall street. *Discovery, 14*, 3.

Bohm, D. (1980). *Wholeness and the implicate order.* London: Routledge & Kegan Paul.

Cantril, H. (1938). The prediction of social events. *Journal of Abnormal and Social Psychology, 33*, 364–389.

Cohen, G. (1973). Hemispheric differences in serial versus parallel processing. *Journal of Experimental Psychology, 97*, 349–356.

Combs, A. (1995). *The radiance of being: Complexity, chaos, and the evolution of consciousness.* Edinburgh, Scotland: Floris Books.

Csanyi, V., & Kampis, G. (1985). Autogenesis: Evolution of replicative systems. *Journal of Theoretical Biology, 114,* 303–321.

Feigenbaum, M. (1980) Universal behavior in nonlinear systems. *Los Alamos Sciences, 1,* 4–27.

Ford, J. (1989). What is chaos, that we should be mindful of it? In P. Davis (Ed.), *The new physics.* New York: Cambridge University Press.

Geschwind, N., & Galaburda, A. (1984). *Cerebral dominance: The biological foundations.* Cambridge, MA: Harvard University Press.

Gleick, J. (1987). *Chaos: Making a new science.* New York: Viking.

Hull, C. (1930). Knowledge and purpose as habit mechanisms. *Psychological Review, 37,* 511–525.

Kant, I. (1958). *The critique of pure reason.* London: MacMillan. (Original work published 1958)

Laszlo, E. (1987). *Evolution: The grand synthesis.* Boston: New Science Library.

Laszlo, E. (1994). *The creative cosmos.* Edinburgh: Floris Books.

Lorenz, E. (1984). Irregularity: A fundamental property of the atmosphere. *Tellus, 36,* 98–110.

Loye, D. (1977). *The leadership passion: A psychology of ideology.* San Francisco, CA: Jossey-Bass.

Loye, D. (1978). *The knowable future: A psychology of forecasting and prophecy.* New York: Wiley-Interscience.

Loye, D. (1980a). Ideology and prediction. *Technological Forecasting and Social Change, 16,* 229–242.

Loye, D. (1980b). Personality and prediction. *Technological Forecasting and Social Change, 16,* 93–104.

Loye, D. (1983a; 1984) *The Sphinx and the rainbow: Brain, mind and future vision.* Boston: Shambhala New Science Library/New York: Bantam New Age.

Loye, D. (1983b). The brain, the mind, and the future. *Technological Forecasting and Social Change, 23,* 267–280.

Loye, D. (1994a). *The psychology of prediction: From Freud to chaos theory.* Work in progress.

Loye, D. (1994b). *Prediction in the dream factory: Creativity and survival in the marketplace.* Work in progress.

Loye, D., & Eisler, R. (1987). Chaos and transformation: The implications of natural scientific nonequilibrium theory for social science and society. *Behavioral Science, 32,* 1, 53–65.

Luria, A. (1973). *The working brain.* New York: Basic Books.

MacLean, P. (1990). *The triune brain in evolution: Role in paleocerebral functions.* New York: Plenum Press.

Maturana, H., & Varela, F. (1980). *Autopoesis and cognition: The realization of the living.* Boston: Reidel.

McClelland, D. (1961). *The achieving society.* Princeton, NJ: Van Nostrand.

McClelland, D. (1975). *Power: The inner experience.* New York: Irvington.

McGregor, D. (1938). The major determinants of the prediction of social events. *Journal of Abnormal and Social Psychology, 33,* 179–204.

Miller, G., Gallanter, E., & Pribram, K. (1960). *Plans and the structure of behavior.* New York: Holt, Rinehart & Winston.

Neuringer, A., & Voss, C. (1993). Approximating chaotic behavior. *Psychological Science, 4,* 113–119.

Pribram, K. (1973). The primate frontal cortex—executive of the brain. In K. Pribram, & A. Luria (Eds), *Psychophysiology of the frontal lobes.* New York, Academic Press.

Pribram, K. (1991). *Brain and perception.* Hillsdale, NJ: Lawrence Erlbaum Associates.

Prigogine, I., & Stengers, I. (1984). *Order out of chaos.* New York: Bantam.

Schwalbe, M. L. (1991). The autogenesis of the self. *Journal for the Theory of Social Behavior, 21,* 269–295.

Selfridge, O., & Neisser, U. (1960). Pattern recognition by machine. *Scientific American, 203,* 2, 60–68.

Simon, H., & Newell, A. (1962). Simulation of human thinking. In M. Greenberger (Ed.), *Computers and the world of the future.* Cambridge, MA: MIT Press.

Stewart, I. (1989). *Does God play dice? The mathematics of chaos.* Cambridge, MA: Basil Blackwell.

Tucker, D. (1981). Lateral brain function, emotion, and conceptualization. *Psychological Bulletin, 89,* 19–46.

Witkin, H. (1972). *Personality through perception: An experimental and clinical study.* Westport, CT: Greenwood Press.

25 Chaos: The Geometrization of Thought

F. David Peat

As a result of the popular books and magazine articles that have appeared over the last few years, the topic of chaos theory has become familiar to many people. Although some psychologists may not be comfortable with the mathematical details of the theory, they are probably acquainted with its broad outlines and general concepts. Thus, for example, the image of "butterfly effect" is often applied to systems so extraordinarily sensitive that a perturbation as small as the flapping of a butterfly's wings produces a large-scale change of behavior. Although chaos theory holds that such systems remain strictly deterministic, they are, nevertheless, so enormously complex that the exact details of their behavior are, in practice, unpredictable, even with the aid of the largest computers.

On the other hand, because such systems remain within the grip of their strange attractor, while the details of their fluctuations appear to be random, nevertheless, their chaos is contained within a particular range of all possible behaviors. Their dynamics may, for example, exhibit a fractal structure in which similar patterns are repeated at smaller and smaller scales of space and intervals of time. As an example, while it is impossible to predict the exact value of a particular share on the stock market at an arbitrary date in the future, one may be able to say something about its general pattern of fluctuation over a month, day, or even an hour.

In a sense, therefore, chaos theory is something of a misnomer for it is not so much the study of systems in which all order has broken down in favor of pure chance but rather of those that exhibit extremely high degrees of order involving very subtle and sensitive behavior. The full description of such systems would require an enormous, potentially an infinite, amount of information. On the other hand, highly complex behavior can sometimes be simulated in very simple ways through the constant repetition of an iteration processes, such as Prigogine's baker's transformation or the nonlinear feedback associated with the changing size of insect populations.

While chaos theory and fractal descriptions are capable of simulating a wide variety of natural processes, it remains an open question as to the extent to which such theories actually offer a full account of the inner workings of nature and society. For example, while repeated iterations can generate complex results, this does not necessarily mean that such iterations are part of the actual generative processes of nature itself. Another pertinent question is to what extent does absolute randomness and chaos occur within the universe. While chaos theory is purely deterministic, may there exist certain natural processes that are essentially chaotic, indeterministic, and random? Quantum theory would be an obvious choice, for the time at which a radioactive nucleus disintegrates is, according to the theory, absolutely indeterministic—it is a matter of pure chance. David Bohm, however, has produced a deterministic version of quantum theory that perfectly accounts for all the empirical findings and predictions of the theory without invoking the assumption of absolute chance.

Another area in which intrinsic randomness occurs is in the sequence of digits of an irrational number. But what is the ontological basis of such numbers in nature? Are they a manifestation of intrinsic randomness in the universe, or do they represent the abstract limits of processes that involve an infinite amount of information? At present, there seems to be no way of deciding whether pure chance and randomness plays a role in the cosmos or if all systems are essentially deterministic in nature.

CHAOS, NON-LINEARITY AND GEOMETRY

Chaos theory is itself a branch of more general fields of study that include nonlinear dynamics and general systems theory. From these come such important concepts as, for example, bifurcation points—a region of phase space (or behavior space) in which a tiny change in external conditions can produce an overall qualitative change in a system's behavior. Nonlinear dynamics also deals with limit cycles and quasi-periodic behavior; that is, with systems that settle down into repetitive behavior highly resistant to external perturbations. Solitons may also be produced in nonlinear systems; these are localized entities that move like particles and are apparently independent yet have their origin in the dynamics of the system as a whole.

A significant characteristic of nonlinear and chaotic dynamics is that, although the underlying theory can be treated in a purely formal way, using abstract equations, it lends itself to an easily visualizable expression in terms of the movement of a system through a landscape of valleys, hills, mountain ridges, saddles, and so on. Although the spaces involved may in fact be multidimensional phase-, configurational-, or behavior-spaces, there is much to be gained from understanding nature in a purely visual way and geometrical way. Thus, for example, the mathematical description of a limit cycle can be easily conceptualized in terms of a system trapped to move within the confines of a deep, circular valley. One can also imagine a system perched on a mountain ridge and about to plunge down one side or the other, depending on the slightest wind. Thanks to computer simulations it is also possible to explore the nature of chaotic motion through the various scales of its strange attractor.

This introduction of geometrical and pictorial images is particularly important when it comes to psychology and sociology, for it opens up new ways of thinking that are not always possible when one deals with nature in purely abstract and numerical ways. Indeed, spatial imagery seems particularly appropriate; after all, we tend to use spatial metaphors when talking about our inner life; we are "up in the air," "in a strange space," "losing direction," "following a path," and "becoming disoriented." That great summing up of the medieval world, Dante's *Divine Comedy,* drew upon a sacred geometry in which everything and everyone had their place. The poem begins with one who has lost his way in a dark wood. By making a journey through a highly structured landscape, the traveler moves toward harmony and balance. Dante's landscape is at one and the same time theological, cosmological, social, and individual; it is an image of the integration of the psyche and of the dynamics of the solar system, for both individual and cosmos are subject to that same love that moves the sun and stars.

This image of a sacred landscape and of a path that must be taken towards wholeness is found in many other cultures. Several of my Native American friends speak of having "a map in the head," and appear to perceive the landscape around them as richly structured and enfolded in space and time. Thus, for example, the land of the Blackfoot was created by Napi as he moved on his journey north. In his other metamorphoses, he created the lands of the Ojibwaj, Cree, and Naskapi. Likewise, during the "Dream Time," the Australian landscape was created by the ancestors and, within certain rock formations, the ancestor, rock, present time, and Dream Time all coexist. Related accounts of creation and the landscape can be found in India where places of pilgrimage are associated with various parts of the body. In all cases, therefore, a sacred geometry exists both internally and externally: it is part geography, part cosmological relationship, part history, part social order, and partly the evolution and nature of human consciousness.

Some of the deepest as well as the earliest ways of understanding ourselves and the cosmos are expressed in geometrical patterns such as the mandala, sacred hoop, four directions, world tree, the snake that consumes its own tail, etc. In all cases, these spatial arrangements have a great numinous power of their own. In our Western society, Carl Jung referred to them as archetypes of the collective unconscious. My Native American friends caution me that these are not mere symbols, representations, or metaphors but are powers in themselves that contain great energy.

Clearly we are touching something very deep in these universal forms and images that are at one and the same time manifestations of the internal dynamics of the cosmos and the structuring of human consciousness. One wonders to what extent the marriage of chaos theory and psychology is beginning to touch on similar ground. Could it be that the images and concepts we are now investigating are not mere abstract conceptual representations or shorthand ways of thinking but possess a numinous power of their own?

Physics has traditionally relied on quantitative measurement, numerical descriptions, and algebraic manipulation for the construction of its theory, but I wonder to what extent this reliance on the quantitative and abstract may be less appropriate within psychology.

Jungian theory suggests that one comes to know the world and oneself by means of the Four Functions. Jung classified Thinking and Feeling as concerned with evaluation and, thus, termed them the "rational functions." By contrast, Intuition and Sensation are "irrational functions," for they do not measure or evaluate but work directly through direct perception. Jung warned of the danger of allowing one of these functions to dominate the others. In this sense, the geometrical or pictorial descriptions that are emerging out of chaos theory could be said to be more perceptive and sensate and, thus, provide an important counterbalance to our prevailing quantitative, evaluative approaches to nature.

And there are even good arguments to suggest that this geometrical, pictorial approach may be an inherently important way of describing the natural world, and our own perceptions of it. In their search for deeper theories at the most fundamental levels of physics, some theoreticians have been looking at new geometries, cohomologies, and topologies as ways of exploring the most fundamental level of physics. The study of loops and knots, for example, has recently been shown to make connections to theories of the subquantum world, such as Edward Witten's axiomatic field theory.

Relationships, such as "inside/outside," "contained in," "next to," "enfolded in," "connected to," "excluded from," etc., can all be expressed in purely topological and geometrical terms without reference to number and measurement. Not only do such relationships appear to be more appropriate at the quantum level of the world, they also lie very close to the ways in which our brains gather and process information about the world. Thus, topological and geometrical relationships may be a more fundamental way of understanding both matter and consciousness.

SOME BURNING QUESTIONS

Thus, it appears that notions of form, pattern, geometry, and structure can be found at the deepest levels of matter and the psyche. It is at this point that a number of questions pose themselves: How are we developing this approach within psychology and the social science? How can we enrich our current pictures and geometries? How will we include such notions as quality and value within the geometrical realm? How are we to deal with the dualities of subjectivity and objectivity? Can we develop new geometries and structures that will both enrich our theoretical understanding of the psyche and serve as integrative function for those who seek an inner development?

THE PSYCHOLOGICAL DIMENSION

Anyone who has dealt with chaos theory will be aware of the associations it evokes in others. The very term brings with it unresolved feelings associated with the break down of order, social chaos, fears at loss of control, anxiety at sudden, disruptive changes, concerns about the transformation of values, and apprehension at the disintegration of our values and the loss of all we hold dear.

To what extent are such profound and disturbing feelings being captured and contained within such concepts as fractals, chaos, bifurcation points, and strange attractors? To what extent are these very forms and patterns becoming charged with a numinous power that can aid in both understanding and healing?

CONCEPTS AND CLUES FROM PHYSICS

In many ways, as we seek to enrich psychology from the perspective of chaos theory, we are all groping in the dark. Since my own background lies in the physical sciences, it is natural that I should look to it for clues and suggestions. Indeed, this approach has tended to be the pattern of the last decades as other disciplines look to physics for their metaphors. I am well aware, however, of the caution needed in this wholesale importation of ideas. I can remember a discussion I had with Stanislav Grof who dreamed of a time when psychology would produce its own deep insights about the worlds of consciousness and matter and that these, in turn, would flow in the other direction and enrich physics and aid in the understanding of fundamental matter. In light of this qualification, the ideas and suggestions outlined in the next several sections should be taken with a generous grain of salt. While they do not all apply directly to chaos theory or the geometrization of thought, I think that each one contains a fruitful germ of enquiry.

Fundamental Law

Often psychology and the social sciences seek fundamental principles and laws, as well as the elementary structures on which behavior and consciousness is based. This approach is clearly taken from physics, which has always sought out the most fundamental laws and most elementary levels of matter structures in its effort to answer such questions as: Why is there something rather than nothing? Why is the universe the way it is?

Such laws have a curious ontological existence, for they appear to stand outside matter and space and have an existence prior to time. Thus, for example, fundamental law is invoked to bring the universe of time, space, matter, and energy into existence within a primordial Big Bang. Now, while physicists like Stephen Weinberg and Stephen Hawking are firm believers in such an ultimate law—and possibly even in a most fundamental level of matter—not everyone agrees with this approach.

Another way of looking at things is that, rather than governing natural processes, these laws are, in fact, generated out of the processes of nature themselves. In this way of thinking, the laws are always provisional and context-dependent; they operate at a certain limited level and break down in more extended contexts. Likewise, "fundamental particles" and ultimate material levels are always subsistent on something beyond them. In this fashion, rather than seeking fundamental laws and equations, one begins to ask how systems generate their own regularities and patterns of behavior.

Take, as an example, the gas laws of Charles and Boyle. At one time they were thought to express the fundamental properties of matter. Later they were discovered to be the result of statistical averages over an enormous number of molecular processes that make up the gas. Later still these molecular processes were discovered to originate in collisions that had to be expressed quantum mechanically.

Today physics seeks to explain one law in terms of behavior at a smaller and presumably more fundamental level. But it could also turn out that processes at the subquantum level are conditioned by the universe in the large, and by large scale, nonlocal processes. Thus, it could be that the regularities or laws that are uncovered at one context, or level, are the result of processes operating at many other levels.

To sum up, physics has traditionally pictured the world as created out of elementary "building blocks" whose behavior is governed by simple, fundamental laws. An alternative approach would be to consider a universe of process and flux out of which unfolds, always within certain limited contexts, a variety of patterns, regularities, and invariances that we take to be "The Laws of Nature."

One wonders if psychology and sociology will ever be based on fundamental laws and levels or if one should seek the patterns and forms that emerge out of complex processes and the interpenetration of levels.

Inertia and Form

It has always struck me that the fundamental behavior of matter and of thought are in many ways similar. Thus, for example, thought tends to cling to forms and patterns as matter clings to its motion.

According to Newton, the motion of matter is always similar to itself. A free body moves in a straight line or remains at rest—at each instant its motion is exactly similar to itself. When, however, this body is acted on by an external force, its motion is not disturbed in an irregular way; rather the change of motion is always exactly similar to itself—uniform acceleration.

Likewise, in relativity, the forms of the laws of nature are always similar to themselves, no matter in which particular frame of motion those laws are expressed. One could even think of the persistence of material bodies as arising in a similar way, for the form of matter is always exactly similar to itself from moment to moment.

Thus, if I were to think of a basic principle of nature it would be this notion of a clinging to form, a principle that seems to occur at all levels of behavior of matter. One wonders to what extent this is also present within consciousness.

Algebras of Thought

Attempts have been made to create algebras of thought and, curiously enough, these same formal structures have currently been shown to have relevance within fundamental physics. The 19th century mathematician, Herman Grassman, created the algebra that bears his name in an effort to show how one thought unfolds out of another. Grassman believed that algebra was not about the physical world but about the movement of thought itself. He observed that each thought contains the trace of that which has gone before and anticipates that which is to come. His algebra reflects that dynamical movement of unfolding and enfolding.

Unfortunately, later mathematicians focused on the static aspects of this work and neglected the more radical nature of his algebra. Grassman's work was, however, revisited by William Kingdon Clifford and William Roland Hamilton, who appeared to understand the radical nature of what he was attempting. Today Grassman and Clifford algebras play an important role in fundamental physics. But, since most mathematicians do not appear interested in fundamental questions of thought, there is little written on this aspect of their work. A colleague of mine, Basil Hiley, who was working with the late David Bohm on the application of these algebras to matter and consciousness, has suggested that the best approach for those interested would be Grassman's *Gasammette Mathematische und Physikalische Werke* (Leipzig, 1894; some of which has been translated into English; see also Hamilton, 1967).

Collective Variables

The relationship between an underlying flux and the appearance of order was investigated by the physicists David Bohm and David Pines in the context of a plasma in a metal. In essence, Bohm showed how, within the apparent random thermal motions of a vast number of electrons, regular, collective oscillations of the plasma are enfolded. Likewise, the random motions of individual electrons are conditioned by the overall motion of the plasma. (Technically speaking, the long-range electrical interactions between electrons are shielded by the plasma so that individual electrons move randomly under short-range forces.)

Bohm and Pines' work seems to me to be full of valuable metaphors for psychology and the social sciences. Take for example, the way in which large scale behavior unfolds out of the random motion of an enormous number of tiny elements and, at the same time, how each individual random motion is conditioned by the collective. Thus, while society emerges out of a group of individuals, individual behaviors unfold out of the collective. One can also speculate on the relevance of this image for the brain—large-scale behavior across the brain develops out of the action of an enormous number of neurological elements. In turn, this large-scale activity conditions the behavior and response of the individual elements and changes their interactions.

I do not know of any nontechnical account of this work. It is described in the original papers, such as David Bohm and David Pines (1953), but these papers are quite mathematical for the nontechnically minded.

Global Behavior

The work referred to in the previous sections demonstrated the way in which a dynamical system can separate itself into two modes of behavior—one dealing with the apparently chaotic motion of individual elements and the other dealing with the large-scale and more regular behavior—yet each dynamic interpenetrates the other and coexists at the same time.

Indeed this raises important questions of how microscopic and macroscopic descriptions can exist side by side and how one and the same system can separate into fast and slow variables. It seems to be of great importance that similar investigations should be made into the functioning of the brain and consciousness, for here both local and global behaviors appear to be performing different yet interpenetrating functions. Thus, it is often said that conscious awareness arises at the global level—yet the global arises out of the local and, in turn, acts to condition the local.

This duality between local and global structure is also connected with the sorts of geometrical pictures that are present in chaos theory and nonlinear theories. In these approaches, a system is treated as a point moving through a richly structured landscape of planes, valleys, saddles, peaks, and fractal-dimensioned strange attractors. Yet the system point itself is not structureless, for it has its own internal dynamics; the fact that it responds to the vagaries of the external landscape means that its internal structure is coupled to that of its outer environment.

David Bohm and Gideon Carmi (1964) looked at the whole question of the way in which a dynamical system divides itself into an internal part and an external environment. The mathematician Roger Penrose has also explored the way in which a series of elements can generate a collective, global order that, in turn, acts back to define the system. For example, Penrose examined the mathematical relationships of a network of quantum mechanical spinors—the most elementary quantum elements possible. He discovered that, when these networks become sufficiently large, they begin to define the first elements of a Euclidian space, namely angles in a three-dimensional space (Penrose, 1971).

Likewise, when groups of harmonic oscillators are coupled together they begin to define structures that mimic those of space and time. The same thing can be done in Hamilton-Jacobi theory in which waves can be brought together and form interference patterns. Out of their "beats," one can begin to define relationships in space and time.

There are many other examples of the ways in which a collection of elements spontaneously defines a global order. Indeed, the orders of space and of time can be generated in this way. In turn, these generating elements themselves need not be a priori primitive but may be the manifestation of some deeper underlying order. It is intriguing to speculate if large scale structures within consciousness and the physical brain could be created in similar ways. Indeed, both human brains and human societies may spontaneously generate global orders that then act back on their elements to order them in new ways.

Coherence

Another approach to this question is that of "coherence." Plasmas, superconductors, and superfluids all exhibit long range, coherent order in which their individual elements work together in response to an overall form. Electrical resistance in a normal metal is caused by the scattering of electrons. An electron in a superconductor, however, will not scatter because its motion is guided by the overall form of the global wave function. Again the notion of pattern and form plays a key role in the physics of coherent systems.

The theoretical physicist H. Frohlich has speculated that examples of coherent systems go beyond that of the laser, superconductor, and superfluid, indeed that they are ubiquitous and a fundamental characteristic of life. Living systems are always open systems, ones that can be pumped to higher energy levels by an influx of matter and energy. In this way, Frohlich argued, a living system is able to maintain a collective and coherent state, one in which a global order prevails and acts backwards to condition the individual elements of the system and coordinate their behavior.

One would suppose that coherence and global coordination would also be present in the brain, consciousness, and society. Coherence would act as an ordering or integrating principle and arise out of the openness of a system to its environment. Isolate such a system from its environment and all its internal coherence will decay.

Coherent systems exhibit long-range order and could be said to respond to global forms, or patterns of information. I have frequently speculated on how such ideas apply to such things as brains and immune systems. When global information is available to the entire system, it becomes possible for distant parts to be coordinated so precisely that tiny disturbances within a system could propagate without dissipation or destructive interference. Ripples at the edge of a pond will normally interfere destructively so that the effects are soon smoothed out. But if these ripples are able to respond to a global pool of information, then it would be possible for them to become coordinated exactly in phase. In such a case, they would interfere constructively, grow in amplitude, and converge towards the center of the pond. By analogy, a brain, or for that matter a neural net, in which global, long-range order prevails—or in which nonlocal correlations are present—could direct disturbances from all over its surface into particular regions. This highly localized activity could then fold back into the entire brain only to appear in a localized form within some other region.

The operation of such a system would require a global field of active and subtle information. But as we know, systems that are termed chaotic are highly sensitive and could be said to carry a large amount of information. By contrast, systems described by limit cycles tend to lose the information of their initial conditions. Hence, a high degree of "sensitive chaos" would appear to be a prerequisite for brains, immune systems, and societies.

Chaos or Madness

In regard to questions of coherence, chaos, and global order, one could ask to what extent should the word chaos be applied in health and sickness? In informal discussions during the conference, the ideas of chaos and mental illness were at times used in an interchangeable way, which, I believe, is confusing and unfortunate.

Healthy individuals exhibit integrated purposeful behavior, there is a center to their existence, they can direct attention in meaningful ways and have a rich sense of inner life. At the same time, they are flexible and adjustable and can be sensitive to what is occurring outside without being swamped or overwhelmed by a sense of mere contingency.

There are also times when that sense of identity diminishes or vanishes, such as when falling in love, being deeply engaged in creative work, or spending time in nature. Some have had been granted mystical experiences. Others, through training and discipline, have been able to enter transcendental or extended states of consciousness in which there is a total loss of the "I" and a deep identification with some transcendent reality. Yet others have acted as "shamans," prepared to take journeys into other worlds for the sake of the society. Yet, even when there may appear to be a total dissolution of boundaries, what could be called the interior sense of integration retains its watchful care over the organism. Thus, there are stories of shamans and medicine people who, at the height of some ceremony involving drumming or the ingestion of drugs, are aware in a very practical sense of the proximity of the central fire and of the welfare of those around them.

In this way, the healthy individual and society is characterized by a strong sense of meaning and direction, by extreme sensitivity and internal order, by an openness to exteriors, by richness of response, by creativity in action and, at the same time, a deep sense of interior integration.

By contrast, the sick person is characterized by a paucity and rigidity of response, by repetitive behavior and inappropriate action. His or her inner experience may range from a sense of loss of connection to that of being overwhelmed by external events and uncontrollable inner promptings. There may a general lack of meaning, an interior blankness and a loss of sensation. Or conversely, the external world may appear violent, overwhelming, and meaningless. In both cases, the normal sense of integration, of openness and appropriate response to the interior and exterior worlds has been compromised.

The question is, how should this be discussed in terms of "chaos theory," and within nonlinear dynamics? Does chaos deal with the mad or with the healthy?

Healthy, organic systems all tolerate a degree of chaos, for they are open and rich in their responses. By contrast, systems that are less sensitive and far from chaos tend to settle into rigid, repetitive behavior, such as limit cycles. For example, a healthy heart exhibits a certain degree of fluctuation in its activity, whereas a strictly repetitive cycle presages a heart attack. Likewise, an individual who is psychically trapped in a Basin attractor will undergo repetitive, mechanical responses. That person's behavior will be obsessional, neurotic, and somewhat predictable.

From an informational point of view, limit cycles are particularly simple, for the information inherent in a system's initial conditions is rapidly lost. No matter where you enter the limit cycle you end up being locked into the same repetitive cycle. Hence, the more you are trapped in a repetitive response the more your personal story becomes impoverished and meaningless. Likewise, your ability to process information in a creative way is diminished. Indeed, to an individual within such a state of mind, there may well appear to be no way of escaping from this predicament. Indeed, it is only by increasing the "dimension" of the system, as it where, that it will ever be possible to enter into a new range of behavior.

The more mechanical the behavior, the less creative and organic is the response and, as a consequence, coherence becomes lost. Coherence is the rich integration of the whole organism that leads to subtle behavior and appropriate response. Coherent systems exhibit a global form in which meanings and perceptions, even those lying far apart, are integrated. By contrast, the person trapped in a limit cycle becomes impoverished. Speech and thought, for example, may become increasingly mechanical. In extreme situations, the lack of internal coherence may suggest what is popularly thought of as "chaos," that is, randomness in thought, speech, and behavior. But it is important to remember that what we take for behavioral "chaos" is in fact the result of a strictly limited, mechanical order in which no inner structure or subtlety is present. True chaos, by contrast, is rich in information and highly sensitive to contexts and changes in the environment.

Thus, mechanical, repetitive behavior, and even "chaotic" and "random" responses are the results of an impoverishment of the organism in response to its environment, an inability to process both interior and exterior information in appropriate ways. The result is a lack of interior coherence, resulting in a breakdown of inner order and outwardly directed behavior.

In other circumstances the boundaries between inner and outer may be become too loose and interior integration so weak that a person becomes overwhelmed by external contingencies. Similarly, the interior can overwhelmed by fear and oppression with a consequent sense of lack of control. Again, all these are examples of the inability to process coherent information in appropriate ways.

Enriching the Geometry

The analogies between physical and mental systems are, of course, strictly limited for human beings, alive with values, feelings, emotions, and other qualities. Bearing these reservations and limitations in mind, is it possible to enrich the current images of chaos theory and nonlinear dynamics to include other qualities?

Similar questions have been raised in elementary particle theories where physicists desire to enrich their current geometrical pictures by referring to "internal symmetries" of the elementary particles. One way in which this can be done is through Gauge theories and Fibre Bundle theories. Here, a rich structure is superposed on each point in space; the theory then explores the nature of the relationships between these structures at different space–time points. One could speculate that something analogous could be constructed on a "behavior" space of consciousness or some sort of "social space."

To take an example, an electron can have either a positive or a negative charge. At first sight, this idea of charge seems to have little to do with the underlying spatial structure, but suppose that, at each point in space, we associate a sort of dual internal structure that corresponds to two internal degrees of freedom—the two possible choices for the sign of its electrical charge. In the absence of an external electrical field, it is quite arbitrary which of the two possible charges is called positive and which negative. There is, therefore, a symmetry associated with electrical change at each point in space. However, once we make a convention of, for example, calling the electron negative at one point in space then this convention must be upheld at all other points.

In other words, we begin with an arbitrary binary structure at each point in space, but now we must introduce a convention or set of transformations or connections between each point in space to ensure that our arbitrary choice of positive or negative is consistent at all points in space. It turns out that the transformations or connections required, called gauge equations, are identical in their form with Maxwell's equations for the electromagnetic field. This is quite a remarkable result for it means that one of the most important fields in physics—the electromagnetic fields—can be derived in a purely geometrical way by considering structures and transformations between space-time points.

It is persuasive to speculate that the behavior spaces associated with psychology and sociology could be enriched by adding a variety of structures, or values, at each point in behavior space. At first sight, this may seem like a tall order but I am encouraged every time I look at a painting by Cézanne. Three-dimensional space can, of course, be portrayed in a more or less mechanical way by means of perspective. Cézanne, however, tried to do something deeper, for by means of color, boundaries, and structures that orient at different angles, axes of rotation, edges, and fields, he was able to associate each region of the canvas with a very rich set of values. In turn, these regions assume new values in relationship to the rest of the canvas. Thus, the whole painting is built up in a very complex way, each region being context-dependent on the whole and the whole being built up out of local and nonlocal relationships between regions. Cézanne was, therefore, able to create a very rich order on a two-dimensional surface, one that employs such relationships as locality and nonlocality, context-dependent value, and the enfolded relationship between the parts and the whole. I think that we could take Cézanne as an example of how rich and satisfying structures can be built up in a formal way.

THE GREAT WORK

Chaos theory has struck such a deep chord in so many different disciplines that it is difficult to account for its attraction in terms of technological advances alone. One reason may be that chaos theory has taken us away from algebraic and numerical abstraction into the geometry of pattern and form. But another, even more compelling reason may be that chaos has an archetypical power of its own.

Chaos theory enables us to touch the irrational elements within our lives, to dialogue with the breakdown of internal order and unforeseen change. Chaos theory suggests that it is still possible to hold on to a certain sort of rationality, even within the breakdown of all order. It suggests that when we are forced to give up control over our lives we may be giving ourselves to a deeper form of wisdom and guiding principle. It implies that, within the heart of chaos, lie new forms of subtle order.

In this respect, I am struck by the remark made by the physicist, Wolfgang Pauli, that physics must learn to accept the irrational in matter. For Pauli, this irrational element was the absolute chance inherent in quantum processes—a chance that transcends all causal accounts or rational explanations. Seeking the irrational can also be seen in Jungian language as an attempt to balance the rational funcfions of evaluation with those of perception.

One can also enter chaos theory through the alchemical door and picture chaos in terms of the spirit Mercury—the trickster of the cosmos. Thus, one experiences the cosmos as a dance between law and order, on the one hand, and chaos and the transformations of the trickster, on the other.

Indeed, it is as if the practitioners of chaos theory were participating in what was once called The Great Work, the *Ars Magna,* or the Royal Road. That is, in the search for spirit within matter. The Great Work seeks to loosen the material bonds of the spirit through the processes of purification, and the spirit that is liberated is not free to return to matter in an act of reanimation and renewal.

Those who practiced the *Ars Magna* in the Middle Ages did not simply believe, as Carl Jung proposed, that they were concerned with their own personal processes of Individuation. Rather, they were participating within the aboriginal act of creation and renewal of the universe. It may seem farfetched to suggest that chaos theory has such elevated goals. Nevertheless, in attempting to touch chaos within matter and psyche, we come in contact with powerful forces and attempt to contain them through a variety of symbols. Chaos is concerned with the breakdown of order, with sudden transitions, with the appearance of the trickster in people's lives, with that last throw of the dice when there is nowhere left to fall. Under such circumstances, one moves from the world of strict causality into that shadowy realm of sycnhronicity where matter and psyche mirror each other. Work on chaos theory may well have begun to touch this new universe.

REFERENCES

Bohm, D., & Carmi, G. (1964). *Physical Review, A133,* 319–331, 332–350.

Bohm, D., & Pines, D. (1953). *Physical Review, 92,* 609–625.

Hamilton, W. R. (1967). Algebras. In H. Halberstarn & R. E. Ingram (Eds), *The mathematical papers* (pp. 15–16). Cambridge, England: Cambridge University Press.

Penrose, R. (1971). Angular momentum: An approach to combinatorial space-time. In T. Bastin (Ed.), *Quantum theory and beyond.* Cambridge, England: Cambridge University Press.

Biographies of Authors

Frederick David Abraham has held faculty positions at San Diego State College and UCLA, and adjunct positions at the University of California, Irvine and the University of Vermont. He has collaborated in research at the Salk Institute and the Friday Harbor Laboratory of the University of Washington as well as in other locations. His research has ranged from concept formation, mathematical learning theory, evoked potentials in auditory discrimination, to EEG work with many species. Recently he has been the *tion to Dynamical Systems Theory for Psychology,* and co-editor of *Chaos Theory in Psychology*, as well as authoring many papers and presentations on chaos theory and psychology.

Peter Ainslie is an ordained minister wirth the Disciples of Christ. He serves churches in Bethesda and Baltimore, Maryland. He holds graduate degrees in religion from Andover Newton Theological School, Union Theological Seminary (New York City), and Catholic University.

Tracy L. Brown, Associate Professor of Psychology at The University of North Carolina at Asheville, received his doctorate in Experimental Psychology from Michigan State University in 1985. Trained in cognition and psycholinguistics, his research focuses on attention, automaticity, and skill learning. Recent work has addressed the role of attention in visual word recognition and its implications for attention theory and reading development.

Michael Bütz is the acting co-director of the psychology department and psychological resident at Wyoming State Hospital in Evanston, Wyoming. Formerly director of Rivendell Psychiatric Center of Billings, Montana, a psychiatric treatment center, as well as assistant professor of psychology at Montana State University, Billings. He has published extensively on the applications of chaos theory to clinical psychology, and is author of a work in press on chaos theory's implications for psychological theory and therapy with Taylor & Francis, as well as lead author of another work in press with John Wiley & Sons, Inc. on applications of chaos theory in family theapy.

Linda Chamberlain is a psychologist in group practice with the Colorado Family Center in Denver, Colorado. She is on adjunct faculty of the University of Denver and the University of Colorado at Denver. Dr. Chamberlain has researched and written on chaos theory's applications in psychology since 1987, is co-author with Michael Bütz of a work in press on chaos theory and family therapy.

Allan Combs is a neuropsychologist and systems theorist at the University of North Carolina at Asheville, and at Saybrook Institute. He is co-founder of The Society for Chaos Theory in Psychology and the Life Sciences, and a member of The General Evolution Research Group. He has written and lectured extensively on chaos theory in psychology, and is author of *Synchronicity: Science, Myth, and the Trickster,* with Mark Holland, the forthcoming *Cognitive Maps in Biology and Culture,* with V. Csanyi, Ervin Laszlo, and Robert Artigiani; editor of *Cooperation: Beyond the Age of Competition,* and author of the forthcoming, *The Radiance of Being: Chaos, Evolution, and Consciousness.*

Eduardo Duran is director of the Family and Child Guidance Clinic, of the Urban Indian Health Board; as well as instructor at the California School of Professional Psychology at Alameda. He is co-author with his wife Bonnie, of *Post Colonial Native American Psychology* (in press).

Stephen E. Francis is a clinical instructor in the department of diagnostic sciences and the attending behavioral medicine specialist at the Pacific Center for Orofacial Pain at the University of the Pacific School of Dentistry in San Francisco. He is the editor of *California Biofeedback* and a Fellow in the American Academy of Pain Management.

Walter J. Freeman studied physics and mathematics at MIT, English at Hamilton College, Philosophy at the University of Chicago, and medicine at Yale University. He interned in internal medicine at The Johns Hopkins Hospital and studied neurophysiology at UCLA with support from the Foundations Fund for Research in Psychiatry. He received the A. E. Bennett Award from the Society of Biological Psychiatry, a Guggenheim Fellowship, Titulaire de la Chaire Solvay in Chemistry from the Universite Libre de Bruxelles, a MERIT Award from the National Institute of Mental Health, and the Pioneer Award from the Neural Networks Council of the IEEE. He was elected President of the International Neural Network Society. He has taught brain science at the University of California at Berkeley since 1959, where he is Professor in the Graduate School.

Sally Goerner has advanced degrees in computer science, counseling and theoretical psychology, specializing in nonlinear dynamics. Her work includes 15 years in research development work for Bell Northern Research Labs, McDonnell Douglas Corporation and NCR as well as private practice in psychotherapy. Author of *Chaos and the*

Evolving Ecological Universe and numerous articles, she is Past-President of The Society for Chaos Theory In Psychology and the Life Sciences, a member of the General Evolution Research Group, the European Academy of Evolutionary Studies and director of the Triangle Center for the Study of Complex Systems.

Ben Goertzel is a lecturer in computer science at the University of Waikatoin Hamilton, New Zealand. He has a doctorate in mathematics from Temple University. He has published three books describing mathematical models of psychological and biological processes, as well as numerous technical papers on chaos, evolution, and the mind. His most recent book is *Chaotic Logic*.

Jeffrey Goldstein is professor of organizational behavior and management at Adelphi University, Garden City, NY. He is author of *The Unshackled Organization: Facing the Challenge of Unpredictability Through Spontaneous ReOrganization*. He has written extensively in the field of nonlinear dynamics applied to psychology and is currently President of the Society for Chaos Theory in Psychology and the Life Sciences.

Gus Koehler is a policy research analyst for the California Research Bureau. His current research involves identifying economic development strategies for the California State Legislature, as well as strategies for preventing community violence. He formerly was a medical disaster response planner for the California Emergency Medical Services Authority. In that capacity he helped manage the state's response to the Loma Perate and Northridge earthquakes, the Los Angeles civil disturbance, and the Cantara hazardous materials train derailment, among other events. He has published his research on organizational learning, political theory and disaster management. His doctorate is in political science and sociology.

Isla E. Lonie is a psychiatrist who has practiced as a psychotherapist for over twenty years in Sydney, Australia. She is a founding member of the New South Wales Institute of Psychotherapy, where she has twice been its president, and has also held the office of President of the Psychotherapy Association of Australia. She has a wide experience in teaching psychotherapy and running workshops as well as contributing many journal articles on this subject.

David Loye is a social psychologist, systems theorist, and futurist. He is the author of many articles and books, including *The Healing of a Nation*, which won the Anisfield-Wolfe Award for best scholarly book on race relations in 1971, *The Leadership Passion*, *The Knowable Future*, and *The Sphinx and the Rainbow*. Recently he has worked with his wife Riane Eisler on *The Partnership Way*, and is presently writing a set of volumes on the psychology of morality.

Terry Marks-Tarlow is a research scientist for the Creativity Research Center of Southern California, and psychotherapist in private practice in Santa Monica, California. She is former President of both the Los Angeles Gestalt Institute and the Los Angeles Society of Clinical Psychologists. Her book, *Creativity Inside Out: Learning through Multiple Intelligences*, is in press.

F. David Peat did his graduate work at Liverpool University and then moved to Canada, where he taught at Queen's University and did research at the National Research Council of Canada. In recent years, he has written or co-written a number of books exploring the relationship between consciousness and the external world, including *The Philosopher's Stone: Chaos, Synchronicity, and the Hidden Order of the World, Synchronicity: the Bridge Between Matter and Mind,* and (with John Briggs) *Turbulent Mirror,* which has become a widely read standard book on chaos theory for the general audience.

Phyllis Ann Perna is a staff psychologist at Eagleville Hospital in Eagleville, Pennsylvania.

Paul E. Rapp did his graduate work at Cambridge University in the department of applied mathematics and theoretical physics as a Winston Churchill Scholar. He has held visiting appointments in the physics department at Bryn Mawr College, the mathematics department at the University of Western Australia, and is currently a professor of physiology of the Medical College of Pennsylvania. He is an editor of *Physica D,* and on the editorial board of the *International Journal of Bifurcation and Chaos.*

Robin Robertson is a clinical psychologist, as well as an actuarial and data-processing consultant in Alhambra, California. He is a former editor and columnist for the Jungian journal *Psychological Perspectives,* and has published numerous books and articles on analytic psychology, the psychological underpinnings of mathematics, and his hobby field of magic. His most recent books are the *Beginner's Guide* series on Jungian psychology, published by Nicolas-Hays.

Hector C. Sabelli is a psychiatrist and Professor of Pharmacology at Rush University. Prior to this appointment he was Professor and Director of the Institute of Pharmacology at the Chicago Medical School. He has received awards in biological psychiatry, neuropharmacology, psychodrama, and cybernetics, and in October of 1994 was awarded the Doctor Honoris Causa from the University of Rosario, Argentina. He has authored numerous articles published in such journals as *Nature, Science, Archives of Internal Medicine, American Journal of Psychiatry,* and written four books, including *Union of Opposites* in 1989.

Linnea Carlson-Sabelli is Director of the Psychodrama program, and Assistant Professor of psychiatric nursing at Rush University. Dr. Carlson-Sabelli is a fellow of the American Society of Group Psychotherapy and Psychodrama, serves on the executive council, and is an executive editor of the organization's journal. She has been active in developing methods to evaluate the effectiveness of psychotherapy. She is also involved in research that enriches sociometry by mathematically quantifying contradiction, ambiguity and ambivalence in interpersonal relationships. She is a member of an interdisciplinary research group currently investigating how emotional states and heart and brain activity reciprocally affect one another.

William Sulis is both a mathematician and psychiatrist. He is an assistant clinical professor of geriatric psychiatry, and an associate member of the psychology department at

McMaster University, where he teaches courses in both psychotherapy, and complex and nonlinear systems theory. He serves as consultant physician to several geriatric psychiatry programs and has written extensively on neural network and complex systems theory.

Benjamin R. Tong is associate professor in the clinical psychology doctorate program at the California Institute of Integral Studies in San Francisco; research associate at the Institute for the Study of Social Change, of the University of California, Berkeley; and visiting lecturer at the School of Ethnic Studies, San Francisco State University. He is also a psychotherapist and organizational consultant in private practice.

Carlos A. Torre is professor at the School of Education of the City University of New York's Queens College and a Fellow at Yale University. He has been a member of the psychology department, and Assistant Dean of the College at Yale University. He is a member of the Academy of Arts and Sciences of Puerto Rico, and has received the Academy's Medal of the Academician. His book, *The Commuter Nation: Perspectives on Puerto Rican Migration*, is in press.

Michael Winkler is a student who has been working with Allan Combs at the University of North Carolina in Asheville. He has presented lectures on chaos theory in psychology at conferences and research institutions around the world, including Brazil, Canada, Chile, and Japan. He is the author of numerous research papers on chaos theory and psychology.

T. R. Young is founder and director of the Red Feather Institute for Advanced Studies in Sociology. He is the author of many articles and books oriented to emancipatory knowledge and participatory science. He was Scholar in Residence at Texas Woman's University in 1991/92 and Distinguished Visiting Professor at Virginia Tech in 1992–1993. As Visiting Professor, he teaches the sociology of law at University of Michigan—Flint this year. He lives and works on Lake Isabella in Central Michigan.

Author Index

Subject Index